Changing National Identities at the Frontier

Texas and New Mexico, 1800–1850

This book explores how the diverse and fiercely independent peoples of Texas and New Mexico came to think of themselves as members of one particular national community or another in the years leading up to the Mexican–American War. Hispanics, Native Americans, and Anglo Americans made agonizing and crucial identity decisions against the backdrop of two structural transformations taking place in the region during the first half of the nineteenth century and often pulling in opposite directions. On the one hand, the Mexican government sought to bring its frontier inhabitants into the national fold by relying on administrative and patronage linkages; but on the other, Mexico's northern frontier gravitated toward the expanding American economy.

Andrés Reséndez is an assistant professor in the Department of History at the University of California, Davis. He is from Mexico City, where he obtained his undergraduate degree in International Relations from El Colegio de México. Reséndez did his graduate work at the University of Chicago and later worked in Mexico as a professional consultant to historically based television programs. Having obtained his Ph.D. in 1997, he returned to the United States as Visiting Assistant Professor in the Department of History at Yale University. The author has traveled extensively throughout Mexico and the American Southwest, and he has written articles about Mexico's northern frontier and the Mexican–American War for leading journals in both Mexico and the United States. He is the editor and translator of *A Texas Patriot on Trial in Mexico: José Antonio Navarro and the Texan Santa Fe Expedition*, forthcoming in the Library of Texas Series. He is also a member of the American Historical Association (AHA), the Organization of American Historians (OAH), and the Latin American Studies Association (LASA).

"The major purpose of Andrés Reséndez's *Changing National Identities at the Frontier* is to examine the complex and overlapping ethnic identities of the peoples in Texas and New Mexico in the decades preceding occupation of the region by the United States. In doing so, Reséndez challenges the traditional historiography of the field that has dealt with the nationalities of Mexicans and Americans as if these were monolithic identities. He argues that individuals and communities in the region struggled with 'enormous ambiguities and constant shifts' in identity because a nation had not yet been constructed where they lived. Through his cogent argument Reséndez makes a splendid contribution to the historiography of the borderlands between the United States. and Mexico."

– John R. Chávez, Southern Methodist University

Changing National Identities at the Frontier

Texas and New Mexico, 1800–1850

ANDRÉS RESÉNDEZ
University of California, Davis

CAMBRIDGE
UNIVERSITY PRESS

CAMBRIDGE UNIVERSITY PRESS
Cambridge, New York, Melbourne, Madrid, Cape Town, Singapore,
São Paulo, Delhi, Dubai, Tokyo, Mexico City

Cambridge University Press
32 Avenue of the Americas, New York, NY 10013-2473, USA

www.cambridge.org
Information on this title: www.cambridge.org/9780521543194

First published 2004
Reprinted 2006

A catalog record for this publication is available from the British Library

Library of Congress Cataloging in Publication data

Reséndez, Andrés.
Changing national identities at the frontier / Andrés Reséndez.
    p. cm.
Includes bibliographical references (p.) and index.
ISBN 0-521-83555-0 – ISBN 0-521-54319-3 (pbk.)
1. Texas – History – To 1846.   2. New Mexico – History – To 1848.   3. Mexican War,
1846–1848 – Social aspects.   4. Frontier and pioneer life – Texas.   5. Frontier and pioneer
life – New Mexico.   6. Texas – Ethnic relations.   7. New Mexico – Ethnic relations.
8. Nationalism – Texas – History – 19th century.   9. Nationalism – New Mexico – History –
19th century.   I. Title.
F390.R46   2004
976.4´05–dc22   2004040651

ISBN 978-0-521-83555-8 Hardback
ISBN 978-0-521-54319-4 Paperback

Dedicated to my parents, to Jaana, and to Vera and Samuel

Contents

Illustrations

Maps

Acknowledgments

Help and enouragement came from many quarters as I went through the marathonlike process of writing a book. At the University of Chicago, Friedrich Katz sparked and nurtured my incipient interest in Mexico's northern frontier, as did Kathleen Conzen, John H. Coatsworth, and Claudio Lomnitz Adler, all supportive teachers and mentors. It was also my great fortune to pass through my graduate years in Chicago accompanied by a large cohort of *compañeros* of the Latin American history program, including Katherine Bliss, Robert Curley, Michael Ducey, Ben Fallaw, Peter Guardino, Tom Passananti, Pablo Silva, Alexandra Stern, Richard Warren, Michael Werner, and others. They were directly responsible for making my experience more challenging but also richer and more fun. In particular, I thank Chris Boyer and Matt B. Karush, whose insights and friendship I have enjoyed all of these years.

In February 1996, in the midst of one of the worst recessions in recent memory, my wife and I went back to Mexico City. At Editorial Clío, Fausto Zerón-Medina and Enrique Krauze generously opened the door and offered me a part-time job that gave me the time and resources to complete my doctoral dissertation. Moreover, the job itself became a unique learning experience as it consisted of helping to write television scripts for historical soap operas. I benefited enormously from the erudition of José Manuel Villalpando, Alejandro Rosas, and Fausto Zerón-Medina, as we gathered sources and explored with fascination the lives of nineteenth-century historical figures whose predicaments and eccentricities easily surpass anything that even the wildest and most imaginative scriptwriter could have concocted.

A series of improbable events led me back to American academia in 1997. I owe a debt of gratitude to several colleagues and friends during this period of transition. David J. Weber has helped at every step, corresponding with an unknown graduate student in Chicago, offering encouragement and sound suggestions over the years, and being exceedingly generous with his time reading the entire book manuscript and improving it substantially in the process. At Yale University, John Mack Faragher, Gil Joseph, Stuart Schwartz, Emilia Viotti da Costa, Robert Johnston, Rick Chavolla, the late Robin Winks, and others provided encouragement and guidance, enabling me to cut my teeth as a visiting assistant professor in one of the great learning centers of the world.

At the University of California at Davis, I have found a most welcoming, collegial, and supportive home. I am privileged to count Arnold J. Bauer, Charles F. Walker, and Thomas Holloway as my fellow Latin Americanists as well as my friends. My special thanks to Arnie and Chuck for reading the book manuscript and for helping with their knowledge of Latin America and of life in general. I am also fortunate to have a group of colleagues and friends interested in the history of borders and borderlands, including Lorena Oropeza, Alan Taylor, and Louis Warren. Lorena and Alan read portions of the manuscript and made perceptive suggestions. I also want to acknowledge Alexandra Puerto and Mark Carey, two of our graduate students, whose formidable research skills added to the final product. Kevin Bryant graciously put at my disposal his boundless technical expertise.

Several other friends and colleagues have kept this project alive over the years. Josefina Z. Vázquez has generously taken the time to read various manuscript chapters, sharing her deep knowledge of early Mexico, pointing me to relevant sources, and urging me to rethink some of my interpretations. Timothy M. Matovina generously opened his home and made available his entire research materials to a perfect stranger. Ross Frank, Ricky S. Janicek, Sandra Jaramillo, Jaime E. Rodríguez, William B. Taylor, Jesús F. de la Teja, Andrés Tijerina, Sam Truett, Eric Van Young, Mary Kay Vaughan, Martina Will de Chaparro, Elliott Young, and others have contributed in one way or another to the completion of this book. At Cambridge University Press, it was my good fortune to work with Lewis Bateman, my editor, and Sarah Gentile. Their professionalism and efficiency have made my experience during the editorial process a fruitful and pleasant one.

Throughout the years I have also incurred many debts of gratitude with librarians and archivists in the United States and Mexico, including those of the New Mexico State Records Center and Archives in Santa Fe, the Center for Southwest Research at the University of New Mexico in Albuquerque, the Rio Grande Historical Collections at the New Mexico State University Library in Las Cruces, the Eugene C. Barker Texas History Center and the Nettie Lee Benson Latin American Collection at the University of Texas at Austin, the Texas State Library at Austin, the General Land Office at Austin, the Daughters of the Republic of Texas Research Library in San Antonio, the Bancroft Library at the University of California at Berkeley, the Regenstein Library at the University of Chicago, the Newberry Library in Chicago, the Beinecke Rare Book and Manuscript Library at Yale University, the Archivo General de la Nación in Mexico City, the Archivo Histórico de la Secretaría de Relaciones Exteriores in Mexico City, and the library at El Colegio de

México in Mexico City. I wish to express my gratitude to the staffs of the following institutions that helped me navigate the complex world of obtaining and securing permissions for the illustrations: the Gilcrease Museum, Editorial Clío, the Texas State Library and Archives, the National Anthropological Archives at the Smithsonian Institution, the Fine Arts Museum of San Francisco, and the Museum of New Mexico in Santa Fe. I am also grateful to Don Agustín Viesca, who allowed me to reproduce the magnificent portrait of his illustrious ancestor. I know well that this is only a partial list of those who rightfully deserve credit and without whom this project would not have been completed.

My greatest debts, not only intellectually but emotionally and otherwise, I owe to four adults and two children. Colonel Samuel R. Martin has been a dear friend for many years. Ever since our fortuitous encounter at a Burger King in Paris in the summer of 1985, the Colonel has stimulated my historical imagination with his wartime stories and memories stretching back to the 1930s. In no small measure, I decided to become a professional historian after being captivated by his conversation and motivated by his unfailing support. Andrés Reséndez Medina not only has been a loving father who has taken time to explore many worlds with his sons, but his devotion to academic endeavors and his intellectual integrity have inspired me from the very beginning. I have no words to express my gratitude to María Teresa Fuentes, my mother, who in addition to her love and encouragement has done everything within her reach to provide me with every opportunity for which I have ever hoped. Her dedication and resolve have been a powerful example throughout my life. Finally, none of this would have happened without Jaana Remes, my wife. We have grown together since our early youth and have shared so much in these years that all of the questions that I ask, my interests and aspirations, are inextricably related to her. As in many other things she does, in this project she reached the perfect balance of being a formidable critic and a fierce supporter. I want to thank her for her time, for her enthusiasm, and for her love. Samuel Reséndez (five years old) and Vera Reséndez (two years old) have completed our happiness. Every single day, they bring sanity, perspective, and joy into my life.

Davis, California
September 2003

Changing National Identities at the Frontier

Texas and New Mexico, 1800–1850

Introduction

This is a book about the shaping of national identities along Mexico's Far North during the tumultuous decades leading up to the Mexican–American War. It grapples with the extraordinarily slippery question of how Spanish-speaking frontier inhabitants, nomadic and sedentary Native American communities, and Anglo Americans who had recently moved to the area came to think of themselves as Mexicans, Americans, or Texans, or adopted some other national or ethnic identification.

This was a world of exceedingly fluid identities. Living at the dawn of various national projects in North America, the men and women residing in what is now Texas and New Mexico molded their national identities in the crucible of anticolonial movements, civil wars, intertribal alliances, utopian schemes, and harebrained land ventures. Just consider the case of the prominent Mexican politician Lorenzo de Zavala (1788–1836). Born a Spanish subject, he spent most of his adult life advocating the cause of Mexico's independence. Yet, having accomplished his lifelong goal, he acquired an enormous colonization contract in Texas, supported a secessionist movement there, and became vice president of the breakaway Lone Star Republic. Zavala helped found not one but two different nations. His difficult journey from Mexican patriot to Texas citizen was hard to fathom even by his own contemporaries, some of whom expressed nothing but contempt: "history will reserve a dark place in its pages for Zavala, the same place accorded to Count Julian, Monk, the American General Benedict Arnold, and Moreau . . . *Quis talia fando . . . temperet à lacrymis?*"[1]

---

[1] José María Tornel, *Tejas y los Estados Unidos* (Mexico City: Ignacio Cumplido, 1837), 57. The Latin quote was abbreviated in the original. The full quote, from Virgil's *Aeneid*, is as follows: "Quis talia fando Myrmidonum Dolopumve aut duri miles Ulixi temperet a lacrimis? Allen Mandelbaum translated this passage as "What Myrmidon or what Dolopian, what soldier even of the harsh Ulysses, could keep from tears in telling such a story?" Allen Mandelbaum, trans., *The Aeneid of Virgil* (Berkeley, CA: University of California Press, 1981), 29. Later

Yet Zavala's experience navigating the turbulent waters of alternative nationalities is far from unique. In fact, most inhabitants of contested frontier regions lived through similar dilemmas. Scores of Mexican-Texans went from Spanish subjects, to Mexican citizens, to Texans, and wound up as Americans, in the short span of a lifetime. To argue that these men and women paid scant attention to such "labels" given that their daily lives changed but little is to gloss over the texture of life in an era when national definitions mattered greatly. At the frontier, choosing one's identity could constitute an exciting business opportunity, a bold political statement, and at times it was quite simply a matter of survival. Not only did "Mexicans" become "Americans," but the reverse trajectory was also possible. Think of the very father of Texas, Stephen F. Austin (1793–1836), who gave up his American citizenship and became a Mexican national in order to validate a colonization contract awarded to his father. Furthermore, as Mexico's most successful colonization entrepreneur, Austin would encourage thousands of fellow Americans to settle in Texas, pledge allegiance to the Mexican constitution, and (at least on paper) convert to Catholicism. Indigenous peoples were just as adept at engaging different national projects, as I shall try to show. Pueblo Indians – let alone nomadic groups – could transmute themselves into fiercely independent peoples, loyal Mexicans, or true American citizens depending on the particular circumstances.

Studying identities is a rewarding but vexing enterprise, as many fellow academics can attest. The study is rewarding because identity is a gateway to many realms of human experience. A person's group loyalty has something to do with biology, religion, language, and shared historical memory; it may be influenced by pecuniary considerations or political preferences; and it may simply be a school lesson or family inheritance. In sum, it is an intricate sentiment borne out of the many wonders and mysteries of human experience. But this very richness makes identity ethereal and impossible to pin down with certainty.

Faced with this intractable problem, when I first embarked on this study, I decided to focus on the various rebellions of the 1830s and 1840s that rocked Texas and New Mexico. My reasoning was that these uprisings, together with the Indian wars and the Mexican–American War, constituted pivotal moments that left little room for ambiguity. Rebellions and wars were occasions when frontier residents faced stark and very public choices and were thus forced to act *as if they were* Mexicans, Indians, Americans, or

authors used this verse to express devastating sadness. Most famously – and possibly Tornel's source – Cervantes wrote:

Muerta, pues, la reina, y no desmayada, la enterramos; y apenas la cubrimos con la tierra y apenas le dimos el último vale, cuando, quis talia fando . . . temperet a lacrimis?, puesto sobre un caballo de Madera pareció encima de la sepultura de la reina el gigante Malambruno, primo cormano de Maguncia, que junto con ser cruel era encantador . . ." (Miguel de Cervantes, *Segunda Parte del Ingenioso Hidalgo don Quijote de la Mancha*, ch. 39).

Texans, however uncertain they privately felt about these categories. Given that many of these uprisings involved matters of sovereignty, they provided brief but fascinating vistas of how different individuals and groups coped with all the contradictory forces swirling about them as they made loyalty decisions of far-reaching consequences.

Of course, such a research strategy assumes that deep within us, some-where in the reptilian portion of our brains, we all belong to one group or another, however reluctant to take a public stance we may be. But after studying the behavior of numerous frontier Hispanics, Indians, and Anglo Americans, I grew less confident of such assumptions. The obvious finally dawned on me, namely, that identity choices almost always follow a situa-tional logic. A person was not a mission Indian *or* a Mexican, a black slave in Mexico *or* an American, a foreign-born colonist *or* a Texan, but could be either depending on who was asking. Hence, judged from the Mexican archival record, the inhabitants of Texas and New Mexico appear as a rather loyal bunch. Ordinary Hispanics, Anglo-American *empresarios*, and indige-nous leaders seeking land grants would all tend to represent themselves as loyal Mexican citizens when addressing higher-ups in the sprawling patron-age system running from Mexico City to these northern communities. Yet these very same individuals were actively involved in numerous commercial and speculative activities that increasingly drew Mexico's Far North into the orbit of the economy of the United States. Accordingly, they occasionally imagined alternative collective identities that harbored the seeds of secession from Mexico or annexation to the United States.

While such seemingly superficial, situational answers may not have ini-tially represented *identity* in any fundamental sense of self-representation, these answers – reiterated over and over in the course of years and decades – inevitably became entangled in crucial family, business, and political matters. What started out as opportunistic or optimizing choices over time acquired a life of their own, and perhaps in this way even seeped into the deeper psyche of frontier peoples. This same phenomenon has been documented in other contested frontiers. Peter Sahlins, who studied Cerdanya – a county in the Pyrenees that was literally split in two halves and divvied up between France and Spain in the seventeenth century – concludes that local peoples consciously appropriated French and Spanish identities, and in the end, as he put it, "their national disguises" wound up "sticking to their skin."[2] Sim-ilarly, the story of how Mexico's Far North became the American Southwest begins in this world of situational answers and alternative imaginations.

Two tsunami-like structural forces swept through this frontier area during the first half of the nineteenth century: state and market. My central argument is that these two forces conditioned the identity choices of frontier residents in

---

[2] Sahlins himself borrowed the phrase from Michel Brunet. Peter Sahlins, *Boundaries: The Making of France and Spain in the Pyrenees* (Berkeley, CA: University of California Press, 1989), 269.

certain fundamental ways. The workings of the Mexican state and American markets collided at the frontier, often pulling in opposite directions, and thus forced the frontier population to confront a remarkably consistent set of identity choices and tensions.

On one side, we have the unfolding of the Spanish and then Mexican national project. The Spanish Crown took possession of this region and slowly introduced institutions, words, and customs that gave a semblance of unity to this otherwise complicated tapestry of societies.[3] Although the Spanish colonial administration laid the groundwork for the process of national transformation, it would only be in the late eighteenth to mid-nineteenth century when this process proceeded in earnest. Mexican nationalists moved decisively to weave the Far North into the national fabric by building on preexisting imperial bureaucracies, promoting new civic and religious rituals, and generally forging an impressive and overlapping patronage network that included the civil administration and the military and Church apparatuses. To be sure, I do not claim that such a nationalizing blitzkrieg resulted in successful or uncontested dominance. But incomplete and fractious as this process of incorporation was, it nonetheless engaged the emerging loyalties of frontier society. This is the glue that kept the northern frontier attached to the rest of the nation, what I airily refer to as the power of the state.

On the other side, the economy of this Spanish/Mexican frontier region experienced a dramatic reorientation toward that of the United States in the early-nineteenth century. During colonial times, the peoples of Texas and New Mexico had been barred from trading with anyone outside of the Spanish Empire. In effect, the frontier population depended on markets and suppliers from the wealthier and larger towns farther south in states such as Durango, Chihuahua, Coahuila, Zacatecas, and San Luis Potosí.[4] Since the 1760s, the Bourbon monarchs began eliminating some trading restrictions, thus spurring the development of regional trading networks throughout northern New Spain. But these incipient, large-scale economic networks shifted dramatically toward the United States in the 1820s. The legal dykes that had kept French, Canadian, and American entrepreneurs more or less in check during the colonial era finally crumbled and gave way to a flood of *americanos del norte*. The newcomers ended up displacing most Spanish/Mexican suppliers and, together with entrepreneurial frontier residents of all ethnicities, launched a host of new economic activities. In

---

[3] For a recent work of synthesis, see David J. Weber, *The Spanish Frontier in North America* (New Haven, CT: Yale University Press, 1992), passim.

[4] For instance, Texas settlements had depended commercially on Coahuila – specifically on the town of Saltillo – since colonial times. See Jesús F. de la Teja, "St. James at the Fair Religious Ceremony, Civil Boosterism, and Commercial Development on the Colonial Mexican Frontier," *Americas* 57:3 (2001), 401–2. For New Mexico's commercial relations with Mexico's interior, see Ross H. Frank, *From Settler to Citizen New Mexican Economic Development and The Creation of Vecino Society 1750–1820* (Berkeley, CA: University of California Press, 2000), 119–75.

the span of a few years, the frontier made the transition from economic backwater to dynamic crossroad of exchange. Communities in Texas and New Mexico no longer lay at the terminus of imperial trading routes starting from Seville and Mexico City but were transformed into strategic way stations between American and Mexican markets. Against the background of a generally stagnant Mexican economy, the Far North inevitably gravitated toward the American economy as frontier residents' livelihoods came to depend on keeping the lines of communication with the United States wide open. I use the term *market persuasion* to refer to this phenomenon, although Mexican nationalists would have been more likely to describe this as the market *nightmare*, as such economic developments in many ways hindered their efforts to fasten the Far North firmly to the rest of the nation.

Thus state and market *conditioned* the identity choices of early-nineteenth century frontier society. Spanish-speaking, indigenous, and Anglo-American peoples of Texas and New Mexico most certainly were not inert clay sculpted by superior forces. At every turn they had choices that they exercised. But frontier inhabitants were compelled to maneuver within powerful political and economic constraints. As they went about their everyday lives, the men and women of the frontier experienced the tensions between state and market in such diverse realms as the organization of ethnic/national spaces, the procurement and consumption of medicine and alcohol, the choice of marrying partners, or the tales that they told about themselves and about others. Time and again, as I will try to show, a person's agonizing identity choices intersected in numerous ways with these two vast structural transformations unfolding simultaneously at the border.

I would like to be very clear at the outset about what is at stake with this argument and what its implications are for the story of how Mexico's Far North became the American Southwest. First, by focusing on how frontier inhabitants interacted with the Mexican state and American market forces, I hope to move beyond simple-minded notions of American expansionism. Now that we live in an era in which the United States projects its influence on a global scale, it is well to examine how this power with its different facets has been deployed historically and what people's reactions to this have been in the past. There is no doubt that during the first half of the nineteenth century the United States expanded demographically, economically, and territorially in a dramatic fashion. United States expansionism *was* a fact of life for all the inhabitants of North America, whether in the United States proper or in Canada and Mexico. The problem is that expansionism is widely used in the contemporary historiography of the United States–Mexico borderlands as the explain-all notion that requires no further elaboration.[5] It is hardly

---

[5] I have made this point before. See Andrés Reséndez, "National Identity on a Shifting Border: Texas and New Mexico in the Age of Transition, 1821–1848," *Journal of American History* 86:2 (Sep 1999), 668–88.

an exaggeration to say that America's *Manifest Destiny* – a catchy phrase invented by journalist John L. O'Sullivan in 1839 for partisan purposes – has remained the interpretive framework of choice among historians for more than a century and a half. And yet, Manifest Destiny – a most ahistorical construct – can hardly be expected to explain just how this process of expansion occurred.

In this book, I try to be more precise about what American expansionism actually meant for those who lived through it in the early-nineteenth century. I try to show that frontier inhabitants experienced America's expansion first and foremost as a powerful economic/cultural phenomenon that ended up affecting their livelihoods and self-perceptions.[6] While the machinations of U.S. politicians to acquire portions of Mexican territory certainly played a role, it is my contention that the de facto economic integration of Mexico's Far North into the American economy during the 1820s and 1830s was far more relevant to the lives of ordinary frontier citizens. American markets provided the medium in which frontier interethnic alliances became not only possible but highly desirable. And more to the point, American markets exacerbated the tensions between Mexico City nationalists bent on control and frontier residents hoping to capitalize on economic opportunities coming from the North. Rather than a simple story of Anglo-American pioneers bent on aggrandizement and backed by their scheming government, I hope to contribute to the telling of a subtler tale in which all frontier inhabitants participated actively and in deeply human ways that did not necessarily conform to implacable national or ethnic lines.

The argument advanced in this book also has implications for the historiography of Mexico. Indeed, this project was conceived very much in dialogue with the recent flurry of works on Mexico's early decades as an independent nation. Long regarded as hopelessly chaotic and inhabited by sycophantic *caudillos*, Mexico's early- nineteenth-century history has come of age as scholars working in different localities throughout Mexico have shed new light on the transition from Spanish colony into independent nationhood. They have examined the articulations of local, regional, and national agents, and have recast liberalism and conservatism as credible, vibrant, and changing political movements, not as timeless ideologies. This scholarship is generally interested in exploring how the Mexican national project unfolded *on the ground*, emphasizing the ways in which colonial and early national institutions anchored the lives of local communities all across Mexico and, conversely, how community members sought to shape these structures

---

[6] What I mean by economic/cultural phenomenon is that I have tried to look at American markets rather broadly, exploring some of their cultural ramifications just as I have done with the Mexican state. My initial inspiration for this came from the pioneering work of Jean-Christophe Agnew, *Worlds Apart: The Market and the Theater in Anglo-American Thought, 1550–1750* (Cambridge, UK: Cambridge University Press, 1986).

according to their wishes and interests.[7] My focus on the Mexican *state* and its impact on identity constitutes an attempt to bring some of these insights to bear on the history of Mexico's Far North at the same time that it seeks to reclaim this region for the overall history of Mexico.

Finally, it is my hope that some of the ideas in this book will further debate about frontier dynamics and their impact on identities around the world. In a work published twenty five years ago devoted to comparing the frontier experiences of the United States and South Africa, Howard Lamar and Leonard Thompson proposed an ambitious agenda that one day would culminate in a grand synthesis – along the lines of the literature on comparative slavery – informed by frontier experiences drawn from around the world.[8] Their vision has yet to come true, but recent research on frontiers and identities along the Pyrenees, on the Ghana–Togo frontier, along the medieval Irish frontier, or in the Ohio valley – just to name a few – gives us a better sense of both commonalities and variation through time and space.[9] Here I will argue that the historical experience of the U.S.–Mexico borderlands in the early-nineteenth century, with state and market pulling in opposite directions, in fact represents a common type of frontier situation in the modern era. Our contemporary, nation-centric mind usually conceives the unfolding of national states and the intensification of capitalism as two complementary and mutually reinforcing developments. Scholars of nationalism have been quick to note that the birth of nations in the eighteenth and nineteenth centuries

---

[7] Peter F. Guardino, *Peasants, Politics, and the Formation of Mexico's National State: Guerrero, 1800–1857* (Stanford, CA: Stanford University Press, 1996); Timothy E. Anna, *Forging Mexico, 1821–1835* (Lincoln, NE: University of Nebraska Press); Michael T. Ducey, "Village, Nation, and Constitution: Insurgent Politics in Papantla, Veracruz, 1810–1821," *Hispanic American Historical Review* 79:3 (Aug 1999), 463–93; Florencia E. Mallon, *Peasant and Nation: The Making of Postcolonial Mexico and Peru* (Berkeley, CA: University of California Press, 1995); Mallon, "Peasants and State Formation in Nineteenth-Century Mexico: Morelos, 1848–1858," *Political Power and Social Theory* 7 (1988): 1–54; Cynthia Radding, *Wandering Peoples: Colonialism, Ethnic Spaces, and Ecological Frontiers in Northwestern Mexico, 1700–1850* (Durham, NC: Duke University Press, 1997); Guy Thomson, "Bulwarks of Patriotic Liberalism: The National Guard, Philharmonic Corps and Patriotic Juntas in Mexico, 1847–88," *Journal of Latin American Studies* 22: 1 (Feb 1990): 31–68; Eric Van Young, "Moving Toward Revolt: Agrarian Origins of the Hidalgo Rebellion in the Guadalajara Region," in Friedrich Katz, ed., *Riot, Rebellion, and Revolution: Rural Social Conflict in Mexico* (Princeton, NJ: Princeton University Press, 1988), 176–204; Richard A. Warren, *Vagrants and Citizens: Politics and the Masses in Mexico City from Colony to Republic* (Wilmington, DE: Scholarly Resources, 2001); among several others.

[8] Howard Lamar and Leonard Thompson, eds., *The Frontier in History: North America and Southern Africa Compared* (New Haven, CT: Yale University Press, 1981), 5–6.

[9] Kim M. Gruenwald, *River of Enterprise: The Commercial Origins of Regional Identity in the Ohio Valley, 1790–1850* (Bloomington, IN: Indiana University Press, 2002); James Muldoon, *Identity on the Medieval Irish Frontier: Degenerate Englishmen, Wild Irishmen, Middle Nations* (Gainesville, FL: University Press of Florida, 2003); Paul Nugent, *Smugglers, Secessionists & Loyal Citizens on the Ghana-Togo Frontier* (Athens, OH: Ohio University Press, 2002); Sahlins, *Boundaries.*

coincided with the rise of industrialism.[10] But when we look closely, we find that states and markets are often out of sync with each other, giving rise to some of the most contentious frontier situations around the world.

Given that this book will tack back and forth rather promiscuously between Texas and New Mexico, I feel compelled to write a few lines about the bases for this comparison. This is all the more relevant given that modern-day readers perceive Texas and New Mexico as two very different areas and will naturally tend to project back such differences historically. This point was brought home to me quite unexpectedly while doing archival research in the mid-1990s. In repositories throughout the American Southwest, people would often ask about my research, to which I would offer a nutshell answer: "Mexican-era Texas and New Mexico." In Texas, my chosen topic came across as rather ordinary. That a Mexican should study Mexican-era Texas caught no one by surprise. But this was not the case in New Mexico. I remember especially one instance when, after hearing my stock answer, a well-meaning lady who was also conducting research at the state archives in Santa Fe patiently explained that New Mexico was largely *Spanish*, having been part of the empire for more than two centuries. By contrast, Mexico's influence had been *minimal* during barely two decades of erratic rule.[11] It is not my intention to read too much into a handful of casual conversations, but it is worth keeping in mind that Texas and New Mexico have indeed experienced strikingly different historical trajectories, especially after 1848, to the point where they now seem quite unrelated to each other.

Against the grain of modern perceptions,[12] in this book I treat Texas and New Mexico simply as two peripheral provinces of Mexico, both similarly exposed to the United States' designs. Of these two northernmost branches of the Spanish/Mexican tree, the one corresponding to New Mexico was

---

[10] Ernest Gellner, for instance, portrays nationalism as a consequence of mankind's passage from the stage of agrarian society into industrialism. He argues that the demands of an industrial social organization prompted the more advanced political and economic centers to incorporate surrounding peasant communities and less developed subgroups into the new economic order. Gellner's story seems to fit well the historical experience of many countries, including Great Britain, France, the United States, and the former Spanish colonies, to name just a few. Gellner, *Nations and Nationalism*, 10, 39–40, 63, 76. Benedict Anderson uses the same logic when he argues that the rise of print capitalism and the codification of languages were key developments in the development of nationalism. Anderson, *Imagined Communities*.

[11] The italics are obviously mine, but I believe they accurately reflect oral emphases.

[12] Indeed, I must confess that I began comparing Texas and New Mexico assuming difference. With the supreme naiveté of a first-year history graduate student, my initial objective was to find a satisfactory explanation of why so much bloodshed had preceded the incorporation of Texas into the United States while the same process had been achieved far more peacefully in the New Mexican case. It did not take me long to find out that I was asking the wrong question. The more digging I did, the more violence I turned up in both areas. Instead, I came away impressed by the remarkably similar political, economic, and national dilemmas that New Mexicans and Texans had to confront.

the older, more established, and more extensive. Albuquerque and Santa Fe were by far the largest Spanish/Mexican settlements anywhere in the Far North. Moreover, the presence of a large sedentary indigenous population, the Pueblo peoples, not only rendered New Mexico superficially similar to Mexico's core provinces but also constituted a propitious substratum for the growth of the ecclesiastical, military, and civil apparatuses. Politically, New Mexico remained directly under the aegis of the federal government throughout the Mexican period as it was administered as a territory, an arrangement that surely contributed to a greater supervision from national authorities than in the case of Texas.

The Texas branch, in contrast, was a more recent and incipient extension into the Far North of Spanish/Mexican peoples and institutions. San Antonio, the Texas capital and the largest Mexican town, was less than a third of the size of either Santa Fe or Albuquerque. Given its more precarious condition as well as its immediacy to settled portions of the United States, it is not surprising that local leaders would conclude early on that the survival of Texas depended on establishing a working partnership with foreign-born colonists. This was a fateful decision that in the 1820s resulted in a rapid and profound Anglo-Americanization of Texas, more so than in New Mexico. Suffice it to say for now that Texas at first emerged as Mexico's most daring, tolerant, and successful colonization scheme. I want to emphasize one final point: In carrying out this unprecedented political and economic experiment, Texans enjoyed considerable freedom of action. Unlike New Mexico, Texas became an autonomous state in 1824 – in partnership with neighboring Coahuila – a political coup that afforded Texans a measure of independence from national authorities that New Mexicans could only dream of attaining.

Some key differences between Mexican-era Texas and New Mexico are especially relevant for our purposes. But the preceding discussion should not obscure the fact that at bottom both Texans and New Mexicans were subjected to very similar pressures from state and market forces and faced "the national question" in remarkably similar ways.

Because Texas and New Mexico were liminal, frontier areas in the past, they are now situated at the crossroads of various academic pursuits. Scholars of Mexican history, historians of the American West, and specialists on Native Americans and Mexican Americans have long dug side by side along the same trenches. In addition, recent scholarly fascination with boundaries, frontiers, and contact zones has generated work beyond the traditional bounds of history and anthropology in such disciplines as sociology, literary criticism, and immigration studies.[13] While this attention across disciplinary

[13] For just a handful of recent appraisals, see Jeremy Adelman and Stephen Aron, "From Borderlands to Borders: Empires, Nation-States, and the Peoples in Between in North American History," *American Historical Review* 104:3 (June 1999), 814–41; David G. Gutiérrez, ed., *Between Two Worlds: Mexican Immigrants in the United States* (Wilmington,

boundaries has resulted in a large scholarly output, it is still unclear whether these different approaches to the "frontier" will ultimately engage one another. Whatever the final outcome, the present state of scholarly fragmentation forced me into a risky eclecticism. I gathered information and shaped my thinking from bits and pieces culled from different fields, and I ended up conceiving an argument with legs that stand on different historiographical traditions. I would like to acknowledge briefly the different intellectual traditions that have contributed to this book.

Trained as a Mexicanist in Mexico and the United States, I first approached the stories of these remote communities in Texas and New Mexico from the south, following the *caminos reales* leading from central Mexico to these outposts. As I pointed out previously, this book has been greatly influenced by the recent historiography of nineteenth-century Mexico. In many ways the insights from this literature also echo and reinforce what historians of Texas and New Mexico were already finding out in the archival record. Their works have also guided my thinking.[14] In addition, American western history furthered my interest in identity – national, ethnic, and otherwise. The widely publicized debates around "old" and "new" western history and its protracted aftermath have underscored the convoluted and nuanced relationships among the different peoples, empires, and nations that have coexisted there.[15] Indeed, one of the strengths of American western

DE: Scholarly Resources, 1996); David G. Thelen, "The Nation and Beyond: Transnational Perspectives on United States History," and additional discussion in the *American Historical Review* (December 1999).

[14] Just to cite a few works, see Nettie Lee Benson, *La diputación provincial y el federalism mexicano* 2 ed. (Mexico City: El Colegio de México, 1994); Gerald E. Poyo, ed., *Tejano Journey, 1770–1850* (Austin, TX: University of Texas Press, 1996); Andrés Tijerina, *Tejanos and Texas Under the Mexican Flag, 1821–1836* (College Station, TX: Texas A & M University Press, 1994). Recent work has highlighted the importance of colonial institutions in the daily lives of frontier residents. See Jesus F. de la Teja, *San Antonio de Bexar: A Community on New Spain's Northern Frontier* (Albuquerque, NM: University of New Mexico Press, 1996); de la Teja, "St. James at the Fair"; Gerald E. Poyo and Gilberto M. Hinojosa, eds., *Tejano Origins in Eighteenth-Century San Antonio* (Austin, TX: University of Texas Press, 1991). For New Mexico, see Charles R. Cutter, *The Legal Culture of Northern New Spain* (Albuquerque, NM: University of New Mexico Press, 1995); Frank, *From Settler to Citizen*, passim; among others.

[15] Even now it is hard not to begin with the foundational essay by Frederick Jackson Turner: "The Significance of the Frontier in American History," in *Annual Report of the American Historical Association for the Year 1893* (Washington, DC, 1894), 199. Recent critiques and new perspectives include, among many others, William Cronon, "Revisiting Turner's Vanishing Frontier: The Legacy of Frederick Jackson Turner," *Western Historical Quarterly* 18 (1987); Cronon et al., eds., *Under an Open Sky: Rethinking America's Western Past* (New York: W. W. Norton, 1992); Patricia Nelson Limerick, *The Legacy of Conquest: The Unbroken Past of the American West* (New York: W. W. Norton, 1987); Limerick et al., eds., *Trails: Toward a New Western History* (Lawrence, KS: Kansas University Press, 1991); Richard White, *"It's Your Misfortune and None of My Own": A New History of the American West* (Norman, OK: University of Oklahoma Press, 1991). White, *The Middle Ground: Indians, Empires, and Republics in the Great Lakes Region, 1650–1815* (New York: Cambridge University

history is that it is a portmanteau term for various scholarly fields with similar concerns – most relevantly for our purposes, the histories of Native Americans and Mexican-Americans. Group identity has been one of the over-riding concerns of the scholarship on Native Americans, as it grapples with the multiplicity of ethnonyms that appear and disappear in the historical record and traces the trajectory of indigenous polities that assume different configurations.[16] To give but one example, in his detailed monograph on the Comanches, Thomas W. Kavanagh emphasized the enormous fluidity and dynamism of Comanche political organizations understood as on-the-ground manifestations of cultural structures by people organized in groups to exploit particular resources. His detailed analysis shows how eastern and western Comanches pursued radically different strategies to obtain state and market resources. His work jibes admirably well with the kinds of tensions explored in this book.[17]

This work has also been decisively influenced by the literature on Mexican Americans. From inception this scholarship has been chiefly concerned with the relationships between Mexican Americans and the dominant Anglo-American society and all the intricacies involved in preserving a cultural heritage while engaging the American economic and political system. I have been greatly influenced by works that, while cognizant of the power of a distinct

---

Press, 1991); David J. Weber anticipated many of the tenets of the New Western history in his landmark book, *The Mexican Frontier, 1821–1846: The American Southwest Under Mexico* (Albuquerque, NM: University of New Mexico Press, 1982). For more recent appraisals, see Lisbeth Haas, *Conquests and Historical Identities in California, 1769–1936* (Berkeley, CA: University of California Press, 1995); Kerwin L. Klein, "Reclaiming the 'F' Word, or Being and Becoming Postwestern," *Pacific Historical Review* 65 (1996), 179–215.

[16] I have found especially useful the following works on Native Americans: Jack D. Forbes, *Apache, Navaho, and Spaniard*, 2 ed. (Norman, OK: University of Oklahoma Press, 1994); William B. Griffen, *Apaches at War and Peace: The Janos Presidio, 1750–1858* (Albuquerque, NM: University of New Mexico Press, 1988); Thomas W. Kavanagh, *The Comanches: A History, 1706–1875* (Lincoln, NE: University of Nebraska Press, 1996); the encyclopedic Edward H. Spicer, *Cycles of Conquest: The Impact of Spain, Mexico, and the United States on the Indians of the Southwest* (Tucson, AZ: University of Arizona Press, 1962); Cheryl Walker, *Indian Nation: Native American Literature and Nineteenth-Century Nationalisms* (Durham, NC: Duke University Press, 1997); White, *The Middle Ground*.

[17] Kavanagh discusses the contrasting arrangements of the two main Comanche divisional organizations. He argues that by the 1830s, Comanches had divided permanently into a western or New Mexico Kotsoteka divisional organization and an eastern division also known as Texas Kotsotekas. Interestingly, the former polity was geared toward furthering the lucrative Comanchero trade with the Pueblo and Hispanic communities of New Mexico. Keeping amicable relations with New Mexican authorities and having access to these markets and other state resources and gifts was central to this group's lifestyle and underpin its collective organization. Meanwhile, the Texas Kotsotekas, unable to secure a comparable stream of supplies from the considerably smaller Texas communities, mined the opportunities afforded by contraband horse trade with merchants from St. Louis and Louisiana and on the basis of a raiding economy focused on Mexican towns. Kavanagh, *The Comanches*, 478–91.

ethnic identity, also consider the layered nature of the Mexican/Mexican-American society.[18] More specifically, I have drawn on the analysis of the insertion of Mexican/Mexican Americans within the American economy. George J. Sanchez, for instance, explores how Mexican immigrants *became* Mexican Americans in Los Angeles by focusing on things like their changing employment and consumer patterns and how these adaptations affected their perception of collective self.[19] I believe that such discreet adjustments, whether among twentieth-century angeleños or among Texans and New Mexicans a century earlier, get us close to the group's longings, plans, dreams, and tribulations as its members go about their everyday lives.

Clearly, I have not mastered all of these fields; but I know enough about them to realize that they are ultimately concerned with some of the same processes and advance similar explanations. This book is an attempt to further an incipient crossdisciplinary dialogue; whether it succeeds in this purpose or falls through the cracks of organized knowledge remains to be seen.

The organization of this book is geared toward advancing along three axes simultaneously: 1) fleshing out the argument, 2) exploring a different facet of frontier life in each chapter, and 3) moving chronologically from the early to the mid-nineteenth century. This structure has caused me many headaches and forced me into difficult compromises, but I hope it makes the book more readable by eliminating repetition. Such a structure also allows readers to move easily from one part of the argument to another, from one topic to another, or from one period to another, although on the last point I confess to considerable backtracking.

Chapter 1 focuses on the alternative conceptions of space coexisting in Texas and New Mexico, thus broadly introducing the topic of loyalty and identity. I briefly survey the different frontier inhabitants and their spatial

[18] For an insightful introduction, see Alex M. Saragoza, "Recent Chicano Historiography: An Interpretive Essay," *Aztlan* 19:1 (1990), 7–10. See also Albert M. Camarillo, *Chicanos in a Changing Society: From Mexican Pueblos to American Barrios in Santa Barbara and Southern California, 1848–1930* (Cambridge, MA: Harvard University Press, 1979). In his study of Anglo–Mexican relations in southern Texas, David Montejano pays particular attention to the ways in which class structures of both Mexican and Anglo communities were related to one another, thus underscoring that affluent and poor tejanos chose very different strategies and had very different experiences in dealing with Anglo society. David Montejano, *Anglos and Mexicans in the Making of Texas, 1836–1986* (Austin, TX: University of Texas Press, 1987). Other works that pay particular attention to gender, class, and immigration cleavages within the community are Armando C. Alonzo, *Tejano Legacy: Rancheros and Settlers in South Texas, 1734–1900* (Albuquerque, NM: University of New Mexico Press, 1998); David G. Gutiérrez, *Walls and Mirrors: Mexican Americans, Mexican Immigrants, and the Politics of Ethnicity* (Berkeley, CA: University of California Press, 1995); Ramón A. Gutiérrez, *When Jesus Came, the Corn Mothers Went Away: Marriage, Sexuality, and Power in New Mexico, 1500–1846* (Stanford, CA: Stanford University Press, 1991); among others.

[19] George J. Sanchez, *Becoming Mexican American: Ethnicity, Culture, and Identity in Chicano Los Angeles, 1900–1945* (Oxford University Press, 1995).

imaginings to underscore the multifarious understandings of space not only between different ethnic groups but also within them. This chapter also prefigures the importance of state intervention and market forces in how space is conceived and organized.

Chapter 2 explores the Spanish institutional background and highlights the continuities and transformations during the early Mexican period. While considerable ink has been devoted to this subject, my specific goal here is to explore how this institutional framework impinged on peoples' loyalties and identities. More specifically, I study how the administrative structure that grew out of the parceling of land in Texas and the Catholic administration in New Mexico influenced frontier residents' notions of collective self. This chapter also highlights the first leg of my argument laying out how state power intersected with peoples' notions of Mexicanness.

Chapter 3 moves from the workings of the Mexican state machinery to the market revolution unfolding in the 1820s and early 1830s along Mexico's Far North. It documents the spread of a commercial ethos not only among Anglo-American residents but also among Spanish speakers and indigenous peoples. This market revolution dramatically changed how frontier peoples procured and consumed vital goods like medicine and alcohol. By showing the extent to which this market revolution impinged on the livelihoods and ultimately the identities of the frontier society, this chapter presents the second leg of the argument.

Chapter 4 illuminates the pull and push of state and market and the characteristic dilemmas faced by frontier residents by focusing on crosscultural marriages. Intermarriages entailed a peculiar set of circumstances. On the one hand, the families involved in such unions could derive tangible benefits by enhancing their political influence, facilitating access to land grants or markets, or consolidating trading partnerships. On the other hand, cross-cultural marriages required a special church dispensation and merited official scrutiny. The particular attractions and difficulties of these marriages shed light on how state and market sought to influence personal and family choices and identities.

Chapters 5 and 6 move squarely into the political arena by examining the pitched ideological battles between federalists and centralists. In Chapter 5, I address the political tensions that culminated in the Texas Revolution of 1835–6, putting special emphasis on how this political fray was inextricably entangled with more profound struggles over national identity. The Texas Revolution was the most successful secessionist movement in the Far North and thus altered politics throughout the region in years to come. As a counterexample, I look at the 1837 Chimayó Rebellion in New Mexico in Chapter 6. The Chimayó Rebellion had its origins in similar tensions that triggered the Texas Revolution, but its outcome was vastly different. My goal in these two chapters is not so much to produce a blow-by-blow account of these events, although I present some new information especially from Mexican and Native American viewpoints, but rather to trace shifting loyalties in the crucible of these tumultuous affairs.

Chapter 7 explores the literary cultures of Hispanics, Kiowa Indians, and Anglo Americans along the frontier. I center my analysis on the many narratives that originated out of the Texan Santa Fe Expedition. This was an expeditionary force launched from the Texas Republic in the summer of 1841, whose mission was to cross Comanche territory to open a direct line of communication with New Mexico. Its objective was to annex a portion of this Mexican province to the Lone Star Republic. The Texan Santa Fe Expedition was so daring and ill-fated that it prompted many tales written in different media revealing the different literary worlds inhabited by frontier peoples.

Finally, Chapter 8 focuses on the "peaceful" military occupation of New Mexico at the start of the Mexican–American War in 1846 and the "Mexicanist" rebellions of 1846–7 aimed at overthrowing the established government by the United States. These dramatic episodes not only mark the end of an era, and thus constitute a fitting end to the book, but also furnish an excellent example of the kinds of national dilemmas faced by the frontier society as the entire area tottered between Mexico and the United States.

I

Carved Spaces

Mexico's Far North, the American Southwest, or Indian Domains?

Compared to many other fearless souls who have offered grand predictions about the world, the Prussian geographer Alexander von Humboldt fares rather well. In 1822 he ventured the opinion that vast territories of North America – not yet completely explored by Europeans and in the midst of an intense imperial race – would ultimately be dominated by two New World nations: the United States and Mexico. A messy imperial board stretching from California and Oregon through New Mexico to Texas and Louisiana would somehow be simplified, and the two remaining contenders would at last be free to lord over this enormous area. Humboldt also predicted the triumph of the United States. He did not imagine the contest as lopsided as it turned out to be. After all, in the early 1800s, Mexico and the United States were still quite comparable in size, total population, and economic output. But in Humboldt's estimation, Mexico would be held back by its indigenous population and abysmal social disparities. A comparatively whiter and more egalitarian United States looked to a bright future, and the only cloud on the horizon was the possibility of a massive slave rebellion.[1]

Humboldt's prescience is sometimes attributed to his uncompromising empiricism and rigorous analysis. Indeed, he is often hailed as a paragon of scientific virtue. Between 1799 and 1803, he led expeditions through some of the most remote corners of South and North America, carrying trunks containing some fifty scientific instruments and painstakingly taking notes on flora, fauna, and topography. For the next two decades, he would weigh the evidence and perfect his totalizing view of the continent, an enterprise that

---

[1] Alexander von Humboldt, *Ensayo Político sobre el Reino de la Nueva España*, 4 vols (Paris, 1822), especially ch. 1. Humboldt makes the comparison of territory and population quite explicit. As for economic output, the gap between the two nations has never been narrower than in 1800, when Mexico produced a little over half as much as its northern competitor. See John Coatsworth, "Obstacles to Economic Growth in Nineteenth Century Mexico," *American Historical Review* 83 (1978), 8–100.

would yield thirty published volumes on America alone. He took nothing for granted and insisted on evidentiary standards that only the most committed geographers could attain.[2]

Yet it is Humboldt's staunchly *European* view of America rather than his empiricism that lies at the heart of his successful prediction. He could not help but be a product of nation-triumphant, modernization-bent Europe. Only in this light can we begin to understand why his vision was so much at odds with the reality of the New World. Only by keeping Europe in mind could one believe that the bewilderingly diverse array of human groups living in this region of North America and the fragmented space that they inhabited would be parceled out between two continental-sized nations. Only after Europe's example (surely idealized) could one imagine that the borders between these human groups, which had remained porous and changing for millennia, would harden into enforceable barriers. And finally, only with this obligatory reference could the Prussian savant assume that only Europeans, or their offspring, would dominate this entire area and that indigenous peoples would be somehow subjected, pushed aside, or exterminated through racial amalgamation or outright physical annihilation in spite of the fact that they controlled some 70 percent of the territory in question and included among their ranks extremely powerful groups like Comanches and Cherokees who were only getting stronger as the nineteenth century wore on.[3]

Humboldt's prescience attests to his ability to articulate a vision of America's geography shared by those who emerged victorious from the continental contest. There was nothing preordained or inherently logical about the map of North America that finally emerged; competing visions were there all along. In an era when the nation-state still was in its infancy, especially in contested areas and borderlands, peoples subscribed to alternative mental maps and admitted several geographic readings, even though agents of the state in the form of mapmakers, boundary commissioners, governors, and other officials did their best to propagate certain geographic interpretations and routinely exposed frontier rustics to "national" or "imperial" maps and treaties. But just as often, local understandings, political expediency, social contacts across borders, international economic networks, and many other circumstances challenged, contradicted, ignored, and even influenced the workings of the state machinery and its geographic requirements. Historians have become increasingly interested in the way in which space is

[2] For an excellent assessment of Humboldt's contributions to the science and geography of America, see Jaime Labastida, *Humboldt: Ciudadano Universal* (Mexico City: Siglo XXI, 1999), passim.

[3] To get a sense of how the continent would look from a Native American perspective, see Jack D. Forbes, *Atlas of Native History* (Davis, CA: D-Q University Press, 1981). Of course, Native Americans were actually making maps of their own. See Malcolm Lewis, ed., *Cartographic Encounters: Perspectives on Native American Mapmaking and Map Use* (Chicago, IL: University of Chicago, 1998).

produced not only by state fiat, but also as the result of multiple forces acting simultaneously on an area.[4] My intention in this chapter is to tease out some of these remarkable alternative geographic readings and perceptions of place offered by peoples living along the Rio Grande in what is now Texas and New Mexico as a way to introduce this book's larger topic of deep-seated struggles over loyalty and identity.[5]

THE NATIONAL IMAGINATION

In the summer of 1824, a bookish Lucas Alamán, recently appointed minister of foreign relations, set out to locate a three-thousand-page report in the national archives in Mexico City. Written by Father José Antonio Pichardo in 1805–8 on commission from the Spanish viceroy, the work documented in excruciating detail the *true* boundary between Texas and Louisiana.[6] Repeated attempts to locate one of the three known copies *en limpio* had resulted in failures, and hence Alamán was forced into a different approach that evinced some desperation. He hired an old priest to piece together as much of the manuscript as possible from a mound of loose sheets and random notes found among the last possessions of the deceased author. Alamán's unpalatable alternative was to obtain a copy of the missing work directly from the Spanish archives; but, alas, Mexico and its former metropolis did not have diplomatic relations.[7]

Alamán's resolve shows more than the Enlightenment's fascination with the written word and drive to preserve the past. He hoped to marshal the book's wealth of data documenting Spain's – and hence Mexico's – sovereignty over Texas into an arsenal of arguments that he could use in

---

[4] See Derek Gregory, *Geographical Imaginations* (Cambridge, MA, 1994); David Harvey, *Justice, Nature, and the Geography of Difference* (Cambridge, MA: Blackwell, 1996); Henry Lefebvre, *The Production of Space*, trans. Donald Nicholson-Smith (Cambridge, MA: Blackwell, 1991); Richard White, "The Nationalization of Nature," *Journal of American History* 86:3 (Dec 1999), p. 977. Ross Frank provides crucial insights into the linkages between economics, identity, and space. Frank, *From Settler to Citizen*. Within the Mexican context, see Raymond B. Craib, "A National Metaphysics, State Fixations, National Maps, and the Geo-Historical Imagination in Nineteenth-Century Mexico," *Hispanic American Historical Review* 82:1 (Feb 2002). For an earlier period, see Barbara E. Mundy, *The Mapping of New Spain: Indigenous Cartography and the Maps of the Relaciones Geográficas* (Chicago, IL: University of Chicago Press, 2000), passim.

[5] I should start out by pointing out that, except for some passing references, I will exclude from my discussion the Laredo-Matamoros and El Paso areas.

[6] For the English version, see Pichardo's *Treatise on the Limits of Louisiana and Texas: An Argumentative Historical Treatise with Reference to the Verification of the True Limits of the Provinces of Louisiana and Texas ... by José Antonio Pichardo* (Austin, TX: University of Texas Press, 1931–46).

[7] Padre José Vicente Sánchez to Lucas Alamán, Mexico City, Ago 7, 1824, in Archivo Histórico de la Secretaría de Relaciones Exteriores (AHSRE): 1-3-808: Acerca de los antiguos límites entre las provincias de Texas y la Louisiana.

his dealings with American diplomats, who had insisted that Texas was part of the Louisiana Purchase.[8] Indeed, throughout the 1820s and early 1830s, the American government relentlessly pursued the acquisition of Texas, even offering to purchase it on several occasions, a delicate and at times insulting subject that topped the list of priorities of the United States' first two plenipotentiary ministers to Mexico, Joel R. Poinsett and Anthony Butler.[9] At the same time, successive U.S. administrations delayed on the ratification of the Adams–Onís Treaty of Limits of 1819, holding out for more territory at the expense of Mexico.[10] Alamán had no illusions about the difficult task that lay ahead of him. General Manuel de Mier y Terán, a close collaborator of Alamán in the late 1820s, best expressed Mexico's challenge:

The North Americans have conquered whatever territory adjoins them. In less than half a century, they have become masters of extensive colonies that formerly belonged to Spain and France, and of even more spacious territories from which have disappeared the former owners, the Indian tribes.... The territory against which their machinations are directed, and which has usually remained unsettled, begins to be visited by adventurers and *empresarios*; some of these take up their residence in the country, pretending that their location has no bearing upon the question of their government's claim or the boundary disputes; shortly, some of these forerunners develop an interest which complicates the political administration of the coveted territory.[11]

Alamán's concerns and actions reveal a particular understanding of borders that was common among diplomats and high-ranking officials in Mexico City and other national capitals. Much like people today, he conceived borders as lines on the ground determined by sovereign states on the basis of actual occupation, historical evidence of possession, and above all competition with rival nation-states. Such notions had evolved over a long period, from Greek and Roman ideas of frontiers to medieval borders to seventeenth-century natural frontiers.[12] By the time the decolonization process got under way in North America in the late-eighteenth

---

[8] At the time, Texas was part of the Mexican state of Coahuila and Texas, as explained later in this chapter.

[9] See Miguel Soto, "Texas en la mira: política y negocios al iniciarse la gestión de Anthony Butler," in Ana Rosa Suárez Argüello, María Marcela Terrazas y Basante, and Miguel Soto, eds., *Política y Negocios: ensayos sobre la relación entre México y los Estados Unidos en el siglo XIX* (Mexico City: UNAM-Instituto Mora, 1997), 15–19.

[10] For a painstaking retelling of these stalling tactics, see Luis G. Zorrilla, *Historia de la relaciones entre México y los Estados Unidos de América, 1800–1958*, 2 vols (Mexico City: Editorial Porrúa, S. A., 1977), I: 91–117.

[11] General Manuel de Mier y Terán to Minister of War, Pueblo Viejo, Nov 14, 1829, from Ohland Morton, *Terán and Texas: A Chapter in Texas–Mexican Relations* (Austin, TX: Texas State Historical Association, 1948), 99. On the thinking of General Terán with respect to Indians and Anglo-American colonists, see Jack Jackson, ed., and John Wheat, trans., *Texas by Terán: The Diary Kept by General Manuel de Mier y Terán on His 1828 Inspection of Texas* (Austin, TX: University of Texas Press, 2000).

[12] Sahlins, *Boundaries*, 4–7, 34–43.

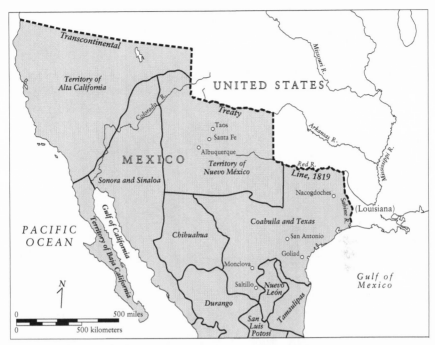

MAP 1.1. Mexico's Far North including Texas and New Mexico

century, frontiers had emerged as central elements in the very definition of the new national states. Mexico was no exception. In the midst of independence festivities in October 1821, Mexico's provisional governing junta expounded on the importance of defining and defending Mexico's natural frontiers. Junta members explained that nature had marked the territory given to each people with deliberate rivers, mountains, and other geographic features: "How many nations are not divided by the Rhine or the Po rivers? Why are Spaniards, French, and Italians wisely separated by the Pyrenees and the Alps?" the junta asked rhetorically.[13]

As far as geographical imagination is concerned, Mexican and American diplomats turned out to have much in common. They may have disagreed about the exact location of the border, but they were of one mind on the need to draw one line, sometimes following the course of a river, sometimes marking an arbitrary line with stones or other monuments placed at regular intervals that would unmistakably separate the two nations (see Map 1.1). After some negotiations, both governments signed a boundary treaty in January 1828. Article 3 required each nation to create a commission to explore, map, and mark the entire length of the borderline. From the start, Mexico's

---

[13] Provisional Governing Junta to citizens of the empire, Mexico City, Oct 13, 1821, Mexican Archives of New Mexico (MANM) 1:177–8.

FIGURE 1.1. Town of San Antonio

government placed the greatest importance on the work of the Boundary Commission. The president promptly appointed General Manuel de Mier y Terán, one of Mexico's most prominent military leaders and a possible contender for the presidency, to head the commission. Other members included mineralogist Rafael Chovell, zoologist and botanist Luis Berlandier, and Lieutenant José María Sánchez, who would serve as draftsman.[10] No expenses were spared as the Boundary Commission enjoyed the service of porters and servants and was protected by a full military escort.

Nowhere was the task of the Boundary Commission more urgent than in the hotly contested Texas–Louisiana area.[11] Demographically, the part of the Texas population called "Mexican" was in fact a small minority. In the early 1820s, this Spanish-speaking population barely surpassed two thousand inhabitants, mostly concentrated in the San Antonio–Goliad region (see Figure 1.1).[12] These two settlements and the string

---

[10] At least three different diaries detail the work of the Boundary Commission: Jean Louis Berlandier, *Journey to Mexico During the Years 1826–1834 by Jean Louis Berlandier*, edited by C. H. Muller and Katherine K. Muller, translated by Shelia Ohlendorf et. al, 2 vols (Austin, TX: Texas State Historical Association, 1980); Jackson and Wheat, *Texas by Terán*; José María Sánchez y Tapia, "A Trip to Texas in 1828," translated by Carlos E. Castañeda, *Southwestern Historical Quarterly* 29 (Apr 1926), 249–88.

[11] Not only had the boundary between Louisiana and Texas been historically murky, but since 1806, confusion arose as local Spanish and American authorities signed a Neutral Ground Agreement. See Donald E. Chipman, *Spanish Texas, 1519–1821* (Austin, TX: University of Texas Press, 1992), 224–41; Odie B. Faulk, "The Penetration of Foreigners and Foreign Ideas into Spanish East Texas, 1793–1810," *East Texas Historical Journal* 2 (Oct 1964), 87–98.

[12] See an exceptional demographic data collection in Tijerina, *Tejanos and Texas Under the Mexican Flag*, 12–18. See also *instrucción formada por el ayuntamiento constitucional.... San*

of *ranchos* that lay in between constituted the extent of the Mexican world in Texas, a sliver of land in the southwestern sector where Catholic churches pointed their crosses to the sky and where allegiance to the Mexican government was accepted. Beyond this core area, was an isolated presidio and town, at the northeastern corner, called Nacogdoches, which was inhabited by a multiplicity of peoples, including some five hundred *tejanos*.[13] But here, according to the overbearing description of Lieutenant Sánchez, the Mexican presence was so weak that it could hardly be recognized:

...these are simple people of good intentions, but they lack education and don't know the culture of our large cities and even ignore the great episodes of our Independence. They imitate the customs of the Americans of the North with whom they deal constantly and cannot be said in truth that they are Mexicans except by birth because they even speak a rather faulty Spanish.[14]

Beyond these three islands where peoples and institutions seemed at least nominally Mexican, commission members found an alien world. In Texas, Native Americans were far more numerous, more diverse, and encompassed a much greater geographic area.[15] Small and large Indian groups crisscrossed the entire province, behaving like independent nations. In 1827 the U.S. consul in Texas reported on the number of warriors of thirty-one Indian nations, including eight thousand Comanches, five hundred Caddos, and three hundred Cherokees. The total number of Indian warriors in the report adds up to more than ten thousand, which we can then multiply by four to get a rough estimate of the total Native American population of some forty thousand – fifteen to twenty times greater than the number of "Mexicans."[16]

Members of the Mexican Boundary Commission were just as disturbed by what they regarded as an uncontrolled flood of Anglo-American immigrants. From 1823 to 1830, Anglo Americans had come to Texas at a rate of nearly

Antonio, Jan 23, 1822, Bexar Archives (BA) 70:388. For simplicity, I will use the name San Antonio. Although such is our current usage, contemporaries had more precise names, using San Antonio de Béxar when referring to the presidio, San Fernando de Béxar to the civilian settlement, and simply Béxar to refer to the whole ensemble. Similarly, I will defer to current usage by calling the second presidio and settlement "Goliad," even though prior to 1828 it was still called Bahía del Espíritu Santo.

[13] The term *Mexican-Texan* or *tejano* is used widely in the literature to distinguish this ethnic group from Anglo Texans or Indians. Yet the protagonists themselves never used it. The term will not be italicized hereafter.

[14] Sánchez y Tapia, "A Trip to Texas in 1828," 26.

[15] See Texas Governor Antonio Martínez, *Estado actual de. . . .* San Antonio, Feb 6, 1822, BA 70:579–80; Sánchez y Tapia, "A Trip to Texas in 1828," passim; Report for the Galveston Bay Company, New York, Nov 15, 1830. Herbert E. Bolton Papers, no. 673, Carton 40, Bancroft Library.

[16] Consul David Dickson to Henry Clay, Jackson, Mississippi, Dispatches from U.S. Consuls in Texas, 1825–44, T 153, 1 roll, National Archives (General Record of the Department of State [RG 59]).

one thousand persons per year. During the early 1830s, that constant stream became a human river of nearly three thousand annually. In 1835, on the eve of the Texas Revolution, the Anglo-Texan and slave population had grown to about 24,700 inhabitants, outnumbering Mexican Texans ten to one.[17] These settlers had practically taken possession of the Texas coast and increasingly blurred the boundary line with Louisiana in a single human continuum.[18] In short, in Texas the Boundary Commission found a diverse ethnic landscape that could hardly be controlled. Mexico seemed to be losing a vital frontier of expansion.

The understanding of borders and national domains espoused by members of the Boundary Commission and other high-ranking Mexican officials can be examined in great detail in the subsequent correspondence and concrete measures undertaken by the Mexican government to refashion Texas along more national lines. In September 1829, the president appointed General Mier y Terán as military commander of the Eastern Interior Provinces, a post that made him responsible for the security of Texas.[19] From his headquarters in the port of Matamoros, Mier y Terán proposed a new plan of action heartily embraced by a new federal administration. First, he called for a new ring of military garrisons that would put the Mexican government in a position to enforce the law and control the Anglo-American and Native American peoples of Texas. Two strategically located garrisons would function as customhouses, one in the Galveston Bay and the other in the Brazos inlet. The customs revenue would then defray the added expenses of the larger military presence. Mier y Terán's second objective was to counterbalance the Anglo-American and Indian numbers by promoting European and Mexican migrants. Cash advances would be offered to Mexican families willing to resettle in Texas, and convicts would serve out their sentences there – rather than "have the majority of them die in the insalubrious jails of Veracruz."[20] These recommendations were discussed in a committee of "territorial integrity of the Republic" in Congress and became the groundwork for the controversial Law of April 6, 1830, which adopted all of Mier y Terán's recommendations and went further in two crucial respects. First, it rescinded all outstanding *empresario* contracts that had not been fulfilled by the date of publication of the law. And second, and most important, it took

---

[17] Data gathered from various sources: Juan Nepomuceno Almonte, *Informe secreto sobre la presente situación de Texas* (1834), edited by Celia Gutiérrez Ibarra (Mexico City: INAH, 1987), 20, 26, 31; Weber, *The Mexican Frontier*, 159–62, 166–7.

[18] Nettie Lee Benson, "Texas as Viewed from Mexico, 1820–1834," 255–6; Morton, *Terán and Texas*, 49–55; Weber, *The Mexican Frontier*, 167–70.

[19] Morton, *Terán and Texas*, 98–116.

[20] Informe del Teniente Coronel Don Constantino de Tarnava al Ministro de Guerra..., Mexico City, Jan 6, 1830, Bolton Papers (BP) 40:673, 2. Mier y Terán sent Lieutenant Colonel Constantino de Tarnava to Mexico City to apprise the minister of war personally of the critical situation of Texas and explain Mier y Terán's plan.

the drastic step of forbidding any further immigration into Texas from the United States.[21]

Frontier garrison soldiers and customs agents were the first to give meaning and teeth to these abstract congressional discussions about imaginary lines on the ground encircling areas where states enjoyed undisputed authority. On October 26, 1830, a sloop anchored at a short distance from a bluff that dominated the upper Galveston Bay. A motley crew of four Mexican officers, twenty recruits from Tamaulipas, and six convict-soldiers waded ashore. To the bewilderment of the local Anglo-American, Indian, and tejano residents, the next day the party began felling trees and laying out plans for a military village and fort. Within six months, one could notice the rough outlines of a hamlet of some fifteen to twenty houses that was purposefully called Anáhuac, the name the Aztecs had given to the center of their empire, and its few streets bore patriotic names as well.[22] The post commander was Colonel Juan Davis Bradburn, an American-born filibuster who after taking part in the wars of independence had become a Mexican citizen with close ties to General Mier y Terán.[23] Little did he and his companions know they were sitting in the midst of a brewing storm over how to define the nation and its borders.

Over the next few months Colonel Bradburn and his men tested the limits of Mexico's sovereignty in Texas. The first serious clash over the enforcement of Mexico's immigration law occurred on February 20, 1831. Two American schooners, the *Crescent* and *Angelia*, pulled into Galveston Bay carrying more than 120 prospective Texas settlers. Colonel Bradburn refused to let the settlers disembark, claiming that there were many Americans among them thereby violating the express prohibition of the Law of April 6, 1830.[24] Colonel Bradburn's steadfast refusal was no ordinary affair. At stake was the most ambitious colonization project conceived in Texas up to that date. The people aboard the *Crescent* and *Angelia* were only the first batch of a much larger pool of immigrants that the Galveston Bay and Texas Land Company – a New York consortium with great resources and influential investors – had signed up for its colonization venture in

[21] Compare Tarnava's report and the Law of April 6, 1830, translated in Malcolm D. McLean, ed., *Papers Concerning Robertson's Colony in Texas*, 16 vols (Fort Worth and Arlington, TX: University of Texas at Arlington Press, 1974–90) 3: 494–9. See also Representación dirijida por el ilustre Ayuntamiento de la ciudad de Bexar al honorable Congreso del Estado..., in J. David Weber, ed., Conchita Hassell Wim and David J. Wober, trans., *Troubles in Texas 1832: A Tejano Viewpoint from San Antonio with a Translation and Facsimile.* (Austin, TX: Wind River Press, 1983), 58.

[22] Margaret Swett Henson, *Juan Davis Bradburn: A Reappraisal of the Commander at Anáhuac* (College Station, TX: Texas A&M University Press, 1982), 51–5. See also Vázquez, "Colonización y pérdida de Texas," 63.

[23] For Bradburn's early life, see Henson, *Juan Davis Bradburn*, 19–47.

[24] Mier y Terán to Alamán, Matamoros, Apr 7, 1831, BP 40:673, 2.

Texas.[25] The Galveston Bay Company made several appeals to General Mier y Terán and urged its Mexican partners to put pressure on Mexico's highest authorities, but to no avail. In the end, the company's ambitious plans were suspended for the time being. The passengers were given temporary plots of land – out of "humanitarian reasons" – in the vicinity of the Mexican military community, where they could be closely supervised.[26] All of this created considerable irritation among Anglo Americans already living in Texas. In a poignant letter to General Mier y Terán, Stephen F. Austin did not hide his disappointment:

> You ask me what I think of the Law of April 6? I will be frank; my objective in coming to Texas was honest, very honest. I have acted in good faith, it has been my ambition to redeem this wilderness and add in this fashion to the prosperity, wealth, and physical and moral strength of this Republic that I have adopted as my own country. My cardinal rule has been faithfulness and gratitude toward Mexico, and this has been the rule of the entire colony as well. It now seems that the Federal Government will reward our faithfulness and services by totally destroying us.[27]

Austin's words paled in comparison to other Anglo-American colonists' active rejection of a federal presence in Texas. More than thirty Anglo-American families living in the Atascosito area – an irregular quadrangle formed by the Atoyac, Sabine, San Jacinto, and Trinidad rivers just in front of Galveston Bay – drew plans to bring reinforcements from beyond the Sabine River to attack the garrison of Anáhuac after learning that Colonel Bradburn's intervention had deprived them of obtaining legal title to the lands they occupied. Only a last-minute agreement prevented bloodshed.[28]

Tariff collection elicited even greater resentment. Texans had been exempted from paying duties for seven years, but the privilege ended in 1830 and was not renewed.[29] In September 1831, Mier y Terán appointed George Fisher, a Serbian-born, naturalized Mexican, as tariff administrator

[25] Anthony Dey, William H. Sumner, and George Curtis to José Antonio Mexía, New York, Jul 1, 1831, BP 40:673, 9.

[26] See Mier y Terán to Alamán, Matamoros, Apr 7, 1831; José Antonio Mexía to Alamán, Mexico City, Jun 19, 1831; Zavala to Alamán, New York, Nov 13, 1831, in BP 40:673, 4; Henson, *Juan Davis Bradburn*, 68.

[27] Stephen Austin to Mier y Terán, San Felipe, Apr 18, 1830, Barker History Center (BHC) 2Q171, 327, 72–3.

[28] Bradburn to Mier y Terán reproduced in Mier y Terán to Alamán, Matamoros, Mar 24, 1831, BP 40:673, 2; Henson, *Juan Davis Bradburn*, 62. For a brief history of the colonization of the Atascosito district, see Jesús F. de la Teja, "El problema de México con los indocumentados en Texas: el distrito de Atascosito, 1821–1836," in *Memorias del primer encuentro de historiadores fronterizos México–Texas* (Saltillo: UAC, 1990–1), 35–40. Bradburn to Mier y Terán reproduced in Mier y Terán to Alamán, Matamoros, Mar 24, 1831, BP 40:673, 2; Henson, *Juan Davis Bradburn*, 62.

[29] Texas colonists were exempted from duties for a seven-year period according to a federal act of September 29, 1823. Yet colonists were supposed to pay tonnage fees, and beginning in 1828 and 1829, various articles – including cotton – were taxed. See *Disposiciones para el*

at Anáhuac.[30] It is clear that Fisher regarded his duty as nothing less than a national crusade, even describing his situation in the Galveston Island to a local priest as being "surrounded by so many enemies of our fatherland" – referring to the local Anglo-American residents.[31] Violence escalated immediately. American merchant ships often ran the blockade located at the mouth of the Brazos River, where the Mexican government had established a collection post called Velasco. In early December 1830, Anglo-American merchants and Mexican guards even exchanged fire. One Mexican soldier was wounded in the action. Later in the month, a group of Anglo merchants threatened an all-out assault on Velasco. Disgruntled by new tariffs, a throng of twenty-five to thirty men armed with sticks and guns protested outside the main customhouse of Texas, located in the treeless and lonely island of Galveston, forcing collector Fisher and his ten-man detachment to keep vigil under arms for three nights in a row.[32] Friction continued unabated for eighteen months until Fisher, fearing for his life, asked to be relieved from Galveston in June 1832. Three weeks later, because of a series of incidents primarily related to tariff collection, a band of Anglo Texans attacked the fort at Anáhuac and succeeded in dislodging the Mexican troops from their post. Within a few days, the Mexican soldiers at Velasco left for Tamaulipas as well.[33] General Mier y Terán remarked with bitterness that every nation in the world collected tariffs, but only in Brazoria did it cause rioting.[34] By assessing taxes on goods brought from *abroad* and turning back American families desiring to settle in Texas, the Mexican federal government asserted its own geographic imagination over Texas.

DOMESTIC CRITICS

It is only natural that Anglo-American colonists and Native Americans resented the Mexican federal government's attempts to assess duties and impose restrictions on them. But perhaps the most consistent critics of the geographic notions advanced by Mexico's federal authorities turned out to be a majority of state and local officials in Texas. Tejanos were fully aware

cumplimiento de la ley del 6 de abril de 1830, Finance Ministry, Mexico City, May 5, 1830, BP 40:673, 2.

[30] Mier y Terán to Jorge Fisher, Matamoros, Sep 25, 1831, in *Testimonio de documentos relativos a la administración de la aduana de Galveston . . .*, Archivo de la Secretaría de la Defensa (ASD), microfilm roll 57, file 1818, Bancroft Library at the University of California in Berkeley (hereafter ASD 57:1818).

[31] Father Miguel Muro quoted in George Fisher to Father Miguel Muro, Anáhuac, Apr 13, 1832, BP 40:686, 1.

[32] George Fisher to Father Miguel Muro, Anáhuac, Apr 13, 1832, BP 40:687, 2.

[33] A detailed account of these events is beyond the scope of this work. The only blow-by-blow account that I know of is in Henson, *Juan Davis Bradburn*, 89–113.

[34] Mier y Terán to Austin, Matamoros, Jan 27, 1832, in Vicente Filisola, *Memorias para la historia de la guerra de Tejas*, 2 vols (Mexico City: Editora Nacional, 1968) 1: 188.

of the importance that the national government accorded to international boundaries as they could glean from treaties and maps sent occasionally from Mexico City, which they dutifully read and filed away in various state archives. But it is also clear that local officials did not share the same level of concern for such national boundary definitions. In his 1825 report on the Texas–Louisiana border, Colonel Antonio Elozúa, military commander of Coahuila and Texas, was revealingly unsure: "[A]s far as I know the boundary treaty was ratified in October of 1820 by King Ferdinand himself and is still in effect.... I don't believe that any changes have been introduced since then."[35] Furthermore, the man directly charged with enforcing the borders of Texas explained with disarming candor that although people generally considered the Sabine River as the boundary line between Mexico and the United States, they did not give a second thought to crossing back and forth. He even added that he did not regard this situation as particularly threatening given that border crossers – especially Anglo Americans – were mostly industrious peoples seeking fertile Texas lands.

To understand the geographic reading that mattered most to tejanos, one must gain some appreciation of their circumstances and self-perceptions. In the course of the eighteenth century, tejanos had come to view themselves as the edge of the Spanish world deep in the heart of North America, the vanguard of Christendom and civilization.[36] Their history had been one of hardship and tenacity in a hostile environment. Tejanos only needed to wander off beyond the protective perimeter of San Antonio or Goliad to find the edges of an alien world dominated by what they defined as heathen, errant, or barbarous nations bent on containing or even rolling back the tejano settlements and jeopardizing their lifelong civilizing work. This sentiment appeared in the instructions that the *ayuntamiento* of San Antonio gave to Father Refugio de la Garza, the first Texas representative to the Mexican Congress in 1822: "Far from advancing in the arts, industry, and the founding of new communities, Texas has lagged behind since it was first settled in 1730 buffeted by constant hostilities from barbarous Indians."[37]

In this struggle to expand the bounds of civilization, tejanos expected a helpful and encouraging national government, not a restrictive one. On

---

[35] Antonio Elozúa, Military Commander of Coahuila and Texas, to *Comisario General* of San Luis Potosí Antonio María Esnaurrízar, Riogrande, Jun 30, 1825, BA 82, 189–90.

[36] Various aspects of eighteenth-century tejano identity are explored in a collection of articles in Poyo and Hinojosa, eds., *Tejano Origins in Eighteenth-Century San Antonio.* See especially Jesús F. de la Teja, "Forgotten Founders: The Military Settlers of Eighteenth-Century San Antonio de Béxar," 27–38; Gerald E. Poyo, "The Canary Islands Immigrants of San Antonio: From Ethnic Exclusivity to Community in Eighteenth-Century Béxar," 41–58; Gerald E. Poyo, "Immigrants and Integration in Late Eighteenth-Century Béxar," 85–103. See also de la Teja, *San Antonio de Béxar.* Both of these essays are in Gerald E. Poyo and Gilberto M. Hinojosa, eds., *Tejano Origins in Eighteenth-Century San Antonio* (Austin, TX: University of Texas Press, 1991).

[37] Instructions to Deputy Refugio de la Garza, San Antonio, Jan 30, 1822, BHC, NA 2q297, 190, 8–17.

these grounds, the first Texas deputy to the National Congress, Father de la Garza, sought freedom of commerce between Texas and the United States. Within a year, the skillful priest had prodded an oblivious Congress into exempting Texans from paying any import duties, a privilege that the *ayuntamiento* deemed crucial for the survival of Texas.[38] Tejanos regarded the federal government's drive to establish military garrisons and customhouses in Texas as beneficial so long as it enhanced security and peace in the area, but were deeply resentful of any attempt to regulate commerce and revoke their trading privileges. Not surprisingly, these influential tejanos regarded the government's efforts to impose duties on trade as a direct blow to their own interests and contrary to the future prosperity of Texas. Even before Mier y Terán's plan went into effect, the national government closed off the preferred entry port of tejanos at Matagorda in 1828, resulting in widespread exasperation among tejanos and a series of petitions that sought to reverse the order.[39]

State and local officials had also concluded that the prosperity of Texas depended on its ability to attract foreign colonists and turn them into law-abiding citizens of Mexico. For nearly a century, tejanos had struggled to populate and pacify a backwater Spanish province the size of continental Spain, France, and Holland put together. Properly monitored, Anglo Americans could speed up this process. The *jefe político* of Texas, Antonio Martínez, put it quite clearly:

...the [Mexican] population in this province is too small, and yet it is absolutely essential to settle Texas so the easiest and least costly way to accomplish this is by admitting *extranjeros*, especially those who are known to us, or have means and properties, or at least can produce certificates of orderly conduct.[40]

Another member of the San Antonio elite was even more forceful: "I cannot help seeing advantages which, to my way of thinking, would result if we admitted honest, hard-working people, regardless of what country they come from... even hell itself."[41]

---

[38] Instructions to Deputy Refugio de la Garza, San Antonio, Jan 30, 1822, BHC, NA 2q297, 190, 8–17; see also Refugio de la Garza to *ayuntamiento* of San Antonio, Mexico City, Apr 30, 1822, BA 71:494–6 and Aug 8, 1822, BA 72:455–7. Decree of Freedom of Commerce in José Antonio Saucedo to Juan Martín de Veramendi, San Antonio, Apr 13, 1825, BA 80:548–9.

[39] Martín de Veramendi to Governor of Coahuila and Texas, Feb 16, 1828, BA 111, 26–8; Ramón Músquiz to Antonio Elozúa, Béxar, Jul 1, 1828, BA 114, 829–30; Antonio Elozúa to Músquiz, Béxar, Jul 4, 1828, BA 114, 957–8; José Benifacio Galán, Customs Officer, to Erasmo Seguín, Goliad, Aug 7, 1829, BA 124, 730–1; José Bonifacio Galán to Erasmo Seguín, Goliad, May 21, 1830, BA 130, 601–3.

[40] *Jefe político* Antonio Martínez, "estado actual de la provincia de Texas," San Antonio, Feb 6, 1822, BA 70, 581–2. See also Jesús F. de la Teja, "Texas: A Tejano Perspective," in Jaime E. Rodríguez O. and Kathryn Vincent, eds., *Myths, Misdeeds, and Misunderstandings: The Roots of Conflict in U.S.–Mexican Relations* (Wilmington, DE: SR Books, 1997), 87–9.

[41] Francisco Ruiz quoted in Weber, *The Mexican Frontier*, 176.

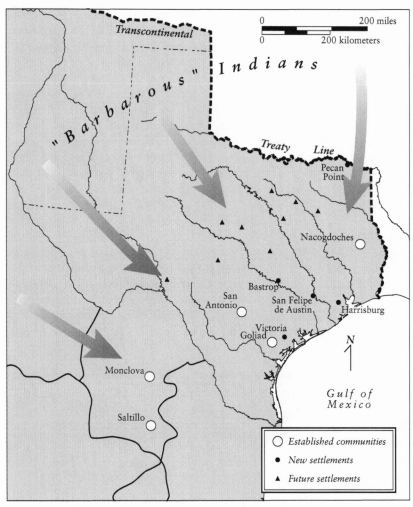

MAP 1.2. Coahuila and Texas as envisioned in the Colonization Law of 1825

The clearest articulation of this vision appears in the 1825 Coahuila and Texas Colonization Law (see Map 1.2). In this notable document, state legislators dreamed of sprawling new communities dotting the entire Texas territory. Any foreigner willing to embrace Catholicism and Mexican rule was free to project a new settlement on unclaimed lands. These new settlements would be located in "the most appropriate places," following the recommendations of state officials, and would be free to pursue all kinds of industrial and mining enterprises. As far as possible, the new settlements would be composed of both Mexicans and foreigners living in stone or wooden houses arranged along straight streets in the Spanish fashion. Lot owners would pay annually one peso that would be applied to the construction of a church. The Coahuila and Texas Colonization Law also reached out to nomadic Indians who were prepared to accept a Christian and sedentary way of life. Indians could establish themselves in any of the new and predominantly Anglo-American or Hispanic settlements. Tellingly, however, the Colonization Law did not set up any explicit mechanism to provide land to entire tribes wishing to establish themselves on their own.

In this fashion, tejano leaders hoped to bring peace to Texas by building a harmonious community composed of different races but united in a common quest for prosperity.[42] By forbidding Americans from settling in Mexican territory, the Law of April 6, 1830, delivered a hard blow to these dreams and generated resentment among tejanos, who objected to meddlesome federal authorities. Tejanos generally understood the geography of Texas and its borders in a way that contradicted the stringent sovereignty notions espoused by Mexico City bureaucrats. While Minister Alamán, having poured over old letters and maps and in light of historical evidence of American expansionism, advocated a strict boundary impervious to goods and peoples coming from the outside, most tejano leaders on the contrary defended a porous border that would allow Texas to prosper.[43]

New Mexico's border with the United States was not nearly as contested as that of Texas. Throughout the Mexican period, the Arkansas River (New Mexicans knew it as the Napeste) had been widely acknowledged as the line separating Mexico from the United States. But nuevomexicanos, like their tejano counterparts, were quite oblivious to national boundaries, subscribing instead to notions of space that had to do more with their immediate surroundings and were far more important to their everyday lives.

A closer look at New Mexico settlements reveals how local inhabitants went about incorporating surrounding space into the colonial/national realm. New Mexico had been the first and ultimately most successful Spanish beachhead in New Spain's northern frontier. Lured by overblown stories of mineral wealth, the Crown sent a reconnaissance expedition as early as 1538 and formally took possession of the region sixty years later. Initially the Crown was able to integrate the upper Rio Grande valley into the empire simply by subjecting the local indigenous population (see Map 1.3). While

---

[42] Colonization Law of the State of Coahuila and Texas, Saltillo, Mar 24, 1825. Translation in McLean, *Papers Concerning Robertson's Colony in Texas*, II: 276.

[43] This was especially the case in Goliad, where residents had a land dispute with Irish *empresario* Green deWitt. See Ana Corolina Castillo Crimm, "Finding Their Ways," in Gerald Poyo, ed., *Tejano Journey, 1770–1860* (Austin, TX: University of Texas Press, 1996) 119–20; Paul D. Lack, *The Texas Revolutionary Experience: A Political and Social History, 1835–1836*. College Station, TX: Texas A&M University Press, 1992, 163; Tijerina, *Tejanos and Texas Under the Mexican Flag*, 123–4; Tijerina, "Under the Mexican Flag," in Poyo, ed., *Tejano Journey*, 44–6.

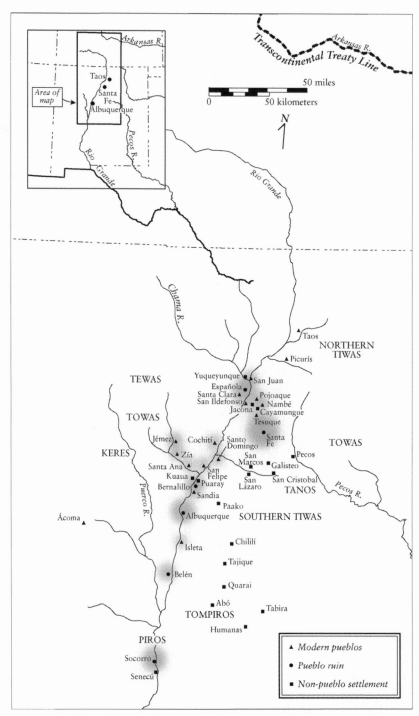

MAP 1.3. Pueblo Indians in the sixteenth century

FIGURE 1.2. Pueblo of Acoma

conquistadors did not find gold and silver, they did encounter sedentary Native Americans living in more than one hundred fixed communities that they called *pueblos de indios*, (see Figure 1.2) or simply *pueblos*.[44] The settled and divided nature of this population greatly facilitated the Spanish conquest

---

[44] Pueblo studies constitute a separate field of inquiry that I am far from having exhausted. Yet monographs of the Pueblos covering the Mexican period are not in abundance. Illuminating works include Gutiérrez, *When Jesus Came*; John L. Kessell, *Kiva, Cross and Crown: The Pecos Indians and New Mexico, 1540–1840* (Washington, DC: National Park Service, 1979). See also Edward P. Dozier, *The Pueblo Indians of North America* (New York: Holt, Rinehart and Winston, 1970); Spicer, *Cycles of Conquest.*

and provided a roadmap for the extent of the Spanish spatial domination in the upper Rio Grande valley. Lack of mineral riches dampened enthusiasm for New Mexico, so Pueblo Indian labor essentially sustained the initial wave of *encomenderos*, crown officials, and missionaries and defined the geographic scope of the Spanish presence in the region. It resembled a discrete point pattern whose periphery was marked by the outermost Indian villages with resident friars.[45]

In the course of the eighteenth century, Hispanic population growth became the principal vehicle to incorporate space into the imperial domain. Originally Pueblo labor had anchored the Spanish activities in the region. But the Pueblos underwent a long-term process of population decline. From a precontact population between 130,000 and 248,000 living in more than one hundred pueblos, by the 1820s it had dwindled to less than 10,000 in twenty remaining settlements.[46] This precipitous decline was coupled with a sustained increase of the nuevomexicano population beginning in the mid-1700s. Whereas in 1750 there were still almost three Pueblo Indians per Hispanic inhabitant, by 1780 the two populations had reached equal numbers; by 1820, the ratio had reversed, with almost three Hispanic inhabitants per Pueblo Indian.[47] These demographic trends dramatically altered relations of power as the Hispanic population went from a powerful minority into an overwhelming and dominant majority. By the time of Mexico's independence, the Hispanic residents of New Mexico had reached 28,000, the largest concentration to be found anywhere in the immense arch of frontier territories dwarfing California and Texas (see Figure 1.3).

Most immediately, this allowed nuevomexicanos to infiltrate Pueblo villages and their lands. In colonial times, the Pueblos had enjoyed a special status as wards and as such had been able to maintain a relatively stable land base. The Spanish monarchy had granted each pueblo a square block of land extending one league running due north, south, east, and west of the mission church and additional communal land for grazing and hunting. Yet Pueblos and Hispanics had always competed for land, especially in northern New Mexico, where the river valleys are narrow and arable land is scarce. As population pressure in the Hispanic settlements built up and pueblos became depopulated, nuevomexicanos appropriated plots within Pueblo grants.[48]

---

[45] Richard L. Nostrand, *The Hispano Homeland* (Norman, OK: University of Oklahoma Press), 54.

[46] Demographic discussion in Thomas D. Hall, *Social Change in the Southwest 1350–1880* (Lawrence, KS: University Press of Kansas), 40, 76.

[47] These numbers do not include the El Paso District and were calculated from the population data in Hall, *Social Change in the Southwest*, table on page 145.

[48] This became legally possible in the early 1820s, when the Mexican government, bent on creating a country of individual property owners, removed the Pueblos' ward status and began to regard them as ordinary citizens. The new land legislation did not settle the enormously

FIGURE 1.3. Town of Santa Fe

Having reached a critical mass, this nuevomexicano population also began to move beyond the immediate basin of the Rio Grande into secondary rivers even in the face of Indian hostility and difficult environmental conditions. An American visitor remarked on this tendency in 1831: "These New Mexicans, with a pertinacity worthy of the Yankee nation, have pushed out into every little valley which would raise half a bushel of red pepper...thus exposing themselves to the Pawnees and Comanches."[49] Richard Nostrand has described New Mexico's process of contiguous expansion as parent settlements gave rise to offspring communities. Typically, stock herders in quest of suitable pasture for their flocks would cross into the next valley, where they would build temporary shelters, irrigate patches of land, and eventually

complex property issues that arose, but it did affect land policies pursued by subsequent national and state authorities. In practice, Pueblo land grants continued to exist, but government officials tended to tolerate irregular and often unlawful land transactions between individual Pueblo Indians and outsiders. Of the twenty remaining pueblos, only Pecos was substantially affected by this onslaught. See G. Emlen Hall and David J. Weber, "Mexican Liberals and the Pueblo Indians, 1821–1829," *New Mexico Historical Review* 4 (Jan 1984), 5–31. See also Malcolm Ebright, "New Mexican Land Grants: The Legal Background," 15–64; G. Emlen Hall, "The Pueblo Grant Labyrinth," 67–138; both in Charles L. Briggs and John R. Van Ness, eds., *Land, Water, and Culture: New Perspectives on Hispanic Land Grants* (Albuquerque, NM: University of New Mexico Press, 1987). For the case of Pecos, see G. Emlen Hall, *Four Leagues of Pecos: A Legal History of the Pecos Grant, 1800–1933* (Albuquerque, NM: University of New Mexico, 1984).

[49] Quoted in Weber, *The Mexican Frontier*, 228. For a detailed discussion of this phenomenon, see Nostrand, *The Hispano Homeland*, 41–6.

attract others.[50] While this process was often spontaneous, local officials also promoted such population dispersion and spatial expansion using land grants to entice residents to establish footholds and pacify the outer perimeter of New Mexico's cluster of settlements. Some of these grants were awarded to entire communities or to groups of at least ten families (see Map 1.4). This was the origin of San Fernando de Taos at the northern edge of New Mexico's settlements; this community gave rise to more than a dozen off-spring communities. Similarly, San Miguel del Vado in the east produced at least a dozen new settlements.[51] On other occasions, proprietary grants were given to individuals who pledged to settle exposed areas. Frances Swadesh has documented how scores of pioneers – including detribalized Indians or *genízaros* (former nomadic Indians who had settled in New Mexico or His-panicized Pueblo Indians) – received grants in the northwestern reaches of New Mexico in the Chama valley, well into the Comanche and Ute frontier. Grants located in areas exposed to nomadic raiding were often made, aban-doned, reopened, and regranted.[52] In any event, by the 1820s, Mexico's area of effective occupation in the upper Rio Grande valley extended well beyond the original pueblo-defined perimeter. The spatial layout of the land grants issued in the late colonial and early national period reflects both population growth pressure and the local authorities' exertions to make inroads into territory beyond the immediate Rio Grande valley controlled by nomadic Indians. Clearly, nuevomexicanos were far less concerned about the border with the United States, which still lay more than one hundred miles north of Taos, New Mexico's northernmost settlement.[53]

The spatial strategy of New Mexican officials was drastically altered af-ter 1821 with the opening of the Santa Fe Trail. The main objective became to develop the areas north and east of New Mexico's original settlements along the increasingly critical trading routes with Missouri. In the 1830s and 1840s, Governor Manuel Armijo, with the approval of the legislature, made grants to Anglo-American and French entrepreneurs alone or in partner-ship with nuevomexicanos. Not only the spatial logic but also the nature of Mexican-era grants was different. Whereas the *sitio* or ranch grants during the Spanish era normally did not exceed one square league and were intended to be settled by the recipient, Governor Armijo's grants were the largest ever issued in New Mexico's history. The Sangre de Cristo and Beaubien-Miranda grants measured a whopping 1,038,195 and 1,714,764 acres respectively

[50] For a detailed discussion of this phenomenon, see Nostrand, *The Hispano Homeland*, 41–8, 71–97.

[51] For the cases of Taos and San Miguel, see Nostrand, *The Hispano Homeland*, 71–2. For a brief discussion of land grants in New Mexico, see Hall, *Social Change in the Southwest*, 94–5.

[52] Frances Leon Swadesh, *Los Primeros Pobladores: Hispanic-Americans of the Ute Frontier* (Notre Dame, IN: University Press of Notre Dame), 33–41.

[53] For a detailed discussion of this phenomenon, see Nostrand, *The Hispano Homeland*, 41–8, 71–97.

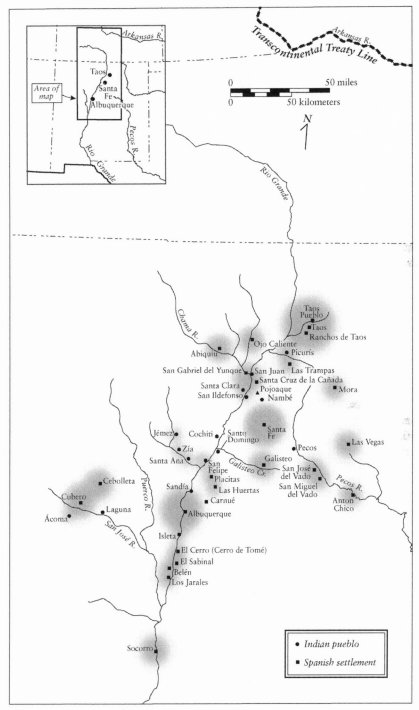

MAP 1.4. Mexico's effective territorial control of New Mexico in the early-nineteenth century

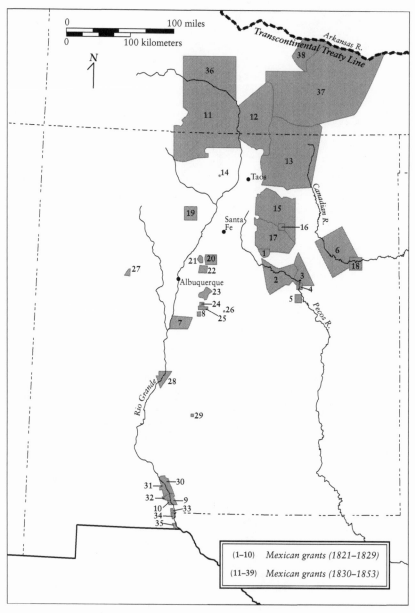

MAP 1.5. Mexican land grants, 1821–53

(see Map 1.5).[54] The motivations behind this liberal land policy were similar to those behind *empresario* contracts in Texas. Far from discouraging Anglo-American settlers or attempting to control the U.S.–Mexico border, New Mexican officials sought to attract enterprising foreign settlers to promote industry and agriculture and above all facilitate New Mexico's commercial exchange with the United States by developing areas along the trading routes. Tejanos and nuevomexicanos clearly understood the space around them in terms of their own experience and needs and welcomed Anglo-American and French entrepreneurs and settlers. A minority of tejanos and nuevomexicanos were quite receptive to the federal government's appeal to control borders and exclude foreigners, especially as the Anglo-American presence became quite dominant particularly in Texas in the mid-1830s. But for the most part, frontier residents continued to reject an impermeable border that they perceived to be contrary to their best interests.

THE SEEDS OF THE AMERICAN SOUTHWEST

The peculiar space that Anglo-American colonists carved out for themselves in Texas in the 1820s and early 1830s reveals yet another reading of the regional geography. In a very incipient form, this spatial understanding is the most direct antecedent of what is today the American Southwest. Anglo-American colonists began moving into Texas shortly before Mexico became independent from Spain. Welcomed initially by the local tejano leadership, this Anglo-American population established itself in communities along the Texas coast and on the Texas–Louisiana border. Although the state colonization law called for mixed settlements composed of both Mexican and foreign immigrants (preferably European), *las colonias*, as Mexicans knew them, were almost completely Anglo-American from the start. These settlements resulted from state land grants offered to colonization entrepreneurs or *empresarios* who, in exchange for land, acquired the obligation to recruit, transport, and settle a certain number of families (usually one hundred or more, typically three hundred) at their own expense. These mostly Anglo-American *empresarios* – the most famous of whom was Stephen F. Austin – quickly found out that it was easier and cheaper to attract settlers from neighboring Kentucky, Arkansas, or Louisiana rather than from the sparsely

---

[54] On the Beaubien-Miranda grant, see Land Grant Records, SG 14, 159, New Mexico State Records Center and Archives (NMSRCA). For a very illuminating article on these intricacies, see Harold H. Dunham, "New Mexican Land Grants with Special Reference to the Title Papers of the Maxwell Grant," *New Mexico Historical Review* 30:1, 1–22. For the extended aftermath of the Maxwell Land Grant and its implications, see María E. Montoya, *Translating Property: The Maxwell Land Grant and the Conflict over Property in the American West, 1840–1900* (Berkeley, CA: University of California Press, 2002), passim.

populated states of northern Mexico.[53] Thus plantations sprang up along the Texas seaboard as woods receded: "a large and valuable portion of the Mexican territory has been redeemed from the wilderness," boasted the *Texas Gazette* in 1830, "and Texas, which was hitherto unknown, even to the Mexicans themselves, is beginning to assume its proper station in the geography of America."[54] A brave new world had emerged.

Although established within Mexican territory, the Anglo-American colonies developed essentially as commercial outposts of Louisiana. As Mier y Terán was quick to observe, Anglo Americans had shunned the Texas interior and established themselves all along the Texas coast and in the Nacogdoches area precisely because of the commercial opportunities and access that these locations afforded.[55] Only a leisurely three-day sailing trip separated New Orleans from the Texas coast. This strategic position propelled Stephen F. Austin's main colony to emerge as "the very center of all maritime and terrestrial communications" in Texas. San Felipe, the most substantial settlement in the area, could be reached through the port of Matagorda, the inlet of the Brazos River, and Galveston Bay, as well as through navigable rivers like the Chocolate and Cíbolo.[56] A cursory examination of a local newspaper like the *Telegraph and Texas Register* – especially the substantial section of commercial notices – reveals the extent to which the rhythms of life at Austin's colony were marked by the arrival of schooners and steam packets from Louisiana. The colonists imported everything from New Orleans, from house frames, china, and silverware to shovels and cotton mills. Conversely, they shipped all the products obtained through their toils – primarily bales of cotton, but also cattle and furs – back to the Louisiana markets, thus closing a trading loop that had little to do with the rest of Mexico. In the mental map of Anglo-American colonists, Texas and Louisiana were inextricably connected, and any attempt to sever those ties constituted a mortal blow to the very livelihood of the colonies (see Map 1.6).

The Nacogdoches area in the northeastern corner of Texas was an even more dramatic illustration of the irrelevance of formal boundary definitions. Quite isolated from other settlements, this area was absolutely dependent on the closest town on the Louisiana side, Natchitoches, where all settlers,

---

[53] The *empresario* system was a contractual agreement between the state government of Coahuila and Texas and a private contractor. The state government would provide the land for the enterprise while the *empresario* bound himself to bring at least one hundred families at his own expense, parcel out the land, and more generally take all the steps necessary to establish a self-sustaining colony within six years. For all his troubles, the *empresario* would be given land.

[54] *Texas Gazette*, San Felipe of Austin, Jun 26, 1830, BHC.

[55] General Mier y Terán to Alamán, Jun 5, 1830, Bolton Papers, no. 637, Carton 40, 312, Bancroft Library.

[56] Mier y Terán to Minister of Internal and Foreign Affairs, Matamoros, Jan 8, 1832, BP 40: 673, 2.

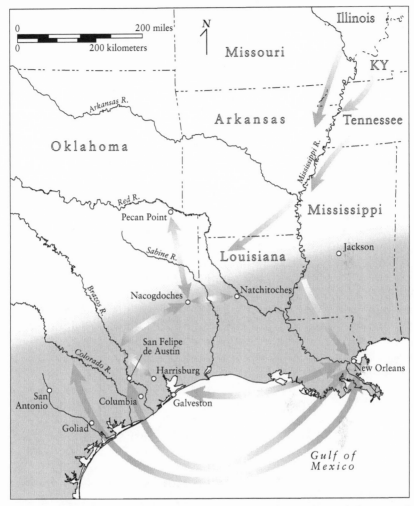

MAP 1.6. The Anglo-Texan colonies and their understanding of the immediate surroundings

both Anglo Texan and tejano, regularly supplied themselves with all manufactured goods and even basic foodstuffs like flour.[57] And such dependency was political as well: Anglo Texans regularly used the courts of Natchitoches and conducted official business there. All of this extended America's de facto jurisdiction into Mexican territory. The military commander of Nacogdoches

[57] Mateo Ahumada, Military Commander of Texas, to Anastasio Bustamante, Commander of the Eastern Interior Provinces, Nacogdoches, Apr 1, 1827, BP 40:673, 7; José de las Piedras, Commander of Nacogdoches, to General Mier y Terán, Commander of the Eastern Interior Provinces, Jan 30, 1832, BP 40:673, 4.

reported with alarm that some Anglo Texans had even organized an American district and half of another within Mexico's boundaries.[58] The geography of this area was all the more difficult to read given that the Nacogdoches-Natchitoches corridor was also an important Indian trading hub. Native Americans in the environs of the Neches and Angelina rivers trapped beaver and otter and sold the pelts on both sides of the border.[59] More importantly, the Nacogdoches–Natchitoches corridor served as a funnel through which virtually all Texas cattle and horses bound for the United States passed. Native Americans were engaged in this trading activity to such an extent that the governor of Coahuila and Texas deemed it necessary to have a vice consul in Natchitoches because, as he put it, "commercial relations in this area have a great influence on peace and war among the barbarous nations of our continent."[60]

In this remote world of east Texas, where no clear national boundaries existed, land ownership was unclear, and international commercial flows affected notions of geography, Mexico experienced the first serious challenge to its sovereignty. On December 21, 1826, a coalition of Anglo Americans and Cherokees proclaimed a new nation called the *Republic of the Red and White Peoples*, also known to history as the *Republic of Fredonia*. Both groups had been propelled into action by what they regarded as exclusionary acts on the part of the Mexican government. And they retaliated by fashioning a spatial arrangement of their own making. The Fredonia uprising reveals very clearly the mechanisms through which Anglo Americans and Native Americans were carving largely independent spaces within Mexican territory.

Much support for the Fredonia uprising came from Anglo-American squatters who had settled on the Mexican side of the Texas–Louisiana border between the Sabine and Atoyac rivers.[61] They began moving into Mexico in 1821, encouraged by announcements in Louisiana newspapers to the effect that the Spanish government had awarded a colonization contract to a fellow Louisianan, Moses Austin, who was looking for three hundred families to settle in Texas. While Stephen F. Austin, Moses's son, lobbied in Mexico City to have the colonization contract ratified – spending more than a year away from Texas – squatters began crossing into Mexican territory. These

---

[58] Colonel Peter Ellis Bean, Military Commander of Nacogdoches, to General Mier y Terán, quoted in Mier y Terán to Alamán, Oct 31, 1830, Bolton Papers, no. 673, Carton 40, 126.

[59] De las Piedras to Mier y Terán, Nacogdoches, Jan 30, 1832, BP 40:673, 4.

[60] Governor of Coahuila and Texas to Minister of War, Saltillo, Dec 27, 1825, General Land Office (GLO) 124:5, 147–9; José Antonio Saucedo, *jefe político* of Texas, to Governor Rafael González, San Antonio, Apr 18, 1825, BA 80, 681. See also Kelly F. Himmel, *The Conquest of the Karankawas and the Tonkawas, 1821–1859* (College Station, TX: Texas A&M University Press, 1999) 40–1.

[61] The story of these settlements is told in Colonel Mateo Ahumada to the Comandante General de los Estados Internos de Oriente don Anastacio Bustamante, Nacogdoches, Apr 1, 1827, Herbert E. Bolton Papers, Carton 40, no. 673, Bancroft Library.

Anglo Americans chose to remain close to the Louisiana border without venturing farther inland as rumors circulated about Stephen Austin's fate – for example, that Austin had died in transit, that the contract had been canceled, and so on. And the presence of squatters right on the Louisiana border encouraged others to follow suit. Even more enticing, Mexico's local authorities initially did not oppose these unregulated settlements. Indeed, James Dill, the first Anglo-American *alcalde* of Nacogdoches who held office during 1821–3, personally gave permission to 168 families to settle in the area.[62]

In 1824, the Mexican government issued its National Law on Colonization specifically prohibiting the settlement of foreigners within twenty leagues (fifty-two miles) of the border with the United States. By then, however, the irregular settlements between the Sabine and the Atoyac had become firmly rooted. Over the years, squatters had cleared woods, built houses, and established a rudimentary system or roads and ferries, and were already planting cotton, maize, and beans. The Mexican commander in Nacogdoches estimated that in 1826 these settlements were already producing some sixteen thousand *arrobas* of cotton sold in Natchitoches, Louisiana for about 4,000 pesos.[63] Removing the squatters would have required a considerable military force. The upshot of all of this was a stark disjuncture between the national imagination and the situation on the ground. Federal legislation may have envisioned a twenty-league boundary preserve devoid of foreign colonists, but in reality the Texas–Louisiana border was becoming blurred as the cotton economy and the complicity of local Mexican officials created a space that was generally beyond the reach of the Mexican government.

The Cherokees – the other main protagonists of the Fredonia insurrection – found themselves in an analogous situation. About sixty Cherokee families first migrated to Texas in 1819–20. Given their bitter experience with American surveyors in Arkansas,[64] these Cherokee immigrants were quite keen on securing a land grant upon entering Texas. The first signs were encouraging. In 1822 Richard Fields, an Anglo-Cherokee chief, journeyed to San Antonio and Mexico City and obtained a provisional approval of the Cherokee settlements and a promise that they would be considered "Spanish-Americans" protected by the law. But the agreement proved somewhat unsatisfactory for both parties. Privately, Mexican officials worried that Chief Fields would use this provisional approval to introduce many more

---

[62] Governor of Coahuila and Texas Ignacio Arispe to Minister of Foreign Relations, Saltillo, Apr 24, 1827, Herbert E. Bolton Papers, Carton 40, no. 673, Bancroft Library.

[63] Colonel Mateo Ahumada to the Comandante General de los Estados Internos de Oriente don Anastacio Bustamante, Nacogdoches, Apr 1, 1827, Herbert E. Bolton Papers, Carton 40, no. 673, Bancroft Library.

[64] Chief Bowles, a Cherokee chief who migrated into Texas, conducted a settlement with the United States and subsequently relocated to Arkansas. But as fate would have it, the Cherokees' chosen settlement was not on land ceded by the United States government.

Cherokee families still residing in Arkansas and delayed the confirmation of the Cherokee grant. For their part, the Cherokees learned with dismay of the colonization law issued by the state of Coahuila and Texas in 1825. Article 19 flatly stated that all prospective settlers needed to convert to Catholicism and declare themselves in favor of Mexico's political institutions. In a letter to the governor of Coahuila and Texas, Chief Fields stated that his belief and hope was that such requirements would apply only to Anglo Americans and other white settlers but not to the Cherokees. Moreover, he pointed out that while *in principle* the Cherokees wished to subject themselves to Mexico's legislation, they did not want to do so immediately.[65] In December 1825, Chief Fields convened a large gathering to discuss the situation and soon thereafter joined the Fredonia rebels.[66] Like the irregular settlements of the Texas–Louisiana border, the Cherokee families were able to carve a space of their own, living at the margins of state authority and posing a very real challenge to the national imagination.

The peculiar netherworld of East Texas finally exploded with the arrival of the Edwards brothers, Haden and Benjamin. In April 1825, the state government in Saltillo gave Haden Edwards a colonization contract to settle eight hundred families in a large area around Nacogdoches adjacent to the border preserve where the squatters lived as well as to the Cherokee-controlled area. By all accounts, the Edwards brothers were brash and determined to succeed in a difficult environment, generating considerable animosities in the process. Most notably, as Haden made preparations to fulfill his colonization contract, he required residents who had arrived before him to produce land titles or face immediate eviction, a move that generated enormous ill will, particularly from tejanos.[67] In the brewing confrontation, Haden Edwards sought to enlist the support of the Anglo-American squatters by offering land within his grant.

The battle lines were already clearly drawn during the elections for *alcalde* of Nacogdoches in December 1825. Residents who had arrived before the Edwards brothers supported the candidacy of Samuel Norris, while the *empresario* threw his lot behind his son-in-law, Chichester Chaplin. The election was controversial. While Edwards immediately certified Chaplin, Norris' supporters contended that many of Chaplin's votes had come from unqualified voters in the irregular border settlements. In the face of indecision, Chaplin took matters in his own hands and forcibly took the archives

[65] Chief Fields to Governor of Coahuila and Texas, Apr 22, 1825, NA, 2q298, 195, 239–41.
[66] Treaty between the imperial government and the Cherokee nation, San Antonio, Nov 8, 1822. GLO 124:5; Minister of Foreign Affairs to General Felipe de la Garza, Commander of the Eastern Interior Provinces, Mexico City, Apr 27, 1823, GLO 124:5; Governor of Coahuila and Texas to War Minister, Saltillo, Dec 27, 1825, GLO 124:5, 147–9.
[67] Expediente sobre los procedimintos del empresario Haden Edwards en le publo de Nacogdoches del estado de Coahuila y Tejas, Mexico City, 1826, Herbert E. Bolton Papers, Carton 40, no. 676, Bancroft Library.

and assumed his duties as *alcalde*. But in March 1826, the *jefe político* in San Antonio, José Antonio Saucedo, reversed the election and directed Chaplin to give the archives to Norris. Revealingly, Chaplin retorted that he took orders only from Saltillo and not from San Antonio and remained defiant for weeks. It was clear that the machine created by the Edwards brothers possessed real power independent from San Antonio authorities. As Norris expressed in a letter to *jefe político* Saucedo:

...no civil officer can discharge his duties nor enforce order nor respect for his authority if he is not supported by regular troops; otherwise he is doomed to be the laughing stock of everybody... if your lordship does not take speedy steps to send regular troops here you may rest assured that oceans of blood will be spilled.[68]

Things finally came to a head when the state government of Coahuila and Texas – the last support of the Edwards machine – conducted its own investigation and decided to revoke Haden's grant in November 1826. The Edwards brothers became incensed. Haden refused to relinquish his newly acquired authority and domain and found strong support to his defiant position from border squatters and settlers already living in his land grant. On November 22, 1826, a group of thirty-six men from the Ayish Bayou area – the largest settlement east of Nacogdoches toward the Louisiana border – seized alcalde Norris, militia Captain José Antonio Sapúlveda, and others, and tried them for oppression and corruption in office.[69] In the meantime, the Cherokees had already concluded that Mexico's delay in confirming their grant could only mean veiled rejection, and they too decided to join a rebellion that was becoming a full-scale secessionist attempt. Chief Fields eloquently explained his motives during the uprising:

In the days of my old age I traveled two thousand miles to the City of Mexico to apply for some lands whereon to establish an orphan tribe of red people who looked on me as their protector. The Mexican government promised me lands for them and after having waited one year in the City of Mexico at a heavy expense I returned to my people where I remained two years longer. ... I am a red man, and a man of honor, therefore I cannot bear such treatment. We will raise the hatchet and fight for lands with other friendly tribes who desire some also. If I am whipped then I shall submit to my fate; if not, I will keep my lands with the assistance of my red warriors.[70]

[68] Samuel Norris to José Antonio Saucedo, Nacogdoches, Oct 17, 1826, NA, 2q298, 197A, 126.

[69] Contract between Haden Edwards and the State Government of Coahuila and Texas, Saltillo, May 19, 1825, GLO 124:3, 61–4. See also file on the conduct of *empresario* Haden Edwards, Ministry of the Interior, 1826, BP 40:676; Declaration of the Republic of Fredonia, Nacogdoches, Dec 21, 1826, BHC, 2q222, 560, 263–5. See also Vito Alessio Robles, *Coahuila y Texas desde la cosumación de la independencia hasta el tratado de Paz do Guadalupe Hidalgo*, 2 vols. (Mexico City: Porrúa, 1979) I, 211–5.

[70] Richard Fields, declaration on behalf of the Cherokee nation in favor of the Fredonian Republic, quoted in Peter Ellis Bean to *jefe político*, Nacogdoches, Dec 21, 1826, NA 2q299, 198, 151–62.

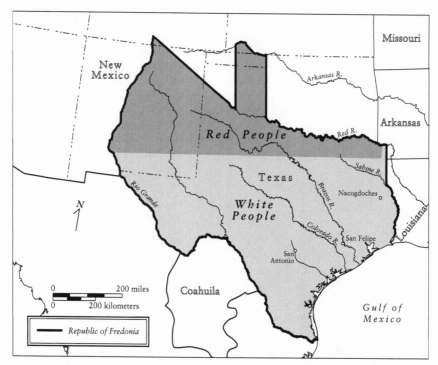

MAP 1.7. The Republic of Fredonia

Just before Christmas of 1826, Anglo-American settlers, Cherokees, and other allied indigenous groups signed a formal declaration refusing to submit their free persons to "the yoke of an imbecile, faithless, and despotic government (erroneously called republic)."[71] The signatories agreed to establish the Fredonia Republic, an entity that would consist of two distinct halves (see Map 1.7). The territory apportioned to the *Red People* roughly comprised the northern half of Texas, from the Red to the Grande rivers. The *White People* would obtain the southern half of Texas and "such other portions of the Mexican United States as the contracting parties by their mutual efforts and resources may render independent, provided the same shall not extend farther West than the Rio Grande."[72]

[71] Declaration of the Republic of Fredonia, Nacogdoches, Dec 21, 1826, BHC, 2q222.
[72] Declaration of the Republic of Fredonia, Nacogdoches, Dec 21, 1826, BHC, 2q222. The exact limits according to Article 3 of the declaration ran as follows:

> The territory apportioned to the Red People (pueblo colorado), shall begin at the Sandy Spring, where Bradley's Road takes off from the road leading from Nacogdoches to the Plantation of Joseph Dust, from thence West, by the Compass, without regard to variation to the Rio Grande, thence to the head of the Rio Grande, thence with the mountains to the head of Big Red River, thence North to the boundary of the United States of North

The movement was short-lived. National troops arrived in Nacogdoches within weeks. The more established colonies of Austin and Dewitt sided with the Mexican government and sent militia forces to reinforce the Mexican regulars. At the same time, government representatives succeeded in persuading the Cherokees to pull out of the secessionist alliance. Mexican forces captured Haden Edwards and the other Anglo-Texan leaders; among the Cherokees, the council of elders turned against Chief Fields and ordered his execution.[73] But in spite of this conclusive ending, the Fredonia Republic stood as a reminder that the geography of Texas admitted several interpretations.

THE EXPANDING INDIAN WORLD

Every time Chief Paruakevitsi entered a Mexican town or gathered with Mexican officials, he produced a copy of a truce that General Anastasio Bustamante had issued in 1827 and insisted that it be read aloud. The Comanche chief enjoyed listening to the Spanish-language reader as he worked his way article by article through the entire document pausing for the simultaneous translator to add his own interpretations. Having heard it before, Chief Paruakevitsi was sensitive to the slightest variation in meaning and emphasis. He seemed pleased after the exercise, pronouncing the document "bueno," and marveling at the thought that this document would command the same recognition in such distant locales as San Antonio, El Paso del Norte, and Santa Fe.[74] Undoubtedly, the Mexican presence reached deep and wide into North America. But it was the indigenous chief and his people, not the local military commander, who were able to travel freely from San Antonio to Santa Fe. Mexicans may have controlled clusters of communities in Alta California, New Mexico, and Texas, but they lacked secure routes connecting these settlements together.[75]

America, thence with the same line to the mouth of Sulphur Fork, thence in a right line to the beginning. The territory apportioned to the White people, shall comprehend all the residue of the Province of Texas and of such other portions of the Mexican United States as the contracting parties by their mutual efforts and resources may render Independent, provided the same shall not extend further West than the Rio Grande.

73 Bean to Saucedo, Nacogdoches, Feb 7, 1827, NA 2q299, 198, 236–7; Alessio Robles, *Coahuila y Texas*, 211–25; Dianna Everett, *The Texas Cherokees: A People Between Two Fires, 1819–1880* (Norman, OK: University of Oklahoma Press, 1990), 46–7.
74 Governor José Antonio Chávez and Comandante Principal Juan José Arocha to Lieutenant Colonel Francisco Ruiz, Bosque Redondo, Jun 26, 1829, MANM 9, 866–8. On the geographic mobility of Chief Paruakevitsi, see Kavanagh, *The Comanches*, 196, 198, 200, 204.
75 On the complex interplay between settled and nomadic communities, see the illuminating works by James F. Brooks, *Captives and Cousins: Slavery, Kinship, and Community in the Southwest Borderlands* (Chapel Hill, NC: University of North Carolina Press, 2002); Jack D. Forbes, *Apache, Navaho, and Spaniard* (1960; reprint, Norman, OK: University of Oklahoma Press, 1994); Hall, *Social Change in the Southwest*, esp. 90–133.

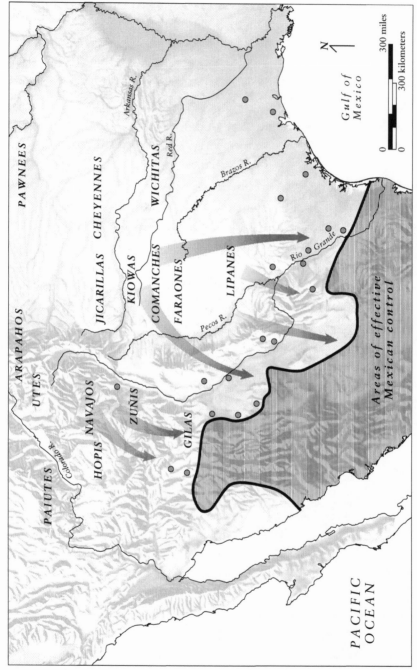

PAWNEES

ARAPAHOS

UTES

PAIUTES

Colorado R.

HOPIS NAVAJOS

ZUÑIS

GILAS

JICARILLAS CHEYENNES

WICHITAS

KIOWAS

COMANCHES

FARAONES

LIPANES

Arkansas R.

Red R.

Brazos R.

Pecos R.

Rio Grande

PACIFIC
OCEAN

Gulf of
Mexico

Areas of effective
Mexican control

N

300 miles

300 kilometers

0

0

MAP 1.8. Indigenous territories expanding at the expense of Mexico in the early-nineteenth century

From the vantage point of nomadic Native Americans, Mexico appeared less like a nation with established borders than clusters of isolated, largely independent, and exposed communities that allowed nomads to move unimpeded through enormous ares where they were far more likely to find other Native Americans rather than Hispanics (see Map 1.8). This was particularly obvious from the mid-eighteenth through the mid-nineteenth century, when nomadism reached its high watermark as the diffusion of horses, the availability of buffalo, imperial and national rivalries, and shifting economic opportunities made life on the horse not only possible but enticing and common. Changing configurations of indigenous territories inside the Spanish Empire and Mexico bore this out. For instance, whereas in the seventeenth century New Mexicans generally thought of the *apachería* as being north and east at some distance from their settlements, in the course of the eighteenth century, various Apache groups moved closer to the Rio Grande valley and literally came to surround it. The Jicarillas moved through the New Mexico–Texas corridor, the Chiricahuas established themselves in a large area west of New Mexico, and various groups known collectively as Western Apaches migrated to what is today eastern Arizona. The upshot was that Apache groups came to occupy territories to the east, west, and south of New Mexico's settlements.[76] A formidable array of indigenous peoples led by Comanches, Kiowas, and Navajos established themselves generally north of New Mexico, pushing Apaches farther south.[77]

In Texas, Native American mobility was comparable if not greater largely because of the American policy to remove Indians east of the Mississippi to the western and southern parts of the Arkansas territory. Lieutenant José María Sánchez of the Boundary Commission reported that just in the vicinity of Nacogdoches he saw a number of bands wandering in all directions.[78] General Mier y Terán, accustomed to the Hispanicized Native Americans of central Mexico, was ill prepared to cope with a constant stream of native visitors who arrived at his improvised quarters (often unannounced, as he pointedly noted) in the hopes of obtaining official recognition for their lands in Texas. After vigorously shaking their host's hand, they sat down

---

[76] Scholarls disagree about the exact migratory routes of Apache groups. See Keith H. Basso, "Western Apache," 463; Morris E. Opler, "Chiricahua Apache," 402–3; Morris E. Opler, "Mescalero Apache," 419; Veronica E. Tiller, "Jicarilla Apache," 447–51; all in William C. Sturtevant, ed., *Handbook of North American Indians*, vol. 10 (Washington, DC: Smithsonian Institution, 1983).

[77] For a general overview of the location of Apaches and Comanches from the pre-horse era through the nineteenth century, see W. W. Newcomb, Jr., *The Indians of Texas: From Prehistoric to Modern Times* (Austin, TX: University of Texas Press, 1961).

[78] Report of José María Sánchez to Minister of Foreign Relations, Nacogdoches, Jun 9, 1828, BHC 2q171, 327, 112.

FIGURE 1.4. Cheyenne

with alacrity on the general's trunks and bed, and those who came later
sat on the dirt floor. Then they lit their pipes and proceeded to negotiate
enveloped by a cloud of smoke in ninety-plus-degree temperatures.[79] As
General Mier y Terán observed, some of these Native Americans had lived
in Texas for decades and had old ties to the Spanish-Mexican communities
and government. Yet others were recent arrivals who had remained quite
independent from the Mexican government (see Figure 1.4).

The Boundary Commissioners were particularly concerned with this recent wave of "foreign" Indians. For instance, sometime between 1806 and
1819, a group of Alabamas entered Texas coming originally from the state
of the same name. The Cherokee Indians moved into Texas in substantial
numbers beginning in 1819 and established themselves in the environs of
the Angelina and Sabine rivers. Groups of Savano and Delaware Indians
also moved south across the Red River. The Savano Indians had lived in
the Illinois plains and moved first into the Arkansas territory and then into
Texas. The Delawares had migrated from Pennsylvania. The Kikapos entered Texas in 1825 having migrated all the way from the Canadian Great

[79] Diary of General Mier y Terán, quoted in report of José María Sánchez to Minister of Foreign
Relations, Nacogdoches, Jun 9, 1828, BHC 2q171, 322.

Lakes region.[80] An Anglo-American newspaper in Texas left no doubt about the likely fallout from such massive migrations:

As appears from the statistical accounts that have been published of them, these Indians exceed one hundred and five thousand. Fears have been entertained by many that the whole body of this discordant mass, composed of the remnants of numberless and distinct tribes who have learned little from civilized man except his vices, would precipitate themselves into Texas. Such an event would be fatal to all that part of the Mexican territory lying east and northeast of a line passing from Matamoros through La Punta de Lampazos, Santa Rosa, etc. for the entrance of the northern Indians would, of course, force the Comanches, Lipans etc. to seek refuge on the borders of the Rio Grande del Norte; and as that country is destitute of buffalo, they would, from necessity, have to subsist on the cattle and other stock of the inhabitants....[81]

Indian groups moved into Mexican territory for different reasons and found themselves in very different circumstances. On the one hand, some eastern Apache groups, once in control of the southern Plains, were simply pushed south by Comanches, Utes, and Wichitas. On the other hand, the powerful Comanche confederation was able to control a large and stable territorial base around the Llano Estacado south of the Arkansas River and expand into Mexico. Through shrewd alliances with Kiowas, Kiowa-Apaches, Arapahos, and Cheyennes, the Horse People retained possession of the Arkansas Basin since the eighteenth century, constituting a formidable barrier to southward-moving Native Americans and westward-moving Anglo Americans well into the 1860s. Unlike Mexico, the Comanche confederation was able to enforce its territorial boundaries, and unlike the fledgling Texas Republic, the confederation was able to remain an autonomous nation throughout this entire period (see Figure 1.5).[82]

One way to reckon the extent to which Native Americans actually controlled this contested territory is by looking at the Spanish and Mexican defensive strategy. Since the 1760s during the *visita general* of José de Gálvez and the military inspection of the Marqués de Rubí, the Spanish Crown had proposed the idea of establishing a line of presidios directly on the Rio Grande that would stop Indian incursions farther into the interior. Tellingly, this strategy left Texas and New Mexico completely outside of the protective military cordon, thus implicitly acknowledging the difficulties of rolling back the Native American presence already there.[83] But even such a retrenchment

---

[80] Report of José María Sánchez, Nacogdoches, Jun 9, 1928, BHC 2q171, 327, 114; Everett, *The Texas Cherokees*, 22; Himmel, *The Conquest of the Karankawas and the Tonkawas*, 7–8.

[81] *Texas Gazette*, San Felipe de Austin, Jun 26, 1830.

[82] Stanley Noyes, *Los Comanches: The Horse People, 1751–1845* (Santa Fe, NM: University of New Mexico Press, 1993), passim.

[83] Whereas the Marqués de Rubí sought to solve the frontier problems chiefly by containing Indian threats through the line of *presidios*, José de Gálvez had a broader international

FIGURE 1.5. Comanche

could not prevent the indigenous advances to the south as various groups, but most notably the Comanches, pushed through the hills and canyons of San Saba across the Rio Grande, "unleashing a powerful offensive that gave them access into Coahuila, Nuevo León, and Tamaulipas eventually forcing the removal of the old presidios of Monclova and Aguaverde to safer locations."[84]

The late-colonial and early-Mexican period witnessed a gradual expansion of the Indian world into Mexico as many indigenous nations, previously isolated and largely dependent on the short supply of powder and

vision concerned with the expansion of other empires into New Spanish territory as well. See discussion in Weber, *The Spanish Frontier in North America*, 237–42.

[84] Miguel Ramos Arizpe to Lucas Alamán, Puebla, Aug 1, 1830, Herbert E. Bolton Papers, Carton 40, no. 673, no page, Bancroft Library.

old weapons provided by the Spanish Crown, came in contact with French and Anglo-American merchants in the aftermath of the Louisiana Purchase. Groups like the Lipan, Jicarilla, Wichita, Comanche, and Kiowa, became invigorated with readily available firearms and powder while New Spain became weakened by internal turmoil that led to emancipation from Spain. According to the authoritative 1830 account of Miguel Ramos Arizpe, the ensuing confrontation unleashed repeated Indian raids throughout Mexico's northeastern provinces, resulting in more than two thousand Mexican men, women, and children being taken captive between 1816 and 1821. In the 1820s, Mexico continued to lose ground as crumbling and undermanned presidios such as Palafox were moved farther south or were abandoned altogether.[85]

Undoubtedly, the Indian world was expanding at the expense of Mexico in spite of contrary appearances. Indian groups occasionally visited Mexican villas to trade, to negotiate treaties, or simply to be *gratified* by the Mexican authorities with blankets, knives, and other trifles. At a more formal level, some of these groups actually pledged allegiance to the Mexican nation and recognized the Mexican government as the highest authority and in return drew salaries and received "authority canes" that chiefs used in their own internal power struggles.[86] But in this landscape of equivocal appearances, a solemn pledge of loyalty to the *capitan grande* in Mexico City did not seem particularly onerous in exchange for real food, trinkets, and land. Tadeo Ortiz, the colonization commissioner in Texas and General Mier y Terán's successor, wrote to the president in 1833, lambasting Mexico's inconsistent Indian policy that sometimes treated nomads as sovereign nations with all the considerations due to powerful governments, but sometimes dealt with them as if they were favorite sons and daughters deserving of all kinds of gifts. In his view, such a strategy, based on the remote hope that nomadic Indians would some day embrace Christianity, had instead nearly devastated Mexico's northernmost tier. Ortiz proposed to conduct an all-out campaign to drive Indians out of Mexican territory and restore national sovereignty, but such a campaign never materialized.[87]

The impact of the expansion of the Indian world was also evident in Mexico's settled communities in the Far North. This phenomenon is impossible to express in spatial terms but nonetheless became quite detrimental to the Mexican national imagination. Tejanos, nuevomexicanos, and

[85] Miguel Ramos Arizpe to Lucas Alamán, Puebla, Aug 1, 1830, Herbert E. Bolton Papers, Carton 40, no. 673, no page, Bancroft Library.

[86] Treaty with the Comanche Nation, Chihuahua, Oct 8, 1826, MANM 5: 425–7. Chief Cuelgas de Castro drew a salary equivalent to that of lieutenant colonel of the Mexican army. Sánchez y Tapia, "A Trip to Texas in 1828," passim.

[87] Report of Tadeo Ortiz, Matamoros, Feb 2, 1833, translated into English by Edith Louise Kelly and Mattie Austin Hatcher, "Tadeo Ortiz de Ayala and the Colonization of Texas, 1822–1833," *Southwestern Historical Quarterly* 32 (Feb and Apr 1929), 322–3.

Anglo-American residents generally conceived the space they inhabited in *opposition* to that occupied by Indians. Official reports and private correspondence invariably depicted Texas and New Mexico as *surrounded* by dozens of Indian nations.[88] Moreover, such sharp spatial portrayals underscored the spiritual differences stated in many polarities such as sedentary versus nomadic, Christian versus heathen, national versus tribal, civilized versus savage.

Notwithstanding this seemingly unbridgeable divide, frontier inhabitants passed from the Mexican to the Indian world and vice versa with relative ease. Consider the saga of José María Crespín and Carpio, two Native Americans of the California missions of San Luis Rey and San Juan Capistrán, who after having escaped their masters in 1833 would spend the next two years drifting westward independently, living with Navajos as well as Gileño and Coyotero Apaches. According to their judicial depositions, they reached Abiquiu sometime in 1835 and settled among a group of *genízaros* for a few months. Wanting to visit and eat in other New Mexican pueblos, the pair spent a few months in Santo Domingo and Isleta but finally grew restless with sedentary life. Sometime in 1836, the twosome departed Isleta and headed west attempting to reach a group of Gileños. On the way, they joined an Anglo-American party that was trading powder, bullets, and *sarapes* in the area; the group hired Carpio and Crespín as guides. That proved to be their undoing, as a Mexican military detachment picked them up for selling arms to wild Indians and took the pair to El Paso for questioning.[89] The story of these two California Native Americans not only shows a formidable indigenous network allowing an active exchange of peoples and ideas spanning all the way from California missions through several nomadic nations to New Mexican pueblos – a network that Hispanics knew imperfectly if at all – but it also reveals how in the eyes of Spanish and Mexican

---

[88] Estimates on the number of nomadic Indians in New Mexico are impossible to obtain for this era, but at least we can get a sense of Indian diversity. In 1831, Antonio Barreiro provided brief descriptions of the main four Indian groups living in New Mexico: Comanche, Ute, Navajo, and Apache. The Apache, in turn, were further divided according to an extensive and often demeaning classificatory scheme including *tontos* or *coyoteros, chiricahuas, gileños, mimbreños, farahones, mezcaleros, llaneros, lipanes, jicarillas,* and others. Antonio Barreiro, "Ojeada sobre Nuevo México...," in H. Bailey Carroll and J. Villasana Haggard, eds., *Three New Mexico Chronicles* (Albuquerque, NM: Quivira Society, 1942), 310–18. Miguel Antonio Lovato supplemented Barreiro's list (in Spanish): *comanches, orientales, yamparicas, sariticas, aa, mansos, flechas rayadas, chiricaguas, arapajoes, tancanos, abajoes, cuampes, comeperros, ampesiz?, sosones, patas negras, caiguas, pananas, guasases, palomos, jumanos, orejones, apaches de la arena, pacanabos, cuhunticas?, cuervos, gente del hígado, lobos, churiques, pelones, and lipanes.* Miguel Antonio Lovato, "Noticioso que da una idea de las diversas y quasi infinitas naciones que circundan a Nuevo México y de algunas otras cosas...," n.p., c1838, Miguel Antonio Lovato Collection, Center for Southwest Research, University of New Mexico.

[89] Judicial proceedings against José María Crespín and Carpio, El Paso, Oct 1, 1836, MANM 22, 461–97.

authorities Indians could move seamlessly from neophyte to nomadic to Pueblo and back to nomadic or even outlaw status.

The three-year saga of Carpio and Crespín itself may have been somewhat extraordinary, but the porous Spanish and Mexican system that allowed them to alter their status was not. During the colonial period, nomadic Native Americans who had become Hispanicized automatically acquired the status of *genízaros*. And *genízaros*, in turn, were able to claim Hispanic *(vecino)* status by virtue of securing a land grant, through loyal service to Spanish individuals, or by marrying into Hispanic families. For instance, in the late-eighteenth century, mission entries at Abiquiu frequently use the term "genízaro vecino" to describe the local population, reflecting the assimilative trend.[90]

In the Mexican period, the process of altering one's status became more streamlined, as official paperwork dropped all mention of racial or ethnic categories.[91] While social disparities and ethnic references persisted in everyday life, in theory at least nomadic Native Americans wishing to become Mexican citizens only needed to settle down, convert to Catholicism, and pledge loyalty. The reverse was also true. Just as nomadic Native Americans could easily become part of Mexico's national polity, individuals regarded as members of the imperial or national body could and did slip out of the fold. One such wave of defections occurred in Texas in the late 1820s, when the last functioning missions were closed down. After having lived for more than one hundred years on mission lands in the vicinity of Goliad, several families of Karankawa and Xaramano Indians were required to move to town and take up residence in Hispanic households as *acomodados* or *arrimados* (servants/additional family members) to complete their assimilation into Mexican society.[92] Contrary to expectations, many former neophytes did take up residence in Goliad; but as fate would have it, a rumor about a Comanche raid a few days later created such commotion that they took to the wilderness and did not return. These movements of individuals in and out of the national community – a phenomenon common in areas that Gonzalo Aguirre Beltrán and Thomas D. Hall have characterized as *regions of refuge* – profoundly defied the national imagination.[93]

Instead of developing into clear territories corresponding to sharp ethnic divisions as described by nuevomexicano officials – the Mexican nation

[90] Swadesh, *Los Primeros Pobladores* 42–6.

[91] Decree abolishing racial categories, Mexico City, Jul 14, 1824, BA 77:485. See also Presidential Decree, Mexico City, May 2, 1826, Spanish Archives of New Mexico (SANM) 1, 6:1341.

[92] Proposal of the *ayuntamiento*, Goliad, Feb 26, 1830, GLO 122:17; Miguel Aldrete to Músquiz, *jefe político*, Goliad, May 18, 1830, GLO 122:18.

[93] While the *region of refuge* notion is better suited to New Mexico during the colonial period, a few traits nonetheless survived into the first half of the nineteenth century, including this considerable passing back and forth of individuals between ethnic communities. See the enlightening discussion in Hall, *Social Change in the Southwest*, 101–2.

FIGURE 1.6. Pueblo of Santa Ana

as opposed to the Karankawa, Navajo, Ute, or Apache nations – Mexico's communities in the Far North seemed to dissolve into contiguous human groups in a pattern of different shades of gray. New Mexico's settled communities provide vivid illustrations of these points of contact between the settled and nomadic worlds. One type of such transitional communities can be found in the *genízaro* settlements located within nomadic Indian areas such as Abiquiu, Ojo Caliente, Los Jarales, and some *ranchos* in the vicinity of San Miguel del Vado.⁹⁴ These settlements attracted itinerant individuals such as the two former California neophytes as well as nomadic peoples who were captured or purchased or who had chosen to live alongside detribalized Pueblo Indians and *vecinos* for other reasons. Such remarkable communities constituted halfway stations or meeting grounds where nomads and settlers could contemplate life in either form.

Pueblos were also meeting grounds where the nomadic and settled worlds came together. Pueblo Indians were formally recognized as Mexican citizens after 1821. But in practice, Pueblos kept a good measure of political, religious, and economic autonomy and preserved ties to neighboring nomadic groups. Pueblo Indians had been traditionally forced to ally themselves with the Spanish and were periodically required to participate in punitive expeditions against the errant nations. Pueblo Indians dreaded these campaigns, as they had to surrender horses and other supplies and, worse still, were often drafted, compelled to leave their families and fields unattended, and forced to risk their lives in faraway skirmishes. But in spite of this pressure, individual

⁹⁴ Angélico Chávez, "Genízaros," in Robert Wauchope, ed., *Handbook of North American Indians*, vol. 9 (Austin, TX: University of Texas Press, 1973), 198–205.

pueblos maintained close trading relations and other contacts with neighboring groups. In an insightful assessment of Pueblo Indian life, Friar Manuel de Jesús Rada characterized them as standing "with one foot in the Church and another in heathenism," and emphasized the frequency with which nomadic Indians could be found in the pueblos, especially in Zuñi, Santa Ana, Zía, Acoma, and Jemez (see Figure 1.6).[95] So strong was this association that New Mexico's authorities feared that Pueblo Indians could "revert" to a "barbaric state" and together revolt against the constituted authority. Such a pan-Indian alliance had impeccable historical precedents going back at least to the Pueblo Revolt of 1680 that had ended in the wholesale expulsion of the Spanish from New Mexico. Allegations of Pueblo-nomadic alliances surfaced in 1837 during the Chimayó Rebellion and again in 1841 during the Texan Santa Fe Expedition.[96]

The greater Rio Grande valley harbored the seeds of many different human projects and competing geographies. Oddly, during the 1820s and early 1830s, these multifarious understandings of place and disparate demographic projects unfolded simultaneously. Mexican federal authorities proceeded to explore, map, and demarcate Mexico's national boundaries. Anglo-American merchants, plantation owners, and ordinary settlers continued to relocate into northern Mexico, establishing commercial ventures and adopting lifestyles that depended on the continuation and accretion of ties to the American markets, especially in the Taos area of New Mexico and along the Texas coast and on the border with Louisiana. For their part, tejanos and nuevomexicanos and their sedentary indigenous allies painstakingly gained ground in their immediate surroundings and attempted to exploit favorable economic conditions created by the integration of this entire area into the American markets. Finally, nomadic Native Americans continued to move deeper into Mexico, pushing other indigenous groups farther south and making inroads into areas that they had not reached before. All of these migratory flows and spatial configurations were possible because of the relatively low population density at the start of the period. But by the mid-1830s, these spatial and demographic projects were beginning to collide with each other, producing a series of rebellions over the question of who was entitled to the bountiful gifts that nature had to offer.

---

[95] Manuel de Jesus Rada to Padre Provincial del Santo Evangelio Fr. José Antonio Guisper, Mexico City, Mar 31, 1829, Microfilm edition of the Archives Históricos del Arcobispado de Durange (AHAD), reel 262, frames 402–7.

[96] For these allegations during the Mexican period, see Manuel Armijo to Ministry of War, Santa Fe, May 7, 1838, MANM 24:899–902. For the historical background of Pueblo–nomadic alliances, see Forbes, *Apache, Navaho, and Spaniard*, 200–24, 250–80.

2

A Nation Made Visible

Patronage, Power, and Ritual

Curious Santa Feans were likely to visit the local post office at any time of the day or night in the final months of 1821. They hoped to get fresh news or at least hear the latest speculations as Spanish garrisons, one after another, capitulated to the insurgent forces throughout New Spain, sparking the infectious rhetoric of emancipation and prompting festivities and jubilation as far north as Chihuahua and Durango.[1] In the midst of all this excitement, New Mexico remained one of the last holdouts. Governor Facundo Melgares had been slow to join the independence bandwagon, and when he finally did, it was less out of his own volition than to follow instructions from higher authority.[2] A portly man of decidedly military demeanor, Colonel Melgares agreed to convey "the sweet voice of freedom" to his fellow New Mexicans sometime in September, but proceeded cautiously, not permitting formal celebrations for three more agonizing months, perhaps fearing (or hoping for) a last-minute revival of Spanish fortunes.

After Christmas, Colonel Melgares began to ponder whether to comply with the detailed instructions that he had received from Mexico City about how

---

[1] *Gaceta Imperial de México*, Mar 1822, Santa Fe New Mexico Records, Box 1, Folder 1, Center for Southwest Research, University of New Mexico (CSR). This document was translated and commented by David J. Weber, "An Unforgettable Day: Facundo Melgares on Independence," *New Mexico Historical Review* 48: 1 (Jan 1973), 29, 36.

[2] In September 1821, Chihuahua's commandant general – with military jurisdiction over New Mexico – suddenly joined the rebel cause. Colonel Melgares claimed that he did not learn about Agustin de Iturbide's entrance into Mexico City until December 26. Yet there is enough evidence to suggest that New Mexicans had found out about the triumph of the independence movement well before and that the governor was only trying to justify his delay. Weber, "An Unforgettable Day," 27. Colonel Melgares' own report provides evidence that pressure had been mounting in New Mexico to declare independence. Governor Melgares was hardly alone in New Mexico in his mistrust of independence. During the entire revolutionary decade of 1810–21, New Mexico remained noticeably uncommitted. See Hubert Howe Bancroft, *History of Arizona and New Mexico, 1530–1888*, vol. 18 (San Francisco, CA: History Company, 1889), 307.

to celebrate independence. Mexico's Provisional Governing Junta did not take things lightly. It required a two-day observance that included several solemn oaths (the exact wording of each question and answer was provided), a parade through town, a formal mass, readings of several independence documents, and a public pledge of allegiance. All of this had to be carried out "with the same magnificence of the old pledges to the King of Spain."[3] Regardless of the outsized hopes of Mexico City bureaucrats, Governor Melgares knew well that in the end independence festivities in Santa Fe would mostly follow the rhythms of local custom and fancy. Indians from Tesuque and other pueblos sent dancers to mark the occasion according to their own celebratory traditions. Three leading citizens of Santa Fe (an alderman, the vicar general, and the military chaplain) provided their own glosses on emancipation by playing each of the three guarantees upon which the Mexican nation had just been brokered: independence, Catholicism, and unity.[4] An American visitor suggested building a flagpole and even volunteered to splice pine trees. It appears that he envisioned a rather solemn affair and did not appreciate the ubiquitous gambling and cathartic fandangos: "[A]ll classes abandoned themselves to the most reckless dissipation and profligacy. No Italian carnival ever exceeded this celebration in thoughtlessness, vice, and licentiousness of every description."[5]

The celebratory contagion reached the Caddo Indians in northern Texas as well. El Gran Cadó received a package with gifts and a letter from Agustín de Iturbide, Mexico's liberator. As the letter was in Spanish and no one in the vicinity could translate it, the Caddo chief and a few warriors set out for Monterrey, as he put it, "toward the house of our father and general chief [the *comandante general* of the Eastern Interior Provinces]."[6] There he found an agreeable host who astonishingly was inviting "all the tribes of the North" to send their children, relatives, and friends to the Imperial Court in Mexico City to witness "the reestablishment of their grandparents' throne."[7] El Gran Cadó accepted the invitation with some trepidation, a decision that

[3] Provisional Governing Junta to Governor Melgares, Mexico City, Oct 6, 1821, MANM 1, 171–4. On the colonial antecedents of such ritual practices, see Cheryl English Martin, *Governance and Society in Colonial Mexico: Chihuahua in the Eighteenth Century* (Stanford, CA: Stanford University Press, 1996), 97–124.

[4] Weber, "An Unforgettable Day," 38.

[5] Thomas James quoted in Weber, "An Unforgettable Day," 33–4, and in Stephen G. Hyslop, *Bound for Santa Fe: The Road to New Mexico and the American Conquest, 1806–1848* (Norman, OK: University of Oklahoma Press, 2002), 232–3. See also David Lavender, *Bent's Fort* (Garden City, NY: Doubleday, 1954), 54.

[6] Gran Cadó to Iturbide, Mar 4, 1822, BHC, 2q220, 552.

[7] Proclamation of Colonel Gaspar López, Saltillo, Nov 3, 1821, quoted in Javier Ocampo, *Las ideas de un día: El pueblo mexicano ante la consumación de su Independencia* (Mexico City: El Colegio de México, 1969), 65.

would split his people into two factions. In the next few weeks, other Native American leaders found themselves making the same journey to the heart of Anáhuac. The Lipan Apache chiefs Castro and Pocarropa (along with two Mexican captives whom the chiefs intended to liberate at the appropriate time) arrived in Monterrey and continued toward the capital. Chief Richard Fields of the Cherokee nation and Botón de Fierro (who claimed to represent the Western Comanches but was in fact a runaway California mission Indian baptized as José Rafael Guadalupe del Espíritu Santo Iglesias y Parra) also secured interviews with the *Gran Capitán* Iturbide.[8] One Creole merchant mockingly commented on these peregrinations: "the good savages are looking for their emperor."[9]

These passages provide precious hints about how different groups and individuals sought to engage, represent, and understand the emerging nation. Conscious of being present at the birth of the nation, contemporaries could not help but feel an overwhelming sense of wonderment and novelty. But in truth, lurking behind these feelings lay the power of colonial institutions. The administrative pressures forcing the hand of Governor Melgares, the Tesuque Indian's desire to celebrate according to tradition, the written instructions from Mexico City reminiscent of royal decrees, and the paternalistic relationship between *El Gran Capitán* and his northern Indian children were all quintessential fixtures of the crumbling colonial world deployed to prop up the new nation. Everywhere in Latin America, colonial institutions provided the skeletal support of newly independent nations. Benedict Anderson has pointed out that such remarkable continuity shows how local imperial agents and Creole provincial elites were the first to create a national imagery through gazettes, decrees, broadsides, and, above all, language. Anderson's claim may be accurate as far as the cultural, almost literary, reading of nations is concerned.[10] Yet it is easy to overlook the obvious, namely that such national imaginings were conveyed through civil, religious, and military administrations, national as well regional and local. Together they supplied the critical links that kept these diverse peoples more or less tied together (see Figure 2.1).

Recent scholarship focusing on Mexico and other Latin American countries has illuminated various aspects of this difficult transition from Spanish colony into independent nation.[11] These works have highlighted the long

---

[8] Gaspar López to Antonio Martínez, Monterrey, Apr 24, 1822, BA 71, 449–51; Antonio Bustamante to José María Parra, Mexico City, Jun 22, 1822, BA 71, 1006–7.

[9] Manuel Márquez y Melo to Andrés de la Viesca, Chihuahua, May 13, 1823, Márquez y Melo Papers, NMSRCA.

[10] Anderson, *Imagined Communities*, 52–65.

[11] Anna, *Forging Mexico*; Guardino, *Peasants, Politics, and the Formation of Mexico's National State*; Mallon, *Peasant and Nation*, and "Peasants and State Formation in Nineteenth-Century

FIGURE 2.1. Paper seal for the years 1844–5

gestation of nationhood, specifically tracing two parallel developments. On the one hand, there is an institutional dimension: a centralizing *state* gradually emerges out of congeries of alternative institutions (Church, *caudillos*, indigenous polities) and is able to exercise authority throughout the national territory. On the other hand, individuals initially committed to ethnic, local, or regional identities gradually come to see themselves as part of a national community. Thus the road to nationhood was dual: the national state had to win out over lesser political organizations and potential challengers; *and* people had to refashion their previous ethnic, corporate, or other subnational loyalties as the nation became their overriding identity.

Both of these processes are at the heart of the story of how Mexico's Far North became the American Southwest. During the critical period leading up to the Mexican–American War, political and cultural centralization remained incomplete in this area. In lieu of a state, Mexico possessed a collection of overlapping civil, military, and religious organizations, some of them purportedly national in scope but often made up of regional power systems.[12] As for cultural nationalism, Creole elites certainly aspired to create a nation, but faced the arduous task of persuading a majority of people to break free from the cocoon of ethnic, local, or at best regional attachments. But incomplete as these processes were, they nevertheless proceeded in earnest at this time. Pueblo Indians, Anglo-American colonists, tejanos,

Mexico," 1–54; Thomson, "Bulwarks of Patriotic Liberalism," 31–68; Charles F. Walker, *Smoldering Ashes: Cuzco and the Creation of Republican Peru, 1780–1840* (Durham, NC: Duke University Press, 1999). Jaime E. Rodríguez O. has reinterpreted the process of emancipation, emphasizing the continuity of political processes and institutions, in *The Independence of Spanish America* (Cambridge, UK: Cambridge University Press, 1998). He has also edited a number of volumes dealing with this period.

[12] Mexico's early political system has been variously characterized as "patrimonial," "personalist," "*caudillista*," and so on. All of these renditions underscore the importance of patronage in forging and maintaining polical control. See discussion in Antonio Annino, "El pacto y la norma: los orígenas de la legalidad oligárquica en México," *Historias* 5 (Jan–Mar 1984), 3–42; Fernando Escalante Gonzalbo, *Ciudadanos Imaginarios* (Mexico City: El Colegio de México, 1995), 97–140.

and nuevomexicanos became linked together through several institutional networks revolving around land, commerce, politics, and religion, forging impressive multi-ethnic local and regional alliances, a great story of national construction that has seldom been appreciated.

Prior to the Texas Revolution of 1836 (an event caused by a premature attempt at institutional centralization in this area, as I will try to argue), a generation of Hispanics, Anglo-American colonists, sedentary Indians, and nomads came to envision a common future emerging out of the wreckage of the Spanish Empire. Frontier residents' visions of community may have been highly stylized and unacceptable to nationalist leaders in Mexico City, but nonetheless, they constituted the building blocks of a Mexican order in this area. For contemporaries in Texas or New Mexico, a future as a part of Mexico was all too real as sources eloquently demonstrate.

And yet it is a world that has been lost to us because of our inability to escape teleology. Most traditional histories tend to skip over the Mexican period rather hastily, aware that incorporation into the United States looms right around the corner. More specifically, these histories have tended to downplay the Mexican context in two crucial respects: first, by depicting Mexico's Far North as largely disconnected from the politics and discussions of central Mexico; and second, by casting the story of this region as a mere prelude to annexation to the United States. Teleology creates the impression that the inhabitants of early-nineteenth-century Texas and New Mexico were simply waiting for the inevitable to occur: revolution and war to break out and the United States to take over.[13] Yet contemporaries believed nothing of this sort. A pervasive set of imperial institutional networks had anchored the lives of the frontier denizens for a long time, an institutional infrastructure that would be substantially transformed and expanded for nationalizing purposes during the Mexican period. Although some individuals did entertain the possibility that the United States might one day acquire portions of New Mexico and Texas, these were bold speculations at most. Thus frontier residents were left to act, live, negotiate, and dream assuming that they would continue to be part and parcel of the Mexican federation and consequently exerted themselves to alter, salvage, resist, and generally shape the emerging order according to their wishes and interests.[14]

---

[13] David J. Weber, "Mexico's Far Northern Frontier, 1821–1854: Historiography Askew," in Weber, *Myth and the History of the Hispanic Southwest* (Albuquerque, NM: University of New Mexico Press, 1988), 94.

[14] I have used and expanded some portions of this chapter pertaining to Texas into an article form. The citation is Andrés Reséndez, "Masonic Connections, Pecuniary Interests, and Institutional Development Along Mexico's Far North," in Jaime E. Rodríguez O., ed., *La Niña Bonita – The Pretty Girl: Constitutionalism and Liberalism in Nineteenth-Century Mexico* (Wilmington, DE: SR Books, forthcoming).

THE ALLURE OF *BALDÍOS*

The parceling out and administration of Texas land constitute the most dramatic examples of how patronage and power brought different peoples together and forged an impressive regional community in northeastern Mexico. In the 1810s, Texas was still a backwater province with enormous *baldíos* (vacant lands), occasionally visited by peripatetic Indians, explorers, trappers, and Spanish officials. Within two decades, this once little-known corner of Mexico would emerge as the most important colonization experiment in the nation, an experiment that would show how the forces of enlightenment and progress could work their magic on a vast and untamed wilderness.

To tell this story of intrigue, high hopes, and political partisanship (a story that would lend itself admirably well to fictional treatment), it is first necessary to say something about an idiosyncratic institution that would play the leading role both in early Mexican politics and in facilitating the colonization of Texas: Freemasonry. Putting aside the reputedly dark underside of these "secret societies" – their conspicuous rituals and secrecy often exaggerated by their Catholic opponents – Masonic lodges were simply social venues where political opinion was shaped in the absence of formal political parties.[15] Masons (invariably men, as no women were allowed) would gather to discuss politics, to exchange information, and – as their political and economic influence increased – to jockey for positions in government and curry economic favors.

In the immediate aftermath of independence, Freemasonry of the Scottish Rite became particularly active in many parts of Mexico. The *escoceses* multiplied largely through the proselytizing efforts of former Mexican deputies to the Spanish Cortes who, after extensive involvement with lodges in Europe, returned to Mexico eager to promote them at home.[16] Initially, the aim of Scottish Rite Masons was to establish a republic and institute

[15] The role of secret societies in early Mexican politics is a crucial but still dimly understood subject. For a brief historiographical assessment, see Jean-Pierre Bastian, "Una ausencia notoria: la francmasonería en la historiografía mexicana," *Historia Mexicana* 175 (Jan–Mar, 1995), 439–60. François-Xavier Guerra contends that Masonic lodges constitute the first modern vehicle of political association. François-Xavier Guerra, *México: Del Antiguo Régimen a la Revolución*, 2 vols (Fondo de Cultura Económica, 1988), I: 157–70. My own work shows that Masonry's role extended far beyond the purely political and encompassed the economic realm as well. Contemporary authors and politicians (and Masons) such as Lucas Alamán and Lorenzo de Zavala provide some evidence of the far-reaching influence of Masonic networks. For a short and balanced introduction to the history of Freemasonry in Mexico, see Lillian Estelle Fisher, "Early Masonry in Mexico (1806–1828)," *Southwestern Historical Quarterly* 40:3 (Jan 1939), 198–214. The most comprehensive study of Masonry in Texas is James David Carter, *Masonry in Texas: Background, History, and Influence to 1846* (Waco, TX: Committee on Masonic Education and Service for the Grand Lodge of Texas, 1955).

[16] The life stories of Miguel Ramos Arizpe and Lorenzo de Zavala illustrate this pattern very well.

some of the reforms advocated by the Spanish Cortes.[17] Early in 1823, after a rapid and highly organized movement, Scottish Rite Masons succeeded in toppling the Mexican Empire headed by Iturbide and lived a brief but crucial heyday in 1823–4. The *escoceses* dominated the Constituent Congress that yielded Mexico's first political constitution in 1824.

But Scottish Rite Masons soon found themselves outflanked by a second Masonic group founded in Mexico City in the summer of 1825. Joel R. Poinsett, the first United States minister to Mexico, was asked to incorporate the newly formed society into the Rite of York by obtaining the regulating patents from the Grand Lodge of New York.[18] Ideologically, the York Rite Masons were more radical than their *escocés* counterparts, favoring popular participation through direct elections and being committed to federalist (understood as home rule) tenets.[19] Their boldness earned them the names of radicals, federalists, or simply *yorkinos*. Moreover, their noticeable proclivity toward the United States stood in stark contrast to the Scottish Rite Masons' distrust of Mexico's northern neighbor. Especially along Mexico's Far North, *yorkinos* had interaction with lodges in the United States and drew support from influential foreign-born residents.[20]

Both brands of Masonry had a tremendous influence on Texas.[21] Texas started its Mexican existence under the aegis of neighboring Coahuila. Coahuila was then a rather backward and empty state, but it was also the cradle of skillful politicians, most notably Miguel Ramos Arizpe, a bespectacled clergyman, former deputy to the Spanish Cortes, and arguably the main

---

[17] On the federalist movement and Ramos Arizpe, see Lucas Alamán, *Historia de México: desde los primeros movimientos que prepararon su independencia en el uño de 1808*, 5 vols (Mexico City: Publicaciones Hornéías, nd.), 5: 357–8; Nettie Lee Benson, *La diputación provincial y el federalismo mexicano* (Mexico City: El Colegio de México, 1955). For a description of the character and influence of Ramos Arizpe, see Lorenzo de Zavala, *Ensayo crítico de las revoluciones de México desde 1808 hasta 1830* (Mexico City: Editorial Porrúa, 1969 [c1831]), 114.

[18] Alamán, *Historia de México*, 5: 411; Zavala, *Ensayo crítico de las revoluciones de México*, 252.

[19] David Brading has noted the inconsistencies between classic liberal doctrines and the *yorkino* movement. Contrary to liberal doctrines, *yorkinos* in south-central Mexico advocated protectionism. David Brading, *The Origins of Mexican Nationalism* (Cambridge, UK: Centre of Latin American Studies, 1985), 71, 92. See also Anna, *Forging Mexico*, 176–7; Guardino, *Peasants, Politics, and the Formation of Mexico's National State*, 122. In the case of the *yorkinos* of Coahuila and Texas, the *yorkino* movement staunchly supported free trade so there were no such inconsistencies. This underscores the fact that, far from a unified political ideology, the *yorkino* movement was very much shaped by regional concerns. Brading, *The Origins of Mexican Nationalism*, 71, 92. See Anna, *Forging Mexico*, 176–7.

[20] Alamán, *Historia de México*, 5, 308, 405, 411–12, 417–18; Zavala, *Ensayo crítico de las revoluciones de México*, 197–8, 252–3, 257. See also discussion in Guardino, *Peasants, Politics, and the Formation of Mexico's National State*, 115–22.

[21] Regino F. Ramón, *Historia general del estado de Coahuila*, 2 vols (Saltillo: Universidad Autónoma de Coahuila, 1990, c1917), 2: 456. On the federalist movement and Ramos Arizpe, see Alamán, *Historia de México*, 5, 357–8; Benson, *La diputación provincial y el federalismo mexicano*.

FIGURE 2.2. Miguel Ramos Arizpe

leader and ideologue of the *escoceses* (see Figure 2.2). Through deft maneuvering at the Constitutional Assembly, Ramos Arizpe managed to pass a law in 1824 that amalgamated his scantily populated Coahuila with the even more deserted province of Texas.[22] He believed that Texas would be better off as a "free and sovereign State" (even though it was only in partnership with Coahuila and with a minority stake at that) rather than "degrade itself" by becoming a territory under the iron grip of the national government.[23] Ramos Arizpe's influence was also decisive in shaping the early political institutions of Texas. In 1824, the citizens of Coahuila and Texas (such was the unwieldy name of the new entity) elected an *escocés*-dominated provincial constituent assembly charged with organizing the state government, drafting a colonization law, and enacting a series of economic reforms.[24]

[22] See Charles A. Bacarisse, "The Union of Coahuila and Texas," *Southwestern Historical Quarterly* 61:3 (Jan 1958), 340–9; Ricki S. Janicek, "The Development of Early Mexican Land Policy: Coahuila and Texas, 1810–1825," Ph.D. dissertation, Tulane University, 1985, 180–99.

[23] Erasmo Seguín, Texas's deputy to the Constituent Congress of 1823–4, had a similar although less sanguine opinion with regard to the union of Coahuila and Texas. See de la Teja, "Texas: A Tejano Perspective," 84–5.

[24] Some of these reforms had already been introduced by the short-lived Provincial Deputation of Texas. See Janicek, "The Development of Early Mexican Land Policy," 136–7. See also Alessio Robles, *Coahuila y Texas*, I: 155–210, 245–69.

But just as the *escoceses* had finished crafting a functioning government, the pendulum swung toward the radical camp. In the elections of 1827 and 1829, York Rite Masons won solid majorities in the twelve-member legislature. More important perhaps was the rise to power of the Viesca brothers. José María Viesca was elected to the governorship of Coahuila and Texas in 1827. A few months later, his brother, Agustín Viesca, was appointed to the Ministry of Foreign Relations during the radical administration of President Vicente Guerrero. Agustín Viesca had been among the founding members of the York Rite Masonry and together with his brother assembled an informal political group with connections stretching from Texas administrators all the way to the highest echelons of the national government. An American witness described the Viesca family as "rich, large, respectable, learned, sensible, and honorable, they believe not in this d——d foolish religion and possess two very fine libraries of miscellaneous and scientific books."[25]

From the start, the *baldíos* of Texas had been considered the very cornerstone of the state's development strategy. The 1824 federal law of colonization essentially left the states free to work out the details of the disposal of their own vacant lands.[26] Hence Coahuila and Texas lost no time in drafting a state colonization law that was approved as early as March 1825, even before the state constitution. The law stated unambiguously that the prosperity of the state hinged on its ability to marshal the energies of entrepreneurial and self-reliant settlers. To achieve this end, the governor and a colonization committee in the state legislature would review all colonization projects and land petitions submitted by national and foreign *empresarios*, Indians, and individuals at large. Those projects deemed "worthy," "sound," and "beneficial to the state" would then be "elevated" to federal authorities for scrutiny. While approval at the federal level was not a foregone conclusion – disagreements sometimes occurred and indeed became a major source of friction in the 1830s – the federal government generally went along with the state authorities' recommendations in the early years.[27]

In essence, the governor and two or three state legislators, after secretive deliberations, were able to confer princely land grants, colonization enterprises, and exclusive rights to navigate Texas rivers and made profitable

[25] Robert Andrews to Stephen Austin, Parras, Sep 5, 1823, quoted in Janicek, "The Development of Early Mexican Land Policy," 195.

[26] Translation of the General Law of Colonization, Mexico City, Aug 18, 1824, in McLean, *Papers Concerning Robertson's Colony in Texas*, 2, 214–17. For an article-by-article analysis of that law, see Janicek, "The Development of Early Mexican Land Policy," 167–79. See also Josefina Zoraida Vázquez, "Colonización y pérdida de Texas," 53.

[27] Janicek, "The Development of Early Mexican Land Policy," 180–216; Ricki S. Janicek, "The Politics of Land: Mexico and Texas, 1823–1836," paper presented at the Texas State Historical Association meeting of 1996. See also the report of José María Díaz de Noriega, Federal Commissioner of Colonization, Monclova, Jun 23, 1834, BP 40:673, 7.

appointments of Texas customs and land officials.[28] Saltillo may have been a dusty small town lost in the Coahuila plains, but after 1825 it attracted a lively cast of land speculators, settlers, *empresarios*, merchants, and politicians of all hues and levels bent on securing Texas land. And in this world prone to the wholesale trafficking of political influence and economic favors, Masonic lodges provided a ready-made network of personal contacts and tacit alliances.[29]

As state legislators discussed the final draft of the state colonization law early in 1825, numerous land developers swarmed into Saltillo. The most successful turned out to be Masons. One of them was Robert Leftwich. Since 1822, Leftwich, representing a group of Tennessee investors, had spent his time dealing with bureaucracies and colonization committees in Mexico City trying to obtain a land grant in Texas. In February 1825, he moved to Saltillo, where he finally clinched the sought-after contract from the state government.[30] Another fellow Mason, Frost H. Thorn, had also followed closely the development of Mexico's land policy both in Mexico City and then in Saltillo, where he too obtained an *empresario* contract to introduce four hundred families.[31] In addition to Leftwich and Thorn, the list of Anglo-American Freemason *empresarios* included David G. Burnet, John Cameron, Benjamin R. Milam, Haden Edwards, and James Power (see Map 2.1).[32]

No *empresario* was more successful than Stephen F. Austin of the Louisiana No. 109 lodge (see Figure 2.3). By early 1825, Austin was already a well-established *empresario* and seasoned operator of the intricate Mexican national and state bureaucracies. Austin had spent all of 1822 and part of 1823 in Mexico City validating a Texas land grant that the Spanish colonial government had conferred on his father.[33] In the course of his lobbying activities, he came in contact with some of the most prominent Mexican politicians as well as other Anglo-American would-be *empresarios*.[34] In June 1825, Austin

---

[28] On the influence of the state legislature, see Alessio Robles, *Coahuila y Texas*, 1: 177–269.

[29] Andreas V. Reichstein had already made this point abundantly clear in his own work: "[Freemasonry] created a bond that brought very dissimilar men together and let them act." Andreas V. Reichstein, *Rise of the Lone Star: The Making of Texas* (College Station, TX: Texas A & M University Press, 1989), 192.

[30] See Leftwich's diary in McLean, *Papers Concerning Robertson's Colony in Texas*, introductory volume.

[31] Mary Virginia Henderson, "Minor Empresario Contracts for the Colonization of Texas, 1825–1834," *Southwestern Historical Quarterly* 31:4 (1928), 298–9.

[32] List of Texas Masons in Carter, *Masonry in Texas*, 425–65.

[33] Moses Austin sought to secure a land grant in Texas claiming rights as a former resident of a Spanish territory (Louisiana). See Vázquez, "Colonización y pérdida de Texas," 50.

[34] José María Tornel describes Austin as that person "with whom we all became acquainted in Mexico [City]." José María Tornel, "Tejas y los Estados Unidos de América" (Mexico City, 1837), in *The Mexican Side of the Texan Revolution*, translated by Carlos E. Castañeda (Dallas, TX: P. L. Turner, 1928), 309.

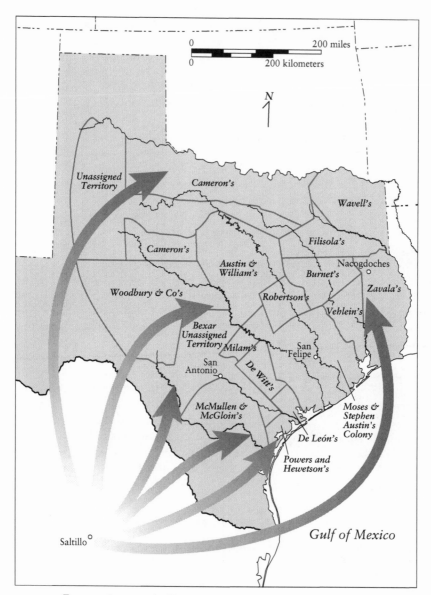

MAP 2.1. *Empresario* grants in Texas

obtained a second grant from the Coahuila and Texas government to introduce five hundred families. It was the beginning of a close relationship, as
Austin was awarded three more colonization contracts: in 1827 to introduce
one hundred families, in 1828 to bring three hundred families, and one more

FIGURE 2.3. *Empresario* Stephen F. Austin

in 1831, in partnership with Samuel M. Williams, to introduce eight hundred families of European and Mexican settlers.[35]

In addition to Anglo-American Masons, prominent Mexican Masons managed to secure *empresario* contracts or eleven-league grants.[36] None other than clergyman Ramos Arizpe himself topped the list. On November 12, 1828, he obtained an enormous colonization contract running along the northern margin of the Rio Grande in an irregular quadrangle comprising between eight hundred and one thousand square leagues of land, or over 4 million acres, according to his own estimates.[37] It is interesting to note that Ramos Arizpe, as a leader of the *escocés* faction, objected to the open-door policies introduced by subsequent *yorkino* administrations that in his view had resulted in the rapid Americanization of Texas. Indeed, Ramos Arizpe justified his own enormous colonization contract as a last-ditch effort to secure a Mexican stronghold north of the Rio Grande:

In November of 1828 I visited the capital of the state of Coahuila and Texas and was dismayed to learn that due to the inconceivable stupidity of three successive *yorkino*

[35] Eugene C. Barker, *The Life of Stephen F. Austin Founder of Texas, 1793–1836* (New York: Da Capo Press, c1968), 89–134, 141–4; Gregg Cantrell, *Stephen F. Austin: Empresario of Texas* (New Haven, CT: Yale University Press, 1999), 132–70; Reichstein, *Rise of the Lone Star*, 32–6.

[36] Benson makes the point that more attention has been given to foreign *empresarios* than to Mexican *empresarios*. See "Texas as Viewed from Mexico," 244–5.

[37] This grant was not included in McLean's list. See report of José María Díaz de Noriega, federal commissioner of colonization, Monclova, Jun 23, 1834, BP 40:673, 7, 637–8; land petition of Miguel Ramos Arizpe to the state government of Coahuila and Texas, Saltillo, Nov 12, 1828, and clarification of Ramos Arizpe's *empresario* contract, n.p., Apr 11, 1830, in BP 40:673, 4.

legislatures, the exclusive rights to navigate the Rio Grande on steamboat were given to a company promoted by Anglo Americans and supported by capitalists of their republic. This privilege extends from the mouth of the Rio Grande or Bravo del Norte, through the states of Tamaulipas, Coahuila and Texas, and Chihuahua, all the way to New Mexico. This disastrous policy in effect puts the line that North Americans have long coveted as the limit of their own territory in the hands of individuals and wealthy capitalists from the United States.[38]

Clearly, the predominance of Anglo-American *empresarios* in Texas constituted one of the main rifts between *escoceses* and *yorkinos*. But the state's *yorkinos*, led by the Viesca brothers, remained very much in control of the land-granting process and continued to favor both Anglo-American entrepreneurs and Mexican leaders who supported an open border with the United States. Indeed, many of the highest-ranking *yorkinos* not only in Coahuila and Texas but also throughout Mexico acquired land in Texas in those years. Texas became something of a haven where liberal politicians pinned their hopes and invested their personal fortunes. In case of a downturn in their political careers, they could always flee to Texas, as many of them did in the mid-1830s. Such prominent York Rite Masons included the grand secretary of the Grand Lodge of Mexico, Colonel José Antonio Mexía. He did not secure a colonization contract, but, with the blessing of Governor Viesca, Colonel Mexía bought a "princely domain" amounting to some fifty-five square leagues or 243,540 acres, far in excess of the eleven square league maximum that Mexican nationals were allowed to purchase by the Colonization Law of Coahuila and Texas.[39]

Another notorious case was that of Lorenzo de Zavala, one of the founders of the first *yorkino* lodges who went on to become governor of the state of Mexico and finance minister. The circumstances in which Zavala obtained his *empresario* contract are indicative of the ruthless wheeling-and-dealing prevalent in Saltillo in those heady years. The colonization contract in question had originally been granted to Colonel Peter Ellis Bean, a naturalized Mexican (possibly *escocés*) whose services had been most valuable in putting down the Fredonia Rebellion of 1826–7. He was offered as a reward, an *empresario* contract to settle Indians. But after the rise to power of *yorkinos* in Saltillo, Colonel Bean was accused of bigamy. (Colonel Bean stated in his land request that he was married to a Mexican woman, doña Magdalena Farfán de los Godos, to bolster his claim to citizenship. But Governor José María Viesca soon found out that the prospective grantee was in fact living

---

[38] Miguel Ramos Arizpe to the state government of Coahuila and Texas, Saltillo, Nov 12, 1828, and clarification of Ramos Arizpe's *empresario* contract, n.p., Apr 11, 1830, in BP 40:673, 4.

[39] Carter, *Masonry in Texas*, 237; Hutchinson, "General José Antonio Mexía and His Texas Interests," 125. On the limitations of private land ownership, see Article 24 of the Colonization Law of Coahuila and Texas. The General Land Office of Texas has defined the *sitio* or square league as 4,428.4 acres.

with an American woman named Candes Marquif.) Judicial proceedings were initiated against him, and even before the verdict had been reached, Colonel Bean was stripped of his grant, which was quickly awarded to Governor Zavala.[40] Zavala's grant remained the most controversial decision made by the state government.

Many other liberal leaders, especially *yorkinos*, acquired land interests in Texas, including Valentín Gómez Farías, the vice president of Mexico, and Father José María Alpuche, an eccentric clergyman from Tabasco, who had also been among the original founders of the *yorkino* lodges together with Zavala and Viesca.[41] Well-connected Masons seemed ubiquitous. Even the Cherokee grant had been arranged through Masonic contacts. When Chief Richard Fields went to Mexico City to negotiate land for his people, he decided to join a lodge.[42] All told, more than half of all land grants in Mexican Texas were awarded to Anglo-American, Mexican, and Native American Masons, while the proportion of Masons within the population of Texas at large was less than 10 percent.[43]

Land and Masonic connections were also vital to the political and economic fortunes of Mexican Texans. While the paucity of records makes it exceedingly difficult to locate individual tejanos as *escoceses* or *yorkinos*, it is possible to identify tejano elite members who favored Anglo-American colonization projects and were ideologically close to the positions adopted by the *yorkino* faction in Coahuila led by the Viesca brothers. The Seguín family is a good example. Erasmo Seguín, the patriarch, had been a consistent supporter of Anglo-American immigration into Texas at least since 1821. He was the first tejano to welcome Stephen F. Austin into Texas; and since that early encounter, the two men struck up a close friendship, economic partnership, and crucial political alliance.[44] Don Erasmo also blazed the way for cooperation with Coahuila politicians. In his quest to advance the interests of Texas, including those of Austin and his Anglo-American colonists, the elder Seguín, as the Texas representative in the Constituent Congress,

---

[40] Peter Ellis Bean's land petition, n.p., May 6, 1826, and Commander of the Eastern Interior Provinces to Ministry of Foreign Affairs, Mexico City, Nov 22, 1828, BP 40:673, 4. See also Governor José María Viesca to Minister of Foreign Affairs, Leona Vicario (Saltillo), May 5, 1828, BP 40:673, 3.

[41] On speculation on eleven-league grants carried out by Masons, see Janicek, "The Politics of Land: Mexico and Texas, 1823–,1836," 9–10. See also C. Alan Hutchinson, "Mexican Federalists in New Orleans and the Texas Revolution," *Louisiana Historical Quarterly* 30 (Jan 1956), 1–47; Hutchinson, "General José Antonio Mexía and His Texas Interests," *Southwestern Historical Quarterly* 85 (Oct 1978), 117–42.

[42] Carter, *Masonry in Texas*, 231.

[43] This figure was determined by comparing McLean's list of Texas land grants with the list of known Masons in Texas provided by Carter, *Masonry in Texas*, 425–65.

[44] For excellent sketches of the lives of Erasmo and Juan Nepomuceno Seguín, see Jesús de la Teja, ed., *A Revolution Remembered: The Memoirs and Selected Correspondence of Juan N. Seguín* (Austin, TX: Texas State Historical Association, 2002), 3–56.

accepted Ramos Arizpe's offer to form a joint state. This arrangement at least kept land decisions within the state. As Ramos Arizpe explained: "[T]he Texas representative and I have agreed to unite our provinces and are of one mind about parceling out our *baldíos* in such a way that this policy will become a powerful lever working in favor of our two provinces."[45] Juan Nepomuceno Seguín continued in his father's footsteps, cultivating close ties with the increasingly influential Anglo-American *empresarios* (especially Austin) and generally maintaining good relations with the *yorkino* leadership in Coahuila. This alliance took concrete form during the Texas Revolution when the Seguíns initially sided with the Viescas and sought to enlist the help of Anglo-American settlers to their cause, as we shall see.

The early life of José María de Jesús Carbajal – one of the most colorful figures of the U.S–Mexico frontier – best illustrates the powerful triangular alliance between tejanos, Anglo-American entrepreneurs, and Coahuila politicians. Carbajal was a native of San Antonio. The first turning point in his life occurred in 1821, when he was sponsored by a newly arrived Austin to spend some years in Kentucky and Virginia learning the tanning and saddle trades. This experience changed Carbajal's life forever. Fluent in English and possessing a demeanor that hinted at something foreign – to the point where fellow tejanos called him "el norteamericano" – when he returned to Texas, Carbajal naturally gravitated toward the camp of his Anglo-American sponsors.[46] Indeed, Austin's intervention continued to be decisive in helping Carbajal to secure employment as a land surveyor and to come in contact with well-known *yorkinos* in Texas (Francisco Madero and Martín de León) and also with the Viesca faction in Coahuila. In 1835, Carbajal was elected as one of the Texas representatives to the state legislature, where he became a fierce supporter of Governor Agustín Viesca.[47]

---

[45] Miguel Ramos Arizpe to *ayuntamiento* of Saltillo, Mexico City, Mar 8, 1824, quoted in Ramón, *Historia General del Estado De Coahuila*, 2: 487. See expanded discussion in Tijerina, *Tejanos and Texas Under the Mexican Flag*, 97–9.

[46] Stephen F. Austin to Mary Holley Austin, quoted in Davenport, "General José María de Jesus Carbajal," 476–7. In a telling letter, Carbajal wrote to his mother explaining that after two years in the United States he had become "verry [sic] wicked," and that he had found consolation in reading the Bible and thus decided to "renounce the doctrines of the Church of Rome" and became a Baptist. Carbajal also asked his mother to send him books in Spanish: "I have nearly lost my language in my own tounge [sic]...." Carbajal to his mother, Lexington, Jul 2, 1826, in Eugene C. Barker, ed., *The Austin Papers* (Washington, DC: Government Printing Office, 1924), II: 1366–7.

[47] Frederick C. Chabot, *With the Makers of San Antonio* (San Antonio, TX: Artes Gráficas, 1937), 33–4. In the early 1830s, Carbajal served as surveyor in the Béxar district until 1834. Carbajal's appointment in records of the General Land Office of Texas [hereafter GLO] 123: 8, 98–9; José Antonio Padilla to *jefe politico* of Texas, Monclova, Jun 13, 1834, GLO 125: 22, 265. See also Ana Carolina Castillo Crimm, "Success in Adversity: *The Mexican Americans or Victoria County*," Ph.D. dissertation, University of Texas at Austin, 1998, 142–4. On the federalist leanings of the de León family, see Castillo Crimm, "Finding Their Ways," 115–18.

The early life of Carbajal shows how prominent tejanos generally remained involved in colonization ventures in Texas as land administrators. With the union of Coahuila and Texas in 1824, the tejano elite in fact lost control of land decisions outside the San Antonio–Goliad region. But some of them made up for this loss by receiving lucrative administrative appointments. Each colonization project required a land commissioner charged with hiring one or more surveyors, collecting the appropriate fees from the colonists, and issuing land titles.[48] Hence the state legislature regularly appointed "well informed, reliable persons," the majority of whom became influential tejanos.[49] These were extremely lucrative jobs. At first, a commissioner negotiated his pay with each colonist. This led to widespread abuse since colonists, eager to obtain land titles, were cajoled into paying large sums of money. A federally appointed official lashed out against them:

> ... bearing the title of commissioners, the state government has sent a bunch of ignorant and destitute men who, under the pretext of giving possession to the colonists, in addition to a stipend of 50 pesos that they receive for each act of possession, conduct a shameful traffic of influence which has resulted in the wholesale transfer of *baldíos* that many foreigners now illegally own.[50]

New regulations were introduced in 1827 whereby commissioners' fees were fixed, but even then a commissioner working on an average-size colony was able to collect what amounted to a small fortune.[51] Not only were commissioners handsomely paid, but also they became key intermediaries between the state government and the *empresarios* who depended on their services. Carbajal's trajectory is quite illuminating in this regard, and he was hardly alone. The roster of land commissioners and surveyors with close ties to Anglo-American *empresarios* and Coahuila politicians includes José Miguel Aldrete and Juan Nepomuceno Seguín.[52]

In the absence of a constituted nation, this vast network of landed interests running from Mexico City, through Saltillo and San Antonio, and to the various colonization projects and land grants throughout Texas is what kept an array of diverse human beings together. Land provided a stake in the nation to a very heterogeneous frontier society that otherwise had little

---

[48] Articles 38 and 39 of the state colonization law.
[49] See José Miguel Aldrete to Ramón Músquiz, Goliad, May 6, 1830, GLO 123:7, 83; Ramón Músquiz to Governor, Béxar, May 24, 1830, GLO 123:7, 87; Appointment of José María Salinas, Béxar, Oct 1, 1831, GLO 123:8, 98–9.
[50] Report of Tadeo Ortiz, Matamoros, Feb 2, 1833, translated by Kelly and Hatcher, "Tadeo Ortiz de Ayala and the Colonization of Texas," 332.
[51] See instructions for land commissioners in GLO 123: 9, 108–9. A commissioner was allowed to collect 15 pesos for each league of *agostadero*, two pesos for each *labor* of *temporal*, and 20 reales for each *labor* of *regadío*. See also GLO 123:7, 77.
[52] For a list of land commissioners and surveyors, see GLO 123, passim.

else in common. Land grants enticed settlers, created new communities, re-stricted the mobility of Indians, and extended the reach of the Mexican government as it brought scattered populations into the orbit of local, state, and national bureaucracies. For instance, *empresarios* initially acted as civil and judicial authorities in their own communities and were required to act as intermediaries between the colonists and the state government. As we think about this impressive protonational administrative network, it is worth keeping three points in mind. First, this nexus of interests not only involved high-ranking Mexican politicians, wealthy Anglo-American developers, and Native American leaders, but also directly affected the common folk. Although the historical record focuses on the actions of prominent speculators and politicians, ordinary foreign-born settlers, Native American families living on land grants, and non-elite tejanos were the most dependent on Texas land and the machinery that validated its distribution and administration. Speculators may have seen their fortunes rise and tumble in spectacular trans-actions, but ordinary individuals literally lived off the land.

Second, this administrative system favored some individuals and restricted access to others, thus generating considerable conflict. Texas was literally parceled out among a few fortunate *empresarios*, whereas aspiring Anglo-American colonists, Indians, and even Mexican Texans could not gain access or at least obtain proper titles to their lands. Anglo-American colonists who had settled beyond colonization grants were perennially at risk of be-ing evicted from their fields and improvements. Regarded as squatters, these colonists often clashed with land commissioners and other Mexican author-ities as they confronted Mexico's land bureaucracy. Similarly, a few Native American groups like the Cherokees were able to secure grants after consid-erable efforts. But most natives had no success, as it was unclear whether to negotiate with state or federal authorities, and there was no established mech-anism comparable to the *empresario* system to give land to Native Americans wishing to settle on their own. Even Mexican Texans complained about lack of access. Since 1826, the *ayuntamiento* of Goliad vigorously protested the decision of the state government to give Irish *empresarios* James Power and William Wilson lands in the extinguished mission of Refugio. *Ayuntamiento* members objected to a land policy that so blatantly favored Anglo-American developers while impinging on the rights of Mexican Texans who had owned these lands "from time immemorial."[53] Understandably, a free-wheeling land administration making controversial decisions generated supporters and antagonists among all ethnic groups. But even as the system was fre-quently challenged, it still came to underpin the political and economic life of Texas.

[53] Members of the *ayuntamiento* of Goliad to Commander of Goliad Juan Manuel Sabariego, Goliad, Jul 25, 1834. Henry R. Wagner Collection of Texas Manuscripts, WA MSS S-339, Box 3, Folder 107, Beinecke Library, Yale University.

The third and final point to bear in mind is that Texas land was rather more than land; it came intertwined with ideology and politics. The entire colonization experiment in Texas was guided by liberal ideals. The state officials' notorious preference for Masonic *empresarios* and Anglo-American settlers stemmed precisely from this faith in the power of liberalism. In the second decade of the nineteenth century, liberalism was on the rise worldwide. Religious and institutional strictures of the past were being cast aside in favor of a new system of freedoms aimed at unleashing the full potential of the human spirit, particularly in the pursuit of economic endeavors.[54] The colonization commissioner for Texas and former Mexican consul in Bordeaux, Tadeo Ortiz, wrote to the president in 1833 explaining that since the French Revolution, Europe had been working relentlessly to abolish all obstacles to the expansion of industry, accumulation of wealth, and commerce. Above all, the commissioner pointed out, the United States furnished indisputable evidence of the validity of these new political doctrines. By bringing hard-working settlers, allowing trade to flourish, and promoting industry, the young republic to the north had become a sprawling and prosperous entity, a *Wunderkind* nation. It was now Mexico's turn to follow suit, and Texas, with its convenient ports, its proximity to the American market, and its enormous *baldíos* was well poised for just that feat.[55] The colonization experiment in Texas thus became a crucial test, an ideological battleground of the virtues of liberalism. The hopes of liberals throughout Mexico rode on its success.

Land in Texas also came to be closely associated with one particular Mexican political movement: federalism. In the nineteenth century, Mexican politics revolved around two political poles: centralism and federalism. The *escocés-yorkino* cleavage was an early expression of this polarity, but it would continue for decades, adopting different names and banners. In the 1820s and 1830s, the main bone of contention between centralists and federalists was the spatial distribution of power. Centralists generally advocated political centralization in Mexico City, whereas federalists championed political autonomy for states and municipalities. The federalist movement was mostly supported by the elites of various states, and chief among them was Coahuila and Texas. Indeed, the Texas *baldíos* constituted the most effective way to propagate federalist ideals. After all, by parceling out land, the state

---

[54] Brading, *The Origins of Mexican Nationalism*, 70. Brading probes the multilayered relationship between liberalism and nationalism. For the articulation and origins of the liberal ideology in Mexico, see Charles A. Hale, *Mexican Liberalism in the Age of Mora, 1821–1853* (New Haven, CT: Yale University Press, 1968), passim.

[55] Tadeo Ortiz to President of Mexico, Matamoros, Feb 2, 1833, BP 40:673, 4. It is important to note that even Mexican politicians who later denounced the expansionism of the United States were initially quite impressed by its success as a nation and ready to follow in its footsteps. See Reynaldo Sordo Cedeño, "El General Tornel y la Guerra de Texas," *Historia Mexicana* 62:4, 934–5.

government of Coahuila and Texas exercised the ultimate attribute of state sovereignty. The bitter disagreements between state and federal authorities over how to distribute Texas land in the early 1830s would go directly to the heart of the federalist–centralist debate. Although not all *empresarios* and settlers in Texas were ardent federalists and many preferred to shun politics altogether, they were well aware that their future was tied to the success of the federalist cause throughout Mexico.

I hasten to add that Mexico was hardly alone in experiencing such sectional tensions. Just as Mexico City and frontier leaders found themselves at loggerheads over issues of tariffs and land sales, so were Washington, D.C., and southern and western states. For instance, in 1831–2, South Carolina – an agricultural and slave-holding state in the South – initiated a legal proceeding known as nullification that in effect repudiated two federal tariff acts, regarding them as contrary to the original constitutional compact. At bottom, nullification was an attempt to preserve the Union by protecting minority rights of southern states against the industrial North. The political debate leading to nullification revealed how difficult it was to strike a balance between states' rights and central authority.[56] More to the point, in 1829–30, the U.S. Senate introduced a motion to restrict land sales in the West, a move denounced by the powerful Missouri Senator Thomas Hart Benton as a sectional attack designed to hamstring the settlement of the West. The question of how and who could dispose of public lands was one that pitted federal and state authorities both in Mexico and the United States. Undoubtedly, sectional tensions colored partisan politics as both national projects seemed headed toward destruction at this time.

NEW MEXICO'S PRIESTLY WEB

A land/civil administration was hardly the only structure of power tying frontier residents to the rest of Mexico. As noted previously, Mexico lacked a unified state during the early decades of the nineteenth century. Instead, it had various chains of command operating more or less independently of each other and sometimes espousing different visions of how the nation should be constituted. The Catholic Church rivaled the civil administration in influence, wealth, geographic reach, and hierarchical and centralizing impulses. And the very incarnation of the Church's administrative might in the north of Mexico was the bishop of Durango, His Illustrious Excellency José Antonio Laureano de Zubiría y Escalante (see Figure 2.4). Bishop Zubiría visited New Mexico for the first time in the summer of 1833. To reach this most distant part of his diocese, the bishop had to brave the Chihuahua desert at its hottest and the *apachería* at its most dangerous in an elegant carriage accompanied

---

[56] William W. Freehling, *Prelude to Civil War: The Nullification Controversy in South Carolina, 1816–1836* (Oxford, UK: Oxford University Press, 1992).

FIGURE 2.4. Bishop José Antonio Laureano de Zubiría y Escalante

by a chaplain, who also performed as singer and master of ceremonies, his personal secretary, and a discrete guard.[57] But these inconveniences could hardly stop him. Since he was appointed bishop two years before, Bishop Zubiría had worked diligently to reassert the Church hierarchy's hold over New Mexico, and the 1833 journey represented a milestone in this process (see Map 2.2). Dressed in full regalia, wielding enormous authority over priests, and self-conscious of the impression that he made on New Mexican parishioners (who had not seen a bishop in seventy-two years), he traveled throughout the far-flung territory painstakingly attempting to connect believers to the Church hierarchy. All kinds of preparations and expectations preceded the bishop everywhere he went. As one Protestant observed:

... the streets were swept, the roads and bridges on the route repaired and decorated; and from every window in the city [Santa Fe] there hung such a profusion of fancy curtains and rich cloths that the imagination was carried back to those glowing descriptions of enchanted worlds which one reads of in the fables of necromancers.[58]

An energetic and at times downright imperious leader, Bishop Zubiría would exert considerable influence on New Mexico for the next two decades.

Franciscan friars had resided permanently in New Mexico since the sixteenth century, and for two hundred years they had attempted to Christianize

---

[57] *Libro en que consta la apertura de la visita general del Obispado de Durango emprendida por el Illmo Sr. Don José Antonio Laureano de Zubiría y Escalante*...New Mexico, Jun–Nov 1833, microfilm edition, 1 reel, NMSRCA (hereafter VGOD).

[58] Josiah Gregg, *Commerce of the Prairies* (Lincoln, OK: University of Nebraska Press, 1967), 255.

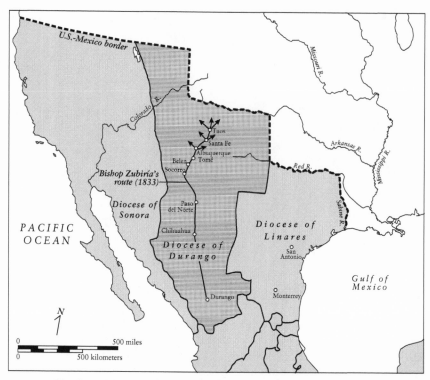

MAP 2.2. Northern Mexico's diocesan division and the route of Bishop Zubiría's trip to New Mexico in 1833

Indians and keep the faith alive among the Spanish settlers. But a period of pronounced ecclesiastical decline in New Mexico began in the late-eighteenth century. The process of secularization (missionaries were required to turn over Indians to the spiritual care of secular or diocesan priests) was part of the reason for this decline. Secularization led to disruptions, as friars retired but were not immediately replaced by parish priests. In 1812, there were still twenty-two active friars and two secular priests; by 1826, nine friars remained, but only five secular priests had taken up residence in the territory.[59] To make matters worse, secularization in New Mexico coincided with the

---

[59] For a general discussion of this decline throughout northern New Spain, see Spicer, *Cycles of Conquest*, 504–6. For evidence of this decline in New Mexico, see Pedro Bautista Pino, "Exposición sucinta y sencilla de la provincia del Nuevo México," 217–18, and Barreiro, "Ojeada Sobre Nuevo México," 162–4, both in Carroll and Haggard, eds., *Three New Mexico Chronicles*. See also Martín González de la Vara, "La política del federalismo en Nuevo México," *Historia Mexicana* 36:1 (Jul–Sep 1986), 102–9; Weber, *The Mexican Frontier*, 59; Marta Weigle, *Brothers of Light, Brothers of Blood: The Penitentes of the Southwest* (Santa Fe, NM: Ancient City Press, 1976), 22.

turmoil of independence. Bishops fled or died and could not be replaced due to lack of relations between Mexico's newly independent government and the Vatican. By 1829, all bishoprics in Mexico were vacant. Religious abandonment became quite apparent in New Mexico. Churches lay in ruins, the sick died without extreme unction, and unbaptized children and unmarried couples proliferated.[60]

Pueblo Indians, who had never been compelled into orthodox Catholicism in the first place, became quite independent in their religious practices, retaining some Catholic elements but altering the meaning. For instance, Pueblos regularly observed Christmas and Holy Week, not solely for the purpose of dramatizing the life of Jesus Christ but to pray for plentiful harvests. In fact, they did not accept Jesus Christ as a central figure but merely as one member of an eclectic pantheon.[61] When Bishop Zubiría visited New Mexico in 1833, his ominous conclusion was that only Pueblo children would reach salvation.[62]

Hispanic New Mexicans were transformed by lack of contact with the official Church as well. They developed a fondness for carved wooden *retablos* and *bultos* (altarpieces and figures representing saints). *Santeros* or craftsmen made impressive works of art, but humbler artisans and even ordinary persons produced figures that had no resemblance to known saint or religious figures, thus raising serious concerns of idolatry. Another expression of local religiosity took the form of penitential brotherhoods. *Penitentes* flogged themselves, carried heavy crosses enacting the passion of Christ, and engaged in other forms of mortification reminiscent of medieval penitential societies (see Figure 2.5). The *Penitente* movement gained a considerable following in northern New Mexico, especially in Santa Cruz de la Cañada, and emerged

---

[60] Barreiro, "Ojeada Sobre Nuevo México," 162. The Mexican government had been eager to fill the bishop vacancies at least since 1827, when it dispatched an envoy to Rome seeking confirmation for the candidates presented by President Guadalupe Victoria. On May 22, 1829, President Vicente Guerrero's administration took definite action to fill the vacant curacies of the nation, insisting on exercising the *patronato real* that the Spanish monarchy had enjoyed, thus infuriating the Vatican. In September 1829, President Guerrero, without waiting for the *patronato* controversy to be settled, requested each cathedral chapter to submit a list of bishop candidates based on "literary accomplishments, exemplary behavior, and patriotism." The Mexican plenipotentiary minister in Rome presented a final selection of candidates on March 5, 1830, already during the administration of Anastasio Bustamante. Apparently the candidates for the bishopric of Durango were sent to Rome later. Bustamante wrote personal letters to Pope Gregory XVI on behalf of those candidates he favored and finally brokered a compromise persuading the Pope to accept five bishopric candidacies, including Zubiría's.

[61] Spicer, *Cyles of Conquest*, 507; William G. Ritch, interview with José Miguel Vigil, and Indian of Pecos living at Jemes, and Pedro José Medina of Zía in relation to Montezuma, n.p., Dec 4, 1877, Ritch Collection, Huntington Library, San Marino, microfilm copy reel 8, NMSRCA.

[62] Bishop José Antonio Laureano de Zubiría y Escalante, pastoral letter on the general conditions of New Mexico, Santa Fe, late Oct 1833, VGOD.

FIGURE 2.5. Procession of *Penitentes*

as an important social and political force at the margins of the official eccle-siastical establishment.[63]

New Mexico's religious abandonment finally gave way to a period of ec-clesiastical reassertion beginning with the appointment of Bishop Zubiría. In 1830, relations between the Mexican government and the Vatican im-proved, and Pope Gregory XVI informally accepted Mexico's candidates for five bishoprics, including that of Father Zubiría.[64] In 1831, a *concurso*

---

[63] The *Penitente* movement of Santa Cruz de la Cañada appears to have centered around the miraculous image of our Lord of Esquipulas. Fray Sebastián Álvarez to Bishop of Durango, Santa Cruz de la Cañada, Nov 16, 1813, Miscellaneous Records, Church Records, Folder 17, NMSRCA. The *Penitentes* of New Mexico appeared sometime between 1790 and 1810. Their story is still shrouded in mystery. Fray Angélico Chávez advances the idea that the *Penitente* Brotherhood appeared in New Mexico "full-blown" and with all the "trappings" of the sixteenth-century penitential societies of Seville. His explanation is simply that one or more individuals who had lived in one part of the Spanish Empire where these penitential societies had long existed took the idea to New Mexico, where it prospered; or, alternatively, some book or manuscript of these societies found its way to New Mexico to inspire the first *Hermandad*. Marta Weigle, while admitting the plausibility of Chávez's notion of a late me-dieval transplant to New Mexico, has nevertheless suggested that the *Penitente* Brotherhood just as easily may have evolved from Saint Francis Third Order, a long-established confra-ternity in New Mexico. The asceticism and plain lifestyle expected from those who joined the Tertiaries, as conceived originally by Saint Francis himself, may have become with the passing of time much more stringent in New Mexico, where brothers resorted to flogging and others forms of mortification that have been so vividly described ever since the early-nineteenth century. See Angélico Chávez, "The Penitentes of New Mexico," *New Mexico Historical Review* 30:3, 119–23; Weigle, *Brothers of Light, Brothers of Blood,* 37–9.

[64] The dispute between the Vatican and Mexico is long and complicated. Here are some high-lights. In 1824, Leo XII issued the encyclical *Etsi jam diu,* exhorting all bishops in the American continent to support King Ferdinand VII. The king had been restored to absolute power, thereby bolstering Spain's claim to its former possessions. The Mexican government responded with heightened rhetoric:

...an ambitious, impotent, and pertinacious [Spanish] government has appealed to the Roman Pontiff thus confounding the spiritual authority of His Holiness with his temporal (competition) of ecclesiastics was held in Durango, resulting in the promotion of several priests for parishes in New Mexico.[65] Bishop Zubiría appointed Father Juan Felipe Ortiz as curate of Santa Fe, and within a year made him *vicario general* (vicar) – that is, the first ecclesiastical authority in the territory. Scion of one of the most prominent New Mexican families and a former student in the seminary of Durango, Father Ortiz became the bishop's most trusted ally in the difficult task of restoring the influence of the diocesan Church in New Mexico.[66]

Bishop Zubiría's Episcopal Visit in 1833 was a continuation of these efforts. For four months, the bishop and his entourage crisscrossed New Mexico from one end to the other, inspecting registries of baptisms, marriages, and deaths, and exhorting all the faithful to "arrange their heavenly affairs," get married properly, baptize their children, and ask for the extreme unction when fearing for their lives.[67] Although joyous and memorable for many, the bishop's Episcopal Visit was also a time of reckoning and naked institutional centralization. Appalled by the poverty of the Church in New Mexico, Bishop Zubiría sought to improve its finances quickly and substantially. Like a shrewd businessman, the bishop counseled priests to maximize burial revenue by dividing the cemetery into five or six plots according to location and then charging differential fees depending on how close each burial site was in relation to the main cross or to the church's entrance. Bishop Zubiría directed all parishioners, under threat of excommunication, to turn their testaments to his secretary so he could ascertain whether any amounts were due to the Church for pious works. Finally, Bishop Zubiría ordered priests to increase the sacramental fees charged for burials, marriages, and baptisms.[68]

authority, mixing religious interests with so-called legitimacy rights for the purpose of destroying the independence and freedom of the American nations. (Ministry of Justice and Ecclesiastical Affairs to *Jefe Político*, Mexico City, Jul 6, 1825, MANM 4, 310).

The Mexican government further infuriated the Vatican by insisting on exercising the *Patronato de Indias*, that is, the right granted to the king of Spain giving him powers to control the Church within his kingdom by governing its finances, deciding which papal decrees would have effect, and, more contentiously, appointing Church officials. For the controversy over the right of *patronato*, see Anne Staples, *La Iglesia en la primera república federal mexicana 1824–1835* (Mexico City: SEP, 1976); Brian R. Hamnett, *Revolución y contrarevolución en México* y el *Perú: liberalismo, realeza, y separatismo, 1800–1824* (Mexico City: Fondo de Cultura Economica, 1978), 362. For the diplomatic aspects of the controversy, see Alfonso Alcalá Alvarado, *Una pugna diplomática ante la Santa Sede: el restablecimiento del Episcopado en México* (Mexico City: Porrúa, 1967).

[65] For a detailed discussion of the secular hierarchy and the ways to advance, see William B. Taylor, *Magistrates of the Sacred: Priests and Parishioners in Eighteenth-Century Mexico* (Stanford, CA: Stanford University Press, 1996), 99–106. For how this system operated in New Mexico, see Santiago Valdez, "Biografía del Reverendo Padre Antonio José Martínez," Taos, 1877, unpublished manuscript, Ritch Collection, Huntington Library, San Marino, microfilm copy roll 1, NMSRCA.

[66] Necrology of Juan Felipe Ortiz, n.p., Jan 22, 1858, Ritch Collection, reel 5.

[67] Bishop Zubiría's visitation, Taos and Santa Cruz de la Cañada, Jul 5, 21, VGOD.

[68] Ibid.

New Mexicans chafed under the impact of these financial reforms. Only four years after the bishop's Episcopal Visitation, New Mexico was rocked by a violent rebellion, and one of the central demands was to reduce or do away with the sacramental fees.

The Church hierarchy's centralizing program for New Mexico went beyond parish finances. When Bishop Zubiría passed through Taos, he objected to the local images and saints so favored by the faithful – "they are so deformed that they are not suitable for heavenly adoration" – and ordered the Taos curate not to bless them "unless they are passable even though they cannot be called perfect."[69] While visiting Santa Cruz de la Cañada, Bishop Zubiría flatly proscribed "a certain brotherhood of penitentes that has existed in this village for some time."[70] In his parting pastoral letter, he dwelt at length on the subject of penance. The bishop explained that penance in moderation was good and indeed necessary for the health of the Church, especially "in this shameful era when we must close our eyes so as not to see and cry over the relaxation of customs leading to the endless multiplication of sin."[71] But he lashed out against the *Penitente* Brotherhoods, directing all parish priests to eradicate them not only for their corporal excesses, but most importantly because their existence had no legal basis.[72] Clearly, Bishop Zubiría attempted to define the contours of the Catholic community in New Mexico. The *Penitente* movement remained very much in force during the next few decades, evincing a strong sense of locality, intimate religiosity, and patriotism, but after 1833 it would have to contend with the centralizing impulses of the Church hierarchy.

Bishop Zubiría also made great exertions to bring Pueblo Indians more fully into the Catholic fold. He exhorted New Mexico's curates to go to any lengths to baptize all Pueblo children, even training two or three adult Indians in each *pueblo* – inclined to ritualism as they were – to perform this sacrament in cases of emergency. The bishop personally vouched for the efficacy of this method. He also reprimanded New Mexico's priesthood for passing up the most propitious occasion to compel Indians to perform the sacrament of confession – that is, right before marriage. By allowing Native Americans to marry without confessing their sins, priests had missed a once-in-a-lifetime opportunity for attempting the salvation of Indians' souls. The bishop urged priests to stop all matrimonial proceedings until confessions had been extracted. He conceded that hearing the confessions of Pueblo Indians was difficult given that many of them did not speak Spanish. But in his estimation, this was not an insurmountable obstacle: "the mute do not possess a language either" – Zubiría pointedly observed – "and yet, they

---

[69] Bishop Zubiría's Visitation, Taos, Jul 5, 1833, VGOD.
[70] Bishop Zubiría's Visitation, Santa Cruz de la Cañada, Jul 21, 1833, VGOD.
[71] Bishop Zubiría's Visitation, Pastoral Letter, Santa Fe, Oct 1833, VGOD.
[72] Ibid.

are able to confess, so it should not be different with Indians."[73] With these measures the energetic bishop tried to weave Pueblo Indians more tightly into the Church and by extension into the Mexican national project.

Finally, Bishop Zubiría addressed the issue of incorporating the foreign-born population of New Mexico. At the outset, this problem did not seem intractable. The French and Anglo-American migration into New Mexico was only a trickle compared to that into Texas, so the foreign-born population never exceeded more than 2 percent of the Hispanic population at any time during the Mexican period.[74] Moreover, while in Texas the foreign-born settled in remote *colonias* of their own, in New Mexico they generally lived in the larger towns, especially Taos and Santa Fe, well within the purview of priests and civil authorities. Yet relations between the Church and foreign-born had been contentious from the start. A critical moment of contact occurred when French and Anglo-American men attempted to marry New Mexican women (see Chapter 4). By the time foreign-born residents made up their minds about marriage, often they had also decided to settle permanently in New Mexico, were interested in obtaining land, and had acquired or contemplated acquiring Mexican citizenship. The system was set in such a way that all of these decisions were intertwined. To become a Mexican citizen, one had to convert to Catholicism. To obtain a land grant, one had to be a naturalized Mexican, and it helped to be married to a Mexican woman. And to get married, one had to be a Catholic. Thus, from the perspective of foreign-born residents, marriage emerged as a crucial step toward legitimizing their economic activities and establishing their social standing within Mexico. And yet marriage entailed a screening process that could be rigorous and contentious, as we shall see. The priest or friar had to conduct a *diligencia matrimonial* (prenuptial investigation) to insure that everything was in order. All of this required patience and money, as the paperwork extended all of the way to the See of Durango, where the dispensations were granted. Since the early 1820s, foreign-born residents and priests clashed over these proceedings.

The Church apparatus in New Mexico was in some ways analogous to the land administration in Texas. Both administrative systems linked exposed frontier provinces to powerful individuals and political groups residing farther south in more populous and wealthier states such as Coahuila and Durango. Patronage underpinned both networks. Just as the governor in Saltillo was able to parcel out land and bestow profitable appointments in Texas, so was the bishop of Durango able to influence priest promotions

---

[73] Ibid.
[74] The Anglo population in New Mexico fluctuated greatly, as it consisted mostly of itinerant merchants, some of whom entered without papers. Passport-holding Anglo Americans in New Mexico never amounted to more than three hundred inhabitants, although this is clearly an underestimation. New Mexico Passport Records Papers, 1825–53, CSR.

and dispose of parish resources in New Mexico. The evidence suggests that Bishop Zubiría used patronage as adroitly as the Viesca brothers, among other things appointing Manuel Armijo as *mayordomo de fábrica* for the parish of San Felipe de Neri in perpetuity, a post that allowed the most successful New Mexican politician of that era to keep 10 percent of the *fábrica* income.[75] Undoubtedly, the most relevant parallel between the Texas land administration and New Mexico's priestly web for our purposes is that they both intended to define the contours of Mexican society in the Far North. Administrators in Texas continuously made decisions about whether to confer land to Native American and Anglo-American settlers, thereby defining the extent of the Mexican community there. Similarly, Church authorities and priests in New Mexico made decisions about who belonged to the Catholic community within the territory, a decision that was closely intertwined to citizenship rights and could give access to marrying partners and land.

But in spite of similarities of function, there were notable differences of emphasis. Guided by notions of progress and development, land administrators in Coahuila and Texas granted privileges to Anglo-American and European settlers and resisted the incorporation of Indians. The Catholic establishment in New Mexico had the exact reverse bias. The conversion of Native Americans had always been the principal objective of the Catholic Church in New Spain, an impulse still in evidence in the early-nineteenth century as shown by Bishop Zubiría's pleas to incorporate Pueblo Indians. This impulse sometimes extended to nomadic Native Americans as well, as in the 1843 letter and call to action of the charismatic priest of Taos, Father Antonio José Martínez, urging the federal government to embark on the grandiose project of teaching nomadic Indians in northern New Mexico to "live in civilized society, cultivating the land, and exercising the various arts and industries."[76] Yet the same enthusiasm did not extend to the Euro-American residents. When Father Manuel Bellido of Taos streamlined the procedure to marry foreign-born residents with New Mexican women in 1823, a fellow priest accused him of being too lenient toward

---

[75] *Fábrica* income referrs to the income derived from the "fabric" or physical plant (buildings, altars, and so on). There was no single dedicated source, so its potential was larger than the sum recorded at any particular time as it often depended on special collections. Normally, *mayordomos de fábrica* were elected, not appointed. Each *mayordomo* had to obtain at least two votes cast by the curate, alcalde, and regidor síndico. The bishop bypassed this method in the case of Armijo. See Bishop Zubiría, Church of San Felipe Neri, Albuquerque, Aug 9, 1833, VGOD. Thanks to William B. Taylor for shedding light on this source of income.

[76] Father Antonio José Martínez to Antonio López de Santa Anna, Taos, 1843, in David J. Weber, ed., *Northern Mexico on the Eve of the United States Invasion: Rare Imprints Concerning California, Arizona, New Mexico, and Texas, 1821–1846* (New York: Arno Press, 1976), imprint No. 5.

foreign-born residents, and the See in Durango promptly removed him from Taos.[77]

For reasons that we shall explore more fully in later chapters, toward the end of the Mexican period many New Mexican priests and the ecclesiastical hierarchy quite openly resisted what they viewed as the wholesale Americanization of the territory. In a prophetic 1845 letter to Bishop Zubiría, Father Martínez makes this defensive Catholic position abundantly clear:

My dearest Father in Jesus Christ,
As I see things over here, this Department will have to belong to the neighboring nation of the North that tolerates all Religions. For some time it has coveted this area, and, according to what I observe, our rulers disregard these perils pretending not to believe what they are told, even though the time of the change of sovereignty is near . . . The changeover to the United States will mean the introduction of diverse religious sects that are tolerated in that country according to their Constitution; but given what little I know by the grace of God, and my determination, I am ready to resist with all my strength the propagation of these sects.[78]

Thus the Catholic Church in New Mexico emerged as the most reliable bulwark of Mexican patriotism construed as defensive Catholicism and sometimes anti-Americanism.

PERFORMING THE NATION

Mexican independence leaders did not delude themselves about the difficulties of bringing the multifarious frontier society into the Mexican fold. Constructing or revamping administrative structures like those revolving around land in Texas and Catholicism in New Mexico constituted one crucial way to extend the grasp of the nation into the Far North. But Mexico's leaders were also aware that beyond developing institutions, they needed to make the Mexican nation present in regions where there were precious few signs of its existence. The nation had to be *shown* or more appropriately *performed* to a heterogeneous frontier audience, and ritual constituted the primary vehicle

---

[77] Father Manuel Rada to don Pedro Millán Rodriguez, gobernador de la Sagrada Mitra, Santa Cruz de la Cañada, Nov 11, 1823; Manuel Rada to Sr. Cura D. Francisco Seiba, Santa Cruz de la Cañada, Feb 22, 1824, both in Archivo Histórico del Arzobispado de Durango (hereafter AHAD), roll 253, 30–1, and 33–5 respectively, Rio Grande Collection, New Mexico State University Library, Las Cruces.

[78] Father Martínez to Bishop Zubiría, Taos, Sep 2, 1845, in Santiago Valdez, Biografía del Reverendo Padre Antonio José Martínez. Apparently, earlier in his life Father Martínez had supported freedom of religion. In his biography of Father Martínez, Fray Angélico Chávez plays down the father's anti-Americanism. He contends that Father Martínez's vitriolic was directed at tejanos and a few unscrupulous land grabbers, not at americanos in general. Angélico Chávez, *But Time and Chance: The Story of Padre Martínez of Taos, 1793–1867* (Santa Fe, NM: Sunstone Press, 1981), 71–7. The examination of Father Martínez's dealings with Anglo Americans does not support this interpretation, as I will try to show.

to transmit this national imagery.[79] In the aftermath of independence, Mexican leaders self-consciously introduced an endless succession of reminders of the nation: flags, coins, seals, medals, letterheads, and commemorations of birthdays and deaths of independence heroes. Leaders like Agustín de Iturbide, Antonio López de Santa Anna, and Maximilian of Hapsburg – all three quite fond of excruciating ceremony and pomp – turned to ritual as an indispensable instrument to rule the country (see Figure 2.6). Between 1821 and 1826, Congress expended considerable time and effort in removing the Spanish heraldry that had heretofore embellished public buildings and carriages and replacing it with new emblems planned to the last detail and always boasting the eagle standing on a prickly pear and devouring a serpent. The legislative branch also took to the task of educating state and local officials and the public at large on such matters as how to write official letters (they were to avoid common wordings like "at your feet" and "other phrases that smell of servility"), how to behave in the presence of the president (no hand kissing or kneeling), and generally how to discharge their civic duties with republican sobriety.[80] Everyday ceremonies like Sunday mass, the occasional wedding, or the routine for initiating court proceedings were suffused with nationalist symbolisms as well. Land possession ceremonies required grantees to shout, "long live the president and the Mexican nation," before they could become legitimate owners.[81]

Independence Day celebration was always the climax of such ritualistic rendition of the nation. Even before the end of the Spanish domination, the Mexican Provisional Governing Junta was prompt to announce that the insurgent army would enter the capital in a triumphal parade on

[79] For an overview of the role of rituals in Mexico, see William H. Beezley, Cheryl English Martin, and William E. French, eds., *Rituals of Rule, Rituals of Resistance: Public Celebrations and Popular Culture in Mexico* (Wilmington, DE: Scholarly Resources, 1994), xiii–xxii. See also Richard Warren, "Ashes and Aerostats: Popular Culture Meets Political Culture in Nineteenth Century Mexico," paper presented at the Latin American Studies Association, Chicago, 1998. On the functions of the *junta patriótica* in Mexico City, see Michael P. Costeloe, "The Junta Patriótica and the Celebration of Independence in Mexico City, 1825–1855," *Mexican Studies/Estudios Mexicanos* 13:1 (Winter 1997), 21–53. On how to understand rituals as politics of celebration, see David Waldstreicher, *In the Midst of Perpetual Fetes: The Making of American Nationalism, 1776–1820* (Chapel Hill, NC: University of North Carolina Press 1997), 3–14, 177–245.

[80] Explanation of the new etiquette in Refugio de la Garza to *ayuntamiento* of Béxar, Mexico City, Aug 8, 1822, BA 72: 455–7. The national symbol, which is still in use in the Mexican flag, was introduced in 1823: Lucas Alamán, Mexico City, Apr 16, 19, 1823, MANM 2:21, 24; Presidential Decree, Mexico City, Mar 21, 1825, MANM 4:248.

[81] For some of these rituals at the northern frontier, see de la Teja, "St. James at the Fair." See also Timothy M. Matovina, *Tejano Religion and Ethnicity: San Antonio, 1821–1860* (Austin, TX: University of Texas Press, 1995), 7–23. On land rituals, see Malcolm Ebright, "New Mexican Land Grants: The Legal Background," in Charles L. Briggs and John R. Van Ness, eds., *Land, Water, and Culture: New Perspectives on Hispanic Land Grants* (Albuquerque, NM, 1987), 54.

FIGURE 2.6. Antonio López de Santa Anna

September 27, 1821, and ordered all towns and villages that had not already sworn independence to do so on that day (see Figure 2.7). The junta provided meticulous instructions to state and local authorities as to what, when, and how to celebrate.[82] But soon both Texans and New Mexicans adapted these festivities to their own ends.

In both provinces, "patriotic committees" labored for months prior to the actual celebration attempting to "excite" the patriotism of all segments of local society. Leading citizens provided substantial outlays of money to pay for lengthy celebrations so that they could show exactly how solvent and patriotic they were. Repetition and anticipation became powerful conduits. Judging by the enthusiasm displayed in San Antonio for the festivities of September 16, 1835, one would not have suspected that Texas was in the throes of a major rebellion. In addition to the usual paraphernalia of bell tolls, pyrotechnics and cannon shots, mass with *Te Deum*, and the party and dance *de rigueur*, an aerostatic globe was released from the main plaza

---

[82] Provisional Governing Junta to Governor of New Mexico, Mexico City, Oct 6, 1821, MANM 1, 171–4.

FIGURE 2.7. Triumphal entrance of Agustín de Iturbide and his troops into Mexico City

to commemorate Mexico's deliverance from Spain. Even more enthusiastic was the Independence Day celebration of 1844 in Santa Fe that lasted six entire days, including three days of bullfights.[83] It is exceedingly difficult to ascertain peoples' real sentiments and motives for their participation. In his report of New Mexico's first Independence Day celebration, Colonel Melgares described the widespread enthusiasm of the people, but somewhat sardonically remarked that it was his hope that these "exteriorities" would translate into genuine support.[84] It is certain that the popular enthusiasm described in many official reports was at least in part a fabrication of zealous local and state officials desiring to show their constituencies in a good light to their superiors.

One of the most obvious features of these early nationalist symbols was the juxtaposition of civic and religious elements. Important civic celebrations always included a solemn mass and *Te Deum*. Three-day public rogations in

[83] Minutes of the patriotic committee for the celebration of Independence Day, San Antonio, Aug 16–22, 1835, BA 166, 363–5; Minutes of the patriotic committee for the celebration of Independence Day, Santa Fe, Jul–Sep, 1844, MANM 37, 564–649. Interestingly, bullfights were a prominent feature of other public occasions, including fairs. De la Teja, "St. James at the Fair," 410–11. More generally on the political uses of the bullfight in Spain, see Adrian Shubert, *Death and Money in the Afternoon: A History of the Spanish Bullfight* (New York: Oxford University Press, 2001), 274–325.

[84] Weber, "An Unforgettable Day," 38.

Texas preceded Congress's first day of deliberations in 1825.[85] Conversely, priests brought the nation to bear in sermons, marriages, baptisms, and other ceremonies. In his Independence Day sermon of 1832, Father Antonio José Martínez of Taos made this connection quite explicit, comparing Miguel Hidalgo, the hero of independence, to no lesser a figure than Jesus Christ. According to the Taos priest, both figures had preached their doctrines to the people courageously, and both had died at the hands of their enemies: "...behold here the mysterious resemblance which gives reason enough evidence to compare Hidalgo to Jesus: the former saved the human race, the latter saved the American people, the continent of Anáhuac."[86] Mexicanness and Catholicism became inextricably intertwined, and indeed Hispanic residents of the frontier used the terms *cristiano* and *mexicano* interchangeably. Religion became a most expedient way to tell Mexicans apart from both Indian pagans and Anglo-American Protestants.

Naturally, not every social group responded in the same way to this national/religious ritual world. Anglo Americans generally avoided Mexican civic occasions. This was especially true in Texas, where colonists were able to insulate themselves from Mexico's ritualistic onslaught as they lived in overwhelmingly Anglo-American communities far from the Hispanic settlements. There is no evidence that patriotic committees in San Antonio or Goliad required representatives from the colonies during Independence Day celebrations or other civic festivities. And when Anglo Americans did become involved, it was strictly out of necessity. The military commander of the heavily Anglo-American district of Nacogdoches, Colonel José de las Piedras, had a chance to test Anglo-American inclination for Mexican ritual at the end of 1827 as he attempted to acquaint the locals with the national and state constitutions. Colonel Piedras summoned all settlers of Ayish Bayou, Sabinas, and Tajaná one morning. Given that the overwhelming majority could not speak Spanish and hence would not be able to utter the customary oath, the Mexican officer chose to have each settler sign a leaf of paper that contained an assertory oath in English. The Mexican officer noted in his report that the public spirit did not seem entirely appropriate: "...their coolness and apathy indicates to me that this act was not to their liking."[87]

Anglo-Texan settlers were also beyond the reach of Catholic priests. Although in theory they had agreed to convert to Catholicism upon settling in Texas, in reality enforcement was lax. The See of Monterrey appointed an Irish priest, Father Miguel Muldoon, as vicar general of the Texas colonies.

[85] Rafael González to José Antonio Saucedo, Saltillo, May 5, 1825, BA 80:963. See also de la Teja, *San Antonio de Béxar*, 148–9; Matovina, *Tejano Religion and Ethnicity*, 20–1.

[86] Sermon of Father Martínez, in Santiago Valdez, *Biografía del Reverendo Padre Antonio José Martínez*, Taos, 1877, unpublished manuscript, Ritch Collection, roll 1, NMSRCA.

[87] Colonel José de las Piedras to General Anastasio Bustamante, Commander of the Eastern Interior Provinces, Nacogdoches, Dec 10, 1827, Herbert E. Bolton Papers 40:673, 2, Bancroft Library.

In the early 1830s, he made occasional whirlwind tours through San Felipe and the other colonies. Father Muldoon emphasized the Catholic fervor of these colonists in a report that was later published: "... they presented to me daily during my visitation, in groups of up to 200 persons to be baptized, to have their marriages confirmed, and to incorporate themselves with enthusiasm to the great Mexican family."[88] Other sources, however, do not support such a sanguine assessment. One colonist described Father Muldoon as a "bigoted old Irishman with an unlimited capacity for drink," and tells how the priest was punched in the face in the midst of an approving crowd, a far cry from the reverence toward religious figures that the Mexican government expected. And even when relations between Father Muldoon and his Texan parishioners were cordial, they were predicated on a nonintrusive form of religion that colonists called "Muldoon Catholicism."[89]

In New Mexico, foreign-born residents were far more involved in civic and religious affairs than in Texas. For example, in New Mexico had a large contingent of Catholic immigrants (of French and Canadian origin) who had obviously less reluctance to participate in religious ceremonies. What is more, some of them became involved in patriotic committees or made financial contributions. Canadian-born Antonio Robidoux was a member of the 1835 *junta patriótica* of Santa Fe, and the American-born merchant Juan Escole (Scollay) took part in the junta of 1844. Immigrants such as Guillermo Esmit, Santiago Col, Santiago Guidens, and Luis Robidoux were generous contributors.[90] Living in towns under the watchful eye of civic and religious authorities, these foreign-born residents could hardly avoid such civic or ritual occasions. Indeed, their participation in patriotic committees may have been a public way to display a national loyalty that was otherwise questioned. But even so, it is fair to say that when it came to nationalizing rituals, foreign-born, Euro-American immigrants to Texas and New Mexico generally preferred to remain on the sidelines.

Pueblo Indians engaged in Mexican ritual in a very different manner. Pueblos possessed their own elaborate ritualistic tradition that had been passed down from generation to generation. A Mexican observer wrote in 1832 that Pueblos engaged in dances and councils inside kivas or underground rooms: "... these rooms are like impenetrable temples where they congregate to consider in secret their misfortunes or successes, their pleasures or sorrows, and the doors are always closed to the Spaniards, for so they call us."[91] But Pueblo Indians also had a long experience dealing

[88] Father Miguel Muldoon, *Gaceta del gobierno supremo del Estado de Coahuila y Texas*, Saltillo, May 27, 1833, BP 40:673, 5.

[89] Cantrell, *Stephen F. Austin*, 238–9; Noah Smithwick, *The Evolution of a State or Recollections of Old Texas Days* (Austin, TX: University of Texas Press, 1983), 46–7.

[90] *Junta patriótica* Proceedings, Santa Fe, Aug 25, 1835, MANM 21, 426; *junta patriótica* Proceedings, Santa Fe, Aug, 1844, MANM 37, 590.

[91] Barreiro, "Ojeada sobre Nuevo México...," 87–8.

FIGURE 2.8. Pueblo of Santo Domingo

with Spaniards and had adapted some of their celebratory manifestations to Spain's imperial mold at the same time that Spanish priests had learned to incorporate Pueblo dances into their calendar of commemorations. Over the course of centuries, Pueblos and Spaniards had sculpted, as it were, a mutually intelligible ritual space.[92] Catholic priests may have complained from time to time about the heretical tendencies of Pueblo dances but accepted them as part of the mutual celebratory repertoire. Conversely, Pueblo Indians took for granted the Spaniards' obsession to commemorate faraway dynastic successions, royal births, weddings, and deaths.

The transition to Mexican sovereignty represented in many ways a continuation of this Spanish-Indian ritual space adapted to a new context. Beginning with New Mexico's very first Independence Day celebration, both Hispanics and Pueblo Indians knew exactly what to expect from each other. In the next few years, Mexican officials left the form unchanged and only tinkered with the content. The Patriotic Committee of Santa Fe in 1844, for example, sent letters to each of the indigenous governors of Tesuque, Nambé, San Ildefonso, Taos, Santo Domingo, and San Felipe, briefly recounting Mexico's ten-year emancipation saga (see Figure 2.8).[93] Interestingly, committee members attempted to engage the addressees by casting the Wars of Independence as a struggle between Indians striving for freedom and Spanish oppressors, and emphasizing the importance of keeping alive the spirit and memory of those who "delivered us from the harsh slavery that we suffered

[92] Here I draw on Richard White's notion of a "middle ground," that is, a space where creative mutual misunderstanding actually forged bridges across cultures. White, *The Middle Ground*.
[93] *Junta patriótica* proceedings, Santa Fe, Aug 23, 1844, MANM 37:590.

for three centuries."[94] But in spite of these novel concepts, the letter concluded very much in the Spanish tradition, urging every Indian governor to organize a dancing group from among his people to commemorate such an important anniversary in the plaza of Santa Fe.

The ritual exchange between the Mexican government and nomadic Native Americans was both the most unpredictable and the most important for preserving amicable relations. It was unpredictable because Mexicans had little control over ritual settings. Nomadic Native Americans surely had opportunities to witness the spectacle of the Mexican nation when they visited Hispanic towns at times of ongoing civic or religious celebrations. But just as often, Mexican envoys and authorities visiting Native American *rancherías* were the ones who found themselves immersed in a totally alien ritual world. It happened to Colonel Peter Ellis Bean when he met a group of three hundred Indians of the Cherokee, Kakapo, Delaware, and other nations in the aftermath of the Fredonia Rebellion.[95] To solemnize a new compact with the Mexican government, the former rebels had already made an arbor of about twenty-five *varas* in length and ten *varas* in width with seats all around, and had placed a buffalo hide in the middle.[96] At the appropriate time, Chief Pata Negra of the Cherokees produced a little box from which he took out twenty-one strings of white beads – symbols left by ancestors – and placed them on the hide while other Native Americans hoisted a white flag in the middle of the round plaza set for the dance.

Material objects were crucial on these ritual occasions. For instance, New Mexico's government began the practice of periodically giving out gifts to Comanches in the late-eighteenth century. A nuevomexicano wrote exultantly about these exchanges in 1812: "...we would never have imagined how beneficial this gift giving policy has been for our province if we hadn't seen it with our own eyes."[97] These gifts consisted of at least two different types of objects. To band chiefs visiting Mexican towns in Texas and New Mexico, the government gave subsistence gifts such as blankets, knives, food, and pottery. In addition, government officials sometimes chose to distinguish certain Native American leaders by giving them *prestige gifts*, such as authority canes, uniforms, medals, and flags, all bearing conspicuous nationalizing symbols. It appears that these two types of objects served to reinforce or possibly even shape Native American social organization, as local bands controlled and distributed subsistence gifts while divisional principal chiefs – one echelon above local bands – obtained the prestige gifts. By

---

[94] *Junta patriótica* proceedings, Santa Fe, Aug 23, 1844, MANM 37:590.
[95] The description of the ritual is in Pedro Ellis Bean to Manuel de Mier y Terán, Nacogdoches, Jul 11, 1828, BHC 2q171, 327, 303–6.
[96] One *vara* was roughly equal to one yard.
[97] Pino, "Exposición," 253. On New Mexico's gifts to Indian nations, see Hall, *Social Change in the Southwest*, 114–15.

investing in subsistence gifts, the Mexican government was in principle able to promote band chiefs and atomize an Indian polity into different bands; by delivering prestige gifts, it could emphasize unity at the divisional level. Thomas W. Kavanagh provides tantalizing evidence of the centrality of these and other political/material exchanges, and argues that Comanches possessed a very fluid and dynamic political organization constantly adapting to exploit particular resources like gifts and commercial flows.[98] For instance, the New Mexico Kotsotecas were able to prosper on the basis of amicable political and commercial relations with Hispanic-Pueblo communities reinforced by regular gift giving, while, in stark contrast, the Texas Kotsotekas, unable to sustain themselves on trade with the smaller Texas towns and more dependent on the horse trade by way of Natchitoches, were forced into an economy geared toward raiding Mexico.[99] Other nomadic Indian groups along Mexico's Far North may have adjusted their political/economic strategies accordingly. If this is the case, then Mexico's gift giving and ritual onslaught (or lack thereof) was absolutely crucial in determining the nature of Mexico's relations with the surrounding Indian communities, thus determining Mexico's chances of preserving its hold over this region.

Prior to the Texas Revolution and the Mexican–American War, Mexico did not possess a full-fledged state. But it did have bureaucracies and systems of patronage that proceeded in earnest with the arduous task of centralizing authority and weaving together disparate frontier social groups. It is time to revise the prevailing narrative of early Mexico as declension from Spanish monarchical institutions, loss of control, and chaos. Since the late-eighteenth century, local and regional powerbrokers throughout Mexico had been experimenting with new ideas and institutions as they coped with the Bourbon reforms.[100] Recent Mexicanist scholarship has emphasized the country's impressive institutional development immediately before and after independence, introducing novel institutions such as elected municipal and provincial governments, attempting to define the proper spheres of the federation and the states, and transforming the relationship between Church and state.[101] This process, difficult as it was in some regions, slowly yielded functioning state and local governments more or less successfully integrated into the national domain.

This same institutional transition began to take place along Mexico's northern frontier, with developments such as the emergence of a land administrative system in Texas in the 1820s and the ecclesiastical reassertion

---

[98] Kavanagh, *The Comanches*, 478–9.

[99] Ibid., 480–1.

[100] Weber provides an overview of these new institutions and ideas in *The Mexican Frontier*, 15–42.

[101] Anna, *Forging Mexico*, passim.

in New Mexico in the 1830s. Although this process of institutional development was never completed before this region ceased to be a part of Mexico,
it nonetheless set the terms of the identity struggles that would rock Texas
and New Mexico in years to come. The story of how Mexico's Far North became the American Southwest begins with these institutions and the ways in
which they impinged on the livelihood of frontier society. Indeed, the Texas
Revolution of 1835–6, the Chimayó Rebellion in New Mexico in 1837, and
the other revolutionary upheavals that broke out in other peripheral regions
of Mexico would be incomprehensible without regard to these determined
efforts at institutional consolidation and centralization and the reactions of
frontier inhabitants. I have also tried to underscore the fact that this institutional development entailed not only systems of control, coercion, and
self-interest, but also various political and ideological meanings. Land in
Texas was associated with ideals of liberalism and home rule, and these very
notions kept the door open to Anglo Americans desiring to settle in Mexico. In contrast, the efforts of the Church hierarchy in New Mexico were
geared toward a different national project far more defensive and reluctant
to incorporate foreign-born residents.

These institutions and ideas created tensions that would have been resolved within the national realm – as they were everywhere else in Mexico –
had it not been for powerful economic forces unleashed at this time linking
Mexico's Far North to the United States.

3

The Spirit of Mercantile Enterprise

The economies of Mexico and the United States were as different as night and day during the first half of the nineteenth century. Between 1800 and 1860, Mexico's total income declined 10.5 percent, whereas that of the United States skyrocketed 1,270.4 percent. In that same period, Mexico experienced little industrialization and saw its exports of bullion plummet while the United States was swept by revolutions in transportation and industry and enjoyed a string of economic booms. In that half century, Mexico's total population hovered around 6 million, while that of the United States grew dramatically from 5 to 32 million. Never again would these two economies diverge so much and seem so utterly disconnected from one another.[1]

And yet, they *were* connected precisely along Mexico's Far North. Unlike its core region, Mexico's northern frontier experienced significant economic growth at this time.[2] But this growth was rather one-sided, as it was propelled chiefly by foreign immigration, the opening of new trading routes to the United States, the availability of cheap import goods, and the exploitation of this region as a crossroads of exchange. For example, New Mexico's economy was radically affected by the opening of the Santa Fe Trail, that is, the establishment of regular trading caravans between Missouri and New Mexico. In 1822, the value of the merchandise imported into New Mexico was estimated at 15,000 dollars; two years later, that figure had doubled, and by 1826 it had doubled again. The declared value of the merchandise taken

---

[1] Coatsworth, "Obstacles to Economic Growth in Nineteenth-Century Mexico," 81–4. John Tutino provides an overview of the economic ups and downs of the Bajío area in *From Insurrection to Revolution in Mexico* (Princeton, NJ: Princeton University Press, 1989). The case for economic stagnation at the core is not conclusive. See Margaret Chowning, *Wealth and Power in Provincial Mexico: Michoacán from the Late Colony to the Revolution* (Stanford, CA: Stanford University Press, 1999).

[2] The economic history of Texas and New Mexico during the Mexican period has yet to be written. See pervasive evidence of economic growth in this chapter. For a general assessment of the economy of the Far North, see Weber, *The Mexican Frontier*, 207–41.

FIGURE 3.1. A caravan on the Santa Fe Trail

to Santa Fe in 1843 was almost half a million dollars, an explosive thirtyfold increase in two decades (see Figure 3.1).[3] Elsewhere in Mexico, the story was much the same: Foreign goods flooded erstwhile-protected markets. In Texas, no momentous event marked the dawn of a new commercial era. Nonetheless, trade rapidly shaped the demography, politics, material culture, and identity of Texas.[4] Trade liberalization had its most dramatic effects in Mexico's Far North, as this region had suffered the most from colonial trading restrictions at the same time that it was tantalizingly close to the dynamic American markets. In brief, Mexico's Far North prospered in the midst of a generally stagnant Mexican economy largely because it gravitated toward the orbit of the expanding American economy (see Map 3.1).

Historians of the United States have emphasized the transformative power of capitalism during the first half of the nineteenth century. First, it touched the lives of those living along the coast and in key trading posts inland. But the transportation revolution early in the century extended the reach of the market, unleashing history's most revolutionary force all across the continent.[5] The distinct subsistence-farming culture of the eighteenth century was profoundly altered by a market onslaught during the Jacksonian era, a

[3] See table in Lansing Bloom, "New Mexico Under Mexican Administration 1821–1486," *Old Santa Fe*, 3 vols (Santa Fe. NM: Old Santa Fe Press) 2:2, 121. Bloom obtained his figures from Josiah Gregg, who was also the original source employed by the United States Congress.

[4] Montejano, *Anglos and Mexicans in the Making of Texas*, 15–21.

[5] Albert Fishlow, *American Railroads and the Transformation of the Antebellum Economy* (Cambridge, MA: 1965); Susan Previant Lee and Peter Passell, *A New Economic View of American History* (New York: W. W. Norton, 1979); Charles Sellers, *The Market Revolution: Jacksonian America, 1815–1846* (New York: Oxford University Press, 1991), esp. 3–33.

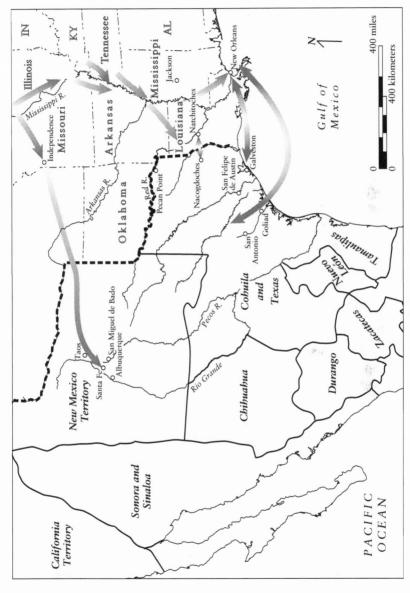

MAP 3.1. Main commercial routes between the United States and northern Mexico

process that ended up transforming gender, race, class, and ethnic relations forever. Mexico's Far North became the outermost perimeter of this same economic revolution. Just as an earlier generation of American merchants, trappers, and land speculators had pushed into the Ohio valley and Louisiana in the 1800s,[6] by the 1820s their successors reached Texas, New Mexico, and California. In all fairness, the arrival of these entrepreneurs did not *open* Mexico's frontier. Since the eighteenth century, Spanish and Creole merchants had linked the economies of Texas and New Mexico to larger markets farther south, constituting regional and even long-distance trading systems.[7] But the lifting of commercial restrictions in the 1820s did accelerate frontier's passage from subsistence to commerce and, most importantly, dramatically reoriented these incipient commercial ties toward the United States.[8]

The tribulations of Manuel Márquez y Melo flesh out this process in vivid detail. Don Manuel was a *criollo* (an individual born in New Spain of Spanish descent) from Guadalajara who had prospered in the final years of the colonial period by selling Spanish wine, aguardiente, mules, and textiles in a large area that encompassed Zacatecas, San Luis Potosí, Coahuila, and Chihuahua. He would spend most of the year riding alongside muleteers and cart men hauling large *barricas* (barrels) filled with spirits and corresponding with a dozen key partners exchanging information about demand, prices, and politics.[9] Having weathered the turmoil of independence, in the early 1820s Márquez y Melo shrewdly expanded his business to southern New Mexico and northern Coahuila. But here he ran into difficulties, and things came to a dramatic halt in 1824. Some of Márquez y Melo's setbacks were purely accidental. In 1823, one *barrica* of *aguardiente* was punctured, spilling more than twenty *arrobas* that quickly disappeared in the thirsty desert sand. Also, the wine reserves of one of his main trading partners went bad during the warm season (fortunately, winter temperatures restored the liquid's original

[6] For the early transformation of the Ohio Valley, see Gruenwald, *River of Enterprise*, 81–100.

[7] On the rise of these intrerregional economic networks during the late colonial period involving Texas and New Mexico, see John O. Baxter, *Las Carneradas: Sheep Trade in New Mexico, 1700–1860* (Albuquerque, NM: University of New Mexico Press, 1987), passim; Frank, *From Settler to Citizen*, 122–75; Gerald E. Poyo and Gilberto M. Hinojosa, "Spanish Texas and Borderlands Historiography in Transition: Implications for United States History," *Journal of American History* 75:2 (Sept 1988), 395–416. For other parts of Mexico, see Eric Van Young, *Hacienda and Market in Eighteenth-Century Mexico: The Rural Economy of the Guadalajara Region, 1675–1820* (Berkeley, CA: University of California Press, 1981); or, in a different context, Radding, *Wandering Peoples*.

[8] On the interlocking of New Mexico's colonial economy with the Santa Fe Trail, see discussion in Frank, *From Settler to Citizen*, 226–8. See also Martín González de la Vara, "La corta mexicanidad de Nuevo México, 1821–1848: un caso de las relaciones entre el gobierno central y la frontera norte," B.A. thesis, UNAM, 1986; Ángela Moyano Pahissa, *El comercio de Santa Fe y la Guerra del '47* (Mexico City: Sep Setentas, 1976), passim.

[9] This account is entirely based on the Márquez y Melo Papers, NMSRCA.

properties).[10] But Márquez y Melo got a first glimpse of the enormity of the challenge ahead on a visit to Parras, Coahuila, in 1822: "I will have to beg your patience for a little longer," he pleaded with one of his disgruntled partners:

... but my goodness here I have found a number of street sellers coming from everywhere and giving away the merchandise that they obtained in this new commerce with the United States ... they're selling *superfinos*[11] of 23 and 24 pesos at 15 and 16. For the moment let us conform ourselves, let us continue our mercantile routine as our European brethren do and we will eventually succeed just like them.[12]

His strategy was doomed from the start. Anglo-American merchants relentlessly drove Márquez y Melo *and* his European (Spanish) brethren out of business in a short time. Geography coupled with Mexico's Byzantine taxation system made it all but impossible for Hispanic merchants to compete. By the time their wares had been shipped from Spain, disembarked at Veracruz, and hauled across half a dozen or more states (each one imposing a state tariff, or *alcabala*), the price had doubled or trebled.[13]

At first it appeared that Anglo-American and a sprinkling of French merchants would merely replace the Spaniards and southern Creoles as the exclusive suppliers of the frontier. Indeed, in the short run a small group of newcomers came to control the new commercial routes and in the process amassed wealth that must have surpassed even their wildest dreams. The Santa Fe Trail, for instance, became inextricably linked to the names of Charles Bent and Ceran St. Vrain. These two partners not only became the largest dealers of the trail, but more strategically coowned Bent's Fort, a necessary stopover on the Arkansas River for the caravans bound for New Mexico. Their business empire would come to include stores in Taos and Santa Fe as well as large colonization enterprises in northern New Mexico.[14] David Waldo was not far behind. By 1846 he had introduced close to one million dollars of merchandise, making a profit of 400,000 dollars. All told, he had outfitted 375 wagons, used 1,700 mules, and 2,000 oxen, and employed around 500 men.[15] To be sure, the Bent brothers, St. Vrain,

---

[10] Manuel Márquez y Melo to Carlos Moya, n.p., Jan 12, 1822; Márquez y Melo to Andrés de la Viesca, Chihuahua, May 13, 1823; Andrés Cárdenas to Márquez y Melo, Parras, Mar 24, 1824; Agustín Viesca to Manuel Márquez y Melo, Parras, Jun 30, 1824. All in Márquez y Melo Papers, NMSRCA.

[11] From the contex, it can be inferred that Márquez y Melo is referring to textiles.

[12] Márquez y Melo to Joaquín Barela, Parras, Jan 12, 1822, Márquez y Melo Papers, NMSRCA.

[13] "The tariff system is such that, if we [New Mexicans] ever find an article from abroad, it is with a 200% markup...," complained Juan Martín Veramendi on behalf of the *ayuntamiento* of San Antonio. Juan Martín de Veramendi to Governor of Coahuila and Texas, Feb 16, 1828, BA 111:26–8.

[14] Harold H. Dunham, "Charles Bent," in LeRoy R. Hafen, ed., *The Mountain Men and the Fur Trade of the Far West*, 10 vols (Glendale, CA: A. H. Clark, 1965–72), 2: 27–48.

[15] Figures taken from Bancroft, *History of Arizona and New Mexico*, 332.

and Waldo constituted the undisputed elite within a heterogeneous community of foreign-born merchants that included all social levels. But it is also true that initially the Santa Fe Trail came to be largely dominated by a surprisingly small number of French and Anglo-American operators. The situation was much the same in Texas, where a handful of Anglo-American dealers not only supplied goods to the fast-growing Anglo-Texan colonies but also gained favor among Mexican Texans and extended their influence into Tamaulipas and Coahuila. By 1826, Anglos completely dominated the trading business in San Antonio and Goliad, introducing merchandise at various times of the year. Some of these Anglo-American traffickers settled in Texas, opened import stores, and married into prominent tejano families.[16]

The initial French and Anglo-American merchants' dominance was a direct result of their unmatched connections to suppliers in the United States and the peculiar vagaries of transportation, all of which slowed down the entry of competitors. Consider the Santa Fe Trail. If Mexican or Native American merchants wanted to enter this business, they had to journey to Missouri and spend weeks or even months dealing and bargaining with suppliers in St. Louis, Independence, Philadelphia, or New York prior to the caravan's departure to Mexico. To succeed in this high-stakes endeavor, these merchants needed time, knowledge or more than a smattering of English or French, and available credit (this could be substituted by cash or precious metals, but this made the venture far riskier). The trail itself, a month-and-a-half odyssey across the continental plains, also favored Anglo Americans,

---

[16] Unlike the highly structured Santa Fe Trail, Texas trade became fragmented into different markets. One group of merchants established a presence at the mouth of the Rio Grande and dominated the trade of the Lower Rio Grande. Another group operated in the San Antonio–Goliad region, while a third group supplied the Anglo-Texan colonies. The best treatment of commerce along the Rio Grande is still an old and unpublished Ph.D. dissertation: LeRoy P. Graf, "The Economic History of the Lower Rio Grande Valley 1820–1875," Ph.D. dissertation, Harvard, 1942. For the other regions, see Juan Nepomuceno Almonte, *Informe secreto sobre la presente situación de Texas, 1834*, edited by Celia Gutiérrez Ibarra (Mexico City: Instituto Nacional de Antropología e Historia, 1987), 20, 26, 31, 60. For the role of Anglo-American merchants in the San Antonio-Goliad region, see notes to the San Antonio census, San Antonio, Jul 31, 1826, NA, 2q298, 197A, 41–3; Chabot, *With the Makers of San Antonio*, 273; Catherine George, "The Life of Philip Dimmitt," M.A. thesis, University of Texas, Austin, TX 1937, 2–16; Sánchez, "A Trip to Texas in 1828," 258. For a list of Anglo traders living in Goliad, see José Miguel Aldrete to Ramón Músquiz, Goliad, Oct 20, 1830, BA 135, 533–4; for a list of Anglo merchants living in San Antonio, see report of Antonio Hernández, San Antonio, Apr 24, 1828, BA 113, 123; report of Francisco Salazar, San Antonio, Apr 24, 1828, BA 113, 122. See also Ramón Músquiz to Erasmo Seguín, San Antonio, Nov 21, 1828, BA 117, 1018–19; José Bonifacio Galán, customs administrator of Goliad, to Erasmo Seguín, Goliad, Aug 7, 1829, BA 124, 730–1. For Anglo-American merchants active in New Mexico, see Howard R. Lamar, *The Far Southwest, 1846–1912: A Territorial History* (New York: W. W. Norton, 1970), 28, 35–55; Ralph Emerson Twitchell, *The Leading Facts of New Mexican History*, 5 vols (Cedar Rapids, IA: Torch Press, 1912), 1: 453.

as it passed through American forts and took place largely inside American territory. Only the last leg of the 2,000-mile trip was conducted in Mexican territory after the caravan had started its breathtaking descent into New Mexico's multicolored desert landscape.

Yet, from these inauspicious beginnings, Hispanic frontier residents gradually chipped away at the Anglo-American commercial stranglehold over the region. Until 1821, places such as New Mexico and Texas had been rather impoverished markets dominated by Spanish and Creole merchants such as Márquez y Melo from farther south. For instance, Chihuahua mercantile houses had long dominated New Mexico's exiguous commerce. However, after 1821, Hispanic residents of the frontier no longer found themselves at the terminus but at the crossroads of new trading routes originating in Louisiana and Missouri and began participating as international merchants in their own right.

In Texas, a group of Hispanic merchants began competing with Anglo Americans within a decade in the San Antonio–Goliad region.[17] The dean among them was José Casiano. Born in 1791 in San Remo (Republic of Genoa) as Giuseppe Cassini, he went to New Orleans in 1816 as a young seaman and became a successful merchant. His business trips took him to Texas, where he eventually set his residence, opening a store in San Antonio in the early 1820s.[18] With his business acumen and contacts, José Casiano not only prospered but initiated other tejanos into the Louisiana–Texas trade as well. Even before he moved to San Antonio, Casiano most certainly had come in contact with a group of tejano exiles in New Orleans. These tejanos had been banished from their native land for their involvement in the independence movements of the early 1810s. This group of émigrés included Colonel Francisco Ruiz and his young nephew, José Antonio Navarro.[19] With Mexico's trade liberalization after 1821, the Ruiz and Navarro families, together with José Casiano, were among the first to engage in the expanding international commerce of West Texas.[20] The stories of Francisco Ruiz and José Antonio Navarro are particularly relevant because they would be the only two tejanos who signed the Texas Declaration of Independence

---

[17] Occupational distinctions are somewhat arbitrary. Merchants were also land owners and ranchers as well as government officials at the same time. Still these individuals described themselves as merchants in the 1830 census. Gifford White, ed., *1830 Citizens of Texas* (Austin, TX: Eakin Press, 1983), 79–112.

[18] There is a brief biographic sketch of don José in the Casiano-Pérez Collection, Daughters of the Republic of Texas.

[19] Joseph Martin Dawson, *José Antonio Navarro: Co-Creator of Texas* (Waco, TX: Baylor University Press, 1969).

[20] The involvement of these tejanos in trading activities in the 1820s was not only a matter of self-interest but also represented the triumph of liberalism over the old system of Spanish privilege and exclusion. See Naomi Fritz, "José Antonio Navarro," M.A. thesis, St. Mary's University, San Antonio, TX, 1941.

fifteen years later. Similarly, José Casiano performed valuable services for the revolution.

Other successful tejano merchants include Ramón Músquiz and Erasmo and Juan Nepomuceno Seguín. Músquiz made frequent business trips to New Orleans with Casiano. He was appointed *jefe político* of Texas in 1827 and 1831, and under his aegis commerce flourished in Texas. Erasmo Seguín also combined a successful administrative career with commercial ventures. Don Erasmo was San Antonio's quartermaster for a decade, a post that made him directly responsible for the collection of import duties, and therefore a key figure in the world of commerce in West Texas. His son, Juan Nepomuceno Seguín, actively participated in the thriving Louisiana–Texas trade, making regular trips to Louisiana since 1826.[21] By the early 1830s, these men not only had developed extensive trading networks comparable to those of their Anglo counterparts – webs stretching from New Orleans suppliers to Texas customs officers and store owners – but also dominated local politics and were very influential in matters of land distribution. By peddling goods, land, and influence, this tejano group became a formidable power.

Similarly, nuevomexicano merchants eventually undermined the virtual monopoly of foreign-born merchants in the Santa Fe Trail. The analysis of New Mexico's customs receipts or *guías* for 1843 – the most complete set of such documents during the Mexican period – gives us a detailed snapshot of the activities and share of the market commanded by nuevomexicanos. That year, New Mexico's total exports to other Mexican states were distributed as follows: 69 percent consisted of European and American goods introduced through the Santa Fe Trail, 17 percent were sheep, and the remaining 14 percent were exports of local products such as wood, wool, and *sarapes*.[22] Out of New Mexico's total exports in the year, Spanish-surnamed individuals appear as owners of 45 percent of all goods departing from New Mexico.[23] But while Anglo Americans were almost exclusively involved in

[21] De la Teja, *A Revolution Remembered*, 5, 16–18, 123–4.

[22] *Guías* yield extremely useful information, such as the name of the owner, the type and quantity of goods, and the destination. Starting in 1839, *guías* included an estimate of the value of the merchandise. *Guía* notebooks for 1835, through 1840 are found on MANM 21:271–363. *Guías* for 1843 are on MANM 34:1200–16, and a few for 1844 are on MANM 37:45–9. The main limitation of this source is that it includes only reported mercantile activities. The statistical analysis was performed on the 1843 set of *guías* only. It can be argued that 1843 was an exceptional year, but unfortunately, it is the only year for which we have virtually complete information.

[23] Contemporary Anglo-American merchants often complained that by the 1840s the trade was falling into the hands of Mexicans. See Mark L. Gardner, ed., *Brothers on the Santa Fe and Chihuahua Trails: Edward James Glasgow and William Henry Glasgow, 1846–1848* (Niwot, CO: University of Colorado Press, 1993), 200 (n.12). See the work of Susan Calafate Boyle, *Los Capitalistas: Hispano Merchants and the Santa Fe Trade* (Albuquerque, NM: University of New Mexico Press, 2000), for the role of native New Mexican and Chihuahuan merchants in the overland trade.

the trafficking of foreign goods, nuevomexicanos were a lot more diversified, controlling 93 percent of the exports of local products and 100 percent of sheep exports in addition to accounting for a full 22 percent of all exports of foreign goods.

These numbers jibe well with anecdotal evidence indicating that New Mexico's old Hispanic elite shrewdly managed to make the transition from land-based, sheep-raising enterprises to the world of international and domestic commerce. Manuel Armijo, three-time governor of New Mexico, is a good example. He rapidly gained a foothold in the Santa Fe Trail, combining his sheep-exporting activities to northern Mexico with the selling of domestic and foreign goods. The United States consul in Santa Fe reported that Governor Armijo was "a very large merchant who has been struggling for some time to monopolize all the commerce of the province."[24] In the same fashion, the prominent Chávez family deftly mixed commercial and livestock ventures. In 1834, Mariano Chávez organized his own caravan to the United States, hiring 150 men for this purpose. Flush with cash from the proceeds, he bought sheep locally; the next year, Mariano and José Chávez decided to go south rather than north exporting twenty-six thousand sheep into Mexico's interior, contributing to the largest herd of animals that ever left New Mexico during the Mexican period.[25] The Otero family followed closely. Antonio José Otero sold 26,100 sheep in Mexico between 1837 and 1843 and imported merchandise from the United States worth more than 3,000 pesos in 1840 bound for the Chihuahua market. Governor Armijo described the Oteros as "the most prominent men in all affairs here in New Mexico and possibly in Chihuahua as well."[26]

Not only traditional oligarchs but also *hispanos* of humbler backgrounds found new avenues of advancement. *Conductores*, the individuals transporting and handling shipments for wealthy merchants unable or unwilling to travel, after a first stint sometimes struck out on their own, becoming owners in their own right. Muleteers' and packers' services were in great demand during these years of rapid expansion of the Santa Fe Trail and were often able to negotiate favorable terms (see Figure 3.2). As the amount of fabrics

---

[24] Manuel Álvarez to Secretary of State, Independence, Missouri, Jul 1, 1843, Dispatches from United States Consuls in Santa Fe, 1830–1846, RG 59. no. 199. If Indeed Governor Armijo had such large operations, he did not report them. Mexican-era *guías* indicate that he was an important trafficker of domestic goods.

[25] Diary of Manuel Álvarez, Santa Fe, Nov 2, 1840, Read Collection, Series II, NMSRCA. José Chávez was a brother of Antonio José Chávez, a merchant who was assassinated on the Trail by a party of Texans in 1843. See Marc Simmons, *Murder on the Santa Fe Trail: An International Incident, 1843* (El Paso, TX: Texas Western Press, 1987). Mariano Chávez was a very consistent livestock exporter. In 1839 he exported 5,000 sheep, in 1840 he sent 5,500 sheep, and in 1843 he reported 4,400 sheep to be sold in Mexico's interior. Data from *guías*.

[26] Manuel Armijo to Donaciano Vigil, Albuquerque, Aug 30, 1848, Donaciano Vigil Collection, NMSRCA.

FIGURE 3.2. Mexican muleteers and their pack mules

circulating in New Mexico increased, so did the need for competent tailors and seamstresses.[27] Many jobs became available in the lodging, food, and entertainment businesses. Consider the case of Gertrudis Barceló. Born to a modest nuevomexicano family, this remarkable woman made a living by organizing gambling soirees in Santa Fe in which patrons played a lottery-like, Spanish game called *monte*. She refashioned herself as doña Tules, and her clientele came to include not only native players but also scores of transient Anglo Americans attracted to New Mexico by the Santa Fe Trail.[28] A volunteer in the U.S. Army described her at the peak of her career:

Madame Toolay nightly displays her glittering piles of gold and silver at Monte. It is amusing to observe her maneuvers during the progress of the game. When fortune favors her, keen small black eyes seem about to start from their sockets, and a melancholy smile covers her wrinkled mouth when losing.[29]

She probably won more often than lost if we are to judge by her possessions. By the time of her death, she owned three houses in Santa Fe, a carriage, silver jewelry, a stock of mules, and an undisclosed amount of cash and debts owed to her.[30] The case of Barceló was exceptional; but there is no doubt that

[27] Calafate Boyle, *Los Capitalistas*, 41, 45.
[28] Janet Lecompte, "La Tules and the Americans," *Arizona and the West* 20:1 (1978), 215-35.
[29] Diary of John North Dunlap, Mar 3, 1847, Santa Fe, Miscellaneous Letters and Diaries, file 4, NMSRCA.
[30] Will (hijuela) of María Gertrudis Barcelo, Oct 13, 1850, Santa Fe, Miscellaneous Records, Wills and Hijuelas, Folder 11, NMSCRA. See also Angélico Chávez, "Doña Tules, Her Fame and Her Funeral," *El Palacio* 58 (1950).

New Mexico commercial activities spawned an entirely new class of store clerks, gambling hall owners, muleteers, *conductores*, trappers, and so on, a few of whom rose to prominence and riches. In the age of commerce, New Mexico's upper crust expanded beyond the traditional oligarchy and came to include successful entrepreneurs of humbler origins, such as doña Tules. Reminiscing about those heady years, Donaciano Vigil, a veteran officer and successful local politician, made the crucial observation that in addition to calicos and scissors, the *spirit of mercantile enterprise* also spread among nuevomexicanos.[31]

That same spirit reached indigenous peoples too. Information on these activities is somewhat spotty but persuasive. As early as the spring of 1822, the Gran Cadó decided to embark on a lengthy trip from northern Texas all the way to Monterrey and Mexico City. His ostensible goal was to pay a visit to Mexico's emperor, hoping to secure land for his people. But the Gran Cadó also viewed the trip as an opportunity to introduce an undetermined amount of tobacco.[32] Beyond introducing products into Mexico, Native Americans profited from a host of activities related to the rising commercial economy of the region. In Texas, Comanches became the principal beneficiaries of the large traffic of mules and horses through the Natchitoches–Nacogdoches corridor. They drove herds of hundreds and even thousands of equines via the *camino real* from the San Antonio–Goliad region into Louisiana. In 1822, the Mexican government allowed the free traffic of mules and horses between Texas and the United States. While the lifting of the ban probably had a negligible impact on an activity that Native Americans had traditionally carried out without regard to Spanish and Mexican legislation, the commercial impetus of Texas–Louisiana trade did increase demand for horses and mules.[33]

Native Americans in New Mexico experienced a comparable windfall with the beaver pelt rush of the 1820s and early 1830s. Abiquiu and Taos became bases for various fur companies dedicated to organizing and outfitting parties of hunters and trappers, sometimes of more than a hundred men at a time, that prowled the rivers of northern New Mexico. These operations required horses and experienced guides generating active trade with neighboring Indians. Utes in particular took advantage of these new commercial opportunities by trapping beaver, selling horses, and offering a range

---

[31] Esposicion de Donaciano Vigil ante la Asamblea Departamental, Santa Fe, Jun 18, 1846, edited and translated by David Weber, *Arms, Indians and the Mismanagement of New Mexico: Donaciano Vigil 1846* (El Paso, TX: Texas Western Press, 1986), 4. My own italics for emphasis.

[32] Gran Cadó to Iturbide, n.p., Mar 4, 1822, in Gaspar López to Ministerio de Relaciones Exteriores, Apr 26, 1822, BHC, 2q220, 552, 9–80.

[33] Decree of the Provisional Governing Junta, Mexico City, Jan 10, 1822, SANM II, 20, 1078–9. See José Gerónimo Huízar to José Antonio Saucedo, Bahía, Aug 11, 1824, BA 77, 665–9.

of services to the fur companies.[34] The scale of these operations rivaled those of the Santa Fe Trail itself. Donaciano Vigil estimated that in 1827 the companies based in Abiquiu produced more than 160 *quintales* of pelts worth close to 100,000 pesos, more than the reported value of the merchandise imported into New Mexico for that same year (85,000). While we ignore how much of those proceeds Native Americans got to keep, we do know that trappers spent considerable sums outfitting their expeditions. That year, the Taos companies spent between 50,000 and 60,000 pesos just on horses and provisions.[35]

Thus the market revolution touched the lives of all frontier residents. For a start, the spirit of mercantile enterprise realigned the interests of all social groups. One the one hand, it facilitated crosscultural alliances based on mutually beneficial arrangements. Although relations between Anglo and Hispanic merchants both in Texas and New Mexico were sometimes contentious, the two groups generally got along quite well and often forged profitable and long-lasting partnerships. In many respects, the two groups of merchants were complementary. While Anglo Americans could make the introductions and pave the way for their Hispanic counterparts with suppliers in Missouri and Louisiana, Hispanic traders could reciprocate helping out their Anglo-American colleagues with Mexican customs officers and other authorities. The two groups were forced to travel together and extend credit to one another. Many Anglo-American merchants ended up marrying into nuevomexicano and tejano families, thus sealing profitable business/personal relationships. Some Mexican-Texan officials, land commissioners, surveyors, and politicians similarly established friendly relations with Anglo-Texan empresarios and settlers based on common pecuniary interests.[36]

On the other hand, those same commercial webs could strain relations and lead to conflict. Generally, the tenuous peace between Hispanics and Native Americans achieved in the last colonial years deteriorated during the Mexican period. New commercial relations were largely to blame for this new wave of hostilities. Historically, Indians had established a barter system with neighboring Spanish settlements in New Mexico and Texas exchanging buffalo hides, chamois, and so on, for rudimentary firearms, knives, and other manufactured goods. Such commercial relations had kept Native American groups weak and somewhat dependent on the Crown.[37] But the

---

[34] Judicial proceedings against Ricardo Cambel, Felipe Tomson, and Vicente Gion, MANM 8, 371–447, and 8, 475–503.

[35] Donaciano Vigil to the Honorable Assembly, Santa Fe, Jun 18, 1846, edited and translated by Weber, *Arms, Indians, and the Mismanagement of New Mexico*, 4.

[36] Andrés Reséndez, "Caught Between Profits and Rituals: National Contestation in Texas and New Mexico, 1821–1848," Ph.D. dissertation, University of Chicago, 1997, ch. 3 and 4.

[37] Weber, *The Mexican Frontier*, ch. 5. Relations between Mexicans and Comanches were characterized by alternating bouts of hostility and attempts at reconciliation. See Kavanagh, *The Comanches*, 201–48.

arrival of French and Anglo-American merchants in the early-nineteenth century shattered that dependency. These new dealers not only made arms and ammunition more readily available to the nomadic tribes but also created a market where Indians could sell spoils of raids (especially horses and sheep) conducted throughout northern Mexico. Indeed, the Comanches, Kiowas, Navajos, and Utes, among others, increased the scope of their raiding activities farther south into Mexico at this time.

Some evidence indicates that Pueblo Indians did not relish New Mexico's commercial turn. They did benefit marginally from increased demand for horses and food, especially in pueblos close to the path of the Santa Fe Trail, and from the trapping activities. For instance, at a camp south of Albuquerque, Pueblo Indians offered to trade melons, eggs, tortillas, and grapes for empty glass bottles carried by a group of Anglo-American merchants.[38] But these contacts were rather sporadic and informal, and whatever benefits accrued to them were offset by tangible disadvantages. Anglo-American and Mexican merchants encroached on Pueblo land as they sought to invest some of their fabulous profits in traditional sheep-raising ventures. Moreover, Pueblo Indians felt the brunt of the increasing hostility from nomadic Indians. All settled New Mexicans suffered from these attacks; but this was especially burdensome on Pueblos and poor *mestizos* who, unlike wealthy New Mexicans, could not buy their way out of military duty.

These changing interethnic relations propelled by the new economic reality of the region coincided with heightened concerns about the ultimate fate of the frontier region. As Mexico's Far North grew ever more dependent on the American economy, inevitably the question of loyalty came to the fore. As early as 1830, New Mexico's Governor José Antonio Chávez informed the minister of the interior that a minority of New Mexicans valued their commercial relations with Anglo Americans so much that they even favored a North American takeover of the territory.[39] Although Governor Chávez went to great lengths to point out that the overwhelming majority of residents remained faithful to Mexico, the report undoubtedly raised some eyebrows in Mexico City as it revealed the extent to which economic interests had a bearing on the loyalty of frontier society. In the same vein, the reports of the Boundary Commission in the late 1820s left no doubts as to the gravity of the situation in Texas, where floods of foreign-born immigrants already outnumbered tejanos; and the sprawling new colonies, turning their backs on Mexico as it were, were totally devoted to pursuing all kinds of commercial ventures with neighboring Louisiana. To be sure, commerce worked in complicated ways and not always against Mexico. As the governor of Chihuahua insightfully observed, the Santa Fe Trail actually

---

[38] Laura Bayer, *Santa Ana: The People, the Pueblo, and the History of Tamaya* (Santa Fe, NM: University of New Mexico Press, 1994), 127–8.

[39] Governor José Antonio Chávez to Minister of the Interior, Oct 2, 1830, MANM 10, 784–5.

bound New Mexico more firmly to the rest of the nation in an indirect way: "...they [nuevomexicanos] cannot sustain their exchange with the Anglo Americans unless they sell their products in this state and others farther west, and this constitutes a tie uniting their interest with those of the other towns in Mexico's interior."[38] Something similar occurred in Texas, as commercial liberalization stimulated trade between Coahuila and Texas and neighboring Mexican states. Still, increased economic interaction with the United States raised the specter of Americanization throughout Mexico's Far North.

GETTING CURED AND GETTING DRUNK: MATERIAL CULTURE
AND NATIONHOOD

Just as delivering and retailing goods affected the very fabric of Mexico's northern society so did *consuming* foreign goods.[39] Every article introduced originated its own little history, creating new needs, displacing local products, and generating new hopes as well as resentments.[40] Of the many objects that flowed into Mexico's Far North in those early decades of the nineteenth century, two items in particular became major sites of nationality struggles: medicine and alcohol.[41] By briefly describing the changing ways in which

---

[38] Governor of Chihuahua to the Minister of Foreign Relations, Chihuahua, May 13, 1825, in sucesos entre México y los Estados Unidos de América 1819–29, AHSRE L-E-1055.

[39] I have expanded this chapter section into a full-length article in "Getting Cured and Getting Drunk: State Versus Market in Texas and New Mexico, 1800–1850," *Journal of the Early Republic* 22:1 (Spring 2002), 668–88.

[40] For some time, anthropologists, sociologists, and historians have analyzed human relations through the prism of material objects. See Fernand Braudel, *Capitalism and Material Life, 1400–1800* (London: Weidenfield and Nicolson, 1973); David W. Kingery, *Learning from Things: Method and Theory of Material Culture* (Washington, DC: Smithsonian Institute Press, 1996); Gerald L. Pocius, "Material Culture Worlds: A Report on Three Conferences," *Material History Review* 46 (Fall 1997), 77–81. Among Americanists, material culture studies have a long pedigree. See Ann Smart Martin and J. Ritchie Garrison, *American Material Culture: The Shape of the Field* (Knoxville, TN: University of Tennessee Press, 1997). Latinamericanists have also become attracted to the field. Alfred Crosby's work tackles the material implications of the Spanish conquest of America: *The Columbian Exchange: Biological and Cultural Consequences of 1492* (Westport, CT: Greenwood Press, 1972). For the more recent past, see Arnold J. Bauer, *Goods, Power, History: Latin America's Material Culture* (New York: Cambridge University Press, 2001); Néstor García Canclini, *Consumers and Citizens: Globalization and Multicultural Conflicts* (Minneapolis, MN: University of Minnesota Press, 2001); Benjamin Orlove, *The Allure of the Foreign: Imported Goods in Postcolonial Latin America* (Ann Arbor, MI: University of Michigan Press, 1997).

[41] Although I treat medicine and alcohol as two separate types of goods for the sake of clarity, early-nineteenth-century men and women were more likely to think of them as belonging to the same general category of objects. Eighteenth-century Americans, for instance, thought of alcohol as nourishment, as something possessing healthful qualities and used not only for drinking in taverns but also rubbed on the skin or mixed with other substances as a cure. Conversely, in Latin America, establishments that offered beverages often sold medicines as well, so there was a clear overlap.

frontier residents procured and consumed medicine and alcohol, I hope to explore how ordinary people experienced the market revolution in their everyday lives and how these objects became endowed with various meanings that reflected national values, aspirations, and dreams.

Before trading relations with the United States began, doctors, medicines, and medical facilities were quite rare in the frontier area. In New Mexico, the only *facultativo de medicina*, don Cristóbal María de Larrañaga, worked for the presidial company of Santa Fe. Being the only accredited physician in New Mexico, Doctor Larrañaga was in theory responsible for the health of more than forty thousand New Mexicans, although in practice his duties consisted mostly of treating ill and wounded presidial soldiers.[42] In San Antonio, Texas, there was a military hospital with sixteen beds as early as 1805. The most striking feature of this medical system was the extent of the state's involvement. Hospitals were run directly by the military. Doctors were licensed by the royal *protomedicato* (medical board) and monitored periodically. And medicines were procured from a network of military hospitals and pharmacies located farther south in New Spain and transported by military escorts. Because medicines were so scarce, transportation costs so high, and frontier residents were generally poor, the Crown was able to effectively dictate who had access to doctors and medicines and who did not.

The Anglo-American settlers who first moved into the area found this system restrictive and insufficient. Recovering from recurrent fevers, William Workman, a merchant living in Taos in 1826, wrote to his brother: "...if it had not a been for Mr. Stanly [Elisha Stanley] I should have died for they was no Doctor hear and not much medisin, and it is one of the meenest Country to be sick in the world for there is no nourishment to be got [sic]."[43] Foreign-born residents were especially concerned because they regarded the border area as a particularly sickly place. Anglo-American authors discussed in newspaper articles and travelers' guides the nature and causes of such prevalence of illness. New Mexico had the advantage of a cool climate, at least in the heavily populated areas encompassing Santa Fe and Albuquerque. Illness there was associated with sudden temperature changes and cold spells that could, it was believed, weaken the body and yield "rheumatic conditions."

In Texas, sickness seemed far more threatening. The heat and the swampy coastal areas produced rotting timber, "umbrageous woods," and "decaying vegetable substances" that released "effluvia" believed to be highly deleterious to human health. Even the upbeat 1835 *Emigrant's Guide to Texas* – a guide for prospective Anglo-American settlers – had to admit that Texas

---

[42] Pino, "Exposición," 222.
[43] William Workman to his brother David Workman, Taos, Feb 13, 1826, in David J. Weber, ed., "A Letter from Taos, 1826," *New Mexico Historical Review* 41 (Apr 1966), 155–64.

residents were prone to suffer bilious attacks and intermittent fevers. And, of course, neither Texas nor New Mexico could escape periodic ravages of epidemics like smallpox and cholera.[44]

Thus foreign-born merchants and immigrants were the first to introduce a host of new medicines; among the most common of these substances were calomel, tartar emetic, and ipecac as well as medical instruments such as lancets.[45] By the 1840s, frontiersmen and women were even able to obtain elaborate and fashionable medicines like blue pills or quinine-based medicines that often bore the names of their inventors: Dr. Champion's Pills, Dr. Sappington's Anti-Fever Pills, and Dr. Thurston's Unrivaled Antifever Pills.[46] A medical exchange of major proportions was clearly under way. Just as Spaniards and Native Americans had borrowed from each other for a long time, now Anglo-American medicine was added to the frontier medical arsenal. This exchange occurred at many levels, as American medicine was far from monolithic. In addition to "orthodox" medicine, there were variants like "Thomsonian," "physiobotanic," "eclectic," and "homeopathic."[47]

One of the most remarkable aspects of the rise of Euro-American medicine along the Mexican frontier is that it was just as ineffective as the previous alternatives. Judged by today's clinical knowledge, early-nineteenth-century medical practices were useless at best and dangerous at worst. The ubiquitous blue pill was in fact a highly toxic, mercury-based compound. Calomel, the most widely prescribed drug, was mercurous chloride, which broke down in the patient's intestine into highly poisonous components that irritated the digestive system and hence acted as a powerful purgative.[48] Medical practitioners did use quinine-based compounds that were quite effective against malaria. But quinine was often prescribed to treat many illnesses for which it had no effect.[49] Of all available medical procedures, nothing came close to attaining the popularity of bloodletting. It is clear that many patients died as a direct result of this medical treatment rather than of the illness that they had often endured for long periods of time.

---

[44] David B. Edward, *The History of Texas; or, the Emigrant's Farmer's, and Politician's Guide to the Character, Climate, Soil and Productions of That Country: Arranged Geographically from Personal Observations* (Austin, TX: Texas State Historical Association, 1990, 1836), 83–4 (hereafter *Emigrant's Guide to Texas*, 83–4).

[45] See set of *guías* for 1835 and 1838, MANM, roll 23, frames 137–58; roll 31, frames 532–64.

[46] William R. Hogan, *The Texas Republic: A Social and Economic History* (Austin, TX: University of Texas Press, 1969), 234; Susan Shelby Magoffin, *Down the Santa Fe Trail and into Mexico: Diary of Susan Shelby Magoffin 1846–1847*, edited by Stella M. Drumm. Lincoln, NE: University of Nebraska Press, 1982), 147.

[47] On the Thomsonian movement and the rise of homeopathy, see Rothstein, *American Physicians in the 19th Century*, ch. 7, 8. See also Jack Larkin, *The Reshaping of Everyday Life* (New York: HarperPerennial, 1989), 89.

[48] William G. Rothstein, *American Physicians in the 19th Century* (Baltimore, MD: Johns Hopkins University Press, 1992), 49–50.

[49] Larkin, *The Reshaping of Everyday Life*, 90.

And yet the imported medicine became eagerly sought after. Foreign-born physicians proliferated in Texas and New Mexico, and unlike their predecessors, they were able to set up private practices that Mexican authorities seldom scrutinized. Some even practiced medicine as a sideline and were men of learning at best and quacks at worst.[50] The proliferation of such practitioners was so rapid that one resident observed that Texas already had a full share of physicians by 1837. He pointed out that the driving force behind such activities was the popularity of Americans among local residents starved for medical services – "with the Mexican as with the Indian, every American is a doctor," – and remarked how Mexicans would not trust the Americans in any commercial transaction involving more than half a cent, and yet they would place their lives in the hands of the *americanos* when it came to medical matters.[51] The unregulated manner in which such "physicians" operated led easily to abuse. Impostors abounded, and nothing prevented anyone with medicines from *becoming* a doctor. John F. Webber decided to impersonate a doctor to cover up his smuggling activities as he traveled in the Rio Grande valley. He would dutifully write down the symptoms of unsuspecting Mexicans, shaking his head and knitting his brows with gravity: "Tartar emetic was the doctor's favorite prescription and his doses were liberal" – wrote Webber's companion:

...and [I] could with difficulty restrain my enjoyment at the situation when the medicine got in its work, seemingly turning the poor devils inside out, they meanwhile swearing and praying alternately. And I felt no twinge of remorse for the monstrous impositions we were practicing upon them when they finally emerged from the doctor's heroic treatment looking as dry and shrunken as so many pods of chili colorado (their favorite article of diet), and loaded him with thanks for his ministrations.[52]

Certainly, these were extreme cases; but the unregimented fashion in which this cadre of physicians worked during the Mexican era stood in stark contrast to the strict standards applied to formal medicine in colonial times.

In retrospect, what is most striking about the rise of Euro-American pharmacopoeia at the frontier is the Mexican government's lack of involvement. After 1821, we find precious few instances in which local or state authorities actually sought to control foreign doctors and substances. Part of the explanation may have to do with the liberal ethos prevalent in early Mexico, especially of frontier officials who regarded imported doctors and medicine as a tangible sign of progress, nothing less than the triumph of science over

---

[50] On the propensity of ordinary Anglo Americans to practice medicine, see Weber, *The Mexican Frontier*, 235–6.

[51] Andrew Forest Muir, ed., *Texas in 1837: An Anonymous, Contemporary Narrative* (Austin, TX: University of Texas Press, 1986), 100, 166.

[52] Smithwick, 30–1.

superstition, civilization over barbarism. Moreover, from the standpoint of ordinary frontier Mexicans, such a flood of foreign medicine only served to underscore the inadequacies of the old and highly regulated medical establishment that had traditionally given access to a handful of officers, soldiers, and well-connected elite members.

For good or bad, the freewheeling new medicine became far more available and greatly increased the dependency of Mexican citizens on foreign-born suppliers and doctors. Even as the two countries plunged into war, frontier Mexicans continued to seek health from those who were now the enemy. James Magoffin, arguably the main architect of the American military occupation of New Mexico, encountered many nuevomexicanos asking for medicine as he traveled south to negotiate the surrender of Chihuahua. "People have been sending in every day for 'remedios,'" wrote Magoffin's wife in her diary. "[S]ickness is great in the country now and *mi alma* [Magoffin] has his name up among the people of the Río Abajo as a skillful *médico*, some of the medicines he has administered to the suffering having been of material service."[53]

Alcohol provides a convenient counterpoint to medicine. The Crown's presence was far less pronounced in this economic activity, and the consequences of the market revolution turned out to be more controversial. Alcohol was one of the commodities widely exchanged in the large commercial areas that flourished throughout New Spain during the eighteenth century under the aegis of the Bourbon economic reforms. Pulque, a popular beverage extracted from maguey, was ubiquitous in central Mexico and quite common in northern cities such as Chihuahua and Durango, which teemed with shanties loaded with jugs and goblets filled with the sweet and fermented liquid during the pulque season.[54] In addition to drinking pulque, northern Mexicans drank other spirits or *caldos*, especially *aguardiente*, rum, and both imported and national wine. Indeed, Parras and El Paso del Norte became important production centers supplying the entire North of Mexico. By 1812, El Paso del Norte boasted very large vineyards, and its wine could be purchased as far away as two hundred leagues.[55] Conspicuous parties of muleteers could be observed on the roads hauling sometimes hundreds of barrels of wine and *aguardiente*, a *giro* controlled mostly by Spaniard and Creole merchants. Spirituous beverages constituted one of the most profitable and flourishing commercial activities to be found anywhere in New Spain.

Yet such freewheeling commercial activity does not mean that the Crown refrained from regulating the consumption of liquor through other means.

---

[53] Magoffin, *Down the Santa Fe Trail*, 183–4.
[54] Gregg, *Commerce of the Prairies*, 255.
[55] Pino, "Exposición," 219. Account book of Márquez y Melo, Márquez y Melo Papers, NMSRCA.

Since the sixteenth century, the Crown had taken a keen interest in curbing public displays of drunkenness, especially Indian overindulgence. In his meticulous study of colonial drinking habits in central Mexico, William B. Taylor has shown how Spanish Crown and Church officials and Spaniards subscribed to a Mediterranean ideal of drinking, extolling the virtues of moderate consumption mostly at mealtimes and praising the individual's ability to "hold" liquor with dignity and without losing control: "... drunkenness to the point of passing out was considered barbarous, disgusting, ridiculous, and a blot on a man's honor."[56] Imperial legislation was modeled after such enduring drinking ideals. A 1796 *bando* spelled out the sentences and punishments for public drunkenness. The Crown was also keen on monitoring the sale of spirits and particularly on guaranteeing the integrity of the liquors offered. In this regard, the Crown promulgated a comprehensive *bando* regulating the sale of alcohol in *vinaterías, cervecerías, cafés, pulquerías, fondas, bodegones,* and other stores.[57] In practice, this legislative corpus gave considerable latitude to local officials to intervene in the sale and consumption of alcohol. The most obvious display of royal authority over spirituous beverages along the frontier was the theatrical spilling of barrels of alcohol in the central plaza. In 1775, Texas Governor Juan Martín de Riperdá ordered the spilling of half a barrel of *mescal* in full view of the locals and in a formal ceremony that required his presence and that of accredited witnesses. The ceremony was intended to send a clear message to dealers that no illegal spirits would be tolerated or sold in Texas.[58] Similarly, on January 7, 1778, the alcalde of San Antonio ordered the spilling of two barrels of *aguardiente* belonging to Juan Joseph Flores de Abrego, who was believed to be passing *chinguirito* (cheap cane alcohol produced locally) for imported *aguardiente.*[59] Even as the commercialization of the alcohol economy proceeded in earnest, the Crown still made efforts to regulate the sale of alcohol, legislated against

[56] William B. Taylor, *Drinking, Homicide, and Rebellion in Colonial Mexican Villages* (Stanford, CA.: Stanford University Press, 1979), 41. See also Solange Alberro, "Bebidas alcohólicas y sociedad colonial en México: un intento de interpretación," *Revista Mexicana de Sociología* 51:2 (Apr–Jun 1989), 349–59; Sonia Corcuera de Mancera, *Del Amor al Temor: Borrachez, Catequésis y Control en la Nueva España, 1555–1771* (Mexico City: FCE, 1994); Teresa Lozano Armendares, *El chinguirito vindicado: el contrabando de aguardiente de caña y la política colonial* (Mexico City: UNAM, 1995).

[57] Manuel Dublán and José María Lozano, *Colección Completa de la Disposiciones Legislativas Expedidas desde la Independencia de la República,* 34 vols (Mexico City: Imprenta del Comercio, 1876), 1: 64, 296, 332. See also Virginia Guedea, "Mexico en 1812: control político y bebidas prohibidas," *Estudios de Historia Moderna y Contemporánea de México* 8 (1980), 23–65.

[58] Auto conducted by Governor Juan María de Riperdá, San Antonio, Oct 16, 1875, BA 11, 661–2. The auto does not specify why half a barrel of mescal was deemed a "bevida prohibida."

[59] This episode is documented in the autos against Juan Joseph Flores de Abrego, San Antonio, 1778, BA 12, 136–8, 287–8.

public drunkenness, and occasionally conducted exemplary punishments by spilling barrels of wines in the central plaza.

The market revolution would ultimately weaken the government's hold on these activities. Import receipts show that Anglo-American merchants immediately recognized the competitiveness of imported spirits. For instance, in San Antonio, John Soe began importing barrels of gin and cases of Bordeaux wine from New Orleans.[60] Just as active were Hispanic entrepreneurs. As early as 1823, Ramón Músquiz (a future *jefe político* of Texas) and Francisco Madero began importing brandy and wine. By 1828, José Antonio Quirós was introducing barrels of whisky, rum, and anisette, and cases of muscatel wine.[61] New Mexico is an even more dramatic example of this phenomenon. Unlike Texas, which could be supplied by sea relatively cheaply, New Mexico was locked inland and therefore merchants had to carry bulky and heavy barrels across the Plains at great peril and cost. But even so, by the 1840s, imported drinks such as French champagne were consumed in elite social gatherings in Santa Fe and Albuquerque.[62] Beyond importing luxury spirits, frontier entrepreneurs became involved in the production of alcohol for local and regional consumption. Mostly Anglo-American businessmen began building distilleries in Texas and New Mexico in the late 1820s and 1830s. In the vicinity of Taos, no less than three distilleries were erected during this period, including an imposing two-story mill belonging to Don Simeon Turley, known among his fellow Anglo Americans as "captain whisky."[63] Indeed, the Taos valley emerged as an important supply center for both Hispanics and neighboring Indians. The American consul at Santa Fe reported that on the American side of the Arkansas River, a number of Anglo Americans without licenses had established a village and carried out a constant traffic with the Indians. He praised the vigilance of American agents in limiting this activity in 1842, but was skeptical that such efforts could dampen alcohol sales, "as the deficiency from our own country is made up from the Valley of Taos and the large parties of Mexicans that are daily selling it to the tribes within our borders."[64] The situation was much the same in Texas. The *Emigrant's Guide* confidently predicted that this little-known corner of

---

[60] Factura de los efectos . . . del comerciante Juan Soe, San Antonio, May 21, 1830, BA 130, 669–70.

[61] Francisco Joseph Bernal to Juan Martín de Veramendi, n.p., Apr 15, 1823, BA 74, 566–7; factura de importación de José Antonio Quirós, San Antonio, Nov 24, 1828, BA 117, 996.

[62] Susan Magoffin, *Down the Santa Fe Trail*, 135–7.

[63] Janet Lecompte, "Simeon Turley," in Hafen, *The Mountain Men and the Fur Trade of the Far West*, 7, 301–14. For the articulation of the liquor trade between the Taos valley and the along the Arkansas River, see Janet Lecompte, *Pueblo, Hardscrabble, Greenhorn: The Upper Arkansas, 1832–1856* (Norman, OK: University of Oklahoma Press, 1978), 87–106.

[64] Manuel Álvarez to Secretary of State, Independence, Missouri, July 1, 1843, Despatches from United States Consuls in Santa Fe, 1830–46, National Archives, RG 59, no. 199.

Mexico would equal Switzerland, France, or Italy in producing "thousands of gallons of most charming beverages," and remarked that Indian drunkenness was directly correlated with distance from established settlements: Those living in the vicinity of towns were often found under the influence of alcohol, whereas those living at some distance could be seen "in their genuine simplicity and worth."[65] Nonetheless, the authors of the *Guide* recommended that settlers turn their exertions toward the making of sugar and rum: "...they will find their recompense, by an unlimited quantity, as it were, of returns to the capital and land employed."[66]

Impressionistic evidence suggests that drinking increased at the border from the 1820s through the 1840s. This trend derived most immediately from the availability of alcohol and the cheap prices due to competition. But it was also related to the profound social transformation caused by the rise of a new commercial economy. For one thing, commerce increased itinerancy. The Santa Fe Trail and the Texas–Louisiana trade brought large groups of men into Mexican cities who needed to be accommodated and entertained for prolonged periods of time – while they waited out the winter or until they sold their merchandise – all of which helped spawn guest houses, hotels, gambling halls, taverns, cantinas, and other meeting places that required steady amounts of liquid lubricant. In this way, a new lifestyle involving not only Anglo-American visitors but Hispanic and Indian residents became conducive to consuming ardent beverages. I was unable to measure relative levels of alcohol consumption for Anglo Americans, Hispanics, and Native Americans in the border region. But we do know that as a nation the United States reached its absolute peak in alcohol consumption precisely in the 1820s and 1830s, when it first came in contact with Mexico. In those decades, every American man, woman, and child drank an average of five gallons of distilled spirits per year, a number that is roughly three times today's levels.[67]

Frontier Mexicans had mixed feelings about the multiplication of distilleries and cantinas, the importation of new spirits, and the rise of consumption. Individuals like New Mexico's Antonio Barreiro emphasized the pecuniary gains to be made through the production of alcohol. Reporting on the construction of a whisky plant in the vicinity of Santa Fe owned by a group of Anglo-American investors, he challenged his fellow nuevomexicanos to follow suit: "Very shortly we shall appreciate how valuable and lucrative such establishments are going to be. How long shall we be strangers on our own soil? How long will it be before we shall recognize the veritable fountains of wealth which we possess?"[68] Other Mexican frontier residents

---

[65] Edward, *Emigrant's Guide to Texas*, 72, 118.
[66] Ibid., 46.
[67] W. J. Rorabaugh, *The Alcoholic Republic: An American Tradition* (New York: Oxford University Press, 1979), charts on pages 23–4.
[68] Barreiro, "Ojeada," 81.

were not nearly as enthusiastic. Some Mexicans decried the availability of alcohol and blamed local Anglo-American producers for its deleterious social consequences. The American consul reported that in those instances when excessive drinking had resulted in thefts, robberies, and murders affecting a Mexican, "he is sure to defer exclusively to the influence of our legally authorized traders instead of the true and natural cause [meaning the peddling of alcohol from all quarters]"[69]

After independence, Mexican authorities continued to subscribe to the colonial ideals of Mediterranean moderation and accordingly regulated increasing alcohol consumption. In contrast to the apparent collapse of governmental involvement in medicine, frontier officials continued to enforce legislation against public drunkenness, although they did so very selectively. I was unable to find cases in which Mexican authorities actually prosecuted Anglo Americans exclusively on charges of public drunkenness, although I did find proceedings for battery and assault in which alcohol surely played a part.[70] This reluctance to proceed against foreign-born residents – if confirmed – is all the more striking given the widespread belief of Mexican authorities about Anglo-American tendencies toward excessive drinking. In 1832, New Mexico's governor wrote privately to the minister of the interior complaining about the riffraff that accompanied the yearly caravan coming from Missouri: "...when drunk they show surprising energy to speak loudly and in a manner offensive toward the Republic to which we all proudly belong."[71] Similarly, a Mexican spy in San Antonio described everyday life in the Lone Star Republic in 1841 as "an unceasing commotion, riot, and abuse conducted by the dregs of Europe and North America under the influence of large quantities of *huizcle* [whisky] *y brandi*."[72] Given such preconceptions, the authorities' reluctance to enforce drinking legislation may indicate unwillingness to antagonize *extranjeros* (foreigners) or the implicit recognition of different cultural norms.

Many frontier residents came to believe that the rise of the market economy had rendered the Mexican government all but powerless to regulate the sale of alcohol and curb excessive drinking with any effectiveness. In particular, the indiscriminate sale of alcohol to Indians emerged as a major problem. In a letter to the State Department, the American consul at Santa Fe described how the thriving alcohol business inevitably led to the "demoralization" of Indians, who were thus forced to "steal, plunder, and murder

[69] Álvarez to Webster, Independence, Missouri, Jul 1, 1843, Despatches from the United States Consuls in Santa Fe, 1830–46, RG 59, 199.

[70] Judicial Proceedings Against the Extranjero Maese for Assault, Santa Fe, Dec 15, 1843, MANM 33, 882–98.

[71] Governor's letterbook of communications sent to Ministerio de Relaciones Interiores y Exteriores, Santa Fe, May 31, 1832, MANM 14, 635–6.

[72] Report of Santiago Vidaurri, Lampazos, May 11, 1841, Box 590, file 87, Herbert E. Bolton Papers, Bancroft Library.

when no better can be done to supply themselves with those indispensable necessities, which they have bartered for intoxicating liquors."[73] Conservative Mexicans were even more adamant on this point. Father Antonio José Martínez, the charismatic priest of Taos, in a public letter and call to action addressed to President Antonio López de Santa Anna in 1843, used similar reasoning.[74] Father Martínez pointed out that during colonial times, the Spanish government had not permitted foreigners from North America to trade with the Indians of northern New Mexico. As he put it, only the misguided liberality of Mexico's early governments had opened the door to these dealers, allowing them to set up a fort (Bent's Fort) on the Arkansas River since 1832. According to the energetic curate, in addition to selling tools and other necessities, Bent's Fort had become the base of operations of unscrupulous dealers who sold liquor to Indians and had succeeded in "demoralizing" them and impelling them to hunt buffalo into extinction and increase their depredations on New Mexico's settlements. The padre forcefully concluded that such liberal policy would sooner or later result in the total devastation of New Mexico.[75]

Some evidence indicates that the deleterious social effects of drinking coupled with the Mexican government's inability to intervene led some frontier residents to take matters in their own hands, especially as Mexico and the United States plunged into war and ethnic and racial tensions mounted. On the afternoon of May 3, 1846, George Bent (brother of Charles Bent) and his friend Francis Preston Blair, Jr., were "in liquor," rambling in the Taos plaza. According to one testimony, they were speaking loudly and possibly insulting passersby. Such public display of drunkenness galvanized the ire of a group of no less than thirty nuevomexicanos, who promptly retaliated by beating the two celebrants and inflicting serious wounds on Blair. Revealingly, the crowd cheered on the assaulters, screaming, "kill the borrachos."[76] The subsequent investigation showed that nuevomexicano authorities were within earshot of the commotion but refused to intervene, preferring to leave the crowd to vent its ire.[77]

73 Álvarez to Webester, Independence, Missouri, Jul 1, 1843, Despatches from the United States Consuls in Santa Fe, 1830–46, RG 59, 199.
74 Father Antonio José Martínez to Antonio López de Santa Anna, "Esposición que el Presbítero Antonio José Martínez, cura de Taos en Nuevo México, dirije al gobierno del Exmo. Sor. General D. . .," Taos, 1843, in Weber, *Northern Mexico on the Eve of the United States Invasion*, imprint No. 5.
75 Ibid.
76 Descriptions of this episode can be found in Bent to Álvarez, Taos, May 3, Read Collection, 86, 87, 88, NMSRCA; Bent to Martínez, May 10, 1846, Read Collection, 89, NMSRCA; Bent to Álvarez, Taos, Jun 1, 1846, Read Collection, 92, NMSRCA. Also José María Martínez to Secretary of Government Juan Bautista Vigil y Alarid, Taos, May 11, 1846, MANM 41, 160–8.
77 See Charles Bent to Álvarez, Taos, May 3, 1846, Read Collection, 86, NMSRCA; Secretary of Government to Prefect of the North District, Jun 6, 1846, MANM 451, 203–4.

Another climactic clash over alcohol took place during the Taos Rebellion in January 1847. Pueblo Indians and nuevomexicanos rebelled against the recently established American government, killing various functionaries in and around Taos, including Charles Bent, the Anglo-American governor appointed by the American army of occupation. After this initial wave of violence, the rebels decided to attack Simon Turley's distillery at Arroyo Hondo, which had become the largest alcohol producing facility in New Mexico. This action can hardly be explained away as the result of wanton violence, as a force of five hundred rebels had to make a twelve-mile foray to Arroyo Hondo and lay siege on a distillery defended by ten well-armed men. The bloody affair lasted two days. At sunset on January 21, 1847, the rebellious party made a successful charge, gaining entrance to the mill. Not content with killing all but two of the defenders who managed to escape, the group of nuevomexicanos and Taos Indians set the place on fire and razed the installation.[78] To be sure, these violent explosions, although clearly revolving around the sale and consumption of alcohol, were also motivated by other factors.[79] These episodes do demonstrate how the newfound availability and consumption of alcohol could generate a popular nationalist backlash and underscore Mexican officials' waning ability to regulate activities unleashed by the market revolution.

The opening of new trading routes linking Mexico's Far North with the American economy severely limited the ability of the Spanish/Mexican government to shape the consumption patterns of Mexicans at the border as scores of foreign-born settlers brought medicines and spirits, became doctors, and built distilleries at the frontier. The proliferation of these goods also challenged the Mexican nation by representing alternative lifestyles and meanings. Some frontier residents regarded Sappington Anti-fever Pills and ipecac as evidence of progress, just as others considered alcohol emblematic of the licentiousness that could be expected from the United States. In fact, these objects were mirrors in which frontier residents were able to project their longings and aspirations that did not necessarily correspond to those

---

[78] George F. Ruxton, *Travels in Mexico* (London: John Murray, 1847), 227–9.

[79] For instance, the roots of the conflict between Father Martínez and the foreign-born alcohol entrepreneurs of Taos were manifold. At one level, this was a classic struggle between border liberals and conservatives over Mexico's openness toward the United States. At another level, it was a struggle for local political control in the Taos area, as the power of the influential Martínez clan was being challenged by a rival political faction led by Charles Bent. At yet another level, this conflict was about land possession, pitting the Pueblo of Taos against land grant recipients, mostly foreign-born. See Dunham, "New Mexican Land Grants with Special Reference to the Title Papers of the Maxwell Grant," 1–22; Lawrence R. Murphy, "The Beaubien and Miranda Land Grant 1841–1846," *New Mexico Historical Review* 42:1, 27–47; David J. Weber, *On the Edge of Empire: The Taos Hacienda of Los Martínez* (Santa Fe, NM: Museum of New Mexico Press), 49–81.

prescribed by government officials. Such were the unspoken tensions behind mundane activities such as getting cured and getting drunk.

MEXICAN OFFICIALDOM FACES THE MARKET REVOLUTION

"In a mercantile century like the one we live in," wrote an exultant commissioner of colonization for Texas in 1833, "it would not be farfetched to imagine that iron rails will someday furrow the land from New Mexico to Galveston accelerating the advancement of civilization and bringing the most remote peoples together through indissoluble bonds of mercantile interest."[80] At the height of the frontier's stunning economic revival in the early Mexican period, there were good reasons to cheer. But development had its own dark underside. Progress yielded unprecedented inequalities, as a handful of French and Anglo-American merchants came to control the lion's share of the profits derived from the Santa Fe Trail and the Texas–Louisiana trade. Mexican conservatives also resented the cast of unsavory characters who, along with respectable foreign businessmen, were attracted to the frontier, espousing alien political ideas, exotic religions, and deleterious goods. But above all, the strong linkage of Mexico's Far North to the economy of the United States raised the specter of territorial loss. Mexican officials at all levels struggled to find a difficult balance between harnessing the full potential of trade with the United States but curbing its worst excesses and forestalling dangerous dependency.

At first, a certain balance was achieved not because of deliberate policy, but as an outcome of bureaucratic infighting. Within every local, state, and federal government, contentious debates erupted over how much to throw open Mexico's northern border. While such discussions continued at all levels, they acquired a characteristic geographic configuration pitting frontier local authorities pushing for more liberalization against a protectionist federal government. The federalist/centralist cleavage defined the politics of the entire nation, but in the Far North it became inextricably intertwined with free commerce and immigration policies.

From the very start, frontier powerbrokers took the initiative to open the border with the United States and maintain it that way. Since 1822, the *ayuntamiento* of San Antonio petitioned for tariff exemptions in Texas. From then on, the San Antonio council members emerged as the most vocal defenders of freedom of commerce. When Congress decided to close the port of Matagorda to foreign vessels in September 1827, Juan Martín Veramendi, on behalf of the *ayuntamiento*, sent a strongly worded letter to the governor

---

[80] Tadeo Ortiz to President, Matamoros, Feb 2, 1833, BP 40:673, 4.

explaining why it would not carry out such an order.[81] The federation re-opened Matagorda in 1828, but not before establishing a customhouse in Goliad. This set the stage for a series of confrontations between *ayuntamiento* members and Goliad's customs officers, with the former openly resisting paying duties.[82]

Similar tensions existed in New Mexico. In spite of the federal government's 1824 order prohibiting foreigners from trapping beaver, Governor Bartolomé Baca (1823–5) took it upon himself to issue licenses provided that at least half of each trapping party was composed of nuevomexicanos. His idea was to allow foreigners to exploit the natural resources of the territory, but in a way that permitted nuevomexicanos to gain expertise and access to trapping equipment.[83] Governor Baca also pioneered international commerce by dispatching commissioners to Missouri and Washington in 1824 and 1825 to put Mexican merchants and American suppliers in contact and facilitate the passage of caravans by seeking peace with Native Americans along the trail.[84] These actions stand in stark contrast to the reluctance of federal authorities to act on an American proposal to conduct a survey and build a road linking western Missouri with New Mexico in 1825.[85] Governor Antonio Narbona (1825–27) continued with the open door policy of his predecessor, supporting the enterprises of several foreign-born residents. William Workman, an Anglo-American merchant who had just settled in Taos, did not fail to notice the improved business climate: "...my chance was never more flattering than it is at present. Chambers has been to Santa Fe and got the holy water put on his head and the governor [Narbona] is a great friend of his, he will assist us in anything that we undertake."[86]

None of these local and state officials were mindless promoters of Anglo-American entrepreneurs. They occasionally expressed reservations about the *extranjeros* and clashed with trappers and merchants unwilling to pay duties or license fees.[87] They also had to reach compromises with a local nationalist

[81] Martín de Veramendi to Governor of Coahuila and Texas, Feb 16, 1828, BA 111, 26–8; Ramón Músquiz to Antonio Elozúa, Béxar, Jul 1, 1828, BA 114, 829–30; Antonio Elozúa to Músquiz, Béxar, Jul 4, 1828, BA 114, 957–8.

[82] José Benifacio Galán, Customs Officer, to Erasmo Seguín, Goliad, Aug 7, 1829, BA 124, 730–1; José Bonifacio Galán to Erasmo Seguín, Goliad, May 21, 1830, BA 130, 601–3.

[83] Donaciano Vigil to the Honorable Assembly, Santa Fe, Jun 18, 1846, edited and translated by Weber, *Arms, Indians, and the Mismanagement of New Mexico*, 4.

[84] Calafate Boyle, *Los Capitalistas*, 58–9.

[85] George C. Sibley. U.S. Commissioner to Governor Narbona, Santa Fe, Jan 5, 1825, Texas State Archives, Archivo General de Mexico, Box 2-22-617, Folder called relaciones exteriores 1815.

[86] William Workman to his brother David Workman, San Fernando de Taos, Feb 13, 1826, in Weber, "A Letter from Taos," 159.

[87] On the mixed feelings of Baca and Narbona, see Daniel Tyler, "Anglo-American Penetration of the Southwest: The View from New Mexico," *Southwestern Historical Quarterly* 75:3 (Jan 1972), 327–30.

opposition. Donaciano Vigil pointed out that in New Mexico, a group of gentlemen "of good intentions but imbued with the doctrines of past centuries," was able to impose a system of exclusion on foreigners for some time.[88] He was referring to the wrangling over beaver trapping of the late 1820s. Several nuevomexicanos denounced foreign-born trappers as law-breakers and usurpers of benefits that belonged exclusively to Mexicans. Mired in protracted legal battles, Anglo-American trappers continued their operations clandestinely or by subcontracting with Native Americans and thereby cutting off nuevomexicanos and New Mexico's treasury from the profit stream.[89]

But these local conflicts should not obscure the fact that frontier officials as a group turned out to be far more supportive of fluid and open relations with the United States than their distrustful counterparts at the federal level. In hindsight, it is easy to understand local motivations. First, local and state officials had to be responsive to a frontier population whose livelihood came to depend on cultivating and expanding economic ties with the United States. Frontier officials not only had to take into account the wishes of a native elite that understood perfectly well the importance of liberal commercial and immigration policies, but also had to accommodate an increasingly prominent foreign-born community whose economic prosperity translated into commensurate political muscle. Second, these local authorities were often involved in trade-related activities themselves and sometimes turned out to be the principal beneficiaries of liberalization. The San Antonio *ayuntamiento*'s free trade leanings are not surprising if we consider that its membership included virtually *all* of the early tejano merchants, including José Casiano, José Antonio Navarro, Angel Navarro, Ramón Músquiz, Juan Martín Veramendi, and Erasmo and Juan Nepomuceno Seguín.

In the same vein, New Mexican officeholders had more than a passing interest in trade with the United States, beginning with Baca, who reportedly invested 1,500 pesos of his own money in the caravan of 1824 and expected to realize a good profit in the Chihuahua trade.[90] Indeed, some New Mexican officials used public moneys to finance their individual business activities by issuing drafts against the territorial treasury. In February 1833, Agustín Durán (treasurer or *subcomisario* of the territory since 1826), Santiago Abréu (the governor since 1832), Ramón Abréu (brother of the former and military commander since 1828), and Jesús María Alarid (also *subcomisario*) were

---

[88] Donaciano Vigil to the Honorable Assembly, Santa Fe, Jun 18, 1846, edited and translated by Weber, *Arms, Indians, and the Mismanagement of New Mexico*, 4.

[89] Proceedings Against Ira A. Emmons for illegal fur trade, Santa Fe, Apr 1827, MANM 7: 207–29; Proceedings Against Ricardo Cambel, Felipe Tomson, and Vicente Gion, MANM 8: 371–447, 475–503; Overall Explanation in Exposition of Donaciano Vigil to the Departmental Assembly, Santa Fe, Jun 18, 1846, edited and translated by Weber, *Arms, Indians, and the Mismanagement of New Mexico: Donaciano Vigil, 1846.*

[90] Bloom, "New Mexico Under Mexican Administration," 170.

accused of misappropriation of public funds. The trial that ensued, the most sensational of that era, showed the extent to which local officials were able to siphon thousands of pesos from the treasury – allegedly for past or future salaries – for personal business ventures and conspicuous consumption.[91] The trial made obvious the close connections between local political power and international commerce. Colonel Albino Pérez, a dashing and somewhat overbearing officer appointed as New Mexico's governor in 1835, would later write about these New Mexican politicians. He pointed out that the objective of Santiago Abréu's brief tenure as governor was merely to "protect foreign smugglers and foster fraud," and explained further:

...since 1828 [Ramón] Abréu struck up the most intimate relations of friendship with foreign merchants, to the extent that he is now their agent and blindly favors their interests regardless of how illicit they are...if it were not for the government's current policy, this man could cause the separation of New Mexico from the Mexican Government.[92]

While these unflattering words were politically motivated, there was some reason for concern. By the 1830s, as much as 70 percent of the entire territorial budget came directly from import revenues from the Santa Fe Trail.[93]

Such cozy arrangements between frontier officials and foreign entrepreneurs only increased the tensions between local and federal governments, a relationship that reached a crucial turning point in the late 1820s as Mexico City embarked on a more assertive course. The situation of Texas best exemplifies these tensions. In 1829, General Mier y Terán's Boundary Commission delivered a damning report on the situation, alerting Congress and the president about the grave perils faced by the nation. In private correspondence, General Mier y Terán explicitly referred to the collusion of local authorities and *extranjeros*. Congress took up the matter and issued a series of decrees establishing military garrisons and customhouses in Texas, forbidding the importation of certain articles, and promulgating the controversial Law of April 6, 1830, which prohibited further Anglo-American immigration into Texas. These measures galvanized public opinion in Mexico City

---

[91] Judicial Proceedings Against Agustín Durán for Misappropriation of Funds, Santa Fe, Feb–Jun, 1833, MANM 16, 943–98; Proceedings Against Jesús María Alarid and Ramón Abréu, Santa Fe, Jul 29, 1833, MANM 16, 1033–4; Correspondence Between *Comisario Substituto* of New Mexico and *Comisario General* of Chihuahua, Santa Fe, Nov 1, 1833, MANM 17, 925–8. See also MANM 17, 936–8, 941–2, 944–7, 973–4.

[92] Albino Pérez to Minister of the Interior (*reservada*), Santa Fe, Jun 10, 1837, AGN, Gobernación, Leg 173, Box 259.

[93] Juan María Alarid, New Mexico's Budget Report for 1832–33, Santa Fe, n.d., MANM 17, 1002–3; Ramón Abréu, New Mexico's Budget Report for 1834–5, Santa Fe, Jun 22, 1835, MANM 21, 420–2; the excellent budget summary from July 1838 through December 1843 in *resúmen estadístico de la tesorería del Departamento del Nuevo México*, n.p., n.d., MANM 34, 1029–31. See also González de la Vara, "La política del federalismo en Nuevo México," 88–9.

and other core regions of the country around the "Texas question," the "scandalous frontier speculation," and the "imprudence" of state and local officials at the frontier.[94] Texas may have been far from Mexico's heartland, but in the symbolic geography of centralist politicians, it was at the center, representing unchecked local and state autonomy even bordering on secessionism.

In this charged political atmosphere, Vice President Anastasio Bustamante staged a coup d'etat against President Vicente Guerrero at the end of 1829. His administration (1830–2) launched an assault on state sovereignty and attempted to purge the *yorkinos*, who controlled most of the state governments.[95] Bustamante's regime also moved to regain control of the economy of the border, initiating a period of bitter local clashes in the Far North.

The Atascosito crisis provides an excellent illustration of the explosiveness of this renewed federal–state rivalry. The conflict began when José Francisco Madero, a state land commissioner, and José María de Jesús Carbajal, his land surveyor, arrived in San Felipe de Austin in January 1831 and published an advertisement in the local newspaper indicating that they would issue legal titles to a group of some thirty Anglo-American families living in front of Galveston Bay in an area known as Atascosito.[96] According to the 1824 National Colonization Law, the federation wielded absolute jurisdiction over land within ten leagues (twenty-six miles) from the coast, and Anglo Americans were not allowed to settle in this federal coastal preserve. In practice, however, Coahuila and Texas authorities had frequently disposed of this area as they saw fit and issued titles to Anglo-American colonists who had a strong preference for coastal property that afforded distinct commercial advantages. This time, however, the federally appointed military commander of Anáhuac, Colonel Juan Davis Bradburn, intervened. Colonel Bradburn reminded the two state officials that they had no authority over the federal coastal preserve and emphasized that, by putting Anglo-American families in possession of lands, they violated Article 11 of the Law of April 6, 1830, that specifically prohibited further Anglo-American immigration into Texas. The state officials countered that the Atascosito settlers had been living in the area prior to 1824 and therefore could not be affected retroactively either by the 1824 Federal Colonization Law or by the April 6, 1830 law. As it turned out, the divergence of interpretation led to a "disagreeable exchange." When the undaunted Madero and Carbajal proceeded with the survey, Colonel Bradburn put them in jail. What made the situation particularly

94 Andrés Reséndez, "Caught Between Profits and Rituals: *National Contestation in Texas and New Mexico, 1821–1848*," Ph.D. dissertation, University of Chicago, Chicago, IL, 141–5.

95 Anna, *Forging Mexico*, 230.

96 For a history of the colonization of the Atascosito district, see de la Teja, "El problema de México con los indocumentados en Texas," 35–40.

volatile was the involvement of the Anglo-American settlers. They had been seeking legal titles for at least four years and saw their prospects dim after Colonel Bradburn's intervention. It appears that Madero and Carbajal openly sought to enlist the support of disgruntled foreign-born colonists in their dispute with the federation. Some of these settlers actually began preparations for an all-out assault on the federal garrison, even bringing reinforcements from neighboring colonies. Colonel Bradburn faced the possibility of a full-scale riot and was able to avert bloodshed only at the last minute by promising a prompt reconsideration of their case by higher authority.[97]

Violence did erupt in the next few months over federal enforcement of tariff collection. In Texas, federal duties, more than any other issue, stood as a powerful political symbol and rallying cry for both sides. The federation regarded tariffs as an essential attribute of federal power and the most obvious way to regulate the frontier's economic activities with the United States. But Texas residents viewed tariffs as a direct blow to their precarious way of life – especially after having enjoyed seven years of duty exemptions – revealing of the highhandedness and lack of understanding of the federal government. Tejano merchants such as Ramón Músquiz referred to the federal government as that "military theocracy," and chafed under tariffs, merchandise seizures, and any other federal attempts to regulate the frontier economy.[98]

But while tejano and Anglo-American merchants alike found the new assessments odious, the most serious altercations during the 1830–2 period involved Mexican customs officers and Anglo-American merchants, thus adding an ominous ethnic and national overtone to this conflict. New Orleans merchant vessels tended to disregard the customhouse at Anáhuac. Ships heading up the Brazos River sometimes ran the Mexican blockade at Velasco at the mouth, and in one instance in December 1830 exchanged fire with the Mexican guards stationed there. After enduring months of continuous hostilities and life-threatening incidents, federal customs collectors and guards in Anáhuac, Velasco, and Galveston Island left Texas in the summer of 1832.[99] Bustamante's government was unable to respond, as it was assailed by a federalist revolution that brought about its downfall a few months later. In Texas, the empty and decaying barracks became reminders of the national government's failure to exercise effective control over the border and underscored the difficulties of undoing entrenched business arrangements that

---

[97] For the legal controversy, see Mier y Terán to Alamán, Matamoros, Mar 24, 1831, BP 40:673, 2; Viesca to Mier y Terán, Leona Vicario (Saltillo), Mar 6, 1831, BP 40:673, 2; Henson, *Juan Davis Bradburn*, 61–2.

[98] Ramón Músquiz to Philip Dimmitt, Goliad, Jun 8, 1835, DP; Tenorio to Ugartechea, Anáhuac, Jun 25, 1835, BA 165, 704–6.

[99] See Henson, *Juan Davis Bradburn*, 89–113.

tied the economies of Texas and Louisiana. These two dramatic years also revealed how such conflicts of interest could be transmuted into struggles defined in ethnic or national terms. General Mier y Terán, the main architect of Mexico's frontier policies, became tormented by Mexico's inability to take control of its vital areas of expansion. On July 3, 1832, standing in front of Iturbide's grave in full-dress uniform, General Mier y Terán pierced his heart by thrusting his body against his sword. "What will become of Texas?" the embattled general asked four times in his last letter, "only God knows."[100]

Before any other revolutions, Mexico's Far North experienced the market revolution. In the midst of a generally stagnant Mexican economy, the frontier gravitated toward the economy of the United States, as the activities of foreign-born entrepreneurs affected the lives of frontier residents. Furthermore, the *spirit of mercantile enterprise* spread among frontier Indians and Hispanics, and their own livelihoods came to depend on continued access to the American markets. It is not easy to characterize the impact of this market revolution. On the one hand, and against the backdrop of Mexico's tepid economic growth, the opening of trading relations with the North improved the standard of living in such places as Texas and New Mexico, creating new business and employment opportunities and providing several avenues for social advancement. Economic growth also became the medium for inter-ethnic alliances between Anglo-American merchants and Native Americans and between Hispanic frontier elites and Anglo-American newcomers. But on the other hand, such material progress came at a cost rendering Mexico's Far North quite dependent on the American economy, creating a powerful clique of foreign-born entrepreneurs whose riches were only matched by growing political influence, and raising concerns about the frontier's wholesale Americanization. Trade liberalization also changed consumption patterns throughout the frontier, as Anglo-American and French entrepreneurs introduced new objects and promoted new industries in the region. Frontier residents projected onto these goods their yearnings and dreams about progress and civilization as well as their fears of Americanization and dependency.

Most threatening, the frontier's market revolution became entangled in the federalist–centralist cleavage unfolding throughout the country. Local officials sought to capitalize on the frontier's economic ties with the United States, prompting alarm among some federal authorities that increasingly branded frontier powerbrokers as secessionists. The frontier society was caught in the middle, torn between the pull of institutions, patronage, orders, and rituals coming from the South and profits flowing from the North.

[100] Mier y Terán quoted in Morton, *Terán and Texas*, 183. See also Josefince Vázquez, "Colonización y pérdida de Texas," in Ma. Esther Schumacher, ed., *Mitos en las relaciones Mexico–Estados Unidos* (Mexico City: Secretarie de Relaciones Exteriores-Fondo de Cultura Economica, 1998), 68.

4

The Benediction of the Roman Ritual

The venerable institution of marriage is an ideal site to examine how the tensions between market and state shaped the lives of flesh-and-blood human beings. A considerable body of scholarship on marriage in colonial and early national Mexico – some focusing specifically on Mexico's northern frontier – has shown the intricacies of formal and informal regulations, factors, and personal decisions implicated in matrimonial arrangements.[1] In teasing out all of the forces at play in marriages – especially in inter-ethnic marriages, hereafter referred to simply as intermarriage – many scholars have emphasized the economic underpinnings of such unions. In sheer economic terms, Anglo-American grooms and their Mexican brides – along with their families – seemed to be meant for each other. But because foreign-born residents regarded intermarriage as the very gateway into Mexican citizenship, social acceptance, and economic security, Church and (to a lesser extent) other officials made efforts to control it and regulate it. (see Figure 4.1) Intermarriage was so enticing that it necessarily invited close official scrutiny, and the state's[2] drive to regulate marital arrangements was squarely justified

---

[1] Asunción Lavrin, *Sexuality and Marriage in Colonial Latin America* (Lincoln, NE: University of Nebraska Press, 1989); Silvia Marina Arrom, *The Women of Mexico City, 1790–1857* (Stanford, CA: Stanford University Press, 1985); Patricia Seed, *To Love, Honor, and Obey in Colonial Mexico: Conflicts over Marriage Choice, 1574–1821* (Stanford, CA: Stanford University Press, 1988); Steve J. Stern, *The Secret History of Gender: Women, Men, and Power in Late Colonial Mexico* (Chapel Hill, NC: University of North Carolina Press, 1995); among others. For marriage at the frontier, see Jane Dysart, "Mexican Women in San Antonio, 1830–1860: The Assimilation Process," *Western Historical Quarterly* 7:4 (October 1976), 365–75; Deena J. González, *Refusing the Favor: The Spanish-Mexican Women of Santa Fe, 1820–1880* (Oxford, UK: Oxford University Press, 1999); Gutiérrez, *When Jesus Came*. Additional references are provided throughout this chapter.

[2] My use of the term *state* in this chapter will be particularly lax. In Chapter 2, I pointed out that in the early-nineteenth century, Mexico did not yet have a consolidated state but rather relied on the overlapping administrative structures of the military, the civil administration, and the Church. In matters of marriages, for example, the Church performed the leading role

FIGURE 4.1. Josefa Jaramillo Carson and child

on nationalist terms. This chapter seeks to explore how economic and institutional transformations engulfing the Far North came to affect very personal and crucial decisions of ordinary individuals.

A MATCH MADE IN HEAVEN

For generations, far-flung communities such as San Antonio, Nacogdoches, Santa Fe, Santa Cruz, and Taos had accepted and incorporated immigrants, whether they were Euro-American, *mestizo* (of mixed ancestry), or Indian. The isolation and hardship of the frontier fostered a remarkable openness toward outsiders and preserved relatively porous racial and ethnic boundaries. Beyond the bedrock of original local indigenous peoples and conquistadors/friars, these frontier outposts experienced several infusions of peoples over the years coming chiefly from the somewhat more populated provinces farther south, such as Coahuila, Nuevo León, Aguascalientes, Chihuahua, and Durango.[3]

of regulation, as will become evident throughout this chapter. Indeed, not until 1857 was the function of registry formally taken out of Church hands and transferred to civil authorities.

[3] By the early-nineteenth century, several tejanos and nuevomexicanos still had relatives and business connections stretching to these places. For New Mexico, see Gutiérrez, *When Jesus Christ Came*; for Texas, see de la Teja, *San Antonio de Béxar*. See also Poyo, "The Canary Islands Immigrants of San Antonio," 41–58. Various aspects of eighteenth-century tejano identity are explored in a collection of articles in Poyo and Hinojosa, eds., *Tejano Origins in Eighteenth-Century San Antonio*. See especially de la Teja, "Forgotten Founders," 27–38; Poyo,

The racial background of these immigrants was extraordinarily diverse, ranging from ordinary *mestizos* and *criollos* to European immigrants – most notably the group of Canary Islanders of San Antonio – to Tlaxcalan Indians from central Mexico, or Apache, Comanche, Navajo, or other indigenous groups of the frontier. Occasionally, Euro-American individuals coming from farther north also established themselves in these remote communities. These foreign families or individuals were valued not only because of their skin color – which automatically placed them in the upper ranges of the racial hierarchy – but also because they frequently had formal education, a trade, or at least good connections. Indeed, most of these colonial-era foreign residents were employees of the state serving in various capacities such as officers, doctors, printers, suppliers, and so on. In such remote and humble communities, where survival depended on the labors of every male and female, *fuereños* were readily embraced and incorporated; any other policy would have been folly.

The attraction worked in the other direction as well. Peripatetic Frenchmen and Anglo Americans had ventured into the interior of North America for generations, establishing casual and not-so-casual relationships with indigenous women in the region. Having left the bounds of their home communities, these pioneers had also forsaken the moral codes, customs, and institutions that traditionally had regulated relationships between men and women. These men faced socially and culturally ambiguous *contact zones* in which such liaisons were not completely regulated by any specific set of norms, and women emerged as inter-ethnic brokers *par excellence*.[4] When French and Anglo-American men reached northern New Spain in the early 1800s, they could turn to a long precedent of Euro-American–indigenous encounters that, for good and evil, would condition subsequent liaisons between Euro-American men and Hispanic and Native American women.

Notwithstanding such mutual attraction, the Spanish Crown erected direct and indirect barriers against sexual or marital relationships between empire subjects and outsiders in frontier areas. Colonial records reveal a small number of liaisons between Euro-American men and Hispanic women. Throughout the eighteenth century, only four or five *extranjeros* – all Frenchmen – appear to have settled in New Mexico and established durable relationships with local women.[5] Intermarriage remained a rare occurrence

---

"The Canary Islands Immigrants of San Antonio," 41–58; Poyo, "Immigrants and Integration in Late Eighteenth-Century Béxar," 85–103.

[4] Sylvia Van Kirk, *Many Tender Ties: Women in Fur-Trade Society, 1670–1870* (Tulsa, OK: University of Oklahoma Press, 1983), esp. ch. 4.

[5] McDowell Craver provides a list of four: Juan Bautista Alarí, Louis Febre, Domingo Labadie, and Jean Mignon. Rebecca McDowell Craver, *The Impact of Intimacy: Mexican–Anglo Intermarriage in New Mexico, 1821–1846*. (El Paso, TX: Texas Western Press, 1982), 16. McDowell Craver derived her information from Fray Angélico Chávez, *Origins of New Mexico Families in the Spanish Colonial Period* (Santa Fe: Museum of New Mexico Press, 1992). To this list

largely because the Crown restricted the commercial and settlement activities in which foreigners could take part, thereby severely limiting their actual physical presence within New Spain. All of this changed after independence. The Mexican government did away with several colonial restrictions and opened the floodgates in the early 1820s, ushering in an economic revolution that brought with it scores of Euro-American men. Between 1820 and 1850, records show at least 122 instances of intermarriage in New Mexico.[6] Texas and California experienced sizeable increases; virtually no place throughout Mexico's Far North was left untouched. While foreign merchants, trappers, and settlers tended to cluster in certain hubs such as Taos, Nacogdoches, and San Felipe de Austin, even remote timber camps and tiny *ranchos* had occasions to interact with the newcomers, giving rise to the possibility of inter-ethnic relationships. Local religious and civil authorities as well as *vecinos* at large were thus left to ponder about the morality and desirability of increasingly common inter-ethnic sexual and marital relationships.

Biological impulse alone would have produced inter-ethnic couplings, as Euro-American men long preceded their female counterparts in reaching Mexican territory. As late as 1846 – at the very end of the Mexican era and fully twenty-five years after the first caravan of Anglo-American men appeared in Santa Fe – Susan Shelby Magoffin was still able to claim (mistakenly) that she was the first Anglo-American woman to have reached New Mexico.[7] Similarly, there is no record of Anglo-American women residing permanently in San Antonio throughout the Mexican period.[8] Even in the Anglo-Texan colonies, Euro-American women were extremely scarce. Noah Smithwick observed that during his entire stay in San Felipe from 1828 to 1831, "there was not a ball or party of any kind in which ladies participated,"

we can add the name of Baptiste Lalande. See David J. Weber, *The Taos Trappers* (Lincoln, NE: University of Oklahoma Press, 1981). New Mexico's prenuptial investigations during the colonial period reveal only one case of a foreign-born resident who went through the formalities of a marriage. It was also something of a special case. In 1792 Enrique Tirrie Corte, native of the city and bishopric of Digne on the Bléone, initiated proceedings to marry María Josefa de la Luz Espíndola. Yet Tirrie had two obvious advantages: He was a Catholic by birth, and he was an employee of the Crown as master armorer of the presidio of Carrizal. Rick Hendrick, ed., *New Mexico Prenuptial Investigations from the Archivos Históricos del Arzobispado de Durango, 1800–1893*, 2 vols (Las Cruces, NM: Rio Grande Historical Collections, New Mexico State University Library, 2000), 1:108–9.

[6] The entire roster of such couples can be found in McDowell Craver, *The Impact of Intimacy*, 49–53.

[7] Historians, including myself, for a long time believed Magoffin. See Margoffin, *Down the Santa Fe Trail*. For earlier instances of Anglo-American women living in New Mexico, see Maria Meyer, *Mary Donoho: New First Lady of the Santa Fe Trail* (Santa Fe, NM: Ancient City Press, 1991). I thank David J. Weber for alerting me of the existence of Donoho.

[8] Margoffin, *Down the Santa Fe Trail*. It is only in 1838 that the first Anglo-American pioneering woman, Mary Maverick, settled in San Antonio. Mary A. Maverick, *Memoirs*, edited by Renu Maverick Green (Lincoln, NE: University of Nebraska Press, 1989), 15.

and the few single women who happened to reach the town were "immediately captured by some aspirant for matrimonial honors."[9] Not surprisingly, a large share of resident Euro-American men established relationships with Hispanic women. William Swagerty has estimated that fully three-quarters of all foreign male trappers who went to New Mexico married Mexican women.[10]

It is extraordinarily difficult to discern how spouses within these interethnic unions regarded each other. We know precious little about how Mexican women regarded their Anglo-American spouses. Notwithstanding the boasts of various *extranjeros* to the effect that Mexican women were irresistibly drawn to their fair skins and adventurous lives, the record shows far less enthusiasm. In some instances, Mexican women and their families rejected marriage proposals from gallant foreigners.[11] At the same time, the evidence indicates that once married, Mexican women remained staunchly loyal to their foreign partners even in the face of considerable pressure from their own families and fellow Mexicans as relations between Mexicans and Anglo Americans deteriorated.[12] We know a lot more about how Anglo-American men felt about Mexican women, for they left several texts detailing their impressions. Beyond commenting on their women's physical traits (copper-colored, Indian-looking, small feet) and peculiar customs (chain-smoking, gambling, and scantily clad), these foreign writers left a decidedly ambiguous portrait. On the one hand, foreign-born males emphasized the romanticism involved in having a Mexican wife, and praised the carefree, sociable, and joyous character of the Mexican woman. A Cincinnatian who reached New Mexico at the time of the Mexican–American War provides a typical vignette:

Though smoking is repugnant to many ladies, it certainly does enhance the charms of the Mexican *señoritas*, who, with neatly rolled-up shucks between coral lips, perpetrate winning smiles, their magically brilliant eyes the meanwhile searching one's very soul. How dulcet-toned are their voices, which, siren-like, irresistibly draw the willing victim within the giddy vortex of dissipation![13]

---

[9] Smithwick, *The Evolution of a State*, 48–9.
[10] William R. Swagerty, "Marriage and Settlement Patterns of Rocky Mountain Trappers and Traders," *Western Historical Quarterly* 11:2 (Apr 1980), 168–9.
[11] McDowell Craver specifically discusses this question in *The Impact of Intimacy*, 12–16.
[12] Here's but one example. Describing his tobacco smuggling activities, Smithwick writes:

> ... we found safe hiding for our wares with an old Mexican woman, Doña Petra, who enjoyed the distinction of being the widow of a white man (one John Smith), and consequently the steadfast friend of all Americans, considering it an honor to have them make her house their home (Smithwick, *The Evolution of a State*, 30).

[13] Leois H. Garrard, *Wah-to-yah and the Taos Trail* (Norman, OK: University of Oklahoma Press, 1955), 171.

But on the other hand – already prefigured in the preceding quote – the *extranjeros* condemned the loose morals, lack of education, and even the crudity of these women. The very same Cincinnatian so admiring of nuevomexicanas explained that once the initial excitement wore off, a more sober reality emerged: "[F]rom the depraved moral education of the New Mexicans, there can be no intellectual enjoyment. The only attractions are of the baser sort."[14] Anglo-American residents often deplored the Mexican character and held very critical opinions of its people. In 1853, the United States attorney for the territory of New Mexico, W. W. H. Davis, penned a fulminating but rather common judgment: "I regret that I am not able to speak more favorably of the morals of New Mexico, but in this particular the truth must be told. Probably there is no other country in the world, claiming to be civilized, where vice is more prevalent among all classes of the inhabitants."[15] As David J. Weber has observed, it is very difficult to tell if those Anglo-American men who regularly expressed unflattering generalizations exempted their own wives (and mothers of their own children) from them, or whether such assessments stemmed precisely out of their own domestic experiences.[16]

Regardless of such emotional tensions, these unions had an inescapable economic dimension. For foreign-born merchants who took up residence in northern Mexico, marriage to a Mexican woman was the easiest and most convenient way to legitimize their economic activities and consolidate their social standing. For a start, marriage gave foreign-born arrivals a set of ready-made alliances through their in-laws. The newcomers could expect to benefit from extended political families that often had connections stretching all the way to the local and regional administrations and to various members of the economic oligarchy and were in a position to exert pressure on behalf of their sons-in-law. More to the point, such unions facilitated the attainment of Mexican citizenship that, in turn, had immediate value as it allowed foreign-born men to bypass onerous regulations restricting their economic activities. For instance, as we saw, in 1826, the authorities of New Mexico issued permits for fur trapping expeditions based on citizenship and required that at least half of each trapping party be composed of Mexicans.[17] Similarly, in 1832, a New Mexican representative insisted that *communal* resources, especially wood, should be free for all national citizens but not so

[14] Ibid., 171. For a sampler of such opinions, see McDowell Craver, *The Impact of Intimacy*, 23–6.
[15] W. W. H. Davis, *El Gringo: New Mexico and Her People* (Lincoln, NE: University of Nebraska Press, 1982), 220.
[16] David J. Weber, "Conflicts and Accommodations: Hispanic and Anglo-American Borders in Historical Perspective, 1670–1853," *Journal of the Southwest* 17:2 (1997), 20–1.
[17] See Proceedings Against Ira A. Emmons for illegal fur trade, Santa Fe, Apr 1827, MANM 7:207–29; Proceedings Against Ricardo Cambel, Felipe Tomson, and Vicente Gion, MANM 8: 371–447, 475–503.

for foreigners, and proposed the imposition of certain restrictions and spe-cial surcharges. This legislation was specifically aimed at a handful of Anglo Americans who were involved in the rum business and were in the process of building distilleries, massive structures that made heavy use of collective resources. Although not enacted in the end, the proposal served as a wake-up call, underscoring the tenuous position of foreign residents perennially exposed to sudden legal changes.[18]

The most vexing and potentially most devastating restrictions imposed on foreign-born residents were related to retail trade. Initially, Anglo-American merchants virtually controlled the Santa Fe Trail and the Louisiana–Texas trade, reaping enormous benefits from these long-distance mercantile activities. Attempting to break into the business and gain a share of the profits, Mexican officials (and their merchant constituents) occa-sionally banned foreigners from selling their wares at the retail level. The idea was to preserve that portion of the business exclusively for Mexican nationals. Anglo Texans faced such regulations in the early 1830s and foreign-born New Mexicans in the mid-1840s, leading to bitter court cases where the tensions between citizenship and financial gain were painfully obvious.[19]

In addition to allowing foreign-born residents to bypass these restrictions, marital ties could also open the door to land acquisition. The imperial colo-nization decree of 1823 invited all industrious foreigners with sufficient capi-tal to settle in Mexico, but pointedly stated that those who married Mexican women "acquired a *special right* to receive their letters of citizenship."[20] Although the exact scope of that special right was not defined, foreign land applicants understandably featured their Mexican spouses prominently in all their dealings with the Mexican bureaucracy. Indeed, an individual's mari-tal status acquired paramount importance and could well be the difference between success and failure when engaged in fiercely competitive bidding processes where foreign land applicants made strenuous efforts to convey their loyalty to Mexico, seriousness of purpose, and stability of their per-sonal circumstances. The gist of Mexico's land legislation was clearly to encourage foreign-born residents to become naturalized and marry Mexican women. Most dramatically, since 1828 a foreigner could not legally purchase rural property except after he became naturalized – which involved resid-ing a minimum of two years in Mexico, being a Catholic, and preferably being married to a Mexican woman. In 1842, Congress seemed to retreat

---

[18] Juan Rafael Ortiz to *jefe político*, Santa Fe, Jul 16, 1832, MANM 14, 970.
[19] For Texas, see Proceedings Against Juan Soe, San Antonio, Sep 15, 1832, BA 152, 865–925. For New Mexico, see Ward Alan Minge, "Frontier Problem in New Mexico Preceding the Mexican War, " Ph.D. dissertation, University of New Mexico, 1997, 118–19, note 36.
[20] Hans Peter Nielsen Gammel, comp., *Laws of Texas, 1822–1897*, 10 vols (Austin, TX: Gammel, 1898), 1: 32.

somewhat by issuing a decree that allowed foreigners to acquire rural and
urban property, but even this law continued to give priority to naturalized
citizens in certain instances.[21]

For their part, Mexican women and their families stood to benefit from
intermarriage as well. Mexican families had traditionally used their kin
ties – children's spouses, godparent relations, cousins, and so on – in ways
that furthered family interests. This was no less true in the harsh environment of the frontier. Naturally, as the economic and political fortunes of
Anglo-American residents improved, so did their attractiveness as marrying
partners. Nuevomexicanas, tejanas, and californias and their families could
benefit immediately from their spouses' and in-laws' access to American
goods, suppliers, credit, and markets. Indeed, the rise of merchant capitalism throughout northern Mexico only made the economic underpinnings of
intermarriage more obvious and compelling. For non-elite Mexican women,
protection and survival were fundamental concerns. Anglo Americans represented themselves as dependable providers and protectors.[22] But for elite
Mexican families seeking to establish a foothold in the lucrative trade with
the United States, a foreign-born son-in-law offered distinct additional possibilities.[23] As Rebecca McDowell Craver notes, this may have been a factor
in the marriage of Juana Ortiz and Santiago (James) Conklin. Juana was
the daughter of Pedro Antonio Ortiz, a wealthy rancher and member of the
Santa Fe oligarchy bent on breaking into the Santa Fe trade. Santiago was
a pioneer of New Mexico's burgeoning international trade and a valuable
partner for any such ventures. Theirs was a match made in heaven that

[21] See ley sobre pasaportes y modo de adquirir propiedades de los extranjeros, Mexico City,
Mar 12, 1828; reglas para dar cartas de naturaleza, Mexico City, Apr 14, 1828; de-
creto del gobierno de la república permitiendo a los extranjeros adquirir bienes raices;
all in Manuel Dublán and José María Lozano, comp., *Legislación mexicana o colección
completa de las disposiciones legislativas expedidas desde la independencia de la República*,
34 vols (Mexico City: Imprenta del Comercio, 1876–1912), 2, 64–5; 2, 66–8; 4, 130–2,
respectively.
[22] For the background on protection of women, see Yolanda Chávez Leyva, "'A Poor Widow
Burdened with Children': Widows and Land in Colonial New Mexico," in Elizabeth Jameson
and Susan Armitage, eds., *Writing the Range: Race, Class, and Culture in the Women's West*
(Norman, OK: University of Oklahoma Press, 1997), 86. On how the law protected New
Mexican women, see Janet Lecompte, "The Independent Women of Hispanic New Mexico,
1821–1846," *Western Historical Quarterly* 12 (January 1981), 20–37; Glenda Riley, *Building
and Breaking Families in the American West* (Albuquerque, NM: University of New Mexico
Press, 1996), 44–5.
[23] Louise H. Pubols provides an in-depth look at how the de la Guerras of Santa Barbara,
California, furthered their business ventures by marrying with Boston merchants during the
Mexican period. She argues that such intermarriage – far from betraying the "traditional"
mores of a *ranchero*, pastoral ethos, as other scholars have asserted – constituted the normal
way of carrying out business in the context of rising merchant capitalism. Pubols, "The De
la Guerra Family: Patriarchy and the Political Economy of California, 1800–1850," Ph.D.
dissertation, University of Wisconsin, 2000.

turned into financial success both for the extended Ortiz clan and for the couple.[24]

The available information for Texas and New Mexico indicates that both foreign-born immigrants and their Mexican women belonged to a wide social spectrum. A full examination of this question lies beyond the scope of this book, but anecdotal evidence coupled with some ideas advanced by scholars of intermarriage point to some interesting regional differences. McDowell Craver has made the interesting observation that in New Mexico, virtually none of the twenty or so *rico* families were involved in intermarriage.[25] Chávez, Perea, Pino, and the other prominent last names – the only exception being Ortiz – are absent from the roster of Anglo-Mexican couples. Interestingly, this apparent reluctance occurs in spite of the fact that these prominent families were becoming Americanized in other ways, such as sending their children to boarding schools in the United States. New Mexican women with foreign spouses included a cross-section of territorial society from soldiers' widows to well-to-do daughters of families, but not quite the upper crust. This may be in contrast to the situation prevalent in California and Texas, where high-profile marriages were more common. In California, the emblematic marriage was that of Anita de la Guerra with Alfred Robinson; in Texas, this trend is epitomized in the marriage of Santiago Buy (James Bowie), the well-known trapper and future martyr, with Ursula Veramendi, daughter of the one-time governor of Coahuila and Texas, Juan Martín Veramendi.[26] As David Montejano has proposed, when Anglo-American men and Mexican women came together, two social hierarchies came to terms with each other in complicated ways that included both racial and social considerations.[27] New Mexico, being the oldest, most established, and wealthiest Mexican province in the Far North, may have had a Hispanic elite with sufficient economic power of its own that it did not need to mix with foreigners, a choice that its less established counterparts in Texas and California did not have.

Did parents' economic and social aspirations play a role in the making of these unions? Intermarriage in the early-nineteenth century took place against the backdrop of changing mores and social attitudes. Briefly stated,

---

[24] McDowell Craver provides a compelling analysis of the economic subtext of inter-ethnic marriages in New Mexico in general and the Ortiz-Conklin marriage in particular. *The Impact of Intimacy*, 19.

[25] Ibid., 6.

[26] Indeed, Bowie had very distinguished Mexican sponsors. Among the witnesses was Angel Navarro, a future *jefe político* of Texas. Bexar County Records. Misc. Papers (Estates, etc.), 1824–85. Bexar County Archives, 1020130, San Antonio, misc. 10, Sampyreac Petition and Misc. Items. Part of recordbook of Charles D. Lytle, Bexar Co. Tax Assessor.

[27] David Montejano has proposed what he calls a "relaxed class analysis," meaning an examination that takes into account both race and social standing. Montejano, *Anglos and Mexicans*, introduction.

throughout the eighteenth and early-nineteenth centuries, the Church – which had long been the principal agent regulating marriage – retreated markedly from aggressive intervention on marital arrangements and even scaled down its basic doctrinal tenets concerning marriage itself.[28] An assertive monarchy quickly moved to fill the authority vacuum. At the level of cultural change, the Crown's ascendancy deeply affected the relationship between parents and children. Allying itself with parents who wished to exercise more control over the marriage decisions of their children, the Spanish Crown promoted a patriarchal order codified in the 1776 Royal Pragmatic on Marriage, a decree forbidding the union of unequal partners and requiring parental consent for those below the age of twenty-five under the threat of disinheritance. Whereas the Spanish Catholic Church had traditionally supported marriages based on the consent of the couple – even intervening to prevent families from interfering in the couple's decision to marry – the monarchy came down on the side of parental authority.[29] And increased parental control naturally facilitated arranged marriages dictated by the need to forge family alliances or consolidate business ventures among elite clans. Many elements of this social order continued well into the postindependence period. As late as 1853, W. W. H. Davis emphasized the peculiarly colonial nature of marital arrangements within New Mexico: "... if a Yankee sets out for the hymeneal altar, he finds himself traveling in a new and untried road."[30] He pointed out that courtship in New Mexico did not entail "sweet good-byes at the door-step, away from ma's searching eyes," but was handled by the parents – preferably by the fathers – exchanging businesslike letters and paying minimal regard for the daughter's affections. In Texas, this same image is best conjured up in the highly readable but somewhat exaggerated recollections of Smithwick:

Old Gaspar Flores was land commissioner [in Texas] and had almost unlimited power in the way of land grants. He offered me any quantity of land, accompanied by the hand of his daughter, a little squatty girl, dark, almost, as an Indian. I was young then and disposed to be fastidious in such matters, and so declined the honor of the alliance, thus throwing away the chance of a lifetime.[31]

To be sure, there are exceptions to the rule. In fact, considerable evidence suggests that during the first half of the nineteenth century, young couples increasingly challenged old traditions and norms. In his landmark study of marriage in New Mexico, Ramón A. Gutiérrez has emphasized the rise of romantic love in the late-eighteenth century greatly complicating parents' attempts to intervene in marriage decisions and marking a decline of the

---

[28] Seed, *To Love, Honor, and Obey in Colonial Mexico*, ch. 11, 12.
[29] Patricia Seed, "The Church and the Patriarchal Family: Marriage Conflicts in Sixteenth-and-Seventeenth-Century New Spain," *Journal of Family History* 10:3 (Fall, 1985), 284–93.
[30] Davis, *El Gringo*, 276–80.
[31] Smithwick, *The Evolution of a State or Recollections of Old Texas Days*, 18.

late-Spanish patriarchal order. Other scholars have reached similar conclusions.[32] But even as patriarchy crumbled, intermarriage along Mexico's Far North continued to be a privileged site where powerful economic factors shaped longings and desires and weighed heavily on peoples' choices. The rise of mercantile capitalism in the region dramatically affected the motivations of Mexican families and Anglo-American immigrants, a mutual attraction that alarmed Mexican authorities.

THE GATEKEEPERS

A bitter quarrel between a priest and a friar that broke out in New Mexico in 1823–4 provides a rare behind-the-scenes look at how early national authorities sought to regulate intermarriage. It all started in December 1823, when the curate of Santa Cruz de la Cañada, Father Manuel Rada, launched into a detailed, scathing, and secret *denuncio* of the resident friar at Taos, Manuel Bellido, for his expeditious manner of marrying foreigners.[33] The most remarkable element of Father Rada's attack is the extent to which it is couched in nationalist terms. The enraged curate forcefully explained that Taos was Mexico's last settlement in the North – the very edge of Christendom – at the same time that it was a powerful magnet for French and Anglo-American settlers. Such a key entrepôt required an energetic spiritual leader willing to abide by his ecclesiastical responsibilities, someone judicious but stern and patriotic. Unfortunately, in Father Rada's opinion, Friar Bellido did not have any of these attributes, but quite the opposite.

Rada cited specific instances of foreigners married in Taos without the proper instruction or requirements and emphasized that some of these men may have been turned down by other priests and wound up with Friar Bellido, who was their last resort. Here was a man of the robe who was rapidly acquiring a reputation for being the most lenient and understanding of all New Mexico's clergy. Father Rada found the friar's reckless marriages not only contrary to the Council of Trent, royal interdictions, and diocesan orders, but frankly repugnant, scandalous, and unpatriotic, as they jeopardized Mexico's possession of New Mexico. Father Rada was particularly appalled by a report indicating that three Frenchmen, in the process of being married by Friar Bellido, took to the plaza of San Fernando carousing and disturbing the neighborhood and discussing loudly what women each of

---

[32] Gutiérrez, *When Jesus Came*, 328–9. See also Maria Raquél Casas, "In Consideration of His Being Married to a Daughter of the Land: Interethnic Marriages in Alta California, 1825–1875," Ph.D. dissertation, New Haven, CT: Yale, 1998. The author shows how conflicts over marriage and female sexuality erupted onto the political arena as californias contested the patriarchal social order and the oligarchy found itself losing moral and political authority.

[33] Manuel Rada to Pedro Millán Rodríguez, gobernador de la sagrada mitra de Durango, (*reservado*) Santa Cruz de la Cañada, Dec 17, 1823, AHAD 253 31–3.

them would get, as if they were referring to horses.[34] He was equally alarmed that New Mexican women would find the prospect of marrying one of those foreign-born arrivals flattering. He pointed out that some women, violating the most basic rules of decency and appropriate behavior, had journeyed to Taos with the only purpose to get acquainted with the *americanos del norte*. To great dramatic effect, Father Rada conjured up the image of a full-fledged meat market where throngs of nuevomexicanas descended upon Taos to pair up with the coveted foreigners.

From the start, Friar Bellido probably knew that his chances of winning the argument and the ensuing bureaucratic maneuvering were close to nil – he was simply a member of the regular clergy up against the secular establishment. But the embattled friar still chose to put up a vigorous defense that ended up spreading the blame widely and exposing a tangle of influences bearing on intermarriage. Friar Bellido admitted to having performed several marriages involving foreign-born spouses, but claimed that these actions had been the result of direct orders from higher-ups in the ecclesiastical and civil administrations. For instance, Friar Bellido pointed out that he had married a Frenchman by the name of José Griné following instructions from his own *padre custodio*, Fray Sebastián Álvarez, and with the blessings of none other than Governor Francisco Chávez, who personally vouched for Griné's solidity of character and Christianity. Indeed, Friar Bellido observed that the *padre custodio* himself would have married Griné had he not been out with a party of Anglo Americans on a trapping expedition.[35] Friar Bellido also rejected the charge that he had both baptized and married an Anglo-American known as Cristóbal Loba without even a smattering of Christian instruction. The friar acknowledged having performed such ceremonies, but once again claimed that his superior had been the one who had determined that Loba was sufficiently Christianized as to receive the Holy Water and, in fact, had given the friar precise instructions to this effect in the presence of the alcalde of Taos, Juan Lobato. With no other impediments, Friar Bellido reasoned, he could hardly be blamed for having married Loba barely two months later.[36] Even more daring, addressing the case of the three loud Frenchmen, Friar Bellido observed that he was not responsible for the actions and words of these individuals who had ultimately been married following proper procedure and with the authorization of the See of Durango itself. These recriminations make quite clear that a clergyman's decision to marry a foreign-born man with a Mexican woman was not only a matter of submitting the appropriate paperwork and paying the fees, but it was a far more complicated affair requiring the sponsorship and acquiescence of various authorities.

[34] Friar Manuel Bellido to Pedro Millán Rodríguez, Taos, Nov 15, 1824, AHAD 252 1043–5.
[35] Ibid., 1043.
[36] Ibid., 1044.

The Church may have retreated from aggressive intervention in marital arrangements in the course of the eighteenth century, but it still retained considerable influence when it came to intermarriage. And the chief tool of ecclesiastical supervision was the *diligencia matrimonial*, or prenuptial investigation. Most prenuptial investigations amounted to little more than a few formalities and were conducted by local friars or parish priests. But in cases where the proposed marriage was prohibited by canon law or raised some ecclesiastical concerns, the *diligencia matrimonial* could turn into a formal inquiry that involved special documentation and testimonials that were then submitted to the seat of the diocese, which would then grant (or deny) a special dispensation or permission. Most commonly, these special cases involved couples related by blood to a prohibited degree (impediments of consanguinity included direct blood relationships to the fourth degree in either traverse or collateral lines). In small frontier communities keen on preserving racial and social boundaries, proposed marriages between second or even first cousins, or adopting other forms of prohibited consanguinity, were quite frequent.[37]

Marriages involving foreign-born bridegrooms constituted another set of special cases that required stringent procedures. For a start, such unions raised the specter of mixed marriages (*matrimonia mixta* or, technically, unions between Catholics and non-Catholics). From inception, the Catholic Church had opposed mixed marriages and had actively discouraged its children from marrying with those outside the Church's pale.[38] Mexico remained an exclusively Catholic nation until 1857 – meaning that one either had to be a Catholic by birth or convert to Catholicism to get married. Therefore, although in theory no mixed marriages were possible, in practice a primary objective of the prenuptial investigation was to ascertain the level of religious instruction of the recently converted spouse. Specifically, those who were not Catholic by birth needed to secure a *certificado de cristiano*, a certification process left in the hands of the parish priest. The process often involved formal religious instruction and the summoning

---

[37] For contexts in which prenuptial investigations were used, see Rick Hendricks, ed., *New Mexico Prenuptial Investigations from the Archivos Históricos del Arzobispado de Durango, 1800–1893*, 2 vols (Lus Cruces, NM: Rio Grande Historical Collections, New Mexico State University Library, 2000), 1:1–2.

[38] The Church's opposition to mixed marriages can be traced back all the way to the teachings of the Apostle St. Paul, who emphasized that a Christian marriage was a symbol of the union between Christ and the Church. Furthermore, the Church elevated marriage to the level of a holy sacrament and hence was very reluctant to allow Catholics to mix with non-Catholics who would not recognize the sacramental character of marriage. The rise of Protestantism renewed the Church's militancy against mixed marriages. Among the reforms introduced in the Council of Trent was the requirement that all marriages be carried out in public and in front of a priest – secret marriages were no longer permitted – in an attempt to discourage mixed unions. Protestant opposition was so strong that the Church was forced to allow certain concessions during the eighteenth century in Holland, Belgium, and elsewhere, while maintaining its basic stance against mixed marriages.

of a witness willing to vouch for the Catholic devotion of the prospective spouse.

While the Mexican ecclesiastical establishment was especially concerned with the recently converted, the prenuptial investigation was set up in such a way that it screened all foreign-born grooms regardless of religion – in fact, there were plenty of *Catholic* foreigners in the Far North including Frenchmen, Canadians, and Irishmen. By far the most onerous requirements of the prenuptial investigation were the *dispensa de extranjería* (dispensation for being foreign) and the *dispensa de vagos* (dispensation for vagrancy), neither of which could be granted locally but required express approval of the diocesan see (the city of Durango for New Mexico and the city of Monterrey for Texas), steps that greatly delayed the process and increased the expenses involved. The dispensation for being foreign was largely an irksome formality that was automatically granted. Far more interesting is the dispensation for vagrancy that reveals both the distrustful attitudes of the ecclesiastical establishment toward foreign immigrants and the fascinating adaptation of old canon regulations to new realities. Foreign-born applicants appear to have dreaded the dispensation for vagrancy more than any other requirement. Friar Bellido observed that foreign-born grooms who initially intended to pursue formal marriages were often discouraged after learning of the *dispensa de vagos*.[39] This particular requirement had its origins in the marriage reforms introduced in the sixteenth century at the Council of Trent urging priests to be very cautious about marrying vagrants:

There are many persons who are vagrants, having no settled homes; and being of a profligate character, they, after abandoning their first wife, marry another, and very often several in different places, during the life-time of the first. The Holy Synod, being desirous to obviate this disorder ... commands parish priests not to be present at the marriages of such persons, unless they have first made a careful inquiry, and, having reported the circumstance to the Ordinary,[40] they shall have permission from him for so doing.[41]

On the surface, the Tridentine's definition of vagrancy could apply to foreign-born immigrants into Mexico's peripheral areas in the 1820s through the 1840s, many of whom were itinerant merchants or had recently relocated, and who could well have spouses in their home communities or along the trail. Understandably, a crucial aim of the prenuptial investigation was to find out whether the applicant had already been married before and what dealings he had conducted with women prior to his arrival in Mexico. If available,

---

[39] Friar Manuel Bellido to Pedro Millán Rodríguez, Taos, Nov 15, 1824, AHAD 252 1044.

[40] In ecclesiastical language, *ordinary jurisdiction* means full jurisdiction, including the power of legislating, adjudicating, and governing. *Ordinary* usually refers to popes and bishops and does not include parish priests.

[41] J. Waterworth, ed. and trans., *The Council of Trent: The Canons and Decrees of the Sacred and Oecumenical Council of Trent* (London: Dolman, 1848), 200.

a testimony from someone who had known the bridegroom before settling in Mexico was a crucial part of the inquiry. While the aim of the *dispensa de vagos* was understandable, the presumption that foreign-born settlers were vagrants was downright demeaning for them. As far as they were concerned, there was a gulf of difference between the sixteenth-century shiftless paupers envisioned by the Holy Synod gathered at Trent and themselves, nineteenth-century mercantile entrepreneurs who were often exceedingly prosperous and moral. But regardless of interpretation differences, the dispensation for vagrancy put a premium on *residency* – living in a particular parish under the spiritual guidance of a priest or friar, and being well known to the local authorities and fellow residents. Although there was no hard-and-fast rule, it appears that the priest conducting the investigation could decide to waive the dreaded *dispensa de vagos* if the applicant had resided long enough (from two to ten years) in the community.

These were the general guidelines for matrimonial proceedings involving foreign-born grooms, but they were creatively adapted to different environments, leading to some variation. Predictably, foreign-born individuals residing in small communities – mining or timber camps, outlying *ranchos*, and so on – were unlikely to resort to formal marriage proceedings. Scarcity of priests, steep sacramental fees, and greater social tolerance for informal unions steered many couples away from formal marriages. Indeed, in the smaller *ranchos* and remote communities that did not possess resident priests, marriage was considered a luxury, even something extraneous and rare. It was not uncommon for officials and priests to arrange massive ceremonies as they traveled about.[42] In contrast, in the large frontier communities dominated by Mexicans, such as Taos, Santa Fe, and San Antonio, the prenuptial investigation was conducted with most if not all of the formalities previously described – allowing for different temperaments among priests. In San Antonio, Father Refugio de la Garza, the parish priest and ecclesiastical judge during the entire Mexican period, was feared for his strictness and high expectations on religious instruction. In 1821, Governor Antonio Martínez wrote to him recommending the marriage of two Anglo Americans identified as señores Banon and Esmit. Father de la Garza proceeded to examine the grooms on "Catholic doctrine, religion, dogma, and faith," but found their answers woefully inadequate and requested a lengthy period of instruction. He then labored strenuously to persuade the applicants "of the Truths that they refused to admit," and went on to "subject them to the authority of Our Lord and our Mother Church ... administering the sacrament of penance and finally that of marriage according to the regulations of the

---

[42] When Governor Albino Pérez visited the pueblo of Zuñi in the winter of 1837, his chaplain, in the span of forty-eight hours, baptized sixty-three children and confirmed thirty-one marriages that were lacking "the benediction of the Roman ritual." Governor Albino Pérez to Comandante General, Santa Fe, Feb 16, 1837, MANM 19, 693.

Council of Trent." Father de la Garza concluded his letter by noting that he had found the instruction of the prospective wives satisfactory, as they were Catholic by birth and had been raised within the Spanish domain.[43] In spite of his high standards, over the course of the years, Father de la Garza acquiesced to numerous intermarriages.

The situation was not very different in New Mexico's principal towns. At Taos, Father Antonio José Martínez was able to strike a delicate balance for some time. On the one hand, Father Martínez came to replace Friar Bellido, who – as we saw – had been removed on the grounds of being too lenient toward Anglo Americans. To avoid a similar fate, Father Martínez needed to exercise considerable rigor and attention to detail in his matrimonial proceedings. But on the other hand, the new curate was able to maintain generally cordial relations with the local foreigners through the 1820s and early 1830s, overseeing their conversions to Catholicism, baptisms, marriages, and other functions. Taking advantage of his close ties to the See of Durango, father Martinez was also able to secure speedy confirmation of his proceedings. Similarly, Father Juan Felipe Ortiz, the parish priest of Santa Fe and *vicario foráneo* (first ecclesiastical authority) of New Mexico, appears to have enjoyed good relations with the foreign-born Santa Fe residents at first. It helped that, during his 1833 visitation to New Mexico, Bishop Zubiría gave Vicar Ortiz the power to grant *dispensas de extranjería*, thus enabling him to provide dispensations more quickly and conveniently.[44]

Yet, by the late 1830s, various circumstances conspired to sour the relationship between New Mexico's men of the robe and their foreign-born parishioners to the point of overt antagonism. Greater local ecclesiastical control of matrimonial proceedings may have expedited the paperwork, but it also made the process more dependent on the wishes of individual priests. The travails of Julián Popa (William Pope) and María Juliana Salazar are quite instructive in this regard.[45] After having lived together for years and having produced two children, the couple decided to go through the formalities of a marriage sometime in the early 1830s. Julián had resided in Taos since 1822; he had been among the first foreign-born settlers to become a naturalized Mexican, and in 1831 took the added step of becoming baptized. María, for her part, was a widow from Taos of known parents, so her only bureaucratic hurdle consisted of obtaining a *constancia*, or certificate of the death, of her first husband before she could remarry. Thus, although facing onerous matrimonial proceedings, the couple had good reasons to feel optimistic; and indeed the marriage went ahead as planned, but with one

---

43 Father Refugio de la Garza to Governor Martínez, San Antonio, Apr 29, 1821, BA 67, 457.
44 Pastoral letter of Bishop Zubiría, Santa Fe, Oct 15, 1833, in Libro en que consta la apertura de la visita general del Obispado de Durango..., microfilm edition, 1 reel, NMSRCA.
45 This episode is based on the diligencia matrimonial of Julián Popa and María Juliana Salazar, Santa Fe and Taos, Dec 20, 1834–Mar 17, 1835, AHAD 391, 320–34.

minor anomaly. Late in 1833, the family moved to Abiquiu and lived there for almost a year, but having resided much longer in Taos, they still chose the latter parish to conduct their matrimonial proceedings. Father Antonio José Martínez of Taos, being well acquainted with the couple, proceeded with dispatch not even requiring from Julián a dispensation for vagrancy. Everything seemed to have gone smoothly for Julián and María – that is, until the couple sought to validate their Taos marriage in its new abode in Abiquiu with Father José Francisco Leyba. Ordained in the waning years of the colonial period, Father Leyba was characteristically distrustful when it came to marrying foreign-born males with Mexican women. The curate of Abiquiu found serious flaws in Julián and María's matrimonial proceedings, declared the marriage invalid, and promptly secured an order through the vicar of New Mexico compelling the Anglo American to give up his wife. In the winter of 1834, Julián Popa was arrested for refusing to surrender María Juliana to the authorities of the Rito Colorado de Abiquiu. He had said that he would much rather suffer the consequences of ignoring the law than face separation from María Juliana. As it turned out, he had to endure both.

In addition to being subject to the temperaments of different priests, aspiring inter-ethnic couples had to contend with political tensions that found their way into matrimonial proceedings, especially as the antagonism between the increasingly centralist New Mexican authorities and the notoriously federalist Anglo-American residents deepened. One such instance occurred during 1841, when New Mexico faced an impending Anglo-American invasion from the neighboring Republic of Texas. Among other preparations, Governor Manuel Armijo requested help from Vicar Ortiz, who did not vacillate:

Your Excellency can rest assured that I will interpose my influence as much as possible both as a private individual and especially as the first ecclesiastical authority of this Department so that all of New Mexico becomes aware of the evils that unavoidably would befall us if we do not resist by all means *the enemy of Mexico's territorial integrity.*[46]

Just a few months before this forceful letter, Vicar Ortiz had ordered all priests within the territory to charge foreign-born grooms 30 pesos in order to receive his *dispensa de extranjería* (above all other customary expenses), thus causing an uproar.[47] Refusing to submit to what was perceived as a surcharge that unfairly targeted only the foreign-born, David W. Spaulding and other Anglo Americans contacted the American consul in Santa Fe, seeking

---

[46] Vicar Juan Felipe Ortiz to Guadalupe Miranda, Peña Blanca, Aug 2, 1841, MANM 28, 1324–6. My emphasis. When the vicar wrote about "the enemy of Mexico's territorial integrity," he was primarily referring to the invading party from Texas; but suspicion inevitably spilled over into the foreign-born residents, many of whom were accused of being collaborators.

[47] U.S. Consul Manuel Álvarez to Guadalupe Miranda, Secretary of Government of New Mexico, Santa Fe, May 22, 1841, MANM 28, 1291–3.

an end to the practice.[48] The matter soon escalated into a full diplomatic row, as Consul Manuel Álvarez turned to the American secretary of state, Daniel Webster, stating in a lengthy *memorial* that such discriminatory surcharge was contrary to Article 9 of the Treaty of Amity and Commerce signed between Mexico and the United States.[49] Vicar Ortiz defended and maintained the surcharge, affirming the independence of the ecclesiastical branch from civil interference. Foreign-born residents continued to complain about exorbitant fees, and their relationship to the Catholic establishment remained contentious until the very end of the Mexican period.

A far more accommodating pattern emerged in the overwhelmingly Anglo-American colonies of Texas. At the outset, lack of resident priests in the *colonias* severely restricted the ability of Mexican ecclesiastics from exercising effective control. In the early 1820s, Father de la Garza was responsible for the spiritual well-being of the *colonos* – at least that was the theory. The San Antonio priest intended to make regular visits to monitor the progress of their learning of Catholicism and minister to this burgeoning population that was newly converted for the most part. But such visits turned out to be sporadic, if they took place at all. In June 1824, *empresario* Stephen F. Austin wrote to the *jefe político* of San Antonio observing that in spite of the enthusiasm of several colonists wishing to marry and have their children baptized, there had been no occasion to do it.[50] Austin exaggerated the religious ardor of his settlers who would much rather have been left alone than have a Mexican priest get involved in their marital and other family decisions. Always a practical individual, the *empresario*'s real aim became apparent in the next paragraph, where he proposed a scheme to avoid the nefarious consequences that would result from the prolonged absence of a priest: "If the padre cannot come, let him give me the necessary authority to perform a kind of provisional marriage until he arrives."[51] This was a plan that fellow Mexican liberals – who had long sought to minimize the role of the Church in everyday life – may have supported, but to which the Church could not have consented. Still, this *was* the system, if only by default. At San Felipe, the Anglo-American alcalde was customarily summoned to "tie the nuptial knot in good American style, but the contracting parties had to sign a bond to avail themselves of the priest's services to legalize the marriage at the earliest opportunity."[52]

---

[48] Manuel Álvarez to Guadalupe Miranda, secretario de gobierno del Departamento de Nuevo México, May 22, 1841, 1291–3. Miranda, in turn, relayed the information to Governor Armijo.

[49] Thomas E. Chávez, ed., *Conflict and Acculturation: Manuel Álvarez's 1842 Memorial* (Santa Fe, NM: Museum of New Mexico Press, 1989), 36–8.

[50] Austin to *jefe polítco*, San Felipe, Jun 20, 1824, Bexar Archives 1824–8, Box 2-23/610. Texas State Archives.

[51] Ibid.

[52] Smithwick, *The Evolution of a State*, 25.

If Father de la Garza himself could not minister to the fast-growing Anglo-American parishioners, then the only alternative was to appoint an ecclesiastic specifically devoted to the *colonos*. It was a most difficult appointment, for such a clergyman would need to find a way to inject himself into the lives of an overwhelmingly Protestant population that had very reluctantly converted to Catholicism to secure Mexican land. (Indeed, it was widely known in San Felipe that a Baptist preacher could quietly make himself available to the colonists. One even opened a school in 1829.[53]) In the early 1830s, the See of Monterrey found a seemingly Solomonic solution by appointing an Irish priest resident in Mexico, Father Miguel Muldoon, as vicar general of the Texas colonies. He did not actually live in the colonies, an arrangement that avoided unnecessary friction, and his tours always involved multitudinous ceremonies for confirmation of marriages and baptisms, thus making the clergyman's brand of Catholicism as collective, diluted, and unobtrusive as possible.[54]

While the Church was unquestionably the main gatekeeper, from time to time military and civil authorities also intervened in matrimonial arrangements. In the course of the eighteenth century, the Crown increasingly asserted its competence to regulate and control marriages. The Royal Pragmatic on Marriage (promulgated in New Spain in the spring of 1778) constituted a milestone in this process.[55] Specifically, the Pragmatic expanded the jurisdiction of the civil judicial apparatus into private life. The royal decree stated that marital abuse and disorder stemmed directly from lack of appropriate civil legislation and from the judges' inability to prosecute offenders. The Pragmatic thus became one important basis for judges and other civil authorities to claim jurisdiction over marital affairs. In addition to expanding the purview of civil authorities, the Royal Pragmatic revealed a deep concern with the mixing of the races and provided rules guiding proper marital arrangements. In effect, the royal decree banned "unequal marriages," defining inequality in strict racial terms. The idea was to compel blacks, Indians, whites, and the various *castas* to remain within their own racial bounds when selecting spouses. But in the practical world of the courts, litigants in effect expanded the scope of the prohibition well beyond race to encompass differences in status, wealth, and political power.[56] In principle, the Royal Pragmatic, signaling a growing civil jurisdiction over marriage and offering guidelines of appropriate matrimonial unions, applied only to subjects within the empire. But it inevitably conditioned attitudes toward marriage with members of other empires and nations and spawned a set of social and political arrangements that would continue into the postindependence era.

---

[53] Ibid., 48.

[54] Father Miguel Muldoon, *Gaceta del gobierno supremo del Estado de Coahuila y Texas*, Saltillo, May 27, 1833, BP 40:673, 5. See also Cantrell, *Stephen F. Austin*, 237–9.

[55] Gutiérrez, *When Jesus Came*, 315–18; Seed, *To Love, Honor, and Obey*, ch. 13.

[56] Seed, *To Love, Honor, and Obey*, 205–8.

In the Far North, state involvement in marital affairs ran along bureaucratic chains of command. Within the military, marriage regulation was an important component of a vast hierarchical system beginning with the president of the Republic and the secretary of war, and stretching all the way to lowly presidial soldiers. Indeed, the president and Congress regularly issued individual marriage licenses or pardons for those who married without a license. These individuals were sometimes minor officers posted as far away as Coahuila and Texas.[57] Within garrisons or presidios, the commanding officer had to give express authorization before any of his subordinates could marry. He was free to pursue his own investigation, and his decision was completely independent of ecclesiastical approval to the point where chaplains or priests who performed marriages without the corresponding military authorization could be sanctioned or prosecuted.[58] Moreover, the remoteness of frontier military outposts generally enhanced officers' control over the marital process, for, in addition to issuing marriage licenses, they also had to grant furloughs or allow the movement of individuals for the purpose of completing all the appropriate bureaucratic requirements of marriage. Foreign-born residents came in contact with military authorities while arranging marriages precisely because their movements, at least initially, constituted a security concern. For instance, an Anglo American residing in Nacogdoches in 1801 was one of the first foreigners who ever attempted to pursue a formal marriage in Texas. Asica – as he was curtly identified in the official documentation – made his marriage plans known to the local authorities and then requested safe passage to San Antonio to "put himself in the state of grace." Almost one month later, the governor's reply came back ordering Asica to remain in Nacogdoches until the *comandante general* returned to San Antonio to make a determination on the matter.[59]

Foreign-born residents could also run into the civil bureaucracy. As is evident in many of the cases presented in this chapter, the sponsorship of the governor, an alcalde, or some other civil authority was key for a successful marriage application. As explained previously, Governor Martínez of Texas wrote a personal letter to Father de la Garza recommending the marriage of two Anglo Americans. Similarly, Governor Francisco Chávez of New Mexico vouched for the Christianity and morality of a foreign-born applicant. As Friar Bellido pointed out, such recommendations and sponsorships carried considerable weight. In addition, there were formal mechanisms of civil control over marriage. Some of these top-down forms of

57 President Guadalupe Victoria, pardon issued on behalf of Hermenegildo Mancebo for marrying without a license, Mexico City, May 7, 1828, BA 115:200–2.
58 See Nemesio Salcedo to Antonio Cordero, Chihuahua, Feb 23, 1809, BA 34, 214. The military *asesor* pointedly questioned the proceedings of Chaplain José Manuel Camacho of La Bahía, Texas, for marrying José Antonio Salinas with María Rafaela Galicia without the license.
59 Bernardo Dortolán to Governor Juan Bautista de Elguía, Nacogdoches, Mar 3, 1801, BA 21 993; Elegía to Dortolán, San Antonio, Mar 28, 1801, BA 17, 1033.

marital control concerned the bureaucrats themselves.[60] Foreign-born residents occasionally became targets of a civil justice system that was in the process of expanding its authority over marital affairs. A civil judge could decide to investigate an unmarried couple living together on his own accord, on a request from the local priest, or because of a specific complaint.[61] But regardless of the triggering circumstance, once involved, civil authorities had no qualms about intervening decisively in private affairs, even using physical force to separate couples or reorganize families.[62]

Abstract notions of state power and market persuasion became all-too-real facts of life in the institution of marriage. For many reasons, most foreign-born men living in Northern Mexico married Mexican women, ranging from the biological (there were no foreign-born women available) to the emotional and social. Economically, such matches seemed to be made in heaven. *Extranjeros* derived immediate tangible advantages from such marriages. The marriages enabled them to bypass onerous legislation that specifically targeted foreigners, increase their opportunities to acquire land and become naturalized, and access ready-made networks in their adopted country through their spouses' extended families. Conversely, Mexican women and

---

[60] The late-colonial period witnessed the emergence of *montepíos*, or committees that decided on pensions for widows and orphans of deceased officials. *Montepíos* clearly functioned as an instrument to enhance royal and then national control over marriage decisions within the civil and military bureaucracy. See D. S. Chandler, "The Montepíos and Regulation of Marriage in the Mexican Bureaucracy, 1770–1821," *Americas* 43:1 (Jul 1986), 47–68.

[61] José Antonio Valdez to Juan Veramendi, Alcalde of San Antonio, Goliad, Jan 23, 1825, BA 55, 354.

[62] For instance, in October 1828, the alcalde of Taos, Vicente Trujillo, examined the case of María Francisca Vargas and foreigner Tomás Boggs. María Francisca had been working as a cook in Boggs' home for some weeks when she began to experience sexual advances – not one or two, but many, she said. On one of these occasions, the foreigner offered to marry María Francisca, an argument that finally persuaded her to put down her guard and "give her body to Boggs," which "he used continuously since June." In the end, the justice system took María Francisca away from the foreigner's house. The alcalde Trujillo then wrote to Governor Armijo, consulting him about how best to restore María Francisca's honor and seek redress from Boggs. Alcalde Vicente Trujillo to Jefe Político Manuel Armijo, Taos, Oct 16, 1828, MANM 7, 1161–3. In another instance, a Santa Fe judge ordered that a three-year-old be taken away from the house of an Anglo-American resident in the Real del Oro and be returned to the mother, María Gertrudis Baca. The Anglo American, known as Don Alejandro Tibu, had forcibly taken the little girl, justifying his actions on the grounds that she was receiving a "bad example" and "no education" from her mother. Judge Antonio Sena of Santa Fe did not dispute this claim, but concluded that Don Alejandro had no legitimacy as a father because he was not lawfully married to María Gertrudis, and that the child was so young that she naturally belonged at her mother's side. Judicial proceedings of María Gertrudis Baca, Santa Fe, Jul 9, 1840, MANM 26, 639–42. Admittedly, these are cases in which the Mexican civil administration would have intervened regardless of the nationality of the spouses. Yet these cases do demonstrate that civil authorities did not hesitate to intervene in marital affairs in certain circumstances.

their families could rely on husbands who often took part in the expanding and profitable trading activities linking northern Mexico to the United States, and therefore had greater access to foreign goods, capital, and markets. These compelling economic considerations, in addition to all the other cultural and social pressures that inter-ethnic couples faced, made inter-ethnic marriage enticing to such couples. Yet it was precisely this remarkable economic fit that invited official scrutiny. The Church, and to a lesser extent other officials, working through a tangle of formal and informal mechanisms, sought to regulate these unions that could potentially damage the religious, political, and territorial integrity of Mexico's exposed frontier areas.

5

The Texas Revolution and the Not-So-Secret History of Shifting Loyalties

Late in the summer of 1836, Orazio de Attelis Santangelo, the notoriously combative and eccentric editor living in exile in New Orleans, received a startling missive from Mexico's interior:

If you exclude the friars, devoid of all common sense; the military commanders, generally hated; and a handful of imbeciles who favor retrograde ideas, the entire population of these states [Tamaulipas, San Luis Potosí, Zacatecas, parts of Jalisco, Nuevo León, Coahuila, Durango, Sinaloa, Chihuahua, and the territories of New Mexico and the Californias] only aspires to secede from the southern half of Mexico.[1]

The letter – signed anonymously by "a Federalist Zacatecan" – forcefully explained how the interests of Mexico's northern states were "diametrically opposed to those of the central metropolis," and in effect called for ending the national compact.[2] Mexico's budding national experiment was living its darkest hour, still reeling from the embarrassing defeat of General Antonio López de Santa Anna's forces at San Jacinto, unable to quell the secessionist movement in Texas, and with a president in captivity who was willing to sign anything to extricate himself.

At first Santangelo was unsure whether to publish the letter. Not that he wished to shy away from controversy; his proverbially radical politics had already resulted in two banishments from Mexico in less than ten years. Rather, he was unsure how the publication of such an incendiary letter would abet his federalist cause.[3] The Naples-born critic knew well that Mexican

---

[1] This letter initially appeared in the *New Orleans Bee* in 1836 and was later reproduced in the *Correo Atlántico*, Mar 6, 1839, and in the *Telegraph and Texas Register*, Apr 10, 1839.

[2] "The Federalist Zacatecan," reproduced in the *Correo Atlántico*, Mar 6, 1839.

[3] A note about terminology: It has been the curse of Mexicanists (and more generally Latin Americanists) working on the nineteenth century to be forced to grapple with notions so malleable and changing, and yet so crucial to the entire historical experience, as liberalism, conservatism, and their forerunners, federalism, centralism, *yorkismo*, and so on. As some scholars have observed, there is no point in treating these notions as fixed political

centralists were in the habit of branding frontier federalists as secessionists, shrewdly blurring the boundaries between political dissent and high treason. The letter would only validate such accusations. And besides such weighty political considerations, there was the practical matter of where to publish the document. Santangelo had been forced to close his own newspaper just a few days before, so he was in the unenviable editorial position of having to surrender such a juicy morsel of information to a rival newspaper. Ultimately, he was won over by his combative streak and forwarded the letter to his nemesis, the editor of the *New Orleans Bee*.[4]

This document was immensely subversive because it made an astonishing leap from domestic partisan bickering to the sacred realm of national loyalty. After leveling the usual accusations against the grasping, multitentacled federal government, the Federalist Zacatecan affirmed that the only viable alternative for the entire North of Mexico was to break free from the Center and South, "where one can see all the propitious elements to perpetuate aristocracy, military tyranny, and the ignominious yoke of superstition." Adding insult to injury, the anonymous writer went on to propose the union of Mexico's northern half (nine states and three territories in total) with the renegade Lone Star Republic, the centralists' very bête noire. To be sure, the Federalist Zacatecan grossly overstated the case in claiming that *all* of Mexico's free thinkers in the Far North advocated separation from the South. But undoubtedly many radical federalists harbored secessionist ideas if there were no other recourse. Tantalizing reports, letters, and newspaper accounts suggest that residents in Coahuila and Texas, Zacatecas, Tamaulipas, Yucatán, Nuevo León, Sonora, New Mexico, Alta California, Baja California, Tabasco, and other states at one time or another sought to dissolve their political connections with central Mexico and embarked on fascinating secessionist schemes with colorful names like the Rio Grande

---

ideas; instead, they should be considered broad and changing political movements. Still, it is possible to get closer to the meaning and membership of these political labels at the regional level and for short periods of time. In this sense, when I write about liberalism in this book, I really mean coahuiltejano liberalism in the 1820s and 1830s, except where otherwise noted.

4 Having lost his citizenship and been condemned to death in his native Naples, Santangelo fled to America, arriving in Mexico in 1825. His distinguished background (he had been married to the Duchess of Pietra d'Oro and was a marquis in his own right) as well as his colorful revolutionary experiences in Europe opened many doors to Santangelo, who quickly made the acquaintance of key political figures, including generals Vicente Guerrero, Santa Anna, Anastasio Bustamante, and Manuel de Mier y Terán. He was banished from Mexico the following year after he published four *disertaciones* about the security of the American republics and the possibility of an aggression from Spain. For Santangelo's life, see Orazio de Attellis Santangelo, *Statement of Facts Relating to the Claim of Orazio de Attellis Santangelo, a Citizen of the United States, on the Government of the Republic of Mexico, Preceded by Some Explanatory Remarks, and Followed by a Certified List of the Accompanying Documents* (Washington, DC: Peter Forge, 1841), 86–7.

Republic or the Republic of the Sierra Madre.[5] Clearly, beleaguered Mexican federalists and other discontents – many of whom were Native Americans and Anglo Americans living in peripheral regions – were willing to go to great lengths to uphold their economic projects and political ideals regardless of the plans and nationalizing rhetoric of politicians in central Mexico.

In the Far North, the linkage between political dissent and secessionism underscores a number of themes that I have attempted to develop in this book. First, the discussion of alternative national configurations shows that Mexicanness did not emerge full-blown immediately after 1821. Communities throughout Mexico remained deeply committed to local or regional attachments and understandably viewed with certain skepticism recent and abstract notions such as *mexicano/a*. Mexico's uneven economic development only deepened such local and regional attachments, putting the interests of such places as the Far North at odds with those of the national government just as similar disparities led to sectional divisions in the United States. Second, in the absence of a constituted state and an established nation, institutions like the civil bureaucracies and land administrations, the army, and the Catholic Church were the principal vehicles to expand the reach of the nation and disseminate a nationalist ideology. It is no coincidence that the Federalist Zacatecan would single out the "friars," "the military commanders," and "a handful of imbeciles" – the latter presumably encrusted in the civil administration. These institutional conduits proved quite effective in building both the nation and a potent centralist coalition, as recent scholarship has demonstrated.[6] And third, the tensions between ideology and loyalty fly in the face of more conventional stories of ethnic clashes between Hispanics, Anglo Americans, and Native Americans in the Far North and mechanistic renderings of relations between "Mexico" and the "United

---

[5] The most complete inventory of these movements was compiled by the Mexican military itself. A sampling of these documents includes the following: Partes relativos al establecimiento de la República del Río Grande en la cual se comprendían los tres Estados, siendo ellos Coahuila, Texas y Tamaulipas, file 1547; Partes y proclamas de los Generales Francisco Vital Fernández y José Cayetano Montoya, gobernador y comandante general del Estado de Tamaulipas, respectivamente relacionados con la expedición organizada en Nueva Orleáns, para formar la República de la Sierra Madre, año de 1848, file 2900; Comunicaciones del Ministerio de Relaciones al de Guerra y Marina, dando cuenta del movimiento rebelde en Matamoros, Tamaulipas, y Broconsoilla para formar la República de la Sierra Madre, año de 1849, file 3007; Movimiento separatista en la Alta California y rebelión en la Baja California, años de 1841–4, file 1888; Plan de los facciosos José Antonio Chávez, Juan Bandini, Manuel Castro, Padre Real, y otros para llevar a cabo la anexión del territorio norte de la Baja California a los Estados Unidos de Norteamérica, año de 1852, file 3215; Movimiento separatista iniciado el 19 de noviembre de 1846 por el General Juan Bautista Traconis, gobernador y comandante general del Estado de Tabasco, file 2273; and many others. All of these files are located in the microfilmed edition of the Archivos Históricos de la Secretaría de la Defensa (hereafter AHSD) in the Bancroft Library at the University of California at Berkeley.

[6] See especially Reynaldo Sordo Cedeño, *El Congreso en la primera república centralista* (Mexico City: Colmex-ITAM, 1993), passim.

States." A more nuanced and sophisticated understanding of how Mexico's Far North became the American Southwest needs to take into account these already existing core–periphery tensions to sketch credibly the peculiar insertion of Anglo Americans and Native Americans and how their actions shaped the ultimate outcome.

In this chapter and the next, I will thus focus on the veiled but dramatic history of shifting loyalties during the Texas Revolution of 1834–6 and the Chimayó Rebellion in New Mexico of 1837–8. I will try to show how the Texas Revolution started out as a remarkable crosscultural movement that would cast a long shadow over subsequent secessionist attempts throughout the region. The Chimayó Rebellion is my contrasting case. Infinitely less known than the Texas Revolution, the Chimayó Rebellion was nonetheless triggered by similar political pressures; its leaders espoused similar ideas, but the outcome turned out to be vastly different.

A TALE OF SUCCESSIVE REVOLUTIONS

"The political character of this country seems to partake of its geological features – all is volcanic," wrote Stephen F. Austin from Mexico City in early 1835, alluding to the distinctive landscape of snow-capped mountains then visible from the capital. Austin pointed out that the situation seemed quiet for the moment, but hastened to add, "to say how long it will remain so would be the same as to say when Vesuvius will or will not explode."[7] In truth, the eruption was well under way when Austin journeyed to Mexico City, and the explosion turned out to be of such force that it would continue to spill out bursts of lava for another thirty years. Mexico's relative stability during its first decade as an independent nation gave way to a difficult stalemate during the first half of the 1830s. The deadlock was finally decided in favor of the centralist project in 1834–6, when the military strongman of Veracruz, Santa Anna, who had hitherto presided over the country with the help of the federalist faction, turned against his erstwhile allies in a dramatic realignment.[8] This maneuver inaugurated a period of conservative ascendancy in Mexico known as the Central Republic.[9]

This momentous political realignment from federalism to centralism lies at the heart of the remarkable tale of shifting loyalties in Coahuila and

---

[7] Austin to James F. Perry, Mexico City, Mar 10, 1835, PTR, 1, 33–6.

[8] See Donald F. Stevens, *Origins of Instability in Early Republican Mexico* (Durham, NC: Duke University Press, c1991).

[9] The traditional liberal interpretation is that Santa Anna himself was at the head of the centralist revolution. See Michael P. Costeloe, *The Central Republic in Mexico, 1835–1846* (Cambridge, UK: Cambridge University Press, 1993). Reynaldo Sordo Cedeño has challenged this idea, arguing that Santa Anna remained in favor of the federation until early 1835, at which time he yielded to the growing influence of the centralist movement in various parts of the country. Sordo Cedeño, *El Congreso en la primera república centralista*, 173, 418.

Texas. By 1830, Coahuila and Texas had emerged as the staunchest bastion of federalism throughout Mexico, the very province chosen as sanctuary by the highest-ranking Mexican federalists, a liberal paradise, and the boldest colonization experiment in the country (see Chapter 2). Not surprisingly, the rise of centralism throughout Mexico had strong repercussions in Coahuila and Texas and ushered in a period of protracted conflict. Traditional histories of the Texas Revolution tend to focus mostly on the deteriorating relations between Anglo-American colonists and Mexican authorities.[10] But this is only the last leg of a much longer saga of successive revolutions that started out early in 1834, a full year and a half before Anglo Texans themselves began considering independence in a series of conventions. A quick survey of the rebellious movement in its entirety reveals the extent to which coahuiltejanos became involved and, wittingly or not, set the course of secession as well.

In its longer and more contextualized version, we can trace the opening shot of the Texas Revolution at least to January 1834. The rebellion started out innocuously enough, when Vice President Valentín Gómez Farías dispatched Colonels José María Noriega and Juan Nepomuceno Almonte to the state of Coahuila and Texas. Colonel Noriega's orders were to journey to Monclova – the capital of Coahuila and Texas since 1833 – to review the labyrinthine maze of Texas colonization contracts and other land transactions. Such instructions were bound to revive old animosities, as federal and state officials had accused each other for years of overstepping their constitutional powers in disposing of Texas land. Colonel Noriega was also directed to investigate the fate of the abandoned Texas customhouses and see to it that they be reopened, another bone of contention between federation and

---

[10] Most traditional interpretations explain the Texas Revolution either in terms of cultural or ethnic incompatibility between Mexicans and Americans or adopt a sweeping Manifest Destiny explanation, casting the revolution as the first episode of the irresistible westward drive of Anglo Americans into Spanish America. See Eugene C. Barker, *Mexico and Texas, 1821–1835* (New York: Russell & Russell, 1965); William C. Binkley, *The Texas Revolution* (Baton Rouge, LA: Louisiana State University Press, 1952); Samuel H. Lowrie, *Culture Conflict in Texas, 1821–1836* (New York: Columbia University Press, 1932). The Manifest Destiny hypothesis has been popular among both Mexican and American historians. See Gene M. Brack, *Mexico Vies Manifest Destiny, 1821–1846* (Albuquerque, NM: University of New Mexico Press, 1975); Frederick Merk, *Manifest Destiny and Mission in American History: A Reinterpretation* (New York: Vintage Books, 1963); and David M. Pletcher, *The Diplomacy of Annexation: Texas, Oregon, and the Mexican War* (Columbia, MO: University of Missouri Press, 1973). Among Mexican historians, see, for example, Gastón García Cantú, *Las invasiones norteamericanas en México* (Mexico City: Editorial Era, 1971). More recently, scholars have focused on Mexico's political strife and its linkage with the Texas secessionist movement. For instance, Andreas V. Reichstein has provided new insights into how the federalist–centralist wrangle, tied to land speculation, fueled revolution. Reichstein, *Rise of the Lone Star*, passim. Similarly, see Miguel Soto, "La disputa entre Monclova y Saltillo y la independencia de Texas," in María Elena Santoscoy, Miguel Soto, and Arturo Eduardo Villarreal, eds., *La Independencia y el problema de Texas: Dos eventos en Coahuila* (Saltillo: Archivo Municipal de Saltillo, 1997), 47–109.

state. Finally, Colonel Noriega bore secret instructions, among them, to spy on the American consul in Matamoros and determine whether the diplomat was encouraging a separatist movement in Texas, and to remove rebellious Anglo-American colonists by offering attractive financial terms to relocate them out of the state.

For his part, Colonel Almonte would travel through Texas to gather relevant geographic, demographic, and military information. He was to "ascertain the opinions of Anglo-Texan colonists concerning separation from Mexico and exploit any differences among them." He would spread the word among black slaves that they could gain their freedom by virtue of "having stepped" on Mexican territory, as stipulated in the Law of April 6, 1830. With regard to Indian tribes, Colonel Almonte was to inform them that the supreme government was willing to give them full possession of the lands that they occupied provided that they unambiguously declare themselves to be members of the Mexican nation.[11] Clearly federal authorities were contemplating an all-out nationalizing blitzkrieg on Coahuila and Texas.

Few would have anticipated the ironic findings of the Noriega-Almonte commission. After a whirlwind six-month tour through Texas, Colonel Almonte penned a remarkably cheery report of the situation on the ground. He found the foreign-born colonists to be thriving economically and content for the most part. Indians were delighted to receive official sanction of their land claims. All in all, Texas seemed generally – almost eerily – quiet in 1834.[12] In the meantime, Colonel Noriega encountered a very different scene in Coahuila. Monclova, the federalist stronghold in the state, turned out to be unwelcome and forbidding. State authorities generally refused to surrender sensitive information about Texas land and customhouses. Moreover, protected by only one corporal and six soldiers, Colonel Noriega felt threatened and had to suffer the ignominy of witnessing helplessly as the state legislature passed laws that flatly contradicted federal legislation.[13] Through the spring of 1834, relations between the Federation and Coahuila and Texas deteriorated dramatically, and the federal commissioner found himself in an increasingly untenable position. On the night of June 25, Colonel Noriega

[11] Report of Almonte to Governor of Coahuila and Texas, Monclova, Sep 23, 1834, BP 40: 673, 5.
[12] Celia Gutiérrez Ibarra, ed., *Cómo México perdió Texas: análisis y transcripción del informe secreto de Juan Nepomuceno Almonte* (Mexico City: INAH, 1987), 13–14.
[13] Colonel Noriega to Francisco Vidaurri y Villaseñor, Governor of Coahuila and Texas, Monclova, Apr 26, 1834; Noriega to Ministry of Interior and Exterior Relations, Monclova, May 26, 1834; both in Herbert E. Bolton Papers, no. 673, Folder 6, Carton 40, no. 36 and 39, respectively. Governor Francisco Vidaurri y Villaseñor and the Permanent Deputation (the ordinary session of the legislature being over) decried the open violation of the state sovereignty as Colonel Noriega began requesting information about land transactions in Texas and Colonel Martín Perfecto de Cos demanded the nullification of a decree that allowed the state to dispose further of Texas land.

wrote a poignant letter to the ministry of the interior and exterior, explaining that he had to leave Monclova immediately: "[T]he circumstances around me are critical, but my conscience is at ease."[14] Later that same night, he wrote to Colonel Almonte, elaborating further: "At any moment now the Government of Coahuila and Texas will withdraw its recognition of the Federation whose laws it has attempted to nullify. We will be the first to go if one takes into consideration that our commissions stem directly from the Supreme Government."[15]

Texas may have been quiescent, but Coahuila was in the throes of revolution. I don't intend to retrace fully this fascinating and bitter story of escalating tensions – Vito Alessio Robles provides the most detailed narrative[16] – but rather I hope to sketch how a classic federalist–centralist dispute affected the loyalties and identities of those involved and ultimately led to secessionism.

Before examining some critical junctures of this story in greater detail, a brief overview of the rebellion and its national context is essential. During the early to mid-1830s federalists and centralists succeeded one another in power and competed ferociously, undercutting each other. In 1833 and early in 1834, the federalists dominated the political process and proceeded to launch a very partisan and reformist program that in essence sought to curtail the privileges of the Church and the army.[17] While President Santa Anna made himself inconspicuous in his hacienda of Manga de Clavo, the acting vice president, Valentín Gomez Farías, together with a newly elected – and quite radical – National Congress, led what amounted to major political transformation pursued aggressively through congressional legislation. As it turned out, such bold initiatives quickly galvanized opposition not only among their intended targets, ecclesiastical and military authorities, but also among "respectable" citizens who were leery of undermining the

---

[14] Noriega to Ministry of Interior and Exterior Relations, Monclova, Jun 25, 1834, Herbert E. Bolton Papers, no. 673, Folder 6, Carton 40, no. 57.

[15] Noriega to Almonte, Monclova, Jun 25, 1834, Herbert E. Bolton Papers, no. 673, Folder 6, Carton 40, no. 59. For the state decree that refused to recognize the authority of the federation, see Governor Francisco Vidaurri y Villaseñor and Secretary José Antonio Padilla, Decree, Monclova, Jun 24, 1834, Bolton Papers, no. 673, Folder 6, Carton 40, Bancroft Library.

[16] The first edition of this two-volume, blow-by-blow account came out in 1945 and is still one of the most authoritative and insightful treatments of the subject. Alessio Robles, *Coahuila y Texas*, I: 499–538. For the dispute between Monclova and Saltillo, which was so crucial to the political polarization of Coahuila and Texas and the eventual secession of Texas, see Soto, "La disputa entre Monclova y Saltillo y la independencia de Texas," 47–109.

[17] My brief overview is largely based on Reynaldo Sordo's recent work, which adds considerable nuance to traditional interpretations. Sordo, *El congreso en la primera república central*, 19–59. See also Josefina Vázquez, "El primer federalism," in Marcello Carmagnani, ed., *Federalismos latinoamericanos: México/Brasil/Argentina* (Mexico City: FCE-Colegio de México, 1993), 36–44.

nation's traditional mainstays. A concerted opposition finally took shape on May 25, 1834, when a group of concerned citizens issued a revolutionary *pronunciamiento* known as the Plan of Cuernavaca. In essence, the Plan of Cuernavaca rejected the ecclesiastical and military reforms, demanded the removal of congressmen and other authorities who had promoted such legislation, and called on President Santa Anna to put a stop to the "irresponsible" federalist adventure.[18]

At first, Mexico's "political regeneration" (as centralists called this political backlash) merely involved the nullification of federalist legislation. But the surprising popularity of the Plan of Cuernavaca – especially in central Mexico – eventually persuaded its leaders that the time was ripe for a change of constitutional order altogether. A new Congress elected in 1835, working alongside an increasingly centralist Santa Anna,[19] introduced a series of measures that undermined the Constitution of 1824, curtailed states rights, and finally promulgated a centralist constitutional compact. It was now the federalists' turn to try to resist the centralist juggernaut.

Not surprisingly, the federalist opposition crystallized especially around peripheral state governments that had enjoyed enormous autonomy under the Constitution of 1824. Silver-rich Zacatecas refused to embrace centralism and was compelled only by threat of force, as General Santa Anna personally took command of a body of federal troops to end Zacatecas's defiance.[20] The states of Guerrero and Yucatán also resisted centralization. Coahuila and Texas followed closely along these same lines. The state legislature in Monclova stood at the epicenter of a staunchly federalist state network that involved the Viesca brothers and their allies, some Anglo-Texan *empresarios*, and many coahuiltejanos connected to the ubiquitous land administration of Coahuila and Texas (see Chapter 2). The dramatic floor debates, poignant letters, and legislative work during 1834–6 have left us a paper trail of the depth of this conflict that ultimately resulted in the separation of Texas from the Mexican Republic.

As far as shifting identities are concerned, three moments are very significant in the unfolding of this story in Coahuila and Texas. The first took

---

[18] Sordo Cedeño, *El congreso en la primera república central*, 57–8.

[19] Initially, President Santa Anna sought to find a political compromise that proved elusive. Then he shut down the National Congress on May 31, 1834, and for the next few months the president gravitated steadily toward centralism.

[20] The traditional interpretation is that the rise of centralism led peripheral states like Zacatecas and Coahuila and Texas to rebel. In contrast, Josefina Vázquez argues that the surprising enthusiasm for a centralist regime in central Mexico stemmed precisely from the unconstitutional defiance of Zacatecas and the specter of secessionism in Texas, thus reversing the causality. Josefina Vázquez, "México y la guerra con Estados Unidos," in Josefina Vázquez, ed., *México al tiempo de su guerra con Estados Unidos 1846–1848* (Mexico City: FCE-SRE-Colegio de México, 1997), 26–8. In fact, one interpretation does not invalidate the other. It is entirely possible – indeed quite likely – that both Mexico City centralists and frontier federalists hardened their positions because they perceived a clear threat from each other.

place in the summer of 1834, when the Monclova legislature clashed swords with the Federation for the first time and began preparing for an impending military clash. As centralism gained adherents in several states and President Santa Anna came to endorse such a momentous shift in national public affairs, the coahuiltejano federalists of Monclova grew hostile and uncompromising. By September 1834, José Antonio Vázquez, the representative of Béxar in Monclova, wrote to his constituents using terse geologic imagery to pin the blame of the nation's political misfortunes on the federal government:

The City of Mexico, that inextinguishable volcano of revolutions, has shaken the whole nation; it has leveled to its foundation the temple consecrated to its liberties, the federal constitution; it has buried beneath its ruins the legitimate authorities of almost all the states, and its disorganizing vibrations must necessarily, within a very short time, reach that remote corner of the Republic which you inhabit.[21]

The first inklings of a concrete secessionist movement in Coahuila and Texas appear in a letter written by the governor of Nuevo León, Manuel M. de Llano, addressed to his coahuiltejano friend and political ally, Agustín Viesca. Governor Llano brooded over the onslaught of centralism in his own state and the "return of the vice regal style of government prevalent in times of our Catholic Spanish government." Governor Llano concluded his letter by suggesting an intrepid plan to avoid a similar fate in neighboring Coahuila and Texas. His three-step proposal was that coahuiltejano federalists decouple Texas from Coahuila, set up a federalist state government in Texas, and then get Anglo-Texan colonists to *uphold* the newly established state government.[22] Governor Llano carefully worded his plan, conceiving the possibility that such actions were impractical due to circumstances beyond his grasp. But he was also well aware that he had stumbled upon a formula that would complicate enormously the national government's efforts to bring Texas into the centralist order. As it turned out, Viesca (who would become governor of Coahuila and Texas a few months later) had either conceived a similar solution independently or found some merit in Governor Llano's daring plan of resistance.

The second critical juncture in the unfolding of this conflict occurred in the spring of 1835. The circumstances could not have been more dramatic. On March 1, a newly elected state legislature began deliberations. Federalist and centralist deputies had reluctantly agreed to work together in one single body, but after ten days of tumultuous debates, shouting matches, and bitter

---

[21] José Antonio Vasquez, Deputy for Texas in Monclova, and Lover Jones, and T. J. Chambers, Superior Judge for Texas, Monclova, Sept 1, 1834, Herbert E. Bolton Papers, no 673, Folder 6, Carton 40, Bancroft Library.

[22] Manuel M. de Llano, Governor of Nuevo León, to Agustín Viesca, Monterrey, Jul 15, 1834, cited in Alessio Robles, *Coahuila y Texas*, I: 509. My italics for emphasis.

FIGURE 5.1. Governor Agustín Viesca

recriminations, the three centralist representatives from Saltillo withdrew.[23] The remaining eight legislators – all of whom were avowed federalists – retaliated promptly by forcing the resignation of the interim governor and nominating Agustín Viesca (see Figure 5.1) as his successor. A few days later, the "Great Sultan," as Viesca's enemies called him, made a dazzling entrance in Monclova and rode to the state assembly to be sworn in. As Alessio Robles has observed, Viesca's accession to power in these critical

---

[23] Journal of the state legislature, Monclova, Mar 12, 1835. Beineke, WA MSS S-266, Western Americana Collection, Beinecke Rare Book and Manuscript Library, Yale University. For a careful treatment of the legislature debates, see Soto, "La disputa entre Monclova y Saltillo y la independencia de Texas," 62–71.

circumstances could only be interpreted as an open challenge to all Mexican centralists, including President Santa Anna himself.[24]

Rather than forming a state government, Governor Viesca immediately set out to organize a war council. And a war it was. Just two weeks prior to Viesca's inauguration, a new National Congress in Mexico City had issued a decree mandating drastic reductions in the size of state militias, the very bulwark of state sovereignty. That decree most directly affected neighboring Zacatecas, which boasted the largest state militia in the country. But Coahuila and Texas closed ranks with Zacatecas, and in the process changed the scope of the conflict from internal political bickering into a full-fledged military showdown between the national army charged with enforcing national legislation and state militias that refused to be disbanded.[25] The essence of the conflict is best captured in the makeup of these two fighting/political forces. On one side, there was the national military, those crumbling federal garrisons located in various towns throughout Coahuila and Texas and organized in an enormous military district called the Commandancy of the Eastern Interior Provinces. Revealingly, its headquarters had recently been moved from Matamoros to Saltillo to bolster the federal presence in Coahuila. Its commander was Colonel Martín Perfecto de Cos, a professional officer and able organizer who also happened to be President Santa Anna's brother-in-law. From Saltillo, Colonel Cos had backed – and at times led – the coahuiltejano centralist movement.

On the other side, there was the state militia, a heterogeneous force gathering in and around Monclova that according to one report amounted to some 150 volunteers in April 1835. The state force included merchants and their dependents as well as thirty or forty Anglo Americans.[26] The federal military and the state *cívicos* had been clashing sporadically in Coahuila for months until things came to a head when Governor Viesca rode into Monclova to stem the tide of centralism in Coahuila and Texas.

We probably will never know how secessionist ideas spread throughout Coahuila and Texas in the intervening year between Governor Llano's provocative letter and the spring of 1835, when secessionism reemerged as a possible course of action. But whatever the exact path of propagation, events on the ground forced coahuiltejano federalists to contemplate

---

[24] Alessio Robles, *Coahuila y Texas*, 532. See also Soto, "La disputa entre Monclova y Saltillo y la independencia de Texas," 77–82.

[25] As Soto points out, the Monclova faction at this time became even more antagonistic toward the Saltillo group when General Cos became temporarily distracted by the conflict between the Federation and Zacatecas. More importantly, the Monclova federalists went on the offensive against the national government itself. Soto, "La disputa entre Monclova y Saltillo y la independencia de Texas," 83–5.

[26] Vicente Arriola, Military Commander of Monclova, to Martín Perfecto de Cos, Monclova, Apr 8, 1835, ASD 23:1095.

retrenching into Texas. By April 1835, the situation of the federalist state government had become untenable. Militarily, the coahuiltejano federalist forces had been reduced to the environs of Parras and Monclova, while centralist troops had gained the upper hand in most other significant towns in Coahuila. Politically, the legitimacy of the Monclova government continued to be challenged by a centralist state government set up in Saltillo and backed up by the Commandancy of the Eastern Interior Provinces. In these desperate circumstances, coahuiltejano federalists in Monclova inched closer to abandoning Coahuila, setting up a new government in San Antonio, and possibly seceding from the rest of the nation, where centralism seemed triumphant. A letter from a centralist informant in Monclova addressed to the political chief in Saltillo gives an idea of the cauldron in which these ideas took shape. It is worth quoting at length:

My Beloved Friend and Sir:
    Unable, due to the unsettled circumstances, to tell you in detail all the evil things that are being perpetrated here, I will only limit myself to describe the wickedness and tortuous maneuverings of the Great Sultan [Agustín] Viesca and his ally [James] Grant. First, they will promulgate a law to take the seat of government to Texas. Second, today they have dispatched a courier to Mexico City demanding the dismissal of Commander [Martín Perfecto de] Cos. Thirdly, they will declare null and void all acts of [José María] Goribar as political chief [the centralist state executive]. Let's move on to other things. [Vice President] Gómez Farías is hiding here and waiting for the infernal Plan of Texca [a federalist rebellion that had just broken out in the state of Guerrero] to take effect. . . .
    They have gathered the civic troops and have made [Juan Antonio] Padilla chief of operations and have appointed as his military assistants Grant and [José María] Uranga. Here you have it, my friend: an advisor, a legislator, and an assassin [Padilla was accused of murder] as commanders; you can judge for yourself how these affairs will turn out.
    Today, a courier has left for the [Texas] frontier to bring one hundred men, I believe our friend Grant has all the show arranged. . . . Your Excellency knows that I'm your friend and will do whatever is in my power to favor that Department [Saltillo] even when I risk my life in so doing. . . . I learned what I told you in a secret session [of the state legislature] except for the stuff about Gómez Farías.[27]

For the next few weeks, Monclova would live through a period of perpetual turmoil with rumors and speculation running amok. Finally, on May 21, after two weeks of secret gatherings, the legislature formally issued the much-anticipated decree changing the seat of government to Texas. That very night, Governor Viesca and his war council rode out of Monclova in the middle of

---

[27] José María de Aguirre to José María Goribar, Monclova, Apr 20, 1835. Microfilmed version of the AHSD files 1095 and 1096 in the Bancroft Library at the University of California at Berkeley.

the night and headed north toward the San Juan road to establish the state government in a more defensible position.[28]

It is also worth emphasizing that at that point coahuiltejano federalists had not only decided to move north, but they had also been relying on Texas resources to carry on the fight. For months, the Monclova government had been requesting militia forces from San Antonio and Goliad. At the same time, Governor Viesca had been pressuring Anglo Texans by playing on their fears: "[T]he party now in power, the same that prohibited the emigration of North American colonists in 1830, has openly declared against all foreigners and secretly favors Spanish policy and Spanish despotism. The law of April 6 is about to be renewed under a still more drastic form."[29] In fact, the Monclova government had no qualms about using Texas land to procure men and arms. Most notably, on May 13, 1835 – in the tumultuous days leading up to the decree changing the seat of government – the legislature alienated twelve hundred leagues or five million acres of Texas land to Samuel M. Williams, Francis W. Johnson, and Robert R. Peebles. In exchange for such enormous tracts of land, the three men were to raise a militia of one thousand men, supply them with arms and ammunition, and keep them in the field for one year.[30] These were momentous decisions that pushed Texas closer toward a complete break with the rest of Mexico, even if Governor Viesca and his followers preferred to think in terms of desperate circumstances and extraordinary measures for political survival.

Before we move to the third and final key moment in this long rebellious movement, it is necessary to pause briefly to examine the impact of these events on the peoples of Texas and on their sense of loyalty and identity. Among the different groups living in Texas, Mexican Texans were the first to get involved in the struggle unfolding in Coahuila. As early as October 1834, the interim political chief in San Antonio, Juan Nepomuceno Seguín, convened nightly social/political *tertulias* largely spent in heated discussions about what course of action Texas should take. An alarmed commander of the San Antonio garrison reported that the San Antonio leadership had agreed to dispatch messengers to the Anglo-American *colonias*, urging them

---

[28] Secret session of the state legislature in Monclova. Copy made in Leona Vicario (Saltillo), May 11, 1835; Vicente Arriola to Cos, Monclova, Jun 1, 1835, ASD 23:1095; Cos to *jefe político* of Béxar, Matamoros, Jun 12, 1835, BA 2q309, 247, 114–15; Judge Daniel J. Toler to M. B. Lamar, n.p., 1844, Lamar Papers (LP) 4, 96–8.

[29] Address to Coahuiltexanos, Monclova, May 4, 1835, Nacogdoches Archives (NA), 2q309, 167–72, 246.

[30] These transaction were complicated and shrouded in mystery. The legislature approved these sales by invoking a state law enacted on April 19, 1834, enabling the governor to dispose of up to four hundred *sitios* to protect the state against Indians. See Judge Daniel J. Toler to M. B. Lamar, n.p., 1844, LP 4, 96–8. This was not the only land transaction in return for support, arms, and men. See Soto, "La disputa entre Monclova y Saltillo y la independencia de Texas," 90–6.

to send representatives for a general meeting, thus showing tejano readiness to act independently.[31]

At the outset, the rise of two rival state governments in Coahuila spelled dire consequences for Texas, as neither Coahuila faction truly represented Texas interests. But the evidence also indicates that Mexican Texans generally leaned toward the Monclova faction.[32] There was certainly a sprinkling of centralism among Mexican Texans, mostly stemming from longstanding land disputes between tejanos and foreign-born colonists or out of general fear of Anglo-American dominance in Texas. Such centralist tejanos – best represented by rancher Carlos de la Garza in the Goliad area and militia captain Vicente Córdova in Nacogdoches – were quite responsive to the defensive patriotic rhetoric of the federal government.[33] But beyond such instances, what is most evident is the dominant tejano support for the federalist movement in the state at least until the fall of 1835. In the San Antonio area, virtually all prominent merchants and landowners – including José Casiano, José Antonio Navarro, the Seguíns, and other elite members represented in the *ayuntamiento* – were supportive of federalism.[34] In one especially dramatic instance in mid-May 1835, the political chief in San Antonio, Angel Navarro, resolutely refused to disband the local civic militia, defying the authority of the National Congress, and went so far as to risk a showdown with the San Antonio garrison by dispatching the Goliad and San Antonio militias to Monclova to support the besieged state government there.[35] Several Mexican Texans distinguished themselves by their unwavering support for the state federalist movement in the early phases of the insurrection. Former political chief Juan Nepomuceno Seguín led a group of some twenty-five volunteers all the way to Monclova and became disappointed after learning that Governor Viesca had given up the struggle in Coahuila and instead

---

[31] Francisco de Castañeda, Commander of San Antonio, to centralist governor José María Goribar, San Antonio, Oct 20, 1834, Daughters of the Republic of Texas (DRT) Spanish Documents Collection; Juan Nepomuceno Seguín to Political Chief of Brazos, San Antonio, Oct 14, 1834, BP 40:673, 5.

[32] For a careful and well-documented discussion of the tejano perspective, see de la Teja, "Texas: A Tejano Perspective," 93.

[33] See Castillo Crimm, "Finding Their Ways," 119–20; Lack, "The Córdova Revolt," 93; Tijerina, "Under the Mexican Flag," 44–6; all in Poyo, *Tejano Journey*. See also Lack, *The Texas Revolutionary Experience*, 163; Tijerina, *Tejanos and Texas Under the Mexican Flag*, 123–4.

[34] This was determined by comparing the list of the largest tejano landowners in the 1840 census to the list of tejano political activists in various gatherings in October 1834 through May 1835. See Gifford White, ed., *The 1840 Census of the Republic of Texas* (Austin, TX: Pemberton Press, 1966), 35–7, and compare that list to the list of signers of the San Antonio declaration, San Antonio, Oct 7, 1834, BP 40:673, 5.

[35] Angel Navarro to Secretary of Coahuila and Texas, San Antonio, May 18, 1835, in John H. Jenkins, ed., *The Papers of the Texas Revolution, 1835–36*, 10 vols (Austin, TX: Presidial Press, 1973), 1: 112–15 (hereafter as PTR); Angel Navarro to Secretary of Government of Coahuila and Texas, San Antonio, May 18, 1835, PTR, 1, 112–15.

had decided to move to Texas.[36] In Victoria, Mexican *empresario* Martín de León and his family were "decidedly opposed to Santa Anna, and all exerted themselves in favor of the constitution of 1824."[37] De León's colonists generally advocated federalism and volunteered in substantial numbers for the Texas army. Meanwhile, the *empresario*'s son, Fernando de León, drove a heard of horses to New Orleans to purchase arms and ammunition for the revolution.[38] The San Antonio representative in the Monclova legislature, José María Carbajal, traveled through Texas in early 1835, offering land to the dispersed Anglo-American and Native American families in exchange for military support for the besieged state government. He later accompanied Fernando de León to New Orleans to purchase arms.[39]

Some evidence also suggests that not only elite members but also ordinary tejanos may have leaned toward federalism. In one instance, at the height of the standoff between the militia volunteers and the San Antonio garrison, members of the *ayuntamiento* decided to assemble the *vecinos* to acquaint them with the nature of the conflict. According to one witness, "such was the popular excitement, that those gathered decided at once to make a bold attempt against the troops."[40] A bloodbath was narrowly averted as cooler heads prevailed at the last minute. Tejano distrust of centralized authority in Mexico City, harking back to the colonial era, may partly explain the popularity of the federalist cause in the San Antonio–Goliad area. But more to the point, since Mexican independence, Texas had evolved as a remarkable liberal paradise promoted by Coahuilan and Texan elites bent on promoting commerce, industry, and colonization policies that welcomed Anglo Americans. Such dominant liberal ideas had restricted the scope of action of nationalizing institutions such as the army and the Church, and had implicated tejanos in many walks of life in a vast network of interests and loyalties created by coahuiltejano federalism.

In contrast to the early involvement of Mexican Texans, Anglo-American colonists remained generally unengaged in the federalist–centralist wrangle

---

[36] Lack, *The Texas Revolutionary Experience*, 22. See also de la Teja, "Texas: A Tejano Perspective," 93–4.

[37] Deposition of James W. Robinson, Victoria, Oct 20, 1849, Unpaid Claims Collection at the Texas State Archives (TSA).

[38] American Consulate in Matamoros to Colonel José Mariano Guerra, Matamoros, Dec 7, 1835, AHDN 48:1657. Castillo Crimm, "Finding Their Ways," 118; Lack, *The Texas Revolutionary Experience*, 161. In spite of these services in favor of Texas, General Thomas Rusk unjustly forced some members of the de León clan to leave Texas. For the full treatment, see Ana Carolina Castillo Crimm, *De León, a Tejano Family History* (Austin, TX: University of Texas Press, forthcoming).

[39] Antonio Tenorio to Ugartechea, San Felipe, Aug 24, 1835, BA 166, 347–9. Músquiz to Dimmitt, Monclova, Mar 5, 1839, Dimmitt Papers (DP).

[40] Angel Navarro to Domingo Ugartechea, San Antonio, May 17, 1835 (at one o'clock in the morning), BA 165–6, 171–2, 225; Angel Navarro to Secretary of Government of Coahuila and Texas, San Antonio, May 18, 1835, PTR, 1, 112–15.

unfolding in Coahuila, at least through the summer of 1835. In truth, neither political faction was able to represent the interests of this community, which had traditionally remained quite detached from the rest of Mexico. To be sure, a handful of foreign-born *empresarios* and land developers had remained close to the Monclova leadership since the very beginning. Governor Viesca's inner circle included foreign-born *empresarios* John Cameron, James Grant, and Benjamin Milam. Moreover, in May 1835, during the last tumultuous days of the Monclova legislature, a handful of Anglo-American speculators became parties to fantastic land deals in exchange for men and arms. But while this small cadre of Anglo-American leaders seemed quite determined to support the federalist state government – and thus protect their own newly acquired pecuniary interests – Anglo Texans at large were either unconcerned, perplexed, or unable to muster enough popular support for concerted action in any direction. In San Felipe, at the heart of Austin's colony, political chief J. B. Miller issued a circular calling on the public to organize and march to the governor's rescue, but no concerted action followed.[41] Other Anglo-American colonies were even less inclined to take sides in Coahuila politics. As details about the Monclova legislature selling-spree became available, enthusiasm for Mexican federalism diminished markedly. In Columbia, Texas, Asa Brigham plainly wrote that it was foolish to rally behind the federalist faction if this only served the purpose of protecting "a few unprincipled land speculators and rescuing one of the most depraved State Legislatures that ever assembled on the continent of North America."[42] Foreign-born colonists may have deemed centralism as tantamount to dictatorship, but coahuiltejano federalism was not more palatable if it meant preserving an arbitrary system of privilege managed by a minuscule group of ruthless politicians and speculators with absolute control over Texas land. These difficult circumstances created a ferment in which incipient ideas of separation from Mexico took hold.

The issue of slavery constituted one aspect of the livelihood, political outlook, and identity of the Anglo-American and black population of Texas that proved very difficult to reconcile with Mexican rule, of either the federalist or centralist varieties. Thus, efforts to preserve slavery contributed at least to some extent to the independentist impulse.[43] Much of the impetus

---

[41] Lack, *The Texas Revolutionary Experience*, 21–2.

[42] Asa Brigham to J. A. Wharton, J. F. Perry, J. H. Bell, and others, Columbia, July 19, 1835, PTR 1, 254–6.

[43] For a fuller treatment, see the excellent book by Randolph B. Campbell. Abolitionists in the early-nineteenth century claimed that the Texas Revolution was in fact a conspiracy by Southern American states to wrest Texas from Mexico to establish slavery fully there. He concluded that although some indirect evidence supports the idea that slavery played a major role in the Texas Revolution, we now lack any direct corroboration. Campbell, *An Empire for Slavery: The Peculiar Institution in Texas, 1821–1865* (Baton Rouge, LA: Louisiana State University Press, 1989), 10–49.

for the colonization of Texas in the 1820s came from the cotton boom in the southern United States that rendered the cheap lands of Texas and their proximity to American markets especially attractive. Cotton was produced on the basis of slave labor, and accordingly, by 1835–6, Texas counted on a black slave population of roughly five thousand, living largely in plantations along the new colonies. Yet this vital economic activity, by far the mainstay of Anglo-Texan livelihood, came repeatedly under attack by Mexican legislation meant to curtail and end outright the Peculiar Institution.[44] While Texan slaveowners and their Mexican allies were successful in shielding Texas from emancipation legislation up to the Texas Revolution, the uncertainty over the future of slavery was a major concern for most Anglo Texans. And once again, as many slaveholders in Texas came to realize, neither Mexican federalists – many of whom were ideologically opposed to slavery – nor centralists – who were bent on enforcing Mexican legislation and controlling Mexico's borders – would be inclined to preserve slavery in Texas in the long run.

The collective identity of the slaves themselves, against the backdrop of these circumstances, remains a most tantalizing matter. Seldom were state and market forces so blatantly at odds with each other and so influential in shaping identity as in the case of the slave population of Texas. In spite of their relative physical isolation as well as formidable linguistic, cultural, and other social obstacles, it is clear that Texas slaves were well aware of the tensions between Anglo-American slaveholders and Mexican officials over the Peculiar Institution. Indeed, some slaves boldly exploited such tensions to secure emancipation. For instance, Mexican judicial proceedings indicate that on April 25, 1832, a black slave by the name of Pita (Peter?) and his son, Thom (Tom?), walked into San Antonio and demanded protection by the Mexican laws from the alcalde, arguing that they had been illegally introduced by Alexander Thomson. Having escaped from a plantation in East Texas, Peter went on to demand that such protection be extended to the rest of his family that had remained in the possession of Thomson.[45] In another expression of this same tension, a group of former black slaves lived

---

[44] Here is a list of the most relevant antislavery legislation affecting Texas: the Legislative Junta convened by Emperor Agustín de Iturbide passed a colonization bill promulgated on January 4, 1823, prohibiting the purchase or sale of slaves within the Mexican Empire; the Constituent Congress of 1823–4 issued a decree on July 13, 1824, prohibiting the slave trade; President Vicente Guerrero issued a decree on September 15, 1829, declaring the immediate emancipation everywhere in the Republic of Mexico. At the state level, the Constitution of the State of Coahuila and Texas promulaged on March 11, 1827, in Article 13, outlawed the introduction of slaves; the State Congress issued a decree on September 15, 1827 regulating Article 13. Discussion in Campbell, *An Empire for Slavery*, 15–34.

[45] Summary of the legal proceedings in *jefe politico* Músquiz to Governor of Coahuila and Texas, San Antonio, Jun 3, 1832, John W. Smith Collection, Box 2, at the Daughters of the Republic of Texas Library at the Alamo in San Antonio.

and worked in San Antonio as free persons in spite of vociferous protestations from their former owners and supported by Mexican authorities. Indeed, in that same year of 1832, Texas officials initiated criminal proceedings against a posse of Anglo Texans led by Henry Brown that kidnapped five emancipated former slaves from the streets of San Antonio.[46] In their own lives, slaves experienced very vividly the clash between state and market.

Native Americans were also drawn into the centralist–federalist wrangle in interesting ways. While much research still needs to be done to understand fully how the ongoing rebellion in Coahuila and Texas played out within the various Indian communities, Native Americans could hardly fail to notice the heightened attention that they received from rival non-Indian factions. The experience of the Texas Cherokees is a good case in point. Since 1831, the federal government had authorized the Cherokee nation to establish a settlement on a fixed tract of land on the headwaters of the Trinity and the banks of the Sabine. But the Cherokees' lack of money and expertise in navigating the Mexican land bureaucracy, as well as Mexico's proverbial political instability and consequent personnel changes, delayed the formalization of the Cherokee grant. Further delays occurred because the projected Cherokee grant overlapped with David G. Burnet's and Vicente Filisola's *empresario* contracts.[47] In August 1834, the Cherokees, on behalf of several Indian groups, complained of this state of affairs to President Santa Anna:

> We, the Red People, brothers of the Mexicans, emigrated to this country about eight years ago, and our Father the President of Mexico promised to give us land in which to raise our children and sent us documents that we have in our hands. We have eagerly kept peace and friendship with our Great Father the President; and since we have been waiting for a long time for our Great Father, the President, to show us the territories that he shall give us, we feel troubled for we have not been able to build good houses nor plow large fields until the land in which we shall live in friendship with our Great Father is shown to us.[48]

By 1835, the Cherokee nation was beset both by encroaching Anglo colonists and by a Mexican land system rendered downright chaotic by the struggle between state and federation. Both federalists and centralists sought to reassure the Cherokees and win them over to their side with land offers and other proposals.[49] For example, in the summer of 1835, the commander of the Eastern Interior Provinces commissioned Vicente Córdova, a resident of Nacogdoches, and Manuel Flores to "raise the Indians as auxiliaries to the National Army." In his report, Córdova claimed that he had obtained

---

[46] Miguel Arciniegas to *jefe político* of San Antonio, Austin, Jun 11, 1832, BA 150, 723–5.

[47] Everett, *The Texas Cherokees*, 62–6.

[48] Shoneys, Cherokees, Kikappus, Muscogas, or Creeks to President Santa Anna, Nacogdoches, Aug 25, 1834, BP 40:673, 5.

[49] *Jefe político* of Nacogdoches to Governor of Coahuila and Texas, Nacogdoches, Feb 6, 1835, BP 40:673, 7.

from the Cherokees a solemn promise to unite with the Mexican government, but gave no details.[50] Barely a few weeks later, James Bowie met with Chief Bowles, asking for an alliance or at least assurances that the Cherokees would remain neutral in the eventuality of a conflict between Anglo-American colonists and Mexican troops.[51] Mexican military agents continued to court the Cherokees for the ostensible purpose of chastising the Comanches, while Anglo-Texan agents – most notably Sam Houston, who boasted a twenty-five-year-long association with the western Cherokees – sought to forestall such an alliance.[52] We can only guess at what transpired within the intervillage council at this turning point. But such contacts and solicitations and the possibility of pursuing different alliances paved the way for the emergence of pro-Mexican and pro-Anglo-Texan wings within the Cherokee nation.[53]

TOWARD SECESSION

The third and final moment in the history of shifting loyalties in Texas took place in the winter and early spring of 1835–6. As President Santa Anna marched toward Coahuila and Texas at the head of six thousand Mexican soldiers to compel obedience from the wayward state, the peoples of Texas pondered many difficult questions ranging from sheer survival and protection of property to weighty considerations of loyalty. While a blow-by-blow account of this tumultuous period is beyond the scope of this book, I do intend to trace a remarkable set of loyalty shifts occurring against the backdrop of repeated military clashes.[54]

The separation of Texas from Mexico occurred during these critical months, but not according to Governor Viesca's original plan. In fact, what little authority Coahuila politicians may have had over Texas all but disappeared through the summer and fall of 1835. Governor Viesca's bold attempt to move the seat of the state government to San Antonio resulted in utter failure. Centralist troops managed to capture Viesca and his entourage before they reached Texas. At the same time, Colonel Cos effectively moved to disband the Monclova legislature. Meanwhile, in Texas, the speculators who had participated in the desperate Monclova land transactions in April and May lost credibility and fell in disgrace. By the fall, few traces of Monclova's power remained. When Governor Viesca – having bribed his way out of prison – finally arrived at Goliad on November 11, 1835, he was unable to

[50] Vicente Córdova to Manuel Flores, n.p., Jul 19, 1835, PTR 1, 256–7.
[51] James Bowie to Rueg, Natches, Aug 3, 1835, BHC 2q309, 249, 112–13.
[52] Everett, *The Texas Cherokees*, 68–70.
[53] Ibid., 75–85.
[54] For a fuller treatment of these events, see Lack's thorough treatment in *The Texas Revolutionary Experience*.

reassert his authority. Philip Dimmitt, the local military commander, simply refused to accord the visitor any official status, let alone recognize him as governor.[55] Texas had completely severed its ties to Coahuila and was ready to act independently. Three groups came to fill the power vacuum: Anglo-American colonists, Mexican federalist leaders of national stature who hoped to use Texas as a springboard for a broad counteroffensive against Santa Anna's centralist regime, and tejanos.

Through the summer and fall of 1835, Anglo-American colonists continued to be gravely split not only between those who wished to continue living under the Mexican flag but upholding the 1824 Constitution, the "peace party," and those who favored independence altogether, the "war party," but also along several other lines: recent arrivals versus old settlers, property owners versus landless volunteers, merchants versus land owners, Department of Brazos versus Department of Nacogdoches, and other such cleavages.[56] Still, most Anglo-Texan colonies perceived the political situation to be dangerous enough as to warrant collective action and thus agreed to send delegates to a grand council to be held in November, where representatives from all Texas communities would discuss the most appropriate course of action.

The electoral process leading up to the November consultation gives us an idea of the sea change taking place among Anglo-Texan colonists with regard to loyalty to Mexico. In essence, the peace party headed by Austin and his allies – many of them landowners with strong ties to the Mexican federalist faction, such as Henry Austin, his brother-in-law James F. Perry, Austin's former secretary and business partner Samuel Williams, James Grant, and others – lost ground. They were depicted as the "gentleman candidates," whereas the war party – directed by William H. Wharton and his brother John, Henry Smith, Carlos Barrett, and others – successfully portrayed themselves as the "People's Ticket."[57] And even beyond the elections, this populist strain remained central to the emerging ideology of emancipation. Recent immigrants such as John Sowers Brooks bluntly spoke against landowners and *empresarios*, whose "influence with the prominent Mexicans enables them to govern the Colony as they desire." As he saw it, independence would secure the public domain "for the General Good of the bone and Sinew of our Country the Actual Settlers."[58]

Although the resolutions of the November consultation were inconclusive, reflecting the parity of forces represented, it is evident that an ideological ferment for independence was taking hold among Anglo-American colonists. By the time of the convention in early March of 1836, the pro-independence

---

[55] Dimmitt to Austin, Fortress of Goliad, Nov 13, 1835, PTR 2, 389–92.
[56] Lack, *The Texas Revolutionary Experience*, 38–74.
[57] Ibid., 45–7.
[58] John Sowers Brooks quoted in Lack, *The Texas Revolutionary Experience*, 58.

sentiment had become so powerful that the heretofore burning question of separation from Mexico was no longer burning, and the faction in favor of the 1824 Constitution managed only a token resistance, if that.[59] Perceived as a landed aristocracy with shady connections to the Mexican political elite, peace party members lost influence. The disrepute of the "speculating party" (as the peace party became known) allowed those who favored complete independence from Mexico to gain the upper hand. For the majority of Anglo Texans, fighting alongside Mexican federalists seemed at best a futile undertaking, and at worst it meant supporting a handful of landowners to preserve a system of privilege. If Mexican federalism was not an option, Mexican centralism was even less so. It is significant that centralism found absolutely no support among Anglo-American colonists in spite of Colonel Cos's initial assurances that the national government merely wanted to restore order and was not ill disposed toward Anglo Americans. Yet centralism was so contrary to the colonists' interests that it was simply beyond their realm of possibilities. Even the Mexican-leaning peace party actually advocated rebellion against the centralist regime. News of Santa Anna's impending occupation of Texas only helped to conjure more forcefully the prevailing images of naked despotism, an imagery that harked back to the American Revolution and the quest for freedom from faraway and oppressive governments. By the time the convention was held, pro-independence ideologues had fashioned a popular rhetoric brimming in parallels to the American epic; Santa Anna was likened to a British monarch, and Anglo Texans were transmuted into harbingers of a new world.[60]

Also, the military engagements that took place in the San Antonio region during the winter of 1835 bolstered the case for independence (see Figure 5.2). Warfare necessarily drew attention to ethnic and racial differences. Even though at least three tejano companies were fighting alongside the colonists, Anglo-American troops, and especially recently arrived American volunteers, grew suspicious as they fought in a predominantly Hispanic setting surrounded by people who spoke a different language. Military men carried into the convention a strong conviction of the ethnic incompatibility between Anglos and Mexicans and brandished theories about the unfitness of the Mexican character for self-government and republican institutions. These ideas were presented as compelling reasons to declare the independence of Texas.[61]

The question of separation from Mexico was much more difficult for Mexican liberals and tejanos. In September 1835, Zavala told Austin that the issue of independence should not be treated at that moment. Zavala

[59] Lack, *The Texas Revolutionary Experience*, 85.
[60] Even contemporary historians are drawn to these parallels. See T. R. Fehrenbach, *Lone Star: A History of Texas and the Texans* (New York: Wings Books, 1968), 174–5.
[61] Lack, *The Texas Revolutionary Experience*, 86.

FIGURE 5.2. The Alamo

proposed instead to draft a declaration to the effect that Texas would defend its rights under the social contract of 1824 and would rejoin the Mexican confederation only as a free and independent state. Zavala's proposal allowed Texas to take independent action, but only if "after the passage of a certain period (say two years) the Mexican states do not recover their freedom."[62] In November, Gómez Farías still defended the national character of the Texas Revolution: "the reports are false, entirely false, that the Texans want to dismember the Mexican territory."[63] As late as December, Mexican federalists still clung to the idea that Anglo Texans were genuinely fighting for federalism. Addressing the citizens of San Antonio, General José Antonio Mexía exclaimed:

Companions! They deceive you who inform you that the Texians [Anglo Texans] wish a separation from the Mexican Federation, therefore do not believe it, what they desire is what I and all Federalists desire, that is the Constitution of 1824 and that we should not be governed neither by friars nor by aristocrats."[64]

When the declaration of independence finally occurred in early March, there was a grave split among Mexican federalists. One high-ranking federalist from New Orleans broke the news to his lover: "I cannot describe to you my anger upon learning that the Texan colonists who had pronounced themselves for the federal constitution now only aspire to become independent."

---

[62] Zavala to Austin, Lynchburg, Sep 17, 1835, PTR 1, 453–54.
[63] Gómez Farías to Estevan Moctezuma, n.p., Nov 7, 1835, PTR 2, 346.
[64] Mexía to the besieged forces in San Antonio, n.p., Dec 1835, PTR 3, 205.

FIGURE 5.3. Lorenzo de Zavala

The writer observed that General Mexía became furious and together with General Martín Peraza left the place saying that "he was Mexican by birth, and would never consent to his country's dismemberment."[65] But the union of federalists and centralists against Anglo Texans and reversion to primeval inter-ethnic warfare, which Austin feared, never materialized. Zavala continued in Texas, became a delegate at the convention of 1836 that declared the independence of Texas, and was then elected vice president of the Republic of Texas (see Figure 5.3). He explained his feelings after the battle of San Jacinto:

Very difficult matters have been offered for our discussion, and I, a Mexican by birth and always partial to my native country, have been torn between opposing duties and sentiments. In the end, I believe I have satisfied my sacred obligations to my new country and my feeling of natural sympathy of the Mexicans.... There is a very strong party here in favor of union with the United States. I am of the same opinion, for by this action, the stability of our government will be assured and because I believe it will be very difficult for Texas to march alone among the other independent nations."[66]

[65] "El desterrado" to his lover, New Orleans, Feb 26, 1836, NA 2q311, 253, 126–9.
[66] Zavala to Mexía, Velasco, May 26, 1836, PTR 6, 384.

FIGURE 5.4. Colonel Juan Nepomuceno Seguín

Many tejanos remained loyal to Texas even as secession from Mexico became permanent. As we saw, tejanos were politically quite active during the early phases of the federalist uprising in Coahuila and Texas through the fall of 1835. As the conflict intensified and as the possibility of military engagements became a reality, some tejanos undoubtedly opted to remain on the sidelines as a logical survival strategy. But still a conspicuous group of tejano leaders made the transition from federalist supporters to backers of independence. The Seguín family provided crucial direction. Old Erasmo Seguín supplied large numbers of cattle to feed the insurgents. Juan Nepomuceno Seguín (see Figure 5.4) raised a tejano volunteer army to fight the national troops.[67]

José Casiano turned over his house and store to the Anglo troops that took possession of San Antonio in the winter of 1835. Casiano's house was used as a hospital, and the wounded were supplied from his store. Posing as a merchant, he went to Matamoros in March of 1836 to spy on the movements of Santa Anna's troops.[68] José Antonio Navarro and Francisco Ruiz, more than anyone else, symbolized the alliance between tejanos and Anglo Texans. They were chosen to represent the Béxar district in the convention in Washington-on-the-Brazos and signed the Texas declaration of

---

[67] Lack, *The Texas Revolutionary Experience*, ch. 10; de la Teja, *A Revolution Remembered*, introduction. For a brief account of the military participation of tejanos, see Stephen L. Hardin, "Efficient in the Cause," in Poyo, *Tejano Journey*, 49–71.

[68] José Casiano to Tribunal for the Adjudication and Settlement of Claims, San Antonio, Feb 26, 1839, Comptroller of Public Accounts Collection, Audited Civil Claims, Box 2, Folder 72, Texas State Archives; *acta levantada por Don José Casiano . . . .*, Apr 16, 1836, Casiano-Pérez Collection, DRT 2: 71.

independence. It is said that Navarro "hesitated in the course which he was about to take, he had an ardent desire to establish a free government for Texas, and yet he trembled at the thought of having to sanction with his signature the eternal separation of Texas from the mother country." In his later years, Navarro was often heard to say that he had been one of the last in the convention to agree to sign the declaration of independence.[69] In December 1836, Francisco Ruiz wrote to his son-in-law: "[D]o not oppose the Texans under any circumstance and advise your friends to do the same, only the power of God will return the territory of Texas to the Mexican government, Texas has arms and money for her defense and will be free forever."[70]

How justified were the high-sounding epithets of "traitors" or "ungrateful" employed by centralist leaders to describe those who acquiesced in the separation of Texas from Mexico? The centralist rhetoric emphasized collective identities based on religion, or linguistic and ethnic solidarity, or merely pointed to the fact that Texas had been an administrative unit of New Spain and Mexico for more than one hundred years. And yet the experience of tejano merchants and landowners and Mexican liberals like Zavala demonstrates that below these collective identities there were deep-running political and ideological convictions as well as pecuniary interests that were also central in determining peoples' loyalties and ultimately their national identity. As much as tejanos were reluctant to forsake their old collective definitions, they were also well adapted to the rough frontier environment where the need to safeguard one's interests and sheer survival had shaped life for generations. If, as Benedict Anderson would have it, the nation is an imagined community, Texas shows that tangible forces underpinned such imaginings. The end of the Texas Revolution did not settle once and for all the identity struggles of Texans. Shifting economic conditions and political instability both in Mexico and in the newly created Republic of Texas continued to plague them for several years, most notably during the two Mexican military occupations of San Antonio in 1842 and in the controversy over the annexation of Texas to the United States.[71] For tejanos, especially, the fundamental tension between their origins, traditions, and culture on the one hand, and the preservation of their interests on the other, continued throughout their lives.

---

[69] Taken from Homer S. Thrall, *A History of Texas* (New York: University Publishing, 1885), 121. Fritz disputes this idea: "José Antonio Navarro," 33–4.

[70] Francisco Ruiz to Blas Herrera, Columbia, Dec 27, 1836, Texas State Archives, Box 2-22/711.

[71] For instance, see Timothy M. Matovina, "Between Two Worlds," and Gerald E. Poyo, "Conclusion," in Poyo, *Tejano Journey*, 73–87, 125–32.

6

The Fate of Governor Albino Pérez

Colonel Albino Pérez had few – if any – inklings of the gruesome fate that awaited him in New Mexico in the summer of 1837. He came from a different world, having spent a lifetime in central Mexico merely trying to jumpstart his sagging military and political career. Before reaching the upper Rio Grande, his most pressing concern had been his seemingly uncanny ability to associate himself with losing factions. In the 1828 presidential election, he had supported the candidacy of Manuel Gómez Pedraza to the extent of commanding a group of thirty dragoons on election day given to the task of "inducing" people to vote for the right candidate.[1] Even though Gómez Pedraza actually won that election, the victorious candidate was quickly and unceremoniously banished from the country. Colonel Pérez then hitched his wagon to the rising political star of General Anastasio Bustamante. He appears as one of the signatories of the *pronunciamiento* issued by the pro-Bustamante reserve army of Jalapa on December 4, 1829. This was his first successful gamble, as Bustamante was catapulted to the presidency, but it turned out to be a short-lived victory. In 1832, we find Colonel Pérez fighting in the environs of the hacienda of Buenavista on behalf of Bustamante's tottering government, once again on the losing side.[2]

Colonel Pérez's big break occurred in the spring of 1835, when President Santa Anna – Bustamante's nemesis, ironically – appointed him both as governor and military commander of New Mexico. We ignore whether Colonel Pérez considered the appointment as a promotion by virtue of the rank or as punishment on account of its geographic remoteness. Whatever the case, he was determined to make the most of his tour of duty in the Far North. He did not hesitate to derive material advantages from his position as governor, coaxing local Anglo-American merchants and rich nuevomexicanos

[1] Zavala, *Ensayo Histórico de las Revoluciones de México desde 1808 hasta 1830*, 2: 48–9.
[2] Ibid., 237, 306; José María Bocanegra, *Memorias para la historia de México independiente, 1822–1846*, 3 vols (Mexico City: ICH-INEHRM-FCE, 1986), 2: 343.

into extending him large loans and generous terms. By all accounts, Colonel Pérez was quite fond of expensive clothes (velvet pantaloons, fur capes, a silver-embroidered jacket, and so on) and imposing furniture.[3] To unsuspecting New Mexicans, Colonel Pérez appeared as an imperious and somewhat extravagant outsider better suited for the fast-paced social life and political intrigue of central Mexico than for the rigors of the frontier.

In addition to enlarging his wardrobe, Colonel Pérez intended to show his political and administrative acumen by weaving New Mexico peacefully but firmly into Mexico's emerging centralist order. Barely a month after his arrival, Colonel Pérez gave an inaugural address in which he congratulated himself for the "thousand proofs of docility, love of order, and subjection to justice" of New Mexicans, reminding them in no uncertain terms of the complete victory that the supreme government's army, commanded by President Santa Anna himself, had obtained over the federalist forces of Zacatecas.[4] In the next few months, Colonel Pérez emerged as an effective political operator. New Mexicans could not help but be electrified by news of the ongoing insurrection in neighboring Coahuila and Texas, but to the governor's credit, the department remained absolutely quiet. Moreover, as President Santa Anna marched with an army to quell the Texas rebels, Colonel Pérez accomplished a major political coup by persuading New Mexicans to pledge allegiance to the centralist constitution. While the governor may have exaggerated somewhat when he stated in his report that New Mexicans had sworn allegiance to the new constitution "with great enthusiasm," at least such ceremonies were not marred by violence or widespread opposition, as happened elsewhere in Mexico.[5] Governor Pérez also deserves credit for preserving the peace in New Mexico through 1836 while the nation experienced the worst string of calamities in its short history: the defeat and capture of President Santa Anna at the battle of San Jacinto, a national government in disarray, and the permanent secession of Texas from Mexico.

Unfortunately, just when Colonel Pérez was getting ready to end a decidedly successful term in New Mexico, his proverbial bad luck struck back with a vengeance. What started out as a local protest in the town of Santa

---

[3] Governor Pérez was not the first nor the last New Mexican governor to borrow against tax receipts. For Governor Pérez's lifestyle, see Janet Lecompte, *Rebellion in Río Arriba, 1837* (Albuquerque, NM: University of New Mexico Press, 1985), 80–3.

[4] Inaugural address of Albino Pérez, Santa Fe, Jun 20, 1835, Read Collection 240, NMSARC. No one in New Mexico was in doubt about Colonel Pérez's political sympathies. But a few days before, he had ordered a gargantuan celebration in Santa Fe over the crushing defeat of the Zacatecas federalists. The celebration had included cannon shots, wild bell tolls (*repique salvaje*), a special lighting to the city, and masses of gratitude. See report of the *ayuntamiento*, Albuquerque, Jul 10, 1835, MANM 19, 836; report of *ayuntamiento*, Abiquiú, Jul 21, 1835, MANM 19, 840–1.

[5] See Albino Pérez to Minister of the Interior and Exterior, Santa Fe, Dec 31, 1835; *acta levantada con motivo del juramento de la nueva constitución*, Santa Fe, Jan 5, 1836; *acta . . .*, Santa Cruz de la Cañada, Dec 14, 1835, all in AGN, Gobernación, Leg 154, Folder 8.

Cruz de la Cañada in the Río Arriba district soon snowballed into a full-fledged anticentralist rebellion that came to engulf the entire northern half of New Mexico. Governor Pérez had little choice but to gather all the forces he could muster – a handful of regular officers and some two hundred volunteers, mostly Pueblo Indians – and attempt to negotiate. On August 7, 1837, Colonel Pérez rode out of Santa Fe at the head of a modest column to meet his fate. As it turned out, upon encountering the rebels, most of his volunteer force deserted on the spot and joined the rebellious party. Miraculously, Colonel Pérez managed a desperate retreat with a few members of his retinue, but was captured the next day in the outskirts of Santa Fe as he was trying to make his way farther south to Albuquerque. According to one account, the governor put up a formidable fight, but was finally brought to the ground, having been lanced and wounded on several occasions. His pulse of life was still beating when the enraged rebels cut off his head and paraded it on a pike near the church of Nuestra Señora del Rosario.[6] The furious crowd surrounded the macabre pole and kept hurling threats and insults at it: "Ah, you robber! You will no longer extort taxes, you will no longer drink chocolate or coffee!"[7]

For a few months in late 1837 and early 1838 New Mexico seemed to be following in the very footsteps of the Lone Star Republic. Comparisons between the Texas Revolution and the Chimayó Rebellion became unavoidable. For Lieutenant Colonel Cayetano Justiniani, commander of a squadron of Chihuahua dragoons dispatched to New Mexico at the height of the rebellion, the "wretched ideas" that had inspired the New Mexican insurgency were "the same as those of the perverse adventurers of Texas."[8] Writing from Mexico City, New Mexico's vicar, Father Juan Felipe Ortiz, ventured a similar opinion:

I almost don't spend an hour of the day without brooding over the lamentable circumstances in which that unfortunate land finds itself . . . it seems evident to me that the people of Río Arriba move hand in hand with the adventurers of Texas, and the conduit to carry out these relations is probably the foreigner [Charles] Bent, of whom there are enough antecedents to believe this and a lot more.[9]

Like Texas, New Mexico was a frontier province that had been fundamentally transformed by the onslaught of Anglo-American commercialism (see Chapter 3). Just like Texans, New Mexicans had agonized over the rise of

---

[6] William Ritch, History of New Mexico from 1527 to 1837, Santa Fe, 1880, Ritch Collection, NMSARC, reel 10.

[7] Lecompte, *Rebellion in Río Arriba*, 34.

[8] Lieutenant Colonel Cayetano Justiniani to Minister of War and Navy, Chihuahua, Sep 12, translated in Lecompte, *Rebellion in Río Arriba*, 110.

[9] Juan Felipe Ortiz to Manuel Armijo, Mexico City, Dec 19, 1837, Donaciano Vigil Collection.

centralism, unveiling a deep-seated antagonism between patriotic and suspicious federal administrators (best represented by Governor Pérez himself)
and some people of the frontier who pressed for greater local autonomy.
And just like Texas, New Mexico finally burst into open rebellion in 1837–
8, rejecting centralism, repudiating the national government, and putting
in the balance the very permanence of New Mexico within the Mexican
fold.

Yet here the similarities end. New Mexico did not embark on a secessionist course, but in fact emerged from this insurrectionary period ever more
firmly attached to the Mexican nation. New Mexico's 1837–8 rebellion galvanized tremendous opposition within the department, helping to revitalize
the military, prompting parish priests to play significant political roles, and
leading to a reorganization of the civil administration that would result in a
durable political coalition that would rule the destinies of New Mexico for
the next ten years. Why such vastly different outcomes?

First, the two provinces differed administratively and demographically
in crucial ways. Whereas Coahuila and Texas had been organized as an
autonomous state since 1824, New Mexico had been ruled as territory directly under federal tutelage. Coahuiltejanos were thus able to claim a sphere
of independent action and self-determination that New Mexicans did not
possess. More importantly, Texas had been a late-blooming and rather impoverished Spanish and then Mexican outpost in the Far North. Its scant
Spanish-speaking population and emerging institutions could barely constitute a significant dike against the concerted action of the majority Anglo-
American and indigenous population. By contrast, New Mexico was a far
more successful extension of Spain in the heart of North America. Not only
was New Mexico Spain's first northern outpost, but it had always been the
largest and most prosperous, and Anglo Americans remained a distinct minority (see Chapter 1).

These considerations partly account for the different revolutionary paths
followed by Texas and New Mexico. But such broad-brush distinctions fail
to capture the deeper parallels and lessons that can be drawn. Ultimately,
Mexico's federalist–centralist rivalry threw the inhabitants of these two frontier provinces into remarkably similar dilemmas about national loyalty and
identity. Moreover, such revolutionary tensions between metropolis and
frontier did not result in clear-cut ethnic antagonisms but led to surprising cross-ethnic coalitions. And finally, the different outcomes of the Texas
Revolution and the Chimayó Rebellion underscore the fact that nothing was
preordained about how these revolutionary upheavals would be resolved.
Instead of interpreting the Texas Revolution as an early expression of Manifest Destiny – that inexorable force that would ultimately give the United
States over half of Mexico's territory – the New Mexican case points to the
historical contingency of such rebellions as they affected the all-too-delicate
balance between centralization and autonomy, between state and market.

CENTRALISM AS LIVED EXPERIENCE

Janet Lecompte, the most insightful student of New Mexico's 1837–8 rebellion, warns us that the rebellion does not have a straightforward explanation: "... it was not a class or race war, not poor against rich, nor Río Arriba against Río Abajo, nor Indian against white, although these tensions existed."[10] What was it then? Let's begin with a puzzling *pronunciamiento*, the only surviving document that spells out the goals of the movement:

Long live God and the Nation and the faith of Jesus Christ, for the most important issues that they stand for are as follows:

1. To be with God and the Nation and the faith of Jesus Christ.
2. To defend our country until the last drop of blood is shed to achieve the desired victory.
3. Not to allow the Departmental Plan.
4. Not to allow any taxes.
5. Not to permit the excesses of those who attempt to carry this out.

God and the Nation, Santa Cruz de la Cañada, August 1, 1837, in camp.[11]

Apart from a tantalizing religious element that we shall soon consider, the *pronunciamiento* amounts to a rejection of the centralist blueprint known in New Mexico as the Departmental Plan. For months, Governor Pérez had been selling the Plan to local skeptics with the argument that New Mexico would no longer be constituted as a second-rate (infant or somehow wanting) administrative unit – that is, a territory without autonomy and ruled from Mexico City – but would instead be "elevated" to the rank of "department" along with all other states.[12]

In principle, the Plan seemed beneficial for territories like New Mexico, as the national government would henceforth stop making demeaning distinctions. But in truth, the Departmental Plan did not so much "elevate" territories to statelike status as "demote" states to something below territorial level. According to the 1836 centralist constitution, "departments" would be ruled by governors appointed from Mexico City and not elected as before, and state legislatures – notoriously independent, as the case of Coahuila and Texas well illustrates – would be replaced by five-person councils or *juntas departamentales* with mostly advisory functions. None of these changes meant much for New Mexicans, who were already under the aegis of the national government. But the Departmental Plan also centralized power *inside* each department, abolishing municipal autonomy and subjecting virtually

---

[10] Lecompte, *Rebellion in Río Arriba*, 45.
[11] This revolutionary proclamation was located in the Benjamin Read Papers. It was a copy made in 1853 from the original. The proclamation was then included in the microfilm edition of the Mexican Archives of New Mexico, MANM 24, 807. The translation is mine.
[12] Governor Pérez to citizens, May 9, 1837, MANM 23, 721.

all communities to the authority of prefects who were directly responsible to the governor.[13]

From the vantage point of fiercely independent New Mexican *ayuntamientos*, the Departmental Plan, far from the much-touted "elevation" heralded by Governor Pérez, turned out to be a precipitous fall and a devastating blow to accepted political practice. Indeed, the rebellion began improbably when the district prefect attempted to suspend Juan José Esquibel, the feisty alcalde of Santa Cruz de la Cañada, for failing to imprison a man who turned out to be a relative of the alcalde. A few days later, Governor Pérez ordered the dissolution of the entire *ayuntamiento* of Santa Cruz de la Cañada on the grounds that some of its members were related by blood. Thus began the Chimayó Rebellion, as Esquibel ignored the interventionist departmental authorities, formed a twelve-member war council known as the *Cantón de la Cañada*, and on August 1, 1837, issued the fateful *pronunciamiento*.

The Departmental Plan was not only intended to centralize power but was also aimed at improving the finances of the national government. New Mexico had been exempted from direct taxation given its territorial status and the peculiar defense burdens of an exposed frontier. Unfortunately, New Mexico's "elevation" to departmental rank also implied, at least formally, the loss of this fiscal privilege, as it would be treated just like all other departments. At first Colonel Pérez was confident that the federal government would ultimately spare New Mexicans from having to contribute to the national treasury. But on April 17, 1837, the national government issued a decree organizing the collection of rents and appointing revenue officials; no exemption was made for New Mexico. Governor Pérez did not acknowledge receipt of a copy of the decree for almost three months, but finally in early July he began discussing the implications of the law with the acting *subcomisario*.[14] It is hard to explain just why taxation unleashed such a fierce storm considering that ordinary New Mexicans and Pueblo Indians like those who became actively involved in the rebellion would have had to contribute modestly if at all. A contemporary Anglo-American merchant attempted to account for this discrepancy by pointing out that New Mexicans were completely unacquainted with the *principle* of direct taxation: "... they would sooner have paid a *doblón* [gold coin worth about sixteen dollars] through a tariff than a *real* [silver coin worth about twelve cents of a dollar] in direct taxes."[15] Other witnesses, and most historians ever since, have emphasized the impact of outlandish rumors circulating among New Mexicans with regard to the new tax code. It was said that the new tax burden would amount to half of a family's property, a third of the fruits of their labor, or it would impose fees for the use of water, pasture, wood; some went so far as to assert that "husbands would be compelled to pay for the

---

[13] Weber, *The Mexican Frontier*, 33–4.
[14] Lecompte, *Rebellion in Río Arriba*, 17–18.
[15] Gregg, *Commerce of the Prairies*, 122.

privilege of sleeping with their wives."[16] Either New Mexicans were very gullible, Governor Pérez made a fatal mistake by failing to communicate effectively and promptly the contents of the new tax code, or political opponents seized on the impending introduction of a new tax to propagate wild rumors meant to discredit the Departmental Plan as a whole. Regardless of their true origin, these rumors did galvanize opposition. While in Coahuila and Texas the loss of state autonomy had been the key rallying cry, in New Mexico taxation made tangible the reality of centralism.

Besides being patently anticentralist, the Chimayó Rebellion possessed obvious religious overtones (another notable difference from the Texas Revolution). In the proclamation of Santa Cruz de la Cañada, the rebels protested to be with God and Jesus Christ. In subsequent communications, the insurgents affirmed that God had inspired the movement and that they had "unsheathed the sword to defend the law and inflict the just punishment ordered by the Omnipotent."[17] On the surface, early priestly participation may account for such recurring religious rhetoric. Had not Father Miguel Hidalgo, in his quest for independence, employed such religious imagery to dramatic effect in 1810? Curate Francisco Madariaga of Tomé became actively involved in the original plot to overthrow Governor Pérez. The curate succinctly stated his political motivations in a letter to his brother in Chihuahua: ". . . on the 9th of this month (and seduced by some people that I leave unnamed since I count myself among them) the First District with all its Indian Pueblos rebelled in favor of the Federation."[18] The parish priest of Taos, Antonio José Martínez, was another early backer of the rebellion, even attending a rebel meeting in the aftermath of the assassination of Governor Pérez.[19] But such early priestly support quickly evaporated when it became clear that a major goal of the rebellion was to challenge the authority of the Catholic establishment itself, specifically with regard to church fees and regulations that forbade burials inside churches. Thus the Chimayó Rebellion opens a fascinating window into the worldviews of ordinary New Mexican Catholics, who were ill at ease with the reforms that the bishopric of Durango had been vigorously introducing in New Mexico for years (see Chapter 2). The protestations to be with God and Jesus Christ and the overall tone of religious self-righteousness stems directly from the movement's affirmation of New Mexican popular Catholicism even as it flew in the face of Church reformism.

---

[16] William Ritch, History of New Mexico from 1527 to 1837, Santa Fe, 1880, Ritch Collection, NMSRCA, roll 10. Lecompte, *Rebellion in Río Arriba*, 18.

[17] Circular to San Francisco del Rancho de Taos, Río Chiquito, Pueblo de Taos, Arroyo Seco, Plaza de San Antonio de Montes y Ranchitos; Santa Cruz de la Cañada, Aug 3, 1837, Donaciano Vigil Papers, NMSRCA.

[18] Curate Francisco Madariaga to Agustín Avellano, Tomé, Aug 12, 1837, in ASDF, File 1225, microfilm edition at the Bancroft Library, reel 28.

[19] Lecompte, *Rebellion in Río Arriba*, 41.

Devout New Mexicans came to believe that the salvation of their souls depended on strict adherence to certain rituals, especially the burial of the dead in the interiors of churches, where the force of prayer and proximity to sacred places could effect the deceased's salvation. New Mexicans had – literally – lived and prayed among the rotting flesh and disintegrating bones of the dead since the sixteenth century.[20] Physical proximity was essential, and so New Mexicans for generations had gone to great lengths and expenses to bury their loved ones underneath their local churches and missions as close to the altar as possible. But, alas, in the late-eighteenth century, a reformist Spanish monarchy and Church hierarchy, driven by public health concerns, began issuing ordinances requiring burials in outlying cemeteries and thus sending shock waves throughout the Spanish Empire. New Mexican Catholics tenaciously resisted the cemetery reforms for half a century. But the vigorous spiritual administration of Bishop Zubiría brought things to a head. Not only did the energetic bishop wish to make New Mexicans comply with the cemetery ordinances once and for all, at the same time he attempted to put the New Mexican Church on firmer financial footing by urging priests to charge higher fees for sacramental services like baptisms, marriages, and burials. These sources of Church revenue became all the more critical after the Mexican government abolished the citizens' legal obligation to pay tithes in 1833.

For ordinary New Mexican Catholics, the upshot was that the eternal salvation of their souls became costlier and more difficult to attain. And their pent-up frustration erupted violently during the Chimayó Rebellion. In Santa Cruz de la Cañada – the very cradle of the rebellion – a group of rebels forced Father Fernando Ortiz, at gunpoint, to allow burials inside the church. They also let the priest know that he should expect no contributions from the faithful except *primicias* (first fruits).[21] In spite of his early support for the rebellion, Father Martínez of Taos fared no better:

On the eleventh of the month [September] I was made to appear in a room in which they had a table with the city councilmen around it, and on all sides were rows of men with their weapons ready and pointed at me: In this way they made me give up the collection of sacramental fees, and the charges for baptisms, marriages and burials; they wanted to eliminate the contributions toward the church building funds, and bury all the dead in the church, to which I said that this was not in my jurisdiction, that if they attempted it by violence and force, I alone could not defend against it.[22]

---

[20] Martina E. Will, "God Gives and God Takes Away: Death and Dying in New Mexico, 1760–1850," Ph.D. dissertation, University of New Mexico, 2000, passim.

[21] Lecompte, *Rebellion in Río Arriba*, 21. Some priests received a share of the tithe revenues. These revenues were known as *primicias*, or first fruits.

[22] Father Martínez to Bishop Zubiría, Taos, Sep 25, 1837, translated in Lecompte, *Rebellion in Río Arriba*, 125.

The Taos rebels also seized the church of El Rancho and the chapel of San Francisco de Asis and "buried a corpse by the steps of the chancel and followed this by doing whatever occurred to them which I could not prevent for no less a reason than I was threatened with death if I opposed it."[23] Faithful New Mexicans were boldly challenging their priests to uphold their own notions of Catholic propriety.

At the heart of popular Catholicism in northern New Mexico was the *Penitente* movement. We lack hard evidence to prove that the *Hermanos Penitentes* as an organization took part in the Chimayó Rebellion, yet some clues point toward them.[24] The *Penitentes* had long sought to fill the vacuum that the formal Catholic establishment had left during decades of neglect, developing a distinct way of dispensing spiritual comfort that included harsh penance and self-flagellation. Not surprisingly, the *Hermanos Penitentes* were among the first casualties of the Church's administrative reassertion of the early 1830s. As we saw in Chapter 2, Bishop Zubiría expressly outlawed the Brotherhood during his visit to northern New Mexico. Interestingly, the religious objectives of the Chimayó Rebellion jibed exceedingly well with those long advocated by the Brotherhood, as both movements stood in opposition to the new religious order imposed from Durango. The geography of the insurrection also matches what little we know about *Penitente* strongholds. Indeed, the epicenter of the rebellion and that of the Brotherhood were one and the same: Santa Cruz de la Cañada. But the most tangible evidence of *Penitente* involvement is a mysterious document that surfaced a few weeks after the assassination of Governor Pérez, entitled "Religious Dissertation." The goal of this text seemed to be to placate the Brotherhood and dissuade its members from taking part in the rebellious movement. The "Religious Dissertation" tells how on November 5, 1837, as the Pope was in the act of celebrating mass in the church of Saint Peter in Rome, a letter from Jesus Christ fell in the pontiff's hands. After brooding over the myriad evils committed in the world, the letter urged those involved in "ugly sin" to present themselves before the "Holly Tribunal of Penance," confess sincerely and with open hearts, and most especially "abstain from using my name in vain" – a likely reference to the allusions to God and Jesus Christ in the *pronunciamiento* of Santa Cruz de la Cañada.[25] The letter ended with a stern admonition against those reluctant to obey:

I will send a multitude of rabid dogs that will tear you to shreds, I will send hunger, pestilence, war ... and not even my Dear Mother nor Saint Catherine of Siena, nor Santa Teresa de Jesús, nor Santo Domingo, nor Saint Francis nor other Saints of Penitence [the entire *Penitente* Pantheon!] will mollify my punishment.[26]

[23] Ibid., 125.
[24] See Harvey Fergusson, *Rio Grande* (New York: Alfred A. Knopf, 1940), 192.
[25] "Religious Dissertation," n.p., Nov 5, 1837, University of New Mexico, Library Collection.
[26] Ibid.

The "Religious Dissertation" is a testament of the efforts of at least one religious leader, possibly a priest, seeking to dissuade *Penitente* participation by resorting to religious imagery.

Anticentralism and popular Catholicism may explain why scores of Creoles and *mestizos* joined the insurgency, but they hardly shed light on the revolutionary ardor of Pueblo Indians. Whatever else it may have been, the Chimayó Rebellion was also an indigenous uprising seemingly supported, in the words of one observer, by "the principal warriors of all the northern pueblos."[27] The eighteen men executed in the turmoil were all white Hispanics of the highest social standing, beginning with Governor Pérez, whereas the men carrying out the executions were overwhelmingly Indian. Understandably, for the duration of the insurrection, whites and *mestizos* were prone to conjuring up images of a race war made all the more real by accounts of the insurgents' weaponry – bows, arrows, and shields – and the gruesome killing of Governor Pérez and his top administrators. Revealingly, even though the governor died after several strokes so that it is impossible to ascertain who really killed him, in the popular imagination the perpetrator was a wiry-built Indian from Cochiti named Manuelito. He died an old man in 1875 and was widely known among nuevomexicanos as "the Indian who killed Governor Pérez." Equally haunting was the fate of the governor's corpse. He was beheaded and his scalp was then taken to Santa Cruz de la Cañada "to dance," an ancient Pueblo custom in which women would scornfully touch their private parts with the scalp or bare their buttocks to it in order to take the power away from the enemy.[28] Why was there such Pueblo antagonism to the established political and religious authorities? One possible answer has to do with the way in which New Mexico's indigenous population experienced the administration of Governor Pérez, especially compulsory and onerous militia service.[29]

The civic militia was a creation of a liberal age impressed with the image of the citizen-soldier who at certain times picked up his gun to defend his country and uphold its liberties and then went back to private life. The Spanish Crown first introduced militia forces in New Mexico, fearing that the veteran troops were not enough to protect the entire province. By 1808, New Mexico boasted three militia companies, each of sixty-nine men, and all three remained active at least for four years.[30] During the wars of independence, militia forces throughout the country grew in importance and acquired new political attributes. In large and independent states such as Zacatecas and

---

[27] Gregg, *Commerce of the Prairies*, 123.
[28] William Ritch, History of New Mexico from 1527 to 1837, Santa Fe, 1880, Ritch Collection, roll 10, NMSRCA; Deposition of Rosario Alvarado, Villa del Paso, Aug 30, 1837, ASDN, File 1225, reel 28. For the meaning of scalp dances, see Gutiérrez, *When Jesus Came*, 19–20.
[29] See also Weber, *The Mexican Frontier*, ch. 6.
[30] Pino, "Exposición," 229–30.

Coahuila and Texas, militias became guarantors of state sovereignty to the point of challenging the authority of the national government in the mid-1830s. In New Mexico, however, the chief task of volunteer forces was to fend off Indian hostilities on the rise since the 1810s. A witness from Chihuahua passed a hard judgment on New Mexico's system of volunteers: ". . . the civic militia, of so much interest in a free country and which is deemed the firmest bulwark of public liberty, is absolutely unknown in New Mexico, for they have not even a conception of it."[31]

The way in which state militias operated in New Mexico made them decidedly oppressive. Once the governor decided to carry out a punitive Indian campaign, he required each town and village to furnish a certain number of men. The alcalde was responsible for fulfilling the town's quota and was empowered to assign heavy fines and even jail those who failed to serve. Sadly, the recruiting system worked in such a way that a disproportionate part of the duty fell on the poor and the Pueblo Indians, as citizens with means generally bought their way out. Governor Francisco Sarracino, after embarking on one campaign, became so appalled that he lashed out against the alcaldes for pressing into service only "the most wretched individuals of their jurisdictions."[32] This was all the more burdensome because those who were pressed into service had to present themselves fully outfitted – some with horses and shotguns, the majority on foot and with bows, arrows, and shields. All were required to pay for their ammunition and food for the duration of the campaign, which was usually forty-five days but could last as long as two or even three months of "continuous and cruel warfare against the barbarous nations some of them already skilled in the use of rifles."[33] Juan Bautista Pino plainly recognized the injustice of the system:

> . . . this burden has no parallel in any other province . . . it is enough to say that many of these unfortunate souls are ruined in one single campaign, they are forced to sell their clothes and their families' clothes to supply themselves with ammunition and food. This horror gets to the point where they even have to sacrifice the freedom of their children to carry out their civic obligations.[34]

By the time Governor Pérez arrived in New Mexico, Pueblo Indians had long endured the militia system. But the mid-1830s witnessed a critical juncture in New Mexico–Indian relations, especially with the Navajo nation, resulting in a dramatic increase in Indian incursions and retaliatory campaigns. After eight years of nominal peace, the Navajos began open hostilities toward New Mexico in 1834. That August, Navajo parties could be spotted in the very outskirts of Santa Fe taking cattle and in one instance

[31] Barreiro, "Ojeada," 158.
[32] Proclamation of Governor Francisco Sarracino, Santa Fe, Jan 9, 1835, MANM 19, 620.
[33] Pino, "Exposición," 225.
[34] Ibid., 225–6.

killing four residents, including one alderman.[35] Governor Sarracino organized one aborted and one effective punitive expedition in 1834. In February 1835, before the planting season commenced, the governor ordered yet another campaign, which ended disastrously with the deaths of New Mexico's military commander, other officers, and scores of volunteers.[36] Upon taking the reins of government in New Mexico, Governor Pérez greatly expanded the war. Preceded by his military reputation and desiring to show New Mexicans and nomadic Indians alike his firm hand, he initially accepted but then rebuffed a Navajo peace offer. Moreover, increasing Apache incursions compounded New Mexico's problems. Between August and October of 1836, Colonel Pérez organized no fewer than three full-fledged military expeditions.[37] As usual, Pueblo Indians suffered the most. They not only were forced into temporary enslavement for the duration of each campaign, but also experienced great losses by virtue of leaving their fields unattended and unwillingly jeopardizing their commercial and other ties with the nomadic groups whom they were forced to fight. At the end of that fateful year of 1836, Governor Pérez organized a fourth expedition in the midst of one of the worst winters New Mexicans could remember.[38] This horrific episode would still be fresh in the mind of many New Mexicans when the Chimayó Rebellion broke out barely six months later.

On December 12, the day of the Virgin of Guadalupe, Governor Pérez departed from Santa Fe with 60 *veteranos* and 730 militia soldiers, a motley column of a few Creole horsemen riding in front, and groups of servants and Indians trailing behind. These were all the men the governor could muster even after threats and exertions. He had hoped to gather two thousand.[39] For almost two weeks, the men braved snowstorms before reaching New Mexico's last settlement to the west, the Pueblo of Zuñi, which was rumored to be in collusion with the Navajo. On Christmas Eve, the troops entered Zuñi and found it at peace. Yet fourteen soldiers were frostbitten and an old draftee, Francisco García, died that same night. Undaunted, Colonel Pérez left Zuñi three days later and headed for the Sierras, trying to engage the Navajo. After Colonel Pérez's troops traveled west of Cubero, storms became constant, and the snow on the ground at times reached up to the soldiers' chests. Horses had to make paths for those who went on foot behind. In early January, the troops finally reached a Navajo *ranchería*, engaging the enemy,

[35] Francisco Sarracino to Ministro de Relaciones Interiores y Exteriores, Santa Fe, Aug 31, 1834, MANM 18, 296–301.
[36] Ministro de Relaciones Interiores y Exteriores to Governor Sarracino, Mexico City, May 23, 1835, MANM 19, 356.
[37] Albino Pérez to Commandant General of Chihuahua, Santa Fe, Nov 1, 1836, MANM 19, 685–7.
[38] Ibid., 687.
[39] The following description is based on the governor's own report. See Albino Pérez to Commandant General of Chihuahua, Santa Fe, Feb 16, 1837, MANM 19, 690–701.

killing twenty, and taking three adult women and six children as prisoners. The volunteer force also recovered 7,300 sheep and a total of 98 horses and mules. But the cost had been enormous: One hundred and forty soldiers were frostbitten so badly that they lost toes and ears. It was so cold that nearly every night, between twenty and thirty of the sheep froze to death. In his report to the commandant general of Chihuahua, Governor Pérez admitted the enormous difficulties: "...if I were to recount to Your Excellency our hardships in detail, they would seem to you incredible."[40] New Mexicans, especially Pueblo Indians, would not easily forget. It is likely that one José Gonzales, who was commanding a group of Indians from Taos, is the same person who six months later would emerge as the leader of the Chimayó Rebellion and, for some time, revolutionary governor of New Mexico.[41]

THREE DEGREES OF SEPARATION

In less than two weeks in early August 1837, the *insurrectos* were rewarded with astonishing and total victory.[42] They dominated the entire Río Arriba district as well as New Mexico's capital and counted on support among the Pueblos of Río Abajo. The extraneous governor, his entire cabinet, and other key collaborators lay dead. And most important, the movement counted on the support of a popular army that some estimates put between three thousand and six thousand men. An individual from the Taos area named José Gonzales, nicknamed *el chepón*, surfaced at the head of the movement.[43] He

---

[40] Ibid., 701.

[41] The background and ethnicity of Governor José Gonzales is still a matter of dispute. See footnote 43. I have kept the original spelling of his name.

[42] By August 7–8, the rebels had soundly defeated the territorial volunteer force and had captured Governor Pérez, his entire cabinet, and several other administrators. Some of them were killed on the spot, whereas others were subsequently tried and executed. See Lecompte, *Rebellion in Río Arriba*, 19–34; deposition of Hugo Estevenson, El Paso, Sep 11, 1837, ASDN, File 1226, reel 28; anonymous, "An account of the Chimayó Rebellion," in Lecompte, *Rebellion in Río Arriba*, 99–100; William Ritch, History of New Mexico from 1527 to 1837, Santa Fe, 1880, Ritch Collection, NMSARC, reel 10; "juicio sobre la conducta de Donaciano Vigil en la revuleta de 1837...," Santa Fe, Jan 4, 1838, MANM 25, 518–20; testimony of Rosario Alvarado, Villa del Paso, Aug 30, 1838, ASDN, File 1225, reel 28; Circular to San Francisco del Rancho de Taos, Río Chiquito, Pueblo de Taos, Arroyo Seco, Plaza de San Antonio de Montes y Ranchitos; Santa Cruz de la Cañada, Aug 3, 1837, Donaciano Vigil Papers, NMSRCA.

[43] Historians have debated for more than a century the origins of this man. Swayed by the marked indigenous participation in the movement, early chroniclers of the rebellion such as W. W. H. Davis and Ralph E. Twitchell pronounced Governor Gonzales to be either a *genízaro* or a Pueblo Indian. More recently, Fray Angélico Chávez identified one José Angel Gonzales, a Taos genízaro, as the ephemeral governor of New Mexico. See Fray Angélico Chávez, "José Gonzales, Genizaro Governor," *New Mexico Historical Review* 30:3, 190–4. Lecompte has disputed this interpretation, claiming that it is probably safer to assume that Gonzales was either a *mestizo* or a Creole, even suggesting that he may have been the famous

had been instrumental in the defeat of Governor Pérez's troops and apparently had "received the custodial staff of the law by unanimous and popular vote."[44] He entered Santa Fe on August 10 and was paraded through the streets on a sedan chair. After making some appointments, he walked to the parish church in the midst of fireworks and public rejoicing. With fitting pomp and circumstance, Gonzales occupied the Palace of the Governors that had been so expensively decorated by his deceased predecessor.[45]

For the next few weeks, the victorious faction attempted to transform a rebellion into a working government. Seeking support from many quarters, the insurgent leaders convened a *junta popular* that would meet in Santa Fe at the end of August. If the Departmental Plan had sought to abolish the authority of New Mexico's communities, the revolution would go out of its way to seek their support and participation. Thus, under the *portal* of the Palace of the Governors, representatives from an unspecified number of New Mexican towns and villages argued openly for three days about the goals of the insurgency and the future of New Mexico. We come closest to hearing the rebels' voices in the minutes of this gathering. The copious marginalia, patches, and scratched-out paragraphs also leave us graphic testimony of profound disagreement and indecision. Ultimately, the Chimayó rebels failed to achieve stability and were only able to hold on to power for a little less than a month. Yet, during these exceptional weeks, New Mexicans enthusiastically broached the subject of New Mexico's precise relationship to the rest of the nation.

The most easily discernible force within the Chimayó movement is comprised of anticentralist politicians and community leaders, mostly Creoles and *mestizos* like Donaciano Vigil, Vicente Sánchez Vergara, and Lieutenant Colonel José María Ronquillo. The final recommendations of the *junta popular* reflected classic anticentralist concerns espoused by such men. For instance, the *junta popular* rejected the legitimacy of Governor Pérez's administration above all for having usurped powers beyond those that the fundamental laws attributed to him, an obvious reference to the high-handed way in which he had abolished the *ayuntamiento* of Santa Cruz de la Cañada. (The rebels were mistaken on this point, as Governor Pérez acted within the broad parameters set by the centralist constitution of 1836 known as the *Siete Leyes*. But as Jane Lecompte has pointed out, when the *junta popular* referred to the *fundamental laws*, they had in mind the *federalist* Constitution of 1824.) In addition, the *junta* emphatically opposed any attempts to levy

---

Taos militia commander who participated in Governor Pérez's disastrous winter campaign against the Navajo. See Lecompte, *Rebellion in Río Arriba*, 36–8, note 54.

[44] Circular to San Francisco del Rancho de Taos, Rio Chiquito, Pueblo de Taos, Arroyo Seco, Plaza de San Antonio de Montes, y Ranchitos; Santa Cruz de la Cañada, Aug 3, 1837, Donaciano Vigil Papers.

[45] Deposition of Hugo Estevenson, El Paso, Sep 11, 1837, AHDN, File 1226, reel 28.

new taxes in New Mexico, pointing out that Governor Pérez was merely seeking to enrich himself and his minions. In effect, the *junta popular*, while incongruously protesting "entire obedience" to the supreme government, in fact rejected the main elements of the centralist order. To be sure, within this broad anticentralist camp, we find different points of view represented. A moderate faction, possibly including the revolutionary governor himself, was trying to avoid a complete break with the national government. Indeed, the initial objective of the *junta popular* had been to choose representatives who would be dispatched to Mexico City to explain New Mexico's desperate circumstances and possibly negotiate a settlement.[46]

But other anticentralists preferred a more assertive course of action whereby New Mexico would remain apart from the Mexican federation until centralists were ousted from power and the federalist constitution of 1824 was reinstated (this plan is identical to the one proposed by Lorenzo de Zavala during the Texas Revolution just a few months before). It appears that the more radical anticentralist faction gained the upper hand when the *junta popular* defiantly declared that Governor Gonzales "ought not to be subject to established laws, but to circumstances as they arise."[47] In this sense, Manuel Armijo, former governor of New Mexico and leader of the counterrevolutionary movement, was entirely correct in observing that "the aim of the faction was, as is evident, to remain independent of the government of the Mexican nation."[48] However carefully worded, the main conclusions of the *junta popular* amounted to an act of secession. But we need to bear in mind that – so far as the anticentralist politicians were concerned – this was only a temporary state of affairs and mostly conceived for the purpose of exerting political pressure on the national government. By rejecting the central government, these New Mexican political activists were merely replicating a strategy pursued by other federalist movements in Zacatecas, Coahuila and Texas, Yucatán, Tamaulipas, and Sonora. Federalist New Mexicans did not shy away from repudiating the national authorities, but they were not questioning New Mexico's ultimate loyalty to the Mexican nation.

Beyond anticentralism, there is scattered evidence of support for permanent secession and even annexation to the United States. One witness remarked that Governor Gonzales invited Anglo-American residents to "march to the United States of the North together with other natives of the country" to secure New Mexico's annexation.[49] On his way to Chihuahua,

---

[46] David Weber speculates that Governor Gonzales probably expected to reach a compromise much like Governor Juan Bautista Alvarado had done in the aftermath of the California revolt of 1836. Weber, *The Mexican Frontier*, 255–60.

[47] Lecompte, *Rebellion in Río Arriba*, 42–3.

[48] Manuel Armijo to Minister of War and Navy, Santa Fe, Oct 11, 1837, translated in Lecompte, *Rebellion in Río Arriba*, 139.

[49] Testimony of Guadalupe Miranda, El Paso, Aug 28, 1837, translated in Lecompte, *Rebellion in Río Arriba*, 115–16.

merchant Hugo Estevenson was told in the Río Abajo district that the objectives of the rebels were to preserve New Mexico as a territory rather than a department, to reject the newly imposed taxes, and not to be subjected to the laws instituted by the centralist constitution. But the merchant also heard that the object was to effect the total separation of New Mexico from the Mexican government, and also heard, "in scattered words," that they wished to annex New Mexico to the United States.[50] Writing one month after the triumph of the Chimayó rebellion, Manuel Armijo described the movement as verging on separatism:

> After ferociously immolating their lawful authorities and many of their fellow citizens, they have put the seal on their iniquity with the greatest of crimes, and renouncing the sacred chains that united them to their country by laws, blood, and religion, they attempt to rend the national colors by substituting the shameful symbol of foreign domination.[51]

None of these tidbits constitute reliable evidence of a concerted plan of secession. Indeed, no documents, either in the New Mexican or the Texan archival record, suggest that the Chimayó rebels established contact with the Lone Star Republic or the United States government in any official capacity. But in the aftermath of a bloody anticentralist insurrection, New Mexicans were unable to ignore the Texas precedent. After all, coahuiltejanos had started out by launching what they believed to be solely an anticentralist rebellion but wound up involved in a full-fledged secessionist movement. New Mexicans could hardly rule out a similar denouement, as border rebellions had a way of acquiring lives of their own. The Texas precedent also made it all but impossible to draw subtle distinctions among shades of secessionism (temporary and for political reasons versus permanent and according to a territorial logic). Before the Texas Revolution, many Mexican citizens, particularly those with federalist sympathies, regarded frontier uprisings within the usual federalist–centralist framework and seldom questioned the motives of foreign-born or indigenous peoples who chose to involve themselves in these struggles. The Texas Revolution complicated things enormously, casting an ominous secessionist shadow over subsequent federalist uprisings. The motivations of even the most patriotic of political dissenters – let alone those of foreign-born or Indian activists – became suspect, as observers throughout the country tended to lump together all frontier rebellions, regarding them as fundamental challenges to the integrity of the national territory.

While annexation to the United States remained a distinct but remote possibility, the outcome that New Mexicans most feared was a massive indigenous uprising that would end up dissolving all political ties with the rest

---

[50] Deposition of Hugo Estevenson, El Paso, Sep 11, 1837, ASDN, File 1226, reel 28.

[51] Manuel Armijo to Military Commander in Chihuahua, Bernalillo, Sep 12, 1837, in Lecompte, *Rebellion in Río Arriba*, 105–6.

of Mexico. New Mexicans had already experienced such a scenario during the Pueblo Revolt of 1680, when Crown authorities, friars, and Spanish residents at large were either massacred or completely driven out of the upper Rio Grande by a powerful alliance of Pueblos and nomadic Indians. It would take Spanish authorities two decades to reconquer New Mexico. It is not my intention to overstate the similarities between these two otherwise distinct insurrections, but like the seventeenth-century movement, the Chimayó Rebellion had resulted in a powerful alignment of Pueblo Indians and nomadic groups, all of whom found good reasons to rid New Mexico of its Hispanic authorities. Since the beginning of the Chimayó Rebellion, all the principal Pueblos in Río Arriba and some in Río Abajo became deeply involved, contributing the lion's share of the insurgent forces that defeated the government's troops. Anglo-American merchant Josiah Gregg dryly observed that the Pueblos had "always been ripe for insurrection."[52] Having achieved military victory, the Pueblo Indians continued to influence the course of the revolution taking part in the *junta popular* and demanding not to be subjected to any authority other than their own.[53] Even after most nonindigenous participants surrendered, various Pueblos vigorously pursued the fight. As late as April 1838, Governor Armijo learned that Indian delegates from the pueblos of Santo Domingo, Cochiti, San Ildefonso, and Santa Clara had met to discuss the best way to rekindle the revolution.[54] A few weeks earlier, Francisco Jaramillo had observed war dances in the Taos pueblo. He reported having the following exchange with three Indians:

Indian: How do you do, friend of Armijo's?
Jaramillo: Fine, why do you ask?
Indian: Because you will see your friend Armijo die like a bird.
Jaramillo: Why?
Another Indian: Do you see that flag over there and those warriors getting ready to fight Armijo?
The third Indian interrupted speaking in their tongue and then the three continued on their way.[55]

---

[52] Gregg, *The Commerce of the Prairies*, 122.

[53] Yielding to the enormous pressure exerted by the Pueblo Indians, the Plan of Tomé specifically stated that the Pueblos would govern themselves not subjected to any authority other than their own, at least until the supreme government settled this point. The Plan also exhorted Pueblo Indians to remain neutral in the rebellion. According to Armijo, when the principal *cabecillas* of the various Pueblos were convened in the capital to discuss the Plan of Tomé in mid-September, they expressed that they "did not wish to live apart but to continue, as always, subjected to the authorities and laws of the same government and as nationals of one single country." Manuel Armijo to alcaldes of Santa Fe, San Ildefonso, Santa Clara, San Juan, Abiquiú, Taos, and Trampas, Santa Fe, Sep 25, 1837, Sender Collection 2:145–6. On Pueblo participation in the *junta popular*, see Philip Reno, "Rebellion in New Mexico, 1837," *New Mexico Historical Review* 40:3, 206, 210.

[54] Tomás Llergo to Manuel Armijo, Santa Fe, Apr 20, 1838, MANM 24, 1185–8.

[55] Santiago Martínez to Governor Manuel Armijo, Taos, Mar 5, 1838, MANM 24, 1168–70.

Such rumblings among Pueblo Indians were all the more threatening given New Mexico's already tense relations with nomadic groups. Immediately after the rebellion broke out, reports poured into Santa Fe confirming the worst. On September 3, 1837, the alcalde of Sevilleta informed that he had been surrounded by a force consisting of Acoma Pueblo Indians and Navajo warriors, and that two residents of Sevilleta had died in the ensuing fight. He also reported that the Pueblo of Zuñi had already established an alliance with the Navajos and that the Pueblo of Laguna may do so shortly.[56] Two weeks later, Judge Julián Lucero of Galisteo reported that two residents of Río Arriba – Bernardo Montoya and Cius Montoya – had attacked the Real del Oro backed by two hundred Gileño and Jicarilla Apaches. He also reported that close to one thousand Apaches were expected to fall on Galisteo within hours. The attack did not materialize.[57] In an address to his fellow New Mexicans, Manuel Armijo painted the gloomiest of prospects: "...the Navajos, reassured by the deplorable condition in which we find ourselves, and in combination with the Pueblos of the frontier, wage a disastrous war that reaches into the very bosom of our families."[58] During the Pueblo Revolt of 1680, escalating intra-Hispanic conflict (a church–state row among other factors) had ended in the total obliteration of the Spanish presence in New Mexico. In the 1830s, the centralist–federalist rivalry provided a similar backdrop. More than anything else, the specter of such a caste war galvanized a powerful counterrevolutionary movement.

Understandably, the Chimayó movement brought together such disparate elements that it bore the seeds of at least three different separatist schemes: temporary rejection of the national government on political grounds, massive indigenous revolt, and permanent secession Texas-style and possible annexation to the United States. All three different paths to separation were possible as the rebellion unfolded. But the last alternative – separation involving scheming Anglo Americans – was the one that caught the fancy of contemporaries (and subsequent historians). The Texas Revolution and its subsequent story have weighed on our historical interpretations in this instance as well. And yet, a balanced assessment of Mexico's effective territorial control in the early-to-mid-nineteenth century would reveal that a large proportion of Mexico's on-the-ground territorial loss – even if temporary – was because of antagonistic local and state governments and assertive indigenous movements, the likely outcomes of the Chimayó Rebellion.

---

[56] *Juzgado Segundo* to *Jefe Político*, Albuquerque, Sep 3, 1837, MANM 23, 421–3; José de Jesús Sánchez to Manuel Armijo, Cochiti, Sep 10, 1837, MANM 23, 439–41.

[57] Julián Lucero, *Juzgado de Policía* of Galisteo, to alcalde Francisco Ortiz y Delgado, Galisteo, Sep 17, 1837, MANM 23, 904–5.

[58] Manuel Armijo to New Mexicans, Santa Fe, Oct 9, 1837, MANM 23, 661.

FIGURE 6.1. Governor Manuel Armijo

FLEXING THE STATE'S MUSCLE

On the eve of the execution of Governor Pérez, a group of anonymous *ricos* agreed to form a government "according to their idea" and began issuing unsigned orders to various alcaldes and community leaders.[59] Working clandestinely at first, the counterinsurgency leadership finally went public on September 8. Curate Francisco Ignacio Madariaga had invited leaders from various towns in Río Abajo to meet in the tiny village of Tomé that day. The resourceful priest had been implicated in the original conspiracy to overthrow Governor Pérez's administration. But since those tragic events, he had experienced a change of heart. Others who had initially been sympathetic to the insurrection were also in attendance, including Vicente Sánchez Vergara, one of the key participants in the revolutionary government up to then, and the "honored citizen" of Albuquerque, Manuel Armijo (see Figure 6.1).[60] Some of the richest men of Río Abajo, including Mariano Chávez, and a sprinkling of municipal authorities who had miraculously survived the uprising completed the roster. After a brief discussion, the group issued a proclamation pointedly signed by the "citizens who love their country and favor

[59] Madariaga to Agustín de Avellano, Tomé, Aug 12, 1837, ASDN, File 1225, reel 28.

[60] Contemporaries, particularly Anglo Americans, accused Armijo of secretly fomenting the rebellion when it was in its initial stages. See Lecompte, *Rebellion in Río Arriba*, 60–1. Further evidence of this interpretation is provided by Ritch, who was told by Donaciano Vigil that: "all documents or papers relating to the revolution and opposition to Pérez were gathered together, as he knew from personal knowledge, and it was well understood that they were destroyed by Armijo." In Chronology of Events by Ritch, Ritch Collection, reel 4.

the Constitution and its laws."[61] The central aim of the Plan of Tomé (as it became known) was to organize a "Liberating Army."

The most remarkable aspect of the counterrevolutionary movement is the unity of purpose and effective collaboration between the military, the Church, and the remnants of the civil administration all represented in Tomé. During the administration of the late Governor Pérez, just a few weeks earlier, such seamless cooperation would have been utterly unthinkable as different branches of government became mired in the federalist–centralist wrangle undercutting each other in sordid struggles for power. But facing the double threat of a secessionism and a large-scale indigenous uprising, cooperation became urgent. The power of the state was effectively deployed in New Mexico, as national, regional, and local members of various administrative machineries and patronage systems brought their resources together to contain the Chimayó Rebellion.

The conduct of New Mexico's veteran army immediately before and during the insurrection speaks volumes of both the limits of state power and also of the state's ability to reconstitute itself and promote a nationalist agenda. According to one detailed report, New Mexico's regular troops had numerous difficulties with Governor Pérez during his administration.[62] The sources of such enmity were multiple. Governor Pérez's continuous Indian campaigns were taxing in the extreme for a small force so ill equipped and dependent on agriculture and its yearly cycle for survival. Moreover, the veteran troops were especially aggrieved by lack of enforcement of the military *fuero* in New Mexico, as veteran soldiers who committed crimes, instead of being tried by a military court, were regularly turned over to the ordinary justice system. As Miguel Antonio Lovato observed, soldiers "receive public beatings even for minor offenses, and rarely enjoy their rightful wages when, in all fairness, these valiant warriors earn their money down to the last maravedí."[63] But the most obvious source of irritation was political. Prominent members of New Mexico's military establishment, including Ensign Donaciano Vigil and Lieutenant Colonel José María Ronquillo – the latter being the highest-ranking officer in New Mexico besides Governor Pérez – had clear federalist sympathies and openly clashed with Governor Pérez's centralist agenda. The governor responded in kind by snubbing and disarming the *veteranos* throughout 1837.

The rebellion gave dissenting officers and soldiers an excellent opportunity to strike back. When Governor Pérez attempted to raise a force to negotiate with the rebels, very few *veteranos* rallied to his side. Worse still, he had to delegate enormous authority to potentially disloyal officers. Most

---

[61] Plan of Tomé, Sep 8, 1837, in Armijo Papers, NMSRCA.

[62] Miguel Antonio Lovato to President, n.p., n.d (maybe 1838 or 1839), Miguel Antonio Lovato Papers, CSR (137).

[63] Ibid.

crucially, when the governor left for Santa Cruz de la Cañada – having to rely mostly on a Pueblo Indian volunteer force – he had little choice but to leave Lieutenant Colonel Ronquillo in Santa Fe acting as New Mexico's top military commander. That may have been Governor Pérez's worst political blunder. Lieutenant Colonel Ronquillo's subsequent actions suggest that he may have colluded with the rebels from the start. He did not intervene in the wake of the crushing defeat sustained by Governor Pérez's volunteer force. More intriguingly, Lieutenant Colonel Ronquillo did not organize any resistance when the rebellious force marched into Santa Fe, but instead rode out to meet the approaching body bearing a white flag and offering his services. The leaders of the insurgency were most favorably impressed, appointing both Lieutenant Colonel Ronquillo and Ensign Vigil to the only two cabinet-level positions in the new administration. Lieutenant Colonel Ronquillo became the military commander of the revolutionary government, whereas Ensign Vigil was named secretary to the new governor.[64] All of these factional disputes and personal maneuverings underscore the limitations of New Mexico's regular troops in upholding a national order. The *veteranos* were not only opposed to Governor Pérez – their nominal commander – but could act entirely independently of the national chain of command.

Another set of personal intrigues would alter once again the role of the regular troops as the rebellion ran its course. Lieutenant Colonel Ronquillo may have sided with the rebels, but some of his subordinates became uneasy about supporting a breakaway government. Just as a Río Abajo went through the motions of mobilizing and fashioning a counterrevolutionary "Liberating Army," the military establishment in Santa Fe went through a reorganization of its own. On September 6, a group of young officers charged Lieutenant Colonel Ronquillo with treason and deposed him.[63] In the ensuing shakeout, the commander of the Santa Fe permanent cavalry, Captain José Caballero, emerged as the de facto military commander. He immediately recalled the presidial troops and managed to put ninety-two men under arms. In addition, 356 *vecinos* attached themselves to the regular troops. Juan Estevan Pino, Juan Rafael Ortiz – and "other men of the highest proportions in all of New Mexico" – as well as some Anglo-American merchants pledged money and supplies.[64] Taking advantage of rebel Governor José Gonzales's absence from the capital, the "Liberating Army"

[64] Lecompte, *Rebellion in Río Arriba*, 21–2, 35, 40.

[63] Lieutenant Colonel Ronquillo was accused of sitting idly during the "darkest days of the rebellion," implying that he had colluded with the rebellious party. Ronquillo left Santa Fe for El Paso the next day. See José Caballero to military commander of Chihuahua, Santa Fe, Oct 2, 1837, ASDN, File 1227, reel 28.

[64] See José Caballero to Commandante General en Chihuahua, Santa Fe, Oct 2, 1837, ASDN, File 1227, reel 28; Miguel Antonio Lovato to President, n.p., n.d (maybe 1838 or 1839), Miguel Antonio Lovato Papers, CSR (137).

of Río Abajo, which had been placed under the command of Manuel Armijo, marched unopposed into Santa Fe on September 14 and joined forces with those under Captain Caballero's command. Armijo – by then only a lieutenant in the Albuquerque militia – was put in command of the combined troops. After several transmutations, New Mexico's veteran troops – along with a force of *vecinos* – once again were playing the role of guarantor of the national constitutional order. By year's end, a detachment from Chihuahua – where the headquarters of the *comandancia general* with jurisdiction over New Mexico was located – would add further strength to New Mexico's newly constituted military and ultimately managed to quell the rebellion. Mexico did not have a fully constituted state, but it did have administrative branches that, under certain circumstances, could act as nationalizing agents.

The Church's role during the Chimayó Rebellion offers another telling illustration of how local, regional, and national administrative resources were deployed to counter separatism in New Mexico. Prior to the uprising, the Church had already been playing an increasingly prominent and partisan political role in New Mexico coinciding with Bishop Zubiría's spiritual administration. Indeed, Zubiría's very ascent to the bishopric of Durango was made possible largely through the good offices of the centralist administration of AnastaSio Bustamante in 1830.[65] In the course of the next few years, the two men would develop a close personal and political relationship. Even during Vice President Bustamante's most controversial action – the capture and execution of former President Vicente Guerrero – Bishop Zubiría's support remained unwavering, as he ordered all priests in New Mexico to sing a *Te Deum* for the arrest of the "*caudillo* and other southern rebels ... in the hope that it will end the country's misfortunes and blood spilling among her

---

[65] As noted in Chapter 2, Vice President AnastaSio Bustamante wrote to Pope Gregory XVI, supporting the appointment of Zubiría for bishop of Durango. Bustamante then used his rapport with Zubiría for political ends. Indeed, Francisco de Paula de Arrangoiz credits Bustamante for bringing about a political alliance that included the "remnants of the *escocés* faction, the respectable part of the *yorkino* faction, the clergy, the army, and in sum all those who wanted justice and order." Francisco de Paula de Arrangoiz, *México desde 1808 hasta 1867* (Mexico City: Editorial Porrúa, 1985), 353–4. Contrary to the traditional interpretation that has viewed the Church as a chief supporter of centralism in Mexico, Josefina Zoraida Vázquez has argued that by the time of independence, the Church was so weakened that it was no longer an important political actor. Vázquez, "Iglesia, Ejército y Centralismo," *Historia Mexicana* 29:1 (1989), 205–34. Her argument may hold for New Mexico during the 1820s, but not for the 1830s–40s, when the vigorous and decidedly partisan ecclesiastical administration of Bishop Zubiría restored the Church's influence over the territory. By focusing on the cases of the Pueblo and Jalisco, Brian F. Connaughton provides evidence for the Church's fragmentation but also of its political influence. Brian F. Connaughton, *Dimensiones de la identidad patriótica: religion, política, y regiones en México* (Mexico City: UAM-Miguel Ángel Porrúa, 2001), 11–29. For an insightful discussion of the Church's weaknesses and strengths in the nineteenth century, see Escalante Gonzalbo, *Ciudadanos imaginarios*, 141–60.

children."[66] Such partisanship made Bishop Zubiría an obvious target when the dominant political winds turned against centralism in 1833, even forcing the "prince of the Church in Durango" to go into hiding.[67] But in 1834, we find the embattled bishop throwing his political weight once again behind the emerging centralist order.[68]

Immediately after learning of the rebellious outbreak in New Mexico, General Bustamante sent a letter to Bishop Zubiría asking him to use his

...considerable influence and that of the parish priests and other ecclesiastics and principal *vecinos* to address the people of New Mexico exhorting them to become peaceful and obedient of the authorities, and to insist on the evils that would befall them if they were to become part of a foreign nation with a different religion and customs so incompatible with the Mexican character. The bishop was urged to send "lengthy admonitions... using the most private and efficacious means and without danger of being intercepted."[69]

The energetic bishop reported back to the ministry of the interior less than two months later noting that he had made sure to contact all priests within New Mexico to urge them not to desist in their efforts to support the established order.[70] Also working from afar was New Mexico's highest ecclesiastical authority after the bishop, Vicar Juan Felipe Ortiz, who at the time of the rebellion was serving as New Mexico's representative in the National Congress in Mexico City. Vicar Ortiz wrote letters in praise of Commander Armijo and all of those "patriotic and sensible nuevomexicanos surrounding him," and predicted a complete victory over the "capricious and tenacious chimayoses," dismissing their movement as merely "a satellite of the ephemeral Republic of Texas."[71] More tangibly, Vicar Ortiz presented

---

[66] Juan Rafael Rascón, Vicar of New Mexico, to Melquiades Antonio Ortega, Santa Fe, Feb 26, 1833, reproduced in Gerald Theisen, "Opinions on the Newly Independent Mexican Nation: Documents from the Archives of the Archdiocese of Santa Fe, New Mexico, 1820–43," *Revista de Historia de América* 72 (1975), 487–8.

[67] In late 1833 and early 1834, a staunchly federalist Congress abolished the citizens' obligation to pay tithes, gave federal and state governments the right to exercise the *patronato real*, forbade priests to discuss political matters in the pulpit, and issued other anticlerical legislation. Refusing to abide by these new laws, Bishop Zubiría, along with other bishops, left Durango in disguise on May 9, 1834, and fled to Zacatecas. Enirque Olavarría y Ferrari, *Episodios históricos mexicanos* 4 vols (Mexico City: ICH-FCE, 1987), 4, 1331–2.

[68] For instance, the bishop wrote an effusive letter to Colonel Blas de Hinojos, then military commander of New Mexico, celebrating his decision to commit New Mexico's troops to the centralist Plan of Cuernavaca. Bishop Zubiría to Colonel Blas de Hinojos, Durango, Sep 30, 1834, MANM 18, 371.

[69] President Bustamante to Bishop Zubiría, Mexico City, Sep 12, 1837, (AGN), Gobernación, Leg 173, Box 259.

[70] Zubiría to Minister of the Interior, Chihuahua, Nov 3, 1837, Archivo General de la Nación (AGN), Justicia, vol. 138.

[71] Vicar Ortiz to Armijo, Mexico City, Dec 19, 1837, Donaciano Vigil Collection. See also Ortiz to Armijo, Mexico City, n.d., MANM 23, 501.

New Mexico's case to fellow congressmen and contacted the Mexican president to request reinforcements from Chihuahua and funds in the order of 25,000–30,000 pesos for New Mexico's newly reconstituted troops.[72]

Whether prompted by higher ecclesiastical authorities or on their own, many New Mexican priests became involved in the efforts to contain the Chimayó Rebellion, even risking their lives. As we saw, Curate Madariaga of Tomé emerged as the leader of the counterrevolutionary movement, coordinating the mobilization of Río Abajo at a time when no other civil or military authority seemed willing to step forward. In his view, New Mexicans not only faced the threat of violence derived from the uprising itself, but also risked becoming a target of expansionist nations (that is, the United States): "... the Almighty will dictate what will happen, I will only tell you that because the Mexican Republic has no troops stationed here, this frontier will be lost to a powerful nation, I believe forever, if God does not intervene."[73] The interim curate of Santa Fe, Father José Francisco Leyba, had reached similar conclusions and also played a crucial role. In fact, his role was so critical that he merited a special mention in Commander Armijo's report to the national government, which described Curate Leyba as "so enthusiastic in the cause of order [a euphemism for sympathizer of centralism] that he offered to confer with the rebels, which was too dangerous considering the class of people composing that *reunión*."[74]

The most detailed information about a priest's efforts to curtail the spread of the revolution comes out of Taos. Father Antonio José Martínez (see Figure 6.2) occupied a privileged vantage point from which to observe the revolution, not only because his parish turned out to be a principal site of rebellious activity, but also because he himself probably sympathized with the movement during the initial stages and became well acquainted with some of its leaders, including José Gonzales. According to Santiago Valdez – one of Father Martínez's pupils who would later write a biography of his teacher interspersed with original documents – many of the father's parishioners joined the rebellion claiming that they were thus "defending Catholicism and the faith of Jesus Christ."[75] But once the anticlericalism and racial elements of the rebellion became evident, Father Martínez became a harsh critic and formidable opponent.[76] He objected particularly to the rebels' liberal use

[72] Ortiz to Armijo, Mexico City, Dec 10, 1837, MANM 23, 501.

[73] Madariaga to Agustín de Avellano, Tomé, Aug 12, 1837, ASDN, File 1225, reel 28.

[74] Provisional Governor Manuel Armijo to Minister of War and Navy, Santa Fe, October 11, 1837, in Lecompte, *Rebellion in Río Arriba*, 141.

[75] Santiago Valdez, *Biografía del Reverendo Padre Antonio José Martínez* ..., Taos, 1877, reproduced from the copy in the Henry E. Huntington Library, Ritch Collection, NMSRCA, reel 1. The following description is based largely on this source except when noted otherwise.

[76] For the role Father Martínez played in the course of the rebellion, see Angélico Chávez, *But Time and Chance*, 51–9.

FIGURE 6.2. Father Antonio José Martínez

of religious rhetoric, which he deemed "very much a propos to seduce an ignorant people."[77] Thus he decided to fight fire with fire and initiated what amounted to a war of images.

During sermons, Father Martínez urged his flock to remain within the "established order," and dwelt at length on "the harsh but necessary punishment that would result from their [the rebels'] transgressions of civil and divine laws."[78] These notions put him tantalizingly close to those expressed in the "Religious Dissertation," the mysterious letter that Jesus Christ addressed to the Pope. Such a blatant counterrevolutionary campaign also put him on a collision course with an increasingly assertive insurrection. At the height of the rebellion, the alcalde of Taos and other citizens held council in the Martínez household and gathered arms and ammunition, seeking to protect themselves against the insurgents. According to the (undoubtedly romanticized) biography by Valdez, Father Martínez resisted until the continuous threats and insults from his parishioners made life impossible and persuaded the embattled priest to flee to Santa Fe for a few days.[79] In the waning phase of the insurrection, Father Martínez maintained an active correspondence with Commander Armijo, keeping him abreast of the activities of the rebellious party in the

---

[77] Valdez, *Biografía del Reverendo Padre Antonio José Martínez...*, 15.

[78] Ibid., 16.

[79] Father Martínez himself tells the same sequence of events. See Martínez to Zubiría, Taos, Sep 25, 1837, in Zubiría to Minister of the Interior, Chihuahua, Nov 3, 1837, AGN, Justicia, vol. 138.

Taos area.[80] During the last military campaign early in 1838, Father Martínez served as chaplain of the government forces and reportedly heard the confession of José Gonzales before the latter faced the execution squad.

Thus the Chimayó Rebellion was quelled, not in one military action but after months of attrition and because of the emergence of a new political alignment in New Mexico decidedly hostile to the rebellion. The process had been slow. After the initial revolt at Santa Cruz de la Cañada in August, another rebellion broke out in Taos in September, and yet another flared up in Truchas in October. It was not until January of 1838 that New Mexico's troops together with reinforcements from Chihuahua were able to rout the rebels in Pojoaque, seventeen miles north of the capital. But more lasting than the sheer military victory was the rare unity of purpose among civil authorities, the army, and the Church – an alliance that, in the short run at least, hinged largely on a nationalist agenda. Indeed, the entire episode had been the occasion for an outpouring of patriotic rhetoric that equated rebellion with secessionism, and counterrevolution with Mexicanness. New Mexico's society would not be the same after 1837. The military and ecclesiastical establishments contributed to this nationalist crusade, insisting on the dangers – real or imagined – of foreign domination and the preservation of the Mexican culture and Catholicism, themes that would loom large in New Mexico in the following years, as we shall see. Sitting at the apex of the civil and military apparatuses, Armijo became the chief beneficiary of this fiercely patriotic symbology, allowing him to become New Mexico's political demiurge for the next decade.

[80] The Armijo-Martínez correspondence is partly reproduced in Santiago Valdez, *Biografía del Reverendo Padre Antonio José Martínez...*, Taos, 1877, Ritch Collection reel 1, NMSRCA. The Church turned out to be an excellent vehicle for collecting detailed and crucial intelligence. For instance, Bishop Zubiría received reports about the progress of the rebellion from at least three parish priests: Juan de Jesús Trujillo from Albuquerque, Fernando Ortiz from Santa Cruz de la Cañada, and Antonio José Marínez from Taos. In turn, Bishop Zubiría transmitted this intelligence to the national government. Zubiría to Minister of the Interior, Chihuahua, Nov 3, 1837, AGN, Justicia, vol. 138.

7

State, Market, and Literary Cultures

On the morning of June 20, 1841, a party of 320 Texans got ready for a perilous venture into neighboring New Mexico.[1] Caught in the last-minute rush, merchants packed their goods and volunteers saddled their horses and checked their bullet-pouches one last time.[2] Hugh McLeod, a twenty-seven-year-old promoted to brigadier general just a few days before, gave the signal and the body started to move. Two companies went ahead as the advance guard, and wagons followed in a single file. Next a company detailed for fatigue duty drove some seventy head of beef cattle, and three companies brought up the rear guard. Starting from Brushy – a spacious camplike rendezvous located twelve miles north of Austin – the mixed party of merchants and soldiers was bound for Mexican territory. Ostensibly it was a commercial venture sponsored by the Texas government to allow Lone Star merchants to tap into the lucrative Santa Fe Trail. Yet several expedition members knew the ulterior and far more important purpose: to claim more than half of New Mexico's territory as part of the expansive Texas Republic.

For weeks, the Texan Santa Fe Expedition (such was its long-winded official name) had generated enormous interest, even to the point of morbidity. For a start, the party would have to cut a swath across a region described by a New Orleans newspaper editor and expedition member as "entirely unknown to the white man."[3] Owing to lack of water and food along the way, the trekkers intended to follow a circuitous route along the Brazos River, through the Cross Timbers pass, skirting the Llano Estacado, and finally

---

[1] Portions of this chapter will appear in article format in Andrés Reséndez, "An Expedition and Its Many Tales," in Samuel Truett and Elliott Young, eds., *Continental Crossroads: Remapping U.S.–Mexico Borderlands History* (Durham, NC: Duke University Press, forthcoming).

[2] George Wilkins Kendall, *Narrative of the Texan Santa Fe Expedition*, 2 vols (New York: Harper and Brothers, 1844), 67. In addition to Kendall's account, I have based this chapter on several other original accounts; see citations throughout this chapter. See also Ángela Moyano Pahissa, *El comercio de Santa Fe y la Guerra del 47* (Mexico City: SepSetentas, 1976), 109–38.

[3] Kendall, *Narrative of the Texan Santa Fe Expedition*, 6.

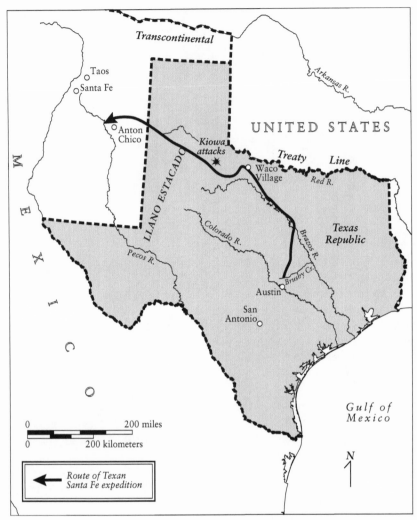

MAP 7.1. The Texan Santa Fe Expedition

along the Red River (see Map 7.1). Anglo Texans vaguely referred to this succession of prairies and deserts as the Comanche Wilderness, one of the most beautiful but harshest landscapes of North America. But the uncharted and forbidding nature of the route was only one of the unusual features of the Santa Fe venture. The reading public's interest was also kindled by the likelihood of contact with "large bands of Indians," as the expedition would pass directly through their known hunting grounds. With characteristic abandon, old Texas campaigners seized on the expedition to reminisce about their own encounters and hairbreadth escapes. Most of these veterans were both fascinated and skeptical about the idea of venturing into the very heartland of the powerful Comanche confederation.[4] Finally, the expedition caused a stir because of its uncertain reception at the other end. The hardy adventurers, although hopeful, could only guess at how New Mexicans would react to their overtures for economic and – as some knew – political incorporation. Certainly the secret instructions given to the commissioners of the expedition were unsettling, as they contemplated the possibility of violent engagements:

... if you are opposed by the troops of the Government of Mexico only, and the people are with you, or indifferent as to the result, the only question for your consideration will be your ability of beating them, of which you and the military officers composing the command, must be the sole judges.[5]

With all of these elements at play, it is no wonder that the Texan Santa Fe Expedition would attract a colorful cast of characters. They included Franklin Combs, son of the governor of Kentucky; Peter Gallagher, a self-described "ex-secretary" of General Sam Houston; Thomas Falconer, an English lawyer "of high literary and scientific attainments"; and George Wilkins Kendall, a journalist and editor who decided that the undertaking was so unprecedented that it would hold the interest of his readers of the *New Orleans Picayune*.[6]

As it turned out, the adventurers got more than they had bargained for. Subjected to punishing summer temperatures, the Texans slowly braved thirteen hundred miles of unforgiving deserts, thick woods, and chasms so deep that only after shedding most of their baggage and heavy carts were they able to reach New Mexico's settlements. The final leg turned into a harrowing free-for-all, as volunteers ran out of food and were reduced to living on frogs, lizards, roots, and "every living and creeping thing."[7] Worse still, the trekkers did encounter Indians, sometimes with fatal consequences, and did not find nine-tenths of New Mexico's population ready to "shake off the tiresome yoke of their [Mexican] task-masters," as had been confidently asserted back in Texas. Instead they found widespread repudiation.[8] The Texans surrendered, and thus began a second and unanticipated phase of the expedition. The hapless prisoners were marched more than two thousand miles toward central and southern Mexico, where they spent months

[4] Ibid. 13–14.
[5] Samuel A. Roberts, Acting Secretary of State of the Republic of Texas, to Commissioners William G. Cooke, Antonio Navarro, Richard F. Brenham, and William G. Dryden, Austin, Jun 15, 1841, in *Letters of Secretary of State Abner S. Lipscomb to Commissioners to Santa Fe* (Austin, TX: G. H. Harrison, 1841), 12–18.
[6] On Kendall's life, see Fayette Copeland, *Kendall of the Picayune*, 2 ed. (Norman, OK: University of Oklahoma Press, 1997).
[7] George W. Grover, "Minutes of Adventure from June, 1841," edited by H. B. Carroll, *The Panhandle-Plains Historical Review* 9 (1936), 28–42.
[8] *Austin City Gazette*, Apr 15, 1840.

in ghastly prisons like San Lázaro, a leper hospital just outside Mexico City, or the notorious fort of San Juan de Ulúa, which was rapidly acquiring a reputation akin to the Count of Monte Cristo's Chateux d'If as described by contemporary novelist Alexandre Dumas.

Because of the colorful personalities involved, the high drama, and the inter-ethnic and international dimensions, it is no wonder that the Texan Santa Fe Expedition would give rise to numerous and largely independent accounts not only in the Lone Star Republic and the United States but also in Mexico and among Kiowas. Taken as a whole, these tales reveal different interpretations of the same episode, and – far more interestingly – they point to widely different literary and print cultures coexisting at the frontier in the 1840s. What we find is a state of literary fragmentation, as different ethnic groups experimented with strikingly different ways of writing, disseminating, and reading stories about themselves and about others. Furthermore, and as in other human realms explored in this book, state and market had a hand in shaping these varied literary cultures. Certainly by the 1840s, print capitalism had made important inroads in this border region, but the Mexican state as well as indigenous pictorial traditions also had a hand in shaping the texts that were being produced and disseminated. What follows is an exploration of the many tales surrounding the Texan Santa Fe Expedition, the literary cultures behind these texts, and the ways in which these stories served to forge collective identities.

THE EVANESCENT AMERICAN-TEXAN JOURNALISTIC AND LITERARY BOUNDARY

The press coverage of the Texan Santa Fe Expedition leaves no doubt that by the 1840s, the "print revolution" that had transformed the northeastern United States had reached the southern frontier and into the Republic of Texas. Especially since the 1820s, newspapers started mushrooming in frontier towns like Louisville, Mobile, Natches, San Felipe de Austin, and Galveston. Judged by the standards of established news organizations like the *New York Herald* or the *National Intelligencer* of Washington, these local newspapers may have seemed crude and amateurish. Their editorial strategy often consisted of liberally clipping articles from other newspapers and spicing them up with local commentary and gossip. Yet these publications fulfilled a legitimate need for cheap local news.

Kendall's *Picayune* is a classic example of this trend. After apprenticeships in Detroit and New York, Kendall set up shop in New Orleans, where journalistic competition was already fierce in a town of seventy thousand. By 1837, no less than ten papers were already in circulation, and eight more – the *Picayune* included – would see launch that year.[9] Kendall and his partner

---

[9] Copeland, *Kendall of the Picayune*, 13–22.

decided to undersell their rivals. Strictly speaking, the Picayune was no "penny press," a term reserved for a couple of sensationalist New York newspapers that were willing to part with a copy for a measly cent. Yet the *Picayune* constituted affordable journalism, as the paper could be purchased with the smallest coin in circulation, the old Spanish "picayon" (six-and-a-quarter cents, or *medio real*), hence its name and motto: "...when we exchange our Picayune for your picayune, and we derive a profit, it will be time enough to touch the Spanish...."[10]

Texas experienced a similar print rush during the Mexican and Republic periods, but along strict language lines. For all the active and critical Spanish-language journalism that would later flourish along the border, no Spanish newspaper was published in Texas prior to the 1850s. Tejanos had to content themselves with publications from neighboring Coahuila, Tamaulipas, and, tellingly, New Orleans, where an eccentric Neapolitan published the radical *El Correo Atlántico*.[11] But while tejanos were forced to peruse out-of-state publications, Anglo Texans had enjoyed local papers since 1829. That year, Godwin B. Cotten pioneered the *Texas Gazette*, a paper of strong homemade flavor that ran for nearly four years.[12] In the early to mid-1830s, a few more English-language newspapers made tentative starts, but the first truly successful Lone Star newspaper was the *Telegraph and Texas Register*. Founded in 1835 under the watchful eye of Gail Borden – a name later associated the world over with soup biscuits and the Gail Borden Eagle brand of condensed milk – the *Telegraph* began publication just in time to chronicle the incidents of the Texas Revolution from a staunchly secessionist perspective. Over the years, the paper kept a distinctive, self-confident, almost boastful expansionist edge and naturally became an early backer of the projected expedition into New Mexico. The *Telegraph* remained in business until well after the Civil War.

The Texan Santa Fe Expedition became a favorite topic of these emerging local and regional newspapers, capturing the imagination of many readers and triggering a flurry of articles, editorials, and public letters discussing all

---

[10] Ibid., 23.

[11] The first newspaper ever printed in Texas, was the *Gaceta de Texas*, published out of Nacogdoches on May 25, 1813. It was meant to promote the filibustering expedition of Bernardo Gutiérrez and Augustus William Magee. A second issue was published on June 19, although it appeared under the title of *El Mexicano*. The prospectus of the *Correo de Texas*, a bilingual newspaper based in San Antonio, came out on April 9, 1823, but the actual newspaper was probably never published. Not until the 1850s did another Spanish-language newspaper appear on the scene again, when *El Bejareño* (1855), *El Ranchero* (1856), and *El Correo* (1858), all three based in San Antonio, began. For a complete compilation of early Texas newspapers, see Thomas W. Streeter, *Bibliography of Texas 1795–1845*, 2 ed. (Woodbridge, CT: Research Publications, 1983), 189–213.

[12] For a description of Cotten, see Smithwick, *The Evolution of a State*, 43–4. For his paper, see Marilyn McAdams Sibley, *Lone Stars and State Gazettes: Texas Newspapers Before the Civil War* (College Station, TX: Texas A & M University Press, 1983), 47–51.

aspects of the expedition and informing on preparations for departure.[13] Indeed, an unprecedented number of news-reporters accompanied the expedition, beginning with Kendall but also including George W. Bonnell, editor of the *Austin Sentinel*, and Commissioner Richard F. Brenham of the *Bulock's Logs* sheets. The expedition commander, General McLeod, became so impressed by the power of the press that five years later, during the war with Mexico, he became the editor of a propagandist semiweekly called the *Republic of the Rio Grande*. The misfortunes of the trekkers, especially their months in captivity in Mexico, only increased public awareness and fostered a sense of outrage vividly expressed in a contemporary broadside published in Austin: "Fellow citizens, the piteous cries, and dying groans of our imprisoned and slaughtered countrymen, come to our ears in every breeze that sweeps over the western prairies...."[14] Expedition member George W. Grover even took to the task of editing a weekly handwritten sheet called *True Blue*.[15]

There is no question that the Texan Santa Fe Expedition, in spite of its misfortunes or precisely *because* of them, became nothing short of a journalistic sensation and a topic of enduring public interest. The release of most expedition members and their return to Texas and the United States prepared the terrain for a second journalistic onslaught. In 1842, Thomas Falconer published an "Extended Account," which first appeared in the *New Orleans Picayune* and was then reproduced in several other newspapers. At about the same time, Franklin Comb's "Narrative" came out in the *Niles' National Register* of Baltimore.[16] A far more significant editorial phenomenon was the publication in 1844 of Kendall's two-volume *Narrative of the Texan Santa Fe Expedition*, an engrossing tale crafted in the "homely, every-day language that is at once understood by all."[17] Kendall's *Narrative* (see Figure 7.1) became an astounding commercial success. It went through seven editions

---

[13] Copeland traces the newspaper coverage of the expedition; see Copeland, *Kendall of the Picayune*, 83–4. For the diplomatic exchange over the prisoners, see *Message from the President of the United States, Communicating ... Copies of Correspondence with the Government of Mexico* (Washington DC: 27th Congress, 2nd Session, SD 325, June 16, 1842). The memoirs of the United States minister in Mexico complete the diplomatic picture. See Waddy Thompson, *Recollections of Mexico* (New York: Wiley and Putnam, 1846). See also George Folsom, *Mexico in 1842* (New York, C. J. Folsom, 1842).

[14] Broadside, Austin, 1842, microfilm of Texas as a province and republic, 1795–1845, reel 9, no. 551.

[15] Sibley, *Lone Stars and State Gazettes*, 131–2.

[16] Thomas Falconer wrote no fewer than three accounts of his experiences in the expedition. All three versions and related documentation can be found in F. W. Hodge, ed., *Letters and Notes on the Texan Santa Fe Expedition 1841–1842* (Chicago, IL: Rio Grande Press, 1963). Comb's "Narrative" appeared in the *Niles' National Register*, Mar 5, 1842. Comb's account has been republished more recently: Franklin Combs, "Narrative of the Santa Fe Expedition in 1841," *New Mexico Historical Review* 5:3, 306–7.

[17] Kendall, *Narrative of the Texan Santa Fe Expedition*, xxix. At least three more firsthand accounts have come to light: Cayton Erhard, "Cayton Erhard's Reminiscences of the Texan

NARRATIVE

OF THE

TEXAN SANTA FÉ EXPEDITION,

COMPRISING A DESCRIPTION OF

A TOUR THROUGH TEXAS,

AND

ACROSS THE GREAT SOUTHWESTERN PRAIRIES, THE CAMANCHE AND
CAYGÜA HUNTING-GROUNDS, WITH AN ACCOUNT OF THE
SUFFERINGS FROM WANT OF FOOD, LOSSES FROM
HOSTILE INDIANS, AND FINAL

CAPTURE OF THE TEXANS,

AND

THEIR MARCH, AS PRISONERS, TO THE CITY OF MEXICO.

WITH ILLUSTRATIONS AND A MAP.

BY GEO. WILKINS KENDALL.

IN TWO VOLUMES.
VOL. I.

NEW-YORK:
HARPER AND BROTHERS, 82 CLIFF-STREET.

1844.

FIGURE 7.1. Cover of Kendall's best-selling book

Santa Fe Expedition, 1841," *Southwestern Historical Quarterly* 66 (1963), 424–56, 547–68; Peter Gallagher, "Journal of the Santa Fe Expedition," in H. Bailey Carroll, ed., *The Texan Santa Fe Trail* (Canyon, TX: Panhandle-Plains Historical Society, 1951), 169–86; Grover, "Minutes of Adventure from June, 1841," 28–42.

in twelve years, selling more than forty thousand copies, which made it the most popular rendition not only of the Texan Santa Fe Expedition but of any (mis)adventures of Anglo Americans in Mexico in the years leading up to the Mexican–American War. In his analysis of America's most popular works, Frank Luther Mott defines a best seller as any book believed to have had a total sale to at least 1 percent of the population of the continental United States. Kendall's *Narrative* is not listed as a best seller, but as a "better seller" or runner-up. Together with Richard H. Dana's *Two Years Before the Mast* (a sailor's account of Alta California) and William H. Prescott's *Conquest of Mexico* (a historical treatment of the first encounters between Spaniards and Aztecs that remains popular to this day), Kendall's work arguably shaped the consciousness of the American reading public toward Mexico prior to the War.[18]

Editors like Bonnell, Brenham, Grover, and Kendall sought to connect with the Anglo-American reading public. They were private entrepreneurs who consciously wrote for the market. They joined the Texan Santa Fe Expedition seeking exciting new material for their readers and hence daringly hoping to gain the upper hand in an already competitive journalistic environment. Thus it is crucial to ask how the market (that is, readers' tastes and expectations) shaped the articles and narratives they wrote. One hundred years later, Claude Lévi-Strauss still marveled at the popularity of such narratives of exotic places like Kendall's, but doubted their value for anthropological purposes: "[Their] desire to impress is so dominant as to make it impossible for the reader to assess the value of the evidence put before him."[19]

The circulation of newspapers like the *Picayune*, the *Gazette*, and *the Telegraph* and works like Kendall's tells much about the nature of the marketplace of readers and its potential impact on texts. Briefly stated, the chain of publications in Missouri, Louisiana, and the Republic of Texas defined the edges of a journalistic domain. Inside this domain (advertisements are especially revealing), one can learn about steam packets plying from port to port, cattle moving back and forth, and people doing business with each other on the basis of familiar assumptions. Beyond this domain, news was sporadic and unreliable, landscapes became blurry and exotic, and people were regarded as alien. Such journalistic domains did not necessarily overlap with formal national boundaries. For instance, the Anglo-American portion of Texas fell under the purview of southern American newspapers, and vice versa. Journalistically, the international border between Texan communities like Austin or Houston and American towns like Natchitoches or New Orleans did not exist. To speed the circulation of information, the United States postal law allowed editors to send and receive exchange papers and copy freely from

---

[18] For a discussion of Kendall's popularity, see Carroll, *The Texan Santa Fe Trail*, 2–16.
[19] Claude Lévi-Strauss, *Tristes Tropiques* (New York: Penguin, 1992), 17.

each other, a privilege that was extended to the Texas Republic.[20] At the same time, the Spanish-speaking section of Texas, the San Antonio–Goliad region, was for the most part excluded. The *Telegraph*, for instance, had a special section on news from "the West." Ethnically different, economically less developed, and immediately adjacent to Mexico and suspected of being mixed up in its rough and tumble politics, the San Antonio–Goliad region was treated almost as a foreign country:

It must be peculiarly painful to every patriot to contemplate the condition of this unfortunate section of our Republic. For more than six years this once favored region has been desolated by a constant train of disasters ... while every other portion of our Republic is enlivened with the cheering influences of industry and enterprise – here every thing languishes and a cheerless blighting torpor spreads its poisonous influence around. The farms are deserted, the villages are sinking under the ravages of decay, and the setters seem rather as sojourners than possessors of their once happy homes.[21]

The coverage of the Texan Santa Fe Expedition reveals that journalistic domains and national boundaries were not coterminous. American newspapers kept their readers abreast of minute logistical details and personalities – often described as if they were one's own next-door neighbors – of this otherwise Texan enterprise. Moreover, the fact that scores of articles meant for local consumption in Texas found their way into southern American newspapers added to the impression of immediacy among readers in Louisiana or Missouri. This explains why Americans such as Kendall and Combs were naturally drawn into the enterprise. In marked contrast, the inhabitants of the San Antonio–Goliad region had no means of keeping abreast of the progress of the expedition and had to satisfy their curiosity mostly through hearsay and rumor. The result was that misinformation predominated in this portion of the Texas Republic. This situation even prompted the president of Texas and main architect of the expedition, Mirabeau Buonaparte Lamar, to visit San Antonio before the party's departure to increase public awareness and support. President Lamar understood that the involvement of tejanos in the expedition was crucial, as they would be able to identify more readily with nuevomexicanos and would be in a better position to persuade them of the joys and advantages conferred by Lone Star sovereignty. A ball was thrown in the president's honor that was attended by virtually all members of the tejano elite, including the mayor of San Antonio, Juan Nepomuceno Seguín, and his wife. But in spite of these social niceties – reaching a climax when President Lamar and Mrs. Seguín opened the ball with a waltz – mistrust seethed. Lack of information had taken a toll, as it was rumored that Mayor

[20] Sibley, *Lone Stars and State Gazettes*, 8.
[21] *Telegraph and Texas Register*, Apr 6, 1842.

Seguín was in close contact with Mexican authorities, informing them of the status of the Texas *invading* expedition.[22]

Beyond creating journalistic domains, newspapers such as the *Picayune* and the *Telegraph* and accounts such as Falconer's and Kendall's helped to forge a national/ethnic imagination by insisting on certain themes that reflected the appetites of potential readers rather than the realities of life at the border. The profits to be derived from the Santa Fe expedition were one such theme. The language of profit and speculative gain dominated the writings of the Texan Santa Fe Expedition from the very beginning. The wealth of the Santa Fe–Chihuahua Trail was enthusiastically discussed in the Anglo-American press. While in reality the total value of declared goods imported into New Mexico for the year of 1841 was a rather modest 150,000 dollars, the *Austin City Gazette* and the *Picayune*, echoing El Dorado, tossed around figures of more than one million dollars.[23] "Conservative" estimates of no less than 75,000 dollars envisioned revenue for Texas that – as one journalist put it – "would certainly tend to patch up our dilapidated finances."[24] And trade was just the beginning. Enormous wealth could be obtained from related agricultural projects, chiefly in cotton, and especially from mining. The *Austin City Gazette* estimated that Chihuahua alone had eight mining towns and one thousand shafts in operation: "... at present, the mines are very ineffectively worked, and the full extent of the Mexican mineral beds will probably never be developed until American or Texian [Anglo-Texan] enterprise carries steam into the bowels of the earth to drag its untold treasures into light."[25]

Such glowing economic prospects have to be understood against the backdrop of the Lone Star's own economic prospects. Real estate values that had soared in the late 1830s plummeted in 1840–1, and paper money was in short supply and circulated at greatly discounted prices; inflation was high, and investment was sluggish.[26] The Santa Fe venture thus appeared as lightning in the dark; it represented, at least partly, the yearnings of a reading public hoping for deliverance from a gloomy economic scenario. Months after the expedition, Falconer admitted as much, pointing out that the value of the trade to Santa Fe had been much exaggerated.[27]

What is particularly fascinating about these trenchant economic analyses is not so much that they exaggerated potential benefits, but that they justified some of the most farfetched schemes of commercial and territorial expansion.

[22] Maverick, *Memoirs*, 49.
[23] These estimates were made by Josiah Gregg in 1843. See discussion in Bloom, "New Mexico Under Mexican Administration" 121.
[24] *Austin City Gazette*, Apr 15, 1840.
[25] *Austin City Gazette*, Jan 20, 1841.
[26] For a more detailed appraisal, see Hogan, *The Texas Republic*, 87–9.
[27] Falconer, "Expedition to Santa Fe: An Account of Its Journey from Texas Through Mexico, with Particulars of Its Capture," in Hodge, *Letters and Notes*, 61.

For instance, the Santa Fe expedition was often construed as a steppingstone into a more comprehensive plan to dominate central and northern Mexico. With an obvious agenda, the editors of the *Austin City Gazette* explained that Chihuahua functioned like a center of distribution for the entire North of Mexico, holding various fairs throughout the year and boasting a seemingly insatiable appetite for foreign goods. Lying far from the Pacific Ocean and from the Gulf of Mexico and locked in by two mountain chains, Chihuahua could not be easily supplied by sea; thus it seemed evident to the newspaper editors that "a golden opening lay ready to be seized upon by Texian enterprise."[28] Thus readers of papers like the *Austin City Gazette* and the *Telegraph* came away with an unmistakable sense that there were sizeable territories in the immediacy of the Lone Star Republic and beyond the southwestern confines of the United States that, by dint of their unrealized economic potential, would ultimately be absorbed. How far these territories extended, nobody knew for certain, although perennial candidates included the entire northeast of Mexico, the Californias, and New Mexico.[29]

The Anglo-Saxon character of the Santa Fe expedition was yet another theme that set imaginary boundaries while reinforcing the self-image of the intended readers. In newspaper articles and accounts of the expedition, the varied human groups that inhabited the border region were classified according to shifting racial categories that placed Caucasians at the top. The venture was thus conceptualized as an attempt to introduce a measure of civilization among a whole spectrum of inferior races. A letter published in the *Columbia Patriot* expressed rather eloquently this point of view:

What field opens up before us for an adventure of the *Anglo-Saxon Nation*! What a wide door for the principles of republican government, of the arts and sciences of morality! . . . what opportunity at hand to raise the Cross and plant the holy institutions of Protestant Christianity! . . . the Bible will find its way to Santa Fe![30]

Such a crusading racial ideology had deep roots stretching back to England and its early colonial experience in America. But more immediately, these notions stemmed from the Lone Star's recent ethnic transformation. A far cry from the multi-ethnic coalition that had made possible the revolution of 1835–6, by the early 1840s Texas had become noticeably Anglo-Saxonized. Basic demography bore this out. Mexican towns and villages on the southwestern tier continued to languish and even decline in population due to unsettled conditions. The indigenous population of Texas had likewise diminished since the halcyon days of Stephen F. Austin, driven out in brutal campaigns waged in 1838–9, especially against the Cherokees, Caddos,

[28] *Austin City Gazette*, Jan 20, 1841.
[29] Among other editorials and articles, those of the *Telegraph and Texas Register*, Aug 14, Sep 11, and Oct 30, 1839, and Jan 1, Apr 15, and Jul 1, 1840.
[30] *Columbia Patriot*, Apr 13, 1839. Copied and translated by Guadalupe Miranda, Santa Fe, Jul 28, 1839, Herbert E. Bolton Papers, Box 41, no. 688, Bancroft Library.

and Comanches. In the meantime, the Anglo-European and slave populations had increased substantially, changing the entire demographic landscape of Texas. Concomitantly, the Anglo-Saxonization of Texas was evident in the very institutions of the country. In 1840, the Texas Congress
finally adopted the English common law for all legal proceedings and re-
pealed most Mexican legislation.[31] And along with institutions came the
question of political personnel. Since the days of the revolution, tejanos had
been sidelined, although a few figures clung to positions of authority at the
local level in an increasingly difficult, ethnic-torn environment. The Santa
Fe expedition took shape in the midst of this sweeping ethnic transformation. Not one Indian was invited, a fact later lamented, and tejanos were
understandably put off by the racial rhetoric.[32] President Lamar had to go
to great lengths to recruit José Antonio Navarro, the tejano patriarch with a
game leg who consented to go – as he later explained to the nuevomexicano
authorities – only to prevent a catastrophe between his present and former
countrymen.[33]

Anglo-Saxonism was not only evident in the practicalities of the expedition but more significantly in how journalists and chroniclers imagined the
human tapestry of this border region. Independent indigenous tribes were
placed in a complicated ranking system. The New Orleans editor placed the
Cherokees and Choctaws high on the list because of their frequent dealings
with the United States; they had their eyes "somewhat opened to the plan
of civil government . . . and had been made to know something of the system
of the Christian religion by the pious zeal of missionaries."[34] In contrast,
Comanches and Wacos did not seem to exhibit any of the "fruits" of civilization in spite of some contacts, and certainly bellicose and roving tribes
like the Kiowa were at the bottom of the Indian hierarchy.[35] Because of the
expedition's itinerary and purpose, it is not surprising that its chroniclers
would devote a great deal of space to classifying Mexicans according to
racial categories. Throughout the southern United States, and especially in
the Texas Republic, it was common to hear racial descriptions of Mexico
like the one offered by the United States Chargé d'Affairs to the Republic of Texas, who regarded Mexicans as "that feeble, dastardly, supersti-
tious priest ridden race of mongrels composed of Spanish, Indian and negro

---

[31] Hogan, *The Texas Republic*, 245.
[32] See "Falconer's Diary," in Hodge, ed., *Letters and Notes*, 108.
[33] Navarro to Armijo, Plaza de San Miguel, Oct 11, 1841, BHC, 2q175, 338, 104.
[34] Kendall, *Narrative of the Texan Santa Fe Expedition*, 181–2. For another detailed effort to
   place the Kiowas vis-à-vis Comanches and other Indians by a contemporary, see George
   Catlin, *Letters and Notes on the Manners, Customs, and Conditions of North American Indians*,
   2 vols (New York: Dover Publications, 1973 [1844]), 2, 73–4.
[35] Kendall, *Narrative of the Texan Santa Fe Expedition*, 281–2.

blood."[36] Beyond a general sense of repugnance at Mexico's mixed racial heritage, all of the expedition accounts introduced racial distinctions that were deemed vital. The *Telegraph*, for instance, likened Mexico to "the Hindoostan," presenting both as semicivilized countries deeply divided into multiple and complicated sects and castes. In the editors' opinion, knowing and exploiting these cleavages was of the utmost importance, for, as Great Britain had demonstrated, it was possible to conquer 50 million souls with only ten thousand to twenty thousand soldiers and a few skillful operators like those of the East India Company. The *Telegraph* estimated that the population of northern Mexico – that is, Nuevo León, Tamaullipas, Coahuila, Durango, Zacatecas, Chihuahua, New Mexico, and the Californias – did not exceed two and a half million, and consisted of "infinitely the best portion of the Mexican nation . . . having more of the Castillian blood and having mixed less with the Indians." Even so, the newspaper estimated that five-sixths of northern Mexicans were of Indian descent, leaving only forty thousand Hispanic whites.[37] New Mexico's population was supposed to mirror this streamlined demographic sketch. The *Austin City Gazette* erroneously affirmed that the inhabitants of New Mexico consisted of a Hispanic minority, mostly isolated from the rest of Mexico, and a majority of Pueblo Indians who nonetheless were "fully as far advanced in civilization as are the Mexicans themselves: they live in villages, cultivate the soil, and practice the different branches of commerce. They are well disposed toward the whites, and in their mode of living imitate them."[38] As we shall see, this rather benign racial portrait

---

[36] Joseph Eve to Richard Southgate, May 10, 1842, reproduced in "A Letter Book of Joseph Eve, United States Chargé d'Affairs to Texas," *Southwestern Historical Quarterly* 43:4 (1940), 494.

[37] *Telegraph and Texas Register*, Apr 10, Aug 28, 1839, and Oct 19, 1840.

[38] *Austin City Gazette*, Apr 15, 1840. A good deal of speculation revolved around how these groups would react to the proposed incorporation into the Republic of Texas. Prior to the denouement of the expedition, the Anglo-American press assumed that the Hispanic elite would simply go along with the Texan scheme. The *Columbia Patriot* confidently stated that for a long time, many of New Mexico's enlightened citizens were not only willing but eager to strengthen their political connections to Texas and had even desired to send deputies to the Texas Congress. See, for instance, the *Columbia Patriot*, Apr 13, 1839; Instructions to Commissioners William G. Cooke, Antonio Navarro, Richard F. Brenham, and William G. Dryden, Austin, Jun 15, 1841, printed in Austin, TX: G. H. Harrison, Printer, 1841, Beinecke, Zc52 841ti. The press was less sanguine about the willingness of the Pueblo Indians, although it was hoped that they too would acquiesce in the end. In a fascinating example of historical revisionism, the *Austin City Gazette* found traces of the Pueblos' readiness to "look into the family of Texian [Anglo-Texan] Freemen" in their crucial participation in the Chimayó Rebellion of 1837. According to the paper, at that time the Pueblo had risen up and "inflicted summary punishment upon thirty of their oppressors," thus revealing a powerful yearning to set themselves free from the shackles of despotism and tyranny. Yet privately some doubts were voiced. The secretary of state of the Republic of Texas, Abner S. Lipscomb, worried that the Pueblo Indians would reject partnership with

of New Mexicans would subsequently change for the worse, but the propagation of these racial categories on the heterogeneous border population
constitutes one of the most critical ideological transformations facilitated by
Anglo-American print culture in this era.

Finally, the uncharted, savage, and exotic nature of the country that was to
be visited by the Texan trekkers was yet another recurrent theme that reified
borders and revealed the close connections between audiences and expedition writers. The latter repeatedly (and mistakenly) stated that no white man
had ever seen the Comanche Wilderness. This argument was sometimes expressed in very precise geographic terms. For Kendall, for example, the Cross
Timbers – a strip of wooded country flanked on the eastern side by clumps
of woodland and on the west by an ocean of prairie – constituted a civilizational divide or an immense natural hedge dividing "the settled portions of
the United States from the open prairies which have ever been the home and
hunting ground of the red man."[39] Peter Gallagher located the Rubicon on a
creek that emptied into the Noland River: "From this spot we knew nothing
of the country as it never before had been traveled by a white man . . . made
12 miles (N.N.E.)[.] All the maps of the country are wrong. . . ."[40] But regardless of the border's exact location, all Anglo-American tales of the expedition
emphasized the primeval character of this region, a world unperturbed by
civilization, living in its own time, and even endowed with mysterious properties; Kendall for one claimed that he had joined the expedition partly in
the hope of correcting a derangement of health.[41]

Of course, what conferred on this area its deepest sense of exoticism was
the presence of the "roaming" Indian in his or her pristine environment.
These Anglo-American narrators could not refrain from engaging a public
that had shown an insatiable appetite for the exotic, pristine, and savage,
whether along Egypt's Nile, in Yucatán, or in the heart of the Congo. The
extent to which the "Indian" stood as a powerful literary device in these accounts can be best gleaned from the contrasting accounts of non-American
and American chroniclers of the Santa Fe expedition. The non-American
Falconer, Gallagher, and Grover tended to dwell on the few violent encounters. The Englishman described in considerable detail the fate of five Texans

---

Texas on the ground that the Texas Constitution enshrined a principle of discrimination toward Indians, who did not enjoy the same protections extended to other citizens. In detailed
instructions, Secretary Lipscomb urged the commissioners to dispel such doubts by stating
that the word "Indian," as used in the Constitution, applied only to "barbarians" but not
to "civilized Indians" who cultivate the soil and profess Christian doctrines. Secretary of
State Lipscomb to Commissioners to Santa Fe, Austin, Apr 14, 1840, in Abner S. Lipscomb,
Letters of Secretary of State to Commissioners to Santa Fe (Austin, TX: G. H. Harrison, Printer,
1841), 26.
[39] Kendall, *Narrative of the Texan Santa Fe Expedition*, 139.
[40] Gallagher, "Journal of the Santa Fe Expedition," 169–86.
[41] Kendall, *Narrative of the Texan Santa Fe Expedition*, 3.

who left camp in search of water and fell in with a group of Kiowas. The Texan Grover focused on the mangled bodies: "some were cut & carved from head to foot, some their brains scattered over the ground on which they fought, & Mayby's heart was cut out of his body. Indeed imagination can scarcely depict the havoc these savage demons made...."[42] The Texan Gallagher highlighted the same tragic episode and also included bizarre and seemingly unimportant occurrences that must have loomed large in his mind, such as the daring approach of a lone warrior whose only purpose had been to get within earshot of the encamped troops to be able to scream in Spanish that "[the Texans] did not know where they were going & their Captain was a Fool."[43]

In contrast, Kendall evinced a more heroic view of Indians. Attuned to the cultural nationalism and romanticism of the American reading public of the era, Kendall presented the Indian as a tragic figure destined to perish in the face of the onslaught of civilization.[44] As the expedition passed through a hastily abandoned Waco village, Kendall remarked the orderly arrangement of wigwams, the aesthetic cornfields and melon patches, and the neatness and cleanliness of the purlieus. He concluded that the Waco had never been "corrupted by association with the whites," nor made "weak and effeminate" by the use of alcohol. After spending an entire morning in this village Kendall's imagination even conjured up images of an Indian Romeo, playing a musical instrument that resembled a fife, discoursing most eloquent music to a "belle of the tribe."[45] The New Orleans editor went on to express his admiration for the likes of Washington Irving and his companions, who had made a trip to the prairies west of the Osage hunting-grounds; for the Honorable Charles A. Murray, who had spent some months "with the buffaloes and the Pawnees" (Kendall had a tendency to write about Native Americans in the same breath as mustangs or tarantulas); and for Sir William Drummond Steward, who year after year left wealth and title to spend his summers high up on the waters of the Missouri among the natives.[46] To be sure, both mindless, horrific violence as described by Falconer or Gallagher and noble innocence by Kendall constituted two sides of the same coin: a world preserved intact, a capsule from a time long vanished in most other regions of the world. But these contrasting portraits of Indians underscore the extent to which authors were guided by the tastes and imaginings of audiences.

---

[42] Falconer, "Extended Account," 39; Gallagher, "Journal of the Santa Fe Expedition," 173–5; Grover, "Minutes of Adventure From June, 1841," 38.

[43] Gallagher, "Journal of the Santa Fe Expedition," 173–5.

[44] Robert F. Berkhofer, *The White Man's Indian: Images of an Idea from Columbus to the Present* (New York: Knopf, 1978), 86–96.

[45] Kendall, *Narrative of the Texan Santa Fe Expedition*, 177–8, 181–2.

[46] Ibid., 3, 76.

The depiction of Mexico also evinced the influence of changing literary tastes. Gallagher, Combs, and Kendall presented Mexico neither as a pristine Indian world nor as a civilized nation, but as disquietingly hybrid, although much closer to savagery than civilization. In Kendall's book, we get a first inkling of this subject even before the expedition's departure, when the New Orleans editor made a quick tour of San Antonio and its environs. The missions, silent and decaying testimonies of a high civilization, particularly impressed Kendall. Yet he found it difficult to reconcile these imposing structures with the "primitive" character of the society that he saw. Kendall reasoned that at first Spain had extended the Catholic doctrines in a decisive and even cruel manner, but that in the course of time the empire had lost some of its initial missionary zeal and in a more humane temper had allowed the "superstitions of the Indian to mingle with the rites introduced among them," thus yielding "anomalous consequences" that were so plainly visible to him.[47] By emphasizing the extent to which the indigenous element had persisted within the bounds of Mexico, chroniclers like Kendall articulated a deeply rooted nexus of beliefs among Anglo-American readers that revolved around the incapacity of Spain as a colonial power. Kendall's talent resided precisely in indulging and to some extent shaping the shifting opinions toward Mexico. In travelogues and memoirs set south of the border during the 1820s and early 1830s, Anglo-American writers still showed considerable sympathy – even when tinged with condescension – for a sister republic that had also managed to escape the clutches of European colonialism.[48] Since the late 1830s, however, Anglo-American authors portrayed the Mexican-Indian world as squarely antagonistic to the civilizing forces springing from both the Texas Republic and the United States. Undoubtedly, some of these notions had been molded in the crucible of the Texas Revolution and its legacy of bitter mistrust enshrined in the tales of the Alamo, Goliad, and San Jacinto.[49] The *Narrative of the Texan Santa Fe Expedition* masterfully incorporated this anti-Mexican ferment of opinion that would soon explode in the penny press and cheap literature of the wartime years.[50]

[47] Ibid., 52–3.

[48] For instance, see the decidedly statistical and generally positive works of the first ministers of the United States and Great Britain in Mexico, respectively: Joel R. Poinsett, *Notes on Mexico, Made in the Autumn of 1822* (New York: F. A. Prager, 1969 [1824]); Henry George Ward, *Mexico in 1827* (London: H. Colburn, 1828). Other works tend toward the idyllic. See Mary Austin Holley, *Texas* (Austin, TX: Texas State Historical Association, 1985 [1833]); and even Richard H. Dana, *Two Years Before the Mast* (New York: Random House, 1936 [1840]).

[49] Other expeditions along the Texas–Mexico border spawned their own anti-Mexican accounts. See, for instance, *Interesting Account of the Life and Adventures of One of Those Unfortunate Men, Who Was Shot at Tampico* (New York, 1836); Thomas Jefferson Green, *Journal of the Texian Expedition Against Mier* (New York: Harper and Brothers, 1845).

[50] For an excellent analysis of how Americans perceived the war with Mexico, see Robert W. Johannsen, *To the Halls of the Montezumas: The Mexican War in the American Imagination* (New York: Oxford University Press, 1985), esp. ch. 6 and 7.

Indeed the transit of Mexico from civilized to savage occurred progressively as these Anglo-American accounts unfolded. The dramatic fate of the expedition afforded a perfect backdrop. At the beginning of their narratives, Falconer and Kendall portrayed Mexicans as inhabiting an intermediate stage in the scale of human development, potentially redeemable through association with more civilized nations, but equally capable of slipping back into barbarity. But the expedition's first dealings with New Mexicans confirmed the worst. Even when these writers occasionally introduced nuance, their texts generally exoticized Mexicans, hereafter associating their character with treachery, cruelty, and servility. Kendall's hyperbolic description leaves no doubt: "...we were now in the power of men who possessed all the vices of savage life without one of the virtues that civilization teaches."[51] Combs reduced New Mexican society to villainous leaders and mindless masses, as he told how Mexican officers "excited the Peons to the highest degree of frenzy," and how the prisoners would have been slaughtered on the spot had they not been huddled together in a small yard enclosed by a mud wall and defended by the regular troops.[52]

Predictably, a popular theme among these writers was Mexico's religious fanaticism, not in the sense of blindly adhering to arbitrary religious precepts, but rather in the more ominous sense of primitiveness and irrationality. Kendall meticulously described a procession staged by the faithful in San Miguel del Vado to give thank for the peaceful surrender of the Texan party.[53] The newsman insisted on the crude Catholic imagery and the quirkiness of the procession led by a balding priest wearing teacup-size glasses and clad in a dirty blanket tied about him with a piece of rope, which would have drawn a smile "even from the gloomiest misanthrope that ever lived." Kendall's most scornful remarks were reserved for the town's patron saint, a wax figure "feathered from head to tow" and with a pair of wings "hanging listlessly from his shoulders;" to complete the "ludicrous *tout ensemble*," the figure's head was covered with a lace cap "of the fashion of our grandmothers."[54] In Kendall's portrait, the procession acquired an air of unreality and silliness against the backdrop of dramatic circumstances in which the lives of hundreds of people hung in the balance.

The new image of "the Mexican" can best be exemplified in a few individual vignettes. With certain balance, Kendall first presented Governor Manuel Armijo as a portly and imposing man. But the governor quickly turned into a conniving, ruthless, and arbitrary egomaniac, just like Santa Anna who, in Kendall's opinion, was the governor's self-conscious role model.[55]

[51] Kendall, *Narrative of the Texan Santa Fe Expedition*, 391.
[52] Combs, "Narrative of the Santa Fe Expedition in 1841," 309.
[53] Kendall, *Narrative of the Texan Santa Fe Expedition*, 455–9.
[54] Ibid., 456.
[55] Combs, "Narrative of the Santa Fe Expedition in 1841," 310; Kendall, *Narrative of the Texas Santa Fe Expedition*, 396–97.

Captain Dámaso Salazar, commander of the rural militia of San Miguel del Vado, fared much worse. Salazar was charged with transporting a group of Texan prisoners from New Mexico to Chihuahua and became notorious for subjecting them to long and arduous marches and keeping food rations to a minimum to induce compliance and forestall escape attempts. Through Kendall's eye, we see a sadistic Salazar taking pleasure in throwing meat cakes high in the air and watching – "with a glee absolutely demoniacal" – the scramble among the suffering throng.[56] Salazar executed at least three Texans who failed to keep the pace, and kept count of the dead by hanging their ears on a string attached to his saddle. He was later court-martialed.[57] Kendall's summary judgment was that the actions of the militia captain marked "a new leaf in the dreadful chapter of human depravity."[58] Salazar's second in command, a man identified only as don Jesús, shared many of his superior's traits. Kendall possessed enough working knowledge of phrenology to affirm that don Jesús's spiritual traits could be easily deduced from his physical appearance; his coarse, dark, hang-dog face, his black eyes, and even the shape of his head revealed a man "destitute of the organs of benevolence and the better attributes of our nature as outer darkness is of light, and if he had a heart at all, it legitimately belonged to a hyena or a prairie wolf."[59] In Kendall's *Narrative*, these characters represent the Mexican world gone haywire, combining an animal ruthlessness and savagery with the wickedness and contrived cruelty worthy of a most decadent society.

From the perspective of the reading public of Texas, Louisiana, and Missouri, the Santa Fe expedition may have been a disastrous commercial and political experiment, but editorially it was a resounding success. The expedition's newspaper coverage and the astounding commercial success enjoyed by writers such as Falconer and above all Kendall reveal the intricate and powerful connections between imagination and market demand, between nationalism and profit-making. However questionable, the texts of the Texan Santa Fe Expedition provided "depth" and "character" to a region of which precious little had been known in Texas and the United States; in the process, journalists and authors found a willing audience. The market had a hand in shaping narratives as New Mexico and the Comanche Wilderness acquired concrete form and texture and became populated by frightful characters like Governor Armijo and his loyal aids, Captain Dámaso Salazar and don Jesús, as well as honorable Waco warriors and bloodthirsty Kiowas.

---

[56] Kendall, *Narrative of the Texan Santa Fe Expedition*, 504.

[57] Judicial Proceedings Against Salazar, Villa del Paso, Nov 6, 1841, Herbert E. Bolton Papers, Box 41, no. 688, Bancroft Library.

[58] Kendall, *Narrative of the Texan Santa Fe Expedition*, 397.

[59] Ibid., 395.

FIGURE 7.2. Chief Dohasan

WINTER CALENDARS: INTIMATE PORTRAYALS OF THE FRONTIER

Kiowas also recorded the passage of the Texan Santa Fe Expedition. Initially this account only circulated within the tribal realm. It would not be until 1892 when James Mooney, an ethnologist living in the Kiowa reservation, obtained four calendars or winter counts and subsequently published them. The oldest work chronicled yearly events beginning in 1833 and covering a period of sixty years.[60] It had been kept for more than three decades by the family of Dohasan (Little Mountain), head chief of the Kiowas, and thus the document became known as the Dohasan Calendar (see Figure 7.2) Set-Tan (Little Bear), a cousin of the great chief, kept a second calendar. The Set-Tan Annual Calendar was almost an exact copy of the Dohasan, but made in greater detail and containing two additional pictographs. Both calendars were originally painted on hides and renewed from time to time

[60] James Mooney, *Calendar History of the Kiowa Indians* (Washington, DC: Smithsonian Institution Press, 1979), 143. Reprinted from the Seventeenth Annual Report of the Bureau of American Ethnology, published in 1898.

as they wore out from age and handling, although the ones acquired by Mooney were already drawn using colored pencils on heavy manila paper. They consist of a series of pictographs arranged in a spiral, beginning in the lower-right corner and ending near the center (see Figure 7.3). An evolving oral tradition was associated with these drawings, as it was customary for calendars to be brought out frequently during the long nights in the winter camp to be exhibited and discussed in the circle of warriors around a fire. At these gatherings, Mooney explained, "the pipe is filled and passed around, and each man in turn recites some mythic or historic tradition, or some noted deed on the warpath, which is then discussed by the circle. Thus the history of the tribe is formulated and handed down."[61] The very existence of the Kiowa texts should alert us to the *limits* of market and state. Even as these vast forces proceeded to transform the lives of frontier peoples in many realms, it was still possible for a literary culture to flourish independently.

It is easy to underestimate the importance of texts in indigenous communities. Of course, archeologists have long been fascinated with the writings of indigenous civilizations of the preconquest era. But oddly, we know far less about the writings of historical – as opposed to archeological – Native Americans of the eighteenth and nineteenth centuries.[62] Notwithstanding nineteenth-century prejudice, Indian peoples kept various writing traditions and acquired new ones under the aegis of print capitalism. Yet researchers have been slow to mine these sources, especially when alternative nonindigenous sources can be used to reconstruct the same historical events. Only recently ethnohistorians have taken a harder look at these texts and have gained awareness of their remarkable amount, quality, and variety.[63]

In the nineteenth century, old forms of indigenous graphic representation coexisted alongside new methods. In the United States, some Native Americans made their first incursions into the world of print, editing newspapers such as the *Cherokee Phoenix and Indian Advocate* or becoming widely recognized authors, such as William Apess and Black Hawk, whose autobiographical accounts first appeared in 1829 and 1833 respectively. In Mexico, an Indian from Tixla, Ignacio Manuel Altamirano, became one of the preeminent literary figures of the 1860s and 1870s.[64] But even as indigenous

---

[61] Ibid., 144–5.

[62] For a recent assessment of scholarly uses of indigenous texts in central Mexico, see James Lockhart, *The Nahuas After the Conquest: A Social and Cultural History of the Indians of Central Mexico, Sixteenth Through Eighteenth Centuries* (Stanford, CA: Stanford University Press, 1992), 5–9.

[63] For a persuasive assessment of the importance of Indian sources – as well as lack of scholarly interest – see George Miles, "To Hear an Old Voice: Rediscovering Native Americans in American History," in William Cronon, George Miles, and Jay Gitlin, eds., *Under an Open Sky: Rethinking America's Western Past* (New York: W. W. Norton, 1992), 52–70.

[64] For an enlightening discussion of Altamirano's patriotism, see David A. Brading, "El patriotismo liberal y la reforma mexicana," in Cecilia Noriega Elío, ed., *El Nacionalismo en Mexico* (Zamora: El Colegio de Michoacán, 1992), 179–204.

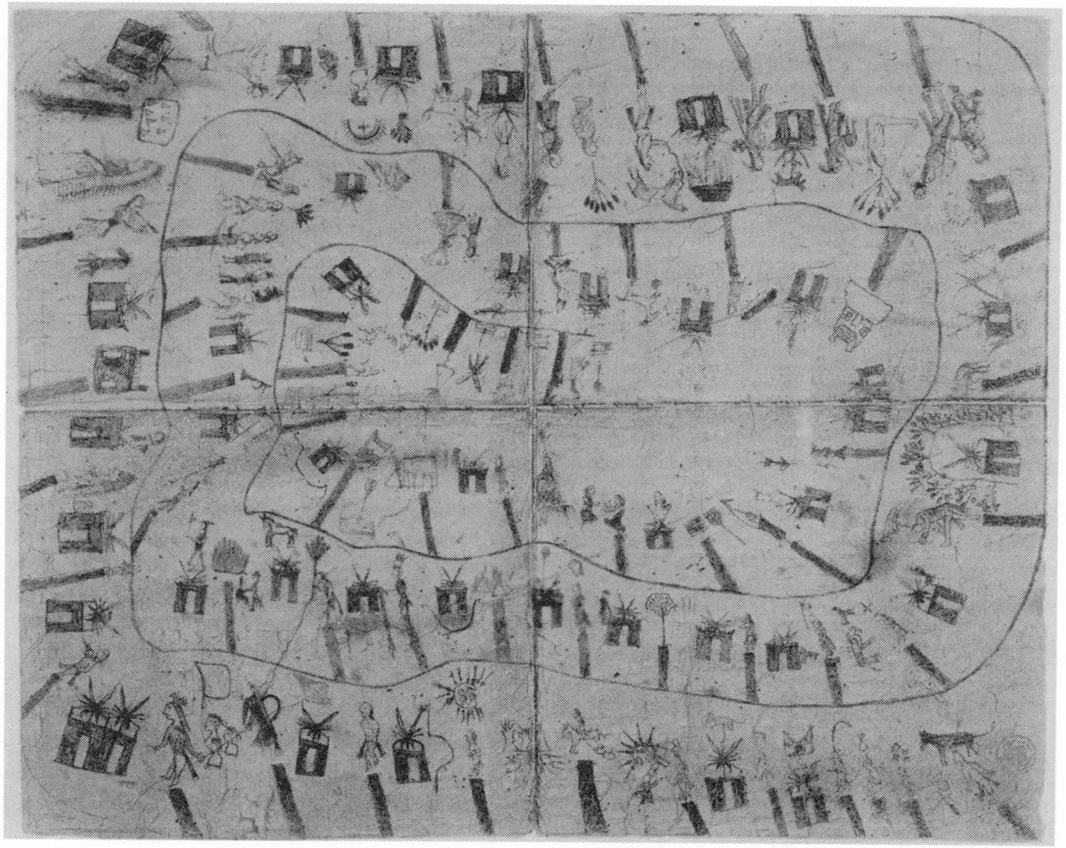

FIGURE 7.3. Set-Tan Annual Calendar

peoples took advantage of modern print capitalism to further their collective and individual interests, old writing traditions persisted throughout much of the century. Among Plains Indians, winter counts continued to exist during this period of transition into modern print. A calendaric culture was evident throughout the plains from North Dakota – where the Sioux kept several chronologies, including the famous Lone Dog's winter count – to the Texas– New Mexico border, where Kiowas and possibly Apaches kept similar spirals of pictographs of memorable events.[65]

Just like any other historical accounts, winter counts derive their power from the particular selection of tales and detail. But while the written word allows for certain latitude in the telling, pictographic writing requires conciseness in the extreme, as pictographs function as mnemonic aids intended to jog the memory of the keeper at a later date. Faced with the impossibility of graphically recording all battles, treaties, and other affairs of paramount importance, pictographic writers had to select one or two yearly events for depiction. Alternate black bars and Sun Dance medicine lodge symbols represented the passage of winters and summers, respectively. Pictographs placed close or on top of a black bar occurred during the cold period, while pictographs adjacent to the Sun Dance medicine lodge symbol happened during the warm season. Here is a partial list of Kiowa pictographs drawn from the Set-Tan Calendar for the 1830s and early 1840s:

1832–3. "Winter when they captured the money." The Kiowas met a small train led by Americans and attacked it. After the scuffle, a few coins were found on the ground that the Kiowas made into disks and wore as hair ornaments.

1833–4. "Winter when the stars fell." Meteoric display was observed throughout North America on the morning of November 13, 1833.

1834–5. "Winter when Bull Tail was killed." A war party was dispatched against the Mexicans of the waterless country – that is, Chihuahua. One morning, they were all surprised by Mexican troops and killed, including Bull Tail.

1835. "Summer of the cattail rush Sun Dance." A Sun Dance was held on the south bank of the North Canadian River, where a great many cattail rushes (*Equisetum arrense*) were growing.

1836–7. "Winter when K'inahiate was killed." K'inahiate (Man) was killed in an expedition against the Mexicans of the timber country – that is, the lower Rio Grande valley.

1837. "Summer when Cheyennes were massacred." As preparations were being made for the Sun Dance, Kiowas discovered, pursued, and massacred forty-eight Cheyennes. Six Kiowa died in the action.

---

[65] Mooney points out that Captain W. P. Clark, in his book on Indian sign language, mentions that Apaches had "picture histories." Mooney, *Calendar History*, 142.

1837–8. "Winter when they dragged the head." Comanche and Kiowa scouts killed one Arapaho Indian and, after scalping and beheading him, dragged his head into camp at the end of a *reata*.

1839–40. "Smallpox winter."

1840. "Red-Bluff Sun Dance." that summer, the confederation of Comanches, Apaches, and Kiowas made peace with the Arapahos and Cheyennes.

1840–1. "Hide-quiver war expedition winter." The old men joined the younger warriors on a war expedition into Mexico, taking along old bows and quivers of buffalo skin.

1841–2. "Winter when A'dalhaba'k'ia was killed." A'dalhaba'k'ia (Sloping Hair) was killed by a Texan detachment.

Calendars like the Set-Tan include some events that outsiders would consider historically significant, such as the devastating smallpox epidemic of 1839 or the 1840 alliance of five nations, a peace that was never broken and single-handedly shaped the geopolitics of the area until the end of the century. But frequently, the Set-Tan Annual Calendar depicts affairs of personal or anecdotal nature, like the deaths of Bull Tail, Man, and Sloping Hair – whose inclusion may still be justified by the importance or promise of these leaders – or the discovery of a handful of coins in 1833, and the killing of a lone Arapaho warrior and the disposal of his body parts in 1837.

Certainly there is no mention of events like the Texas Revolution or the Mexican–American War, events that unquestionably had tremendous repercussions on Kiowas and Comanches. These omissions do not imply that the Kiowas were disconnected from the Texas Republic, Mexico, and the United States. On the contrary, Kiowas for a long time had become part and parcel of this fluid international space, as their livelihood had come to depend on the ebb and flow of civil wars and international disputes in this area. Kiowas regularly sent parties that operated in an enormous geographic area from California through Texas and sometimes ventured as far as Tamaulipas, Chihuahua, and Durango. In these forays, Kiowas gathered a great deal of information from captives, allies, and other sources. Moreover, since the eighteenth century, Kiowas had established regular trade relations with New Mexican *comancheros* and Pueblo Indians and beginning in 1835 maintained periodic contacts with American trading houses.[66] Thus lack of information does not explain the absence of events like the Texas Revolution or the Mexican–American War in these chronologies.

Neither do these absences imply arbitrariness on the part of winter count keepers. The peculiar mix of historical and individual affairs depicted in these Indian chronologies puzzled early ethnographers such as Garrick Mallery

[66] See Mildred P. Mayhall, *The Kiowas*, 2 ed. (Norman, OK: University of Oklahoma Press, 1971), 85–91.

(discoverer of the Lone Dog Calendar) and Mooney. Mallery was persuaded that winter counts were not intended to be continuous histories,
but simply constituted sets of unusual or peculiar happenings well suited
for depiction or particularly dear to the keeper. He was most impressed
by the fact that the Sioux winter count did not even mention Colonel
George Armstrong Custer's campaign of 1868, which ultimately compelled
the southern tribes to go on a reservation for the first time, and barely
made reference to the pitched battles of 1874, which terminated in the Sioux's
final confinement in reservations. After careful consideration of pictographs
covering more than sixty years, Mooney too concluded that the Kiowa calendars resembled the personal reminiscences of a garrulous old man rather
than the full-fledged history of a nation.[67] This may have been the case. Yet,
for all the seeming randomness, once chosen, these events acquired great
saliency, as they served to fix all ordinary activities of the group. For instance, a person was said to have been born in the winter when the stars fell
or a couple started living together in the winter when A'dalhaba'k'ia was
killed, and so on. While we know little about how winter counts were actually written, it seems likely that some discussion preceded the final choice of
pictographs given their significance in the collective tribal memory. We know
that at least some of the events depicted had seized the collective imagination from the very beginning, and it was generally agreed that they best
evoked a particular winter or summer. A German captive who was but a
little boy when the bleeding head of the Arapaho warrior was dragged into
camp in the winter of 1837–8 still recalled the thrill of horror fifty years
later.[68]

Having worked with only Kiowa calendars and informants, Mooney later
came to the realization that the pictograph for the winter of 1841–2 corre-
sponded remarkably well with an Indian encounter narrated in Kendall's
book of the Santa Fe expedition. The pictograph in question refers to the
killing of Chief A'dalhaba'k'ia and shows a warrior with the right side of
the head shaved and the left side with the hair at full length, a hairstyle that
allowed the wearer to display ear pendants (see Figure 7.4). A bird on top of
the warrior's head represents a characteristic ornament of red woodpecker
feathers. A stain on his body indicates that A'dalhaba'k'ia died of a bullet
wound. According to oral tradition, the entire Kiowa tribe was camping
on a small stream when it was discovered that a party of Texan soldiers
was moving toward them. The Kiowas managed to surprise and kill five
Texans who were ahead of the main body; the Kiowas captured the Texans'
horses, but lost A'dalhaba'k'ia. The Kiowas then abandoned their camp,
but remained vigilant of the main body of intruders; returning a few days
later, they found a Texan who had strayed from the group and then killed

[67] Mooney, _Calendar History_, 146.
[68] Ibid., 273.

FIGURE 7.4. Chief A'dalhaba'k'ia

him.[69] This fateful encounter took place in the fall of 1841 on a small stream near the Llano Estacado that Kiowas named Pabo P'a (American Horse River).

Virtually all of these details match Anglo-American descriptions. The first five Anglo Americans massacred are identified as Lieutenant Geo R. Hull and four companions. Anglo-American witnesses also agree that over the next few days parties of Kiowa scouts monitored the progress of the Texan

---

[69] Winter counts constitute invaluable historical sources, but one has to bear in mind that the original pictographs are then interpreted by the keepers, the translators, and ethnologists like Mooney. See Melburn D. Thurman, "Plains Indian Winter Counts and the New Ethnohistory," *Plains Anthropologist* 27 (1982), 173–5. For other winter counts among Plains Indians, see N. A. Higginbotham, "The Wind-Roan Bear Winter Count," *Plains Anthropologist* 26 (1981), 1–42; Garrick Mallery, "Picture-Writing of the American Indians," in *10th Annual Report of the Bureau of American Ethnology, 1888–89* (Washington, DC: U.S. Government Printing Office, 1893).

party. They also state that another expedition member, a Mexican simply identified as Ramón, was murdered a few days later. Finally, Anglo-American sources amply justify the Kiowa usage of "American Horse River," for, as Falconer and Gallagher explained, on the morning of September 4, 1841, Kiowa horsemen were able to stampede all the cattle and eighty-three horses of the expedition. Immediately pursued, the Kiowas were forced to leave the cattle behind, but took all the horses.[70] We know something more about what transpired in the main Kiowa camp after the first violent encounter with the Texans. Some New Mexican *comancheros* were trading among Kiowas when a group of warriors came dashing in with enemy scalps and entrails, as well as the dead bodies of eleven fellow warriors, including that of a principal chief (presumably A'dalhaba'k'ia). The *comancheros* reported that immediately all manner of ceremonies and performances was under way. Warriors danced around the Texan scalps, and women smote and cut their breasts and ran naked through thorns and prickly pear bushes to show their grief and affection toward the deceased.[71]

The Kiowa calendars in general and the depiction of the encounter with the Texans more specifically reveal a different way of seeing, interpreting, and writing about themselves and the people around them. Consider the notion of territory. Winter counts make it clear that the Kiowas, unlike depictions in American and Mexican sources, did not regard themselves as a shiftless wandering tribe, but understood the area where they lived as a homeland. Like many other prairie Indians, the Kiowas had originally migrated from the northern Plains driven out by the Dakota Sioux and Cheyennes. According to oral tradition, by the late-eighteenth century, Kiowas ranged between the forks of the Platte River, advancing along the base of the mountains and pushing Comanches from the northern head streams of the Arkansas. Some years of war ensued, but finally a settlement was reached sometime around 1790.

It was a stunning feat of diplomacy. Instead of more years of uncertainty and violence, Kiowas and Comanches occupied together the territory along and south of the Arkansas, holding it in common for decades. In the course of these years of relative peace, Kiowas and Comanches became even closer allies, often camping, hunting, trading, and conducting expeditions together, although Kiowas tended to make their home camps toward the northwestern portion of the river whereas Comanches kept near the Llano Estacado and along the Texas frontier.[72] From the early 1830s until reservation days in

---

[70] Thomas Falconer, "Extended Account," in Hodge, *Letters and Notes*, 38–41; Kendall, *Narrative of the Texan Santa Fe Expedition*, 257–85; Gallagher, "Journal of the Santa Fe Expedition," 174–5; Grover, "Minutes of Adventure from June, 1841," 35.

[71] Kendall later met these same *comancheros*. Kendall, *Narrative of the Texan Santa Fe Expedition*, 352.

[72] Mooney, *Calendar History*, 164.

the late 1860s, the Kiowa homeland remained remarkably stable, although this did not preclude Kiowa bands from moving about within this large domain in patterns dictated by lifestyle, depletion of animals and plants, and military considerations. Still, Kiowas developed strong emotional ties to specific locations to which they regularly returned. The Set-Tan mentions that a place on the south bank of the North Canadian River at the Red Hills with a great many cattail rushes was a favorite spot for holding Sun Dances. A nearby location was so frequently used for that purpose that it was given the name of Sun-Dance Creek. Other sites, such as the American Horse River, evoked deeds that were tragic but always meaningful to the collectivity. In 1867, Kiowa chief Satanta eloquently spoke of this sense of attachment: "All the land south of the Arkansas belongs to the Kiowas and Comanches, and I don't want to give away any of it. I love the land and the buffalo, and will not part with any."[73]

While it is clear that Kiowas developed a strong sense of territoriality in the early to mid-nineteenth century, it is also evident that they did not conceive boundaries as permanent demarcations guaranteed by formal treaties but merely as temporary expressions of relations of power (see Figure 7.5). Thus the main narrative thrust of the Dohasan and Set-Tan calendars revolves around the vital geopolitics of this fractious region. The Kiowas had been able to maintain control over one area due first and foremost to skillful diplomacy. The smoking of the pipe with the Comanches had been a decisive event ending a period of internecine warfare and ushering in a new era of relative peace and stability. In 1840, the Kiowas helped to broker another momentous alliance, joining five nations – Kiowa, Comanche, Kiowa-Apache, Arapaho, and Cheyenne – ensuring Kiowa possession of the Arkansas Basin and forming a veritable barrier to westward- and southward-moving Indians (attracted by the prospects of trading horses with the Mexican settlements) as well as to encroaching whites from the northeast.[74] But sometimes negotiation was not enough. These calendaric accounts also underscore the enormous energy and determination of the Kiowas to pursue, kill, and repel trespassers like the Osages, Pawnees, and Texans. The latter in particular emerged as a serious threat. In the late 1830s, Texans conducted a war of extermination and removal in an area that Comanches and Kiowas had long regarded as their own. The Kiowa-Comanche alliance was driven out of its best hunting grounds in violation of treaties and without compensation. In the spring of 1840, the Comanches suffered losses at the Council

---

[73] Satanta's speech at the Treaty of Medicine Lodge, Kansas, in 1867, as reported by journalist Henry M. Stanley. Quoted in Colin G. Calloway. ed., *Our Hearts Fell to the Ground: Plains Indian Views of How the West Was Lost* (Boston, MA: Bedford Books of St. Martin's Press, 1996), 114. Like Kiowas, Comanches had a keen sense of place. See Daniel J. Gelo, "Comanche Land and Ever Has Been: A Native Geography of the Nineteenth-Century Comanchería," *Southwestern Historical Quarterly* 103:3 (Jan 2000), 273–310.

[74] Mayhall, *The Kiowas*, 92–3.

FIGURE 7.5. Kiowa warrior

House Fight at San Antonio and along the edges of the white settlements at the hands of Texas Rangers. Kiowas and Comanches retaliated in the summer, raiding the Texas coast around Victoria and Linville.[75] The Texan Santa Fe Expedition of 1841, the Kiowa victories over this advancing body of Texans, and the death of Sloping Hair have to be understood against the backdrop of this deep-seated enmity and quest to preserve a homeland free of encroachment.

Always pragmatic, Kiowas regarded peoples around them neither as impossibly large nations nor as ethereal races, but as discrete human groupings. Breaking down these human aggregates into tribes served Kiowas well, allowing them to cope effectively with changing configurations of Americans, Mexicans, and Texans. Kiowas made a clear distinction between "Americans" – that is, emigrants from the North or Kansas side and generally regarded as friendly – and "Texans," whom Kiowas called *Tehaneko*, a word probably derived from the Spanish *tejano*. Indeed, Kiowas continued to make this distinction long after Texas became annexed to the United States.[76] Large polities like the United States and Mexico were cut down to

[75] Ibid., 93.
[76] While Kiowa animosity toward Texans was deep-seated, distinguishing between Texans and Americans was difficult in practice. American merchant Josiah Gregg points out that in 1839 his party encountered a group of Comanches who immediately prepared for war and pointedly refused to smoke the pipe. After some time, it became clear that the Comanches

size according to their actual presence in the area. Revealingly, Kiowas called Americans *Hanpoko*, or "trappers", given the primary occupation of Americans with whom they regularly came in contact. With regard to Mexicans, winter counts distinguish between various groups, such as "Mexicans of the waterless country" (the people of Chihuahua) or "timber Mexicans" (those living in the lower Rio Grande valley). In fact, Kiowas not only wrote about but also dealt with Mexico in subnational terms, making war on half a dozen Mexican states while keeping friendly relations with New Mexico, where they found a brisk market for war spoils.[77] Kiowas were not disposed to judge nations by formal attributes and grandiose statements. Great chiefs and captains as far away as Mexico City and Washington may have claimed the allegiance of incredibly large numbers of people and sovereignty over vast territories, but what mattered most to Kiowas were the actual conditions on the ground and the actions of flesh-and-blood human beings.

Kiowa calendars constitute fine-grained glimpses of human affairs. These portraits were made almost at a microscopic scale where individual gestures and chance encounters mattered greatly both for the consequences for the individuals involved as well as for their potential to disrupt delicate tangles of alliances and counteralliances that were so central to the well-being of human beings living in this contested space. The dragging of the head of an Arapaho warrior, the accidental encounter with a group of Texans, or the kidnapping of a young child acquires great significance when viewed in the context of a fluid human landscape where a faux pas is the difference between peace and war. Dohasan and Set-Tan did not depend on the vagaries

---

had mistaken the Americans for their Texan enemies, as the caravan was traveling outside the limits of the United States and over a hundred miles from the trail normally used by American merchants bound for Santa Fe. Texans sometimes used this confusion to their own advantage, traveling through Indian territory with American flags to avoid difficulties. Gregg, *The Commerce of the Prairies*, 197–211.

77 Peace with the Comanches had been the cornerstone of New Mexico's survival for over seventy years. New Mexicans had kept peace with the powerful Comanche-Kiowa-Kiowa Apache confederation, even though the latter was periodically at war with Tamaulipas, Chihuahua, Durango, and Zacatecas. So dear was this alliance to New Mexicans that they had repeatedly refused to join all-out campaigns against the Comanche, preferring to incur widespread condemnation from half a dozen Mexican states and the national government rather than have to experience a devastating war of attrition. See Governor of New Mexico to Departmental Assembly, Jun 27, 1845, Santa Fe, MANM 38, 740–5. In the spring of 1841, Governor Armijo was ordered to break New Mexico's alliance with the Comanche. The crafty governor gave various excuses to postpone any such action. See Armijo to Almonte, Santa Fe, Mar 3, 1841, MANM 27, 1116–20. Mistaken reports to Governor Armijo stated that the Comanches had signed peace treaties with the United States, with the Anglo Americans of Bent's Fort, and with the Republic of Texas. See Buenaventura Lovato to Armijo, Taos, May 31, 1841, Herbert E. Bolton Papers, Box 41, no. 688, Bancroft Library; Armijo to Almonte, Jun 3, 1841, MANM 28, 1432–4; Buenaventura Lovato to Armijo, Santa Fe, Jun 3, 1841, BHC, 2q175, 339, 202–3.

of market fashions in the way Kendall, Falconer, and the other chroniclers of the Santa Fe expedition did. Yet these calendar keepers did seek a connection with their people, striving to re-create the human, and sometimes the supernatural, universe in which Kiowas operated, and offering lessons ranging from the character of other groups to the wisdom and limits of negotiation and warfare. Finally, calendars served as conventional histories of a people, keeping a tally of how Kiowas had managed the collective enterprise of survival. Already an old man in 1892, Set-Tan took out the calendar that he had kept for a long time and gave it to Mooney without asking for any payment in return. Complaining that the young men were already forgetting their own history, Set-Tan asked Mooney to take the calendar to Washington so that the white people might always remember what the Kiowas had done.

THE MEXICAN STATE AND ITS TEXTS

Understandably, Mexicans composed several texts about the Texan Santa Fe Expedition. Ever since 1838, when rumors of an invading expedition from Texas first reached Mexico, military and civil officials spilled liters of ink in patriotic *pronunciamientos* and correspondence denouncing the Lone Star interlopers.[78] The Mexican press hailed the capture of the party of Texans as Mexico's most brilliant victory since the days of the Alamo and Goliad. In a letter that first appeared in *El Pigmeo* of Chihuahua and was later reproduced in *El Siglo Diecinueve* of Mexico City, editors marveled at how a determined but disorganized crowd of New Mexicans, barely armed with spears and slings, had been able to cow a well-armed force of invasion into surrender.[79] Carlos María de Bustamante, arguably the most influential historian of the time, joined the choir of lore, writing a commentary of

---

[78] Mexican officials received the first inklings of an invasion in the summer of 1838, when James Kirker, an Irish merchant and scalp hunter, informed Governor Manuel Armijo that two thousand Texan soldiers would invade New Mexico in the following spring. General Military Commander Simón Elías to Governor Armijo, Chihuahua, Aug 29, 1838. This intelligence seemed to be confirmed in early 1839 by a newspaper article from Missouri announcing that a body of five hundred men under the command of Colonel Henry Karnes was headed for Santa Fe to establish "friendly alliances" with Mexicans and indigenous groups along the way. *Columbia Patriot*, Missouri, Apr 13, 1839, translated into Spanish by Guadalupe Miranda, Secretary of Governor Armijo, Santa Fe, Jul 28, 1839, Herbert E. Bolton Papers, no. 688, Carton 41, Folder 37, Bancroft Library. In 1840 New Mexicans were subjected to another false alarm due to a private letter: John Tennyson to Parker and Kelly, New Orleans, Apr 20, 1840, translated into Spanish by Angel Farías, Chihuahua, Jun 16, 1840, BHC, 2q 175, 339, 88-9. See also Armijo to Almonte, Santa Fe, Jul 31, 1840, MANM 26, 401-3. The expedition finally materialized in the fall of 1841. See the rest of this chapter for correspondence and addresses.

[79] *El Siglo Diecinueve*, Nov 1, 1841. See also *El Cosmopolita*, Mar 2, 1842, and Mar 12, 1842.

Governor Manuel Armijo's capture of the Santa Fe expeditioners that went along with an anonymous *memoria* from New Mexico.[80]

Bustamante's account became the standard Mexican version of the fate of the Santa Fe expedition. Yet it was not meant for the masses. Unlike Kendall's book – deliberately crafted to appeal to average readers – Bustamante's commentary and *memoria* targeted the influential few. His writing style was that of the consummate insider, peppered with cryptic references and political lessons aimed at settling old scores and laying out fault lines emerging from the Texan Santa Fe Expedition.[81] These stylistic differences between Kendall and Bustamante in fact indicate vastly different literary cultures. In the case of Mexico, it was the state and not so much the market that was deeply implicated in the production and dissemination of texts on the Texan Santa Fe Expedition.

Printing flourished in Mexico, especially in the course of the eighteenth and early-nineteenth centuries. Its value as a political weapon became all too clear during the wars of independence, as anticolonial rebels, critical literati, and imperial bureaucrats desiring to quell dissention turned presses into propaganda tools.[82] Yet it was in the tumultuous decades after emancipation when political printing reached a new plateau that would have been unimaginable just a half a century before. Every army commander of importance, every bishopric and religious order, every state and local government of note, every self-respecting *caudillo* and regional strongman, and every revolutionary leader required the services of printing presses. Collectively, these opinion leaders issued a prodigious amount of loose sheets in the form of broadsides, *pronunciamientos*, open letters, accounts, satirical stories, sermons, *folletos*, and many other literary formats.[83] These publications were so

---

[80] "Espedicion de los tejanos rendida a las fuerzas del general don Manuel Armijo, el 5 de octubre de 1841," in Carlos María de Bustamante, *El Gabinete Mexicano* (Mexico City: Imprenta de José M. Lara, 1842), reprinted as *Cuadro Histórico de la Revolución Mexicana de 1810*, 8 vols (Mexico City: INEHRM, 1985), 8, 216–25. Bustamante and Governor Armijo were close political allies. In fact, Bustamante dedicated the second volume of his *El Gabinete Mexicano* to the embattled governor.

[81] As his detractors were quick to point out, Bustamante's political involvement made objectivity impossible. Wearing two hats as congressman and self-appointed national historian, Bustamante could hardly refrain from using his writings to advance his political career and, conversely, his political influence to gain access to government documents and publish his work. For an incisive portrait of Bustamante, see *Sembranzas de los Representantes que Compusieron el Congreso Constituyente de 1836* (Mexico City: Imprenta D. Manuel R. Gallo, 1837), 8–9.

[82] For a brief appraisal of the critical role played by these publications in the eighteenth and early-nineteenth centuries, see Rodríguez O., *The Independence of Spanish America*, 36–44.

[83] The scarcity of printing presses made them a particularly coveted commodity, because having one automatically conferred status to the owner and showed commitment and seriousness. Reporting on the progress of the centralist insurrection of 1833, Antonio Barreiro, New Mexico's deputy to the National Congress, thought it important to include the intelligence

ubiquitous that Carlos María de Bustamante was convinced that the entire history of Mexico, from its most famous episodes down to its inconsequential details, could be pieced together from this torrent of paper. In fact, he made it his lifelong task to preserve these texts for posterity before they became irretrievably lost, as pharmacists and storeowners used these printed sheets for everything except reading. Firework makers were notorious for transmuting broadsides and *folletos* into smoke and dazzling pyrotechnics in the aftermath of every successful revolution.[84]

Unlike Texan and American editors and printers, who sought to hold the interest of the largest number of readers to make a profit, their Mexican counterparts wrote chiefly for the local, regional, and national political figures of their day. Mexican publications could not depend on their readers for survival; the reading public was simply too small. Instead, Mexican editors and printers had to rely on the largesse and protection of career politicians, military figures, and ecclesiastical leaders, and constantly curried their favor and patronage. Not surprisingly, the most obvious feature of these texts is their unrelenting political nature. The enormous body of Mexican texts composed of a host of provincial and national newspapers as well as the *folletería* of the first half of the nineteenth century is *almost exclusively* political.[85] Bustamante himself, who valued these publications so much, readily admitted that they were written primarily for the purpose of criticizing antagonistic political groups or flattering the victorious party. Typically state governments acquired printing equipment for ostensibly official purposes – like publishing regulations – but state and local politicians also used them to launch their careers, broadcast their opinions, and pass judgment on all public matters. The reverse trajectory was also common. Opposition leaders gathered around fleeting editorial projects that lasted until resources ran out or censorship took its toll. New Mexico provides a fitting example of the Mexican printing world. Prior to 1841, there was only one operating printing press in the entire territory. From its plates came New Mexico's first

---

that the rebel army of Generals José Durán and Mariano Arista possessed a printing press and was in the habit of releasing a daily bulletin to the public. He also underscored that the Marquis of Vivanco, who had joined the rebellion, carried a press as well, operated by none other than the minister of Guatemala in Mexico. Antonio Barreiro to Blas de Hinojos, Mexico City, Jul 24, 1833, Ritch Collection, reel 3, NMSRCA New Mex. State Records Center and Archives as cited before.

[84] Bustamante, "Advertencia al que Leyere," in Bustamante, *Cuadro Histórico de la Revolución Mexicana*, 23–27.

[85] Broadsides, public letters, sermons, and *pronunciamientos* were obviously and unabashedly political. Similarly, in the 1820s and 1830s newspapers were published by political institutes such as Masonic societies and constituted platforms for political fencing rather than vehicles of information. Lucas Alamán considered newspapers as little more than propaganda machines. For instance, he points out that in the aftermath of Iturbide's downfall, *El Sol* was being published by a homonymous Scottish Rite Lodge and *El Aguila Mexicana* by a competing York Rite Lodge. Alamán, *Historia de México*, 5, 204, 383.

newspaper in 1835, defiantly called *El crepúsculo de la libertad* (the twilight of freedom). Yet this staunchly liberal paper was discontinued after only four issues, for it came out just as a new centralist administration was taking charge.[86] Subsequently, the press served to print a handful of government *bandos* and decrees, and in 1837 it was acquired by the influential priest of Taos, Father Antonio José Martínez, who went on to publish textbooks and personal essays until 1844.[87]

It is only natural that the topic of Texas would find its way to Mexico's printing presses. Years before the Santa Fe expedition got under way, Texas had already become the bête noire of Mexico's politics and occupied a prominent place in Mexico's constant editorial squabbles. No other subject – with the possible exception of Santa Anna's political maneuverings – incited such passions and polarized the editorial world of Mexico so much. Since the late 1820s, the fate of Texas had been fiery journalistic fodder. Radical federalists regarded the liberal policies adopted in Coahuila and Texas as the best hope of Mexico's future development, expounding their views in numerous *folletos* and newspapers such as *El Águila Mexicana* and later *El Cosmopolita*, as well as provincial newspapers of similar persuasion. Centralists countered that Texas constituted the worst example of speculation and utter disdain for the imperative of preserving the territorial integrity of the nation, charges that appeared in virulent *pronunciamientos* and letters published in centralist publications such as *El Sol* and later *El Mosquito Mexicano, La Lima de Vulcano*, and others.

The secession of Texas from Mexico in 1836 brought things to a head and sharply redrew political and journalistic battle lines. *El Correo Atlántico* (O.A. Santangelo resurrected the paper from his exile in New Orleans) and *El Cosmopolita*, both of which had initially supported the federalist insurrection in Texas, turned to criticize Texan secessionism, implicitly vindicating the centralist position. Yet the secession of Texas did not end Mexico's journalistic squabbles; if anything, it added another bone of contention. After 1836, the national political scene became an active cauldron threatening to boil over every time prominent military officers such as Generals Nicolás Bravo, Mariano Arista, and Santa Anna issued earnest *pronunciamientos* vowing to conduct campaigns to reconquer Texas. Although no immediate action was taken, speculation ran rampant in cafes, along promenades, and in evening gatherings or *tertulias*. Some believed that Texas had been lost forever, others that reconquest was imminent, and yet others feared that such a campaign would ultimately draw the United States into the fray.[88]

---

[86] See article by E. Boyd, CSR, "New Mexico Imprints, 1835–1853," MSS 197.

[87] Father Martínez sold the press to the government to print an official periodical called *La Verdad*, which appeared in 1844–5. Simultaneously, another newspaper, called *El Payo de Nuevo México*, became available in New Mexico.

[88] *El Mosquito Mexicano*, Mexico City, Aug 14, 1837.

The press stoked the fire with fresh revelations, especially as federalist uprisings broke out in 1838–41 and Anglo Texans became involved. The rebellion was centered in northern Tamaulipas, immediately adjacent to Texas, and its leaders had no qualms about raising funds and recruiting Anglo-Texan volunteers with the blessings of the Lone Star government. These incidents quickly catapulted Texas to the center of public debate. In Tamaulipas itself, a battery of anti-Texas newspapers blossomed in the 1830s and 1840s, among them *El Ancla, La Brisa,* and *El Mercurio de Matamoros.* Especially rabid was *El Látigo de Tejas* (the whip of Texas), whose sole purpose was to chastise those "perfidious" Anglo Texans and their "ungrateful Mexican minions."[89] In the meantime, *El Cosmopolita* lamely defended the Tamaulipas insurgents, emphasizing that the presence of Anglo-Texan "auxiliaries" did not imply a formal political connection of any kind with the Lone Star Republic.[90] Although the uprising was ultimately quelled, Mexico's politics increasingly hinged on the outcome of the "Texas question." Authors and editors wrote about Texas aware of painful memories and deep-running political and moral associations. This was especially the case in neighboring New Mexico, which had lived under the shadow of the Lone Star Republic since the insurrection of 1836.

Ordinary New Mexicans were not only exposed to these printed sources, but more commonly came in contact with handwritten texts copied and circulated by state and local governments. Such texts included addresses or regulations posted in prominent places in central plazas and often read aloud on Sundays and in other special days. Due to the dearth of printing equipment, New Mexicans learned about the "Texas question" and debated its implications in this fashion. For four years – ever since 1838, when an invasion from Texas became a distinct possibility – New Mexicans heard various handwritten addresses and orders on the subject.[91] On each occasion,

---

[89] *El Látigo de Tejas*, Matamoros, Sep 9, 1844, Newberry Library, Matamoros Collection, vol. 49: 45–7.

[90] *El Cosmopolita*, Apr 11, 1840. See also Jan 1, 1840, and Jan 15, 1840.

[91] In 1838 Santiago Kerker (James Kirker), an Irish trader and trapper who was working as an Indian scalp hunter for the governor of Chihuahua, informed Armijo that two thousand Texan soldiers were headed for New Mexico to claim the territory, as stipulated in the treaty of Velasco, which Santa Anna had signed to save his life. See Manuel Armijo to Chihuhua's Military Commander, Santa Fe, Nov 29, 1838, microfilmed edition of the MANM, reel 24, Frame 1279 (hereafter MANM 24, 1279); Manuel Armijo to Ministro de Guerra y Marina, Santa Fe, Aug 18, 1839, Barker History Center, Box 2q175, 339 (hereafter BHC 2q175, 339) at the University of Texas at Austin. In 1839, New Mexican officials received newspaper clippings from the United States about a military company being raised in Texas under governmental sanction for the purpose of exploring the route to New Mexico and forming friendly alliances with the Comanche nation and other tribes along the way. See *Columbia Patriot*, Apr 13, 1839. Copied in Santa Fe by Guadalupe Miranda on July 28, 1839, Herbert E. Bolton Papers, Box 41, Folder 688, Bancroft Library. In the spring of 1840, a New Orleans resident wrote to the authorities in Chihuahua informing that one hundred

the chain of events would start when Governor Armijo received confidential information about the possibility of an invasion and rumors started to spread. The governor would then convene a meeting in Santa Fe with the leading men of the territory. These conclaves ended with pledges of loyalty to the nation, a plan of defense, and written addresses – the governor's included – intended to stimulate the patriotic zeal of the people at large. In putting together his anti-Texas coalitions, Governor Armijo enlisted the help of key military and ecclesiastical leaders who, in turn, sent instructions and letters to their subordinates. In 1841, the governor pleaded in particular with the vicar of New Mexico, Juan Felipe Ortiz, to "display his influence over all classes," and by virtue of his dignity exhort all the faithful to help in the defense.[92] From Santa Fe, many of these addresses, religious sermons, letters, and instructions were copied and sent to other communities – not only Hispanic towns, but also Indian pueblos and Anglo-American ranches.

What happened next depended on local authorities. Sometimes local authorities just affixed the document to a wooden beam of the municipal building, the local church, or the most prominent structure. Other authorities, like Judge Miguel Mascareñas of Mora, a town in eastern New Mexico and likely stopover of the Texan party, went to greater lengths, gathering all residents in the central square to read aloud the governor's address. Judge Mascareñas reported that the people responded "in one voice" and with "Spartan will" to be united forever with the nation.[93] Sometimes the documents themselves – especially official communiqués, or *bandos* – contained specific instructions about how they should be made known to the public: "... to be read aloud on Sunday after being received," or – as in the case of Armijo's 1840 proclamation concerning the Texas invasion – "to be published as *bando* in this capital city for three consecutive Sundays, and displayed in public places, and thereafter every first Sunday of the month in all political districts."[94] Thus state-sponsored texts circulating in central plazas and supply stores reached ordinary New Mexicans, even those who were subliterate or downright illiterate.[95]

Texans had gathered together and armed themselves with rifles, pistols, swords, and lances and were headed for New Mexico. See John Tennyson to Parker and Kelly, New Orleans, Apr 20, 1840, translated by Angel Farías in Chihuahua, Jun 16, 1840, BHC 2q175, 339, 88–9.

[92] Armijo to Almonte, Santa Fe, Aug 4, 1841, MANM 28, 1443–6. See acceptance in Vicar Juan Felipe Ortiz to Gudalape Miranda, Peña Blanca, Aug 2, 1841, MANM 28, 1324–6.

[93] Judge Miguel Mascareñas to Guadalupe Miranda, Mora, Aug 31, 1841, MANM 28, 1335–7.

[94] Governor Armijo's 1840 proclamation to the people concerning the Texas invasion was issued as a *bando*.

[95] E. P. Thompson still provides the most compelling case of how texts were used and appropriated by subliterate workers. Thompson, *The Making of the English Working Class* (New York: Vintage Books, 1963), 724–49.

From this repertoire of harangues, addresses, and accounts of the Texan Santa Fe Expedition, it is possible to isolate two recurrent themes that served both to repudiate the Texas Republic and to affirm elite views about what constituted Mexico's national identity. One had to do with the morality of Texans, generally introduced with epithets like "criminal," "corrupted," "depraved," and "perfidious".[96] These words were far more than random adjectives. In a secret report that Governor Armijo undoubtedly used to compose his invective against the Santa Fe expedition, a Mexican spy operating in San Antonio presented a more detailed account of Texan morality:

Texas is composed of the most famous criminals vomited up by Europe, North America, and others parts of the world. Seeking to escape punishment for past crimes, these men have come to Texas looking for a new country and have turned the old Mexican province into a den of thieves afflicted by the most depraved vices.[97]

The spy stressed the point that life in Texas was a daily riot and commotion, abuse, and assassination, and that even though severe legislation had been enacted to curtail these offenses, the judicial system discriminated against Mexicans who were hanged even for seemingly minor offenses and on the basis of hearsay evidence. As we saw in Chapter 3, a closely related strand revolved around the prodigious quantities of whisky and brandy that Texans supposedly imbibed.[98] This view resonated with great force in New Mexico because Anglo Americans owned the largest distilleries of the territory and were frequently blamed for perceived drunkenness and lowering moral standards. Indeed, two out of three Anglo-American agents commissioned by the president of Texas to start preparing the terrain in New Mexico before the arrival of the Santa Fe expedition sold whisky for a living. John Rowland and William Workman were naturalized Mexican citizens who had lived in the Taos area since the 1820s.[99] Their advocacy on behalf of the Texas Republic together with their thriving whiskey business was not lost on New Mexico's priesthood, which had long noted the deleterious effects of Anglo-American modernity. Fearing retaliations, Workman and Rowland sold their entire

---

[96] For instance, see Armijo's proclamation to the people of New Mexico, Santa Fe, Jul 16, 1840, MANM 27, 1265.

[97] Report of Santiago Vidaurri, Lampazos, May 11, 1841, Box 590, file 87, Herbert E. Bolton Papers, Bancroft Library. New Mexicans received copy of a second spy report. Spy Rafael Uribe to Mariano Arista, Monterrey, Jul 25, 1841, Box 590, file 87, Herbert E. Bolton Papers, Bancroft Library.

[98] Report of Santiago Vidaurri, Lampazos, May 11, 1841, Box 590, file 87, Herbert E. Bolton Papers, Bancroft Library.

[99] In 1837, Workman was accused of contraband trade. See Proceedings Against William Workman, Santa Fe, July 21–30, 1837, MANM 23, 963–75; Letter from a Member of the Santa Fe Expedition, Mexico City, Feb 20, 1842, in *Telegraph and Texas Register*, Apr 20, 1842.

stock of liquor at half price and left for California before the expedition reached New Mexico.[100]

Catholic fervor constituted the second recurrent theme in these harangues, addresses, and instructions. Even before the Texas Revolution, many Mexicans had viewed Anglo Texans as irreverent opportunists. Anglo Texans – just like Anglo Americans in New Mexico – were required to convert to Catholicism in order to obtain Mexican citizenship and be allowed to purchase land and conduct other transactions. Most complied out of necessity, but their level of participation in Catholic ritual, with a few exceptions, remained notoriously low or nonexistent. Indeed, the extent of Anglo-Texan repudiation of Catholicism became evident after Texas seceded from Mexico. Pious nuevomexicanos learned with dismay that the parish priest of San Antonio, Refugio de la Garza, was suspended from his ministry, cheated out of his properties, and even chained and paraded through the streets of San Antonio like an ordinary criminal.[101] Such were the perils of becoming prey of a heretic or Protestant people. In New Mexico, Vicar Ortiz had already taken concrete steps to limit the number of foreign-born residents who acquired Mexican citizenship via marriage with Mexican women by insisting on strict procedures to grant dispensations and by mandating a thirty peso surcharge for the paperwork.[102] As New Mexicans grappled with real or imaginary invasions from Texas, Catholicism emerged as a cornerstone of resistance: "New Mexicans, will you look on with indifference as a handful of foreign adventurers march all the way to our communities to take away our freedom and interest, to pollute our innocent traditions, and to do away with our true and loved Religion . . . ?"[103]

Were ordinary New Mexicans receptive to these public exhortations and accounts? It is exceedingly difficult to tell. Although the commercial success of Kendall's *Narrative* and the arduously discussed and evolving oral tradition that accompanied winter counts provide at least an inkling of how these texts played out to wider audiences, we have no comparable gauge for Mexican proclamations. Still, we have some tantalizing clues. In the summer of 1840, in the midst of an anti-Texas propaganda campaign, a conspiracy was discovered in the Río Abajo district. A group of laborers and peons had secretly set out to burn all account books and traces of their indebtedness since the year of 1830. Captured before the plan went into effect, the leaders – all members of the "lower classes," according to Armijo's report – revealingly explained in their judiciary depositions that they welcomed a Texan

---

[100] For an account of Workman's distilling activities, see Lecompte, "Simeon Turley," 301–14.

[101] Report of Santiago Vidaurri, Lampazos, May 11, 1841, Box 590, file 87, Herbert E. Bolton Papers, Bancroft Library.

[102] The U.S. consul in Santa Fe protested this measure. See Manuel Álvarez to Guadalupe Miranda, Secretary of Government of New Mexico, Santa Fe, May 22, 1841, MANM 28, 1291–3.

[103] Armijo to the People of New Mexico, Santa Fe, Jul 16, 1840, MANM 27, 1265.

takeover, as it would result in their deliverance from debt. The insurgents somehow believed that Texans would favor a more equitable distribution of power and money.[104] Indeed, Governor Armijo, who so many times had tried to puse the patriotic zeal of ordinary New Mexicans, privately worried that non-elite New Mexicans could easily be persuaded to support Texas if they saw the slightest advantage in such a course.[105] But at the same time, it is also evident that Governor Armijo was able to marshal a respectable and heterogeneous force of resistance consisting of a few wealthy individuals – who raised what amounted to private armies – ecclesiastics, political allies of the governor, less affluent civil and military officers, as well as an unspecified number of ordinary New Mexicans who enlisted in the army of resistance without receiving any compensation or salary.[106]

It is possible that these latter citizens agreed at least with some of the ideas expressed in the many passionate addresses denouncing the Lone Star Republic that circulated in the territory. Perhaps the most convincing evidence of this concern is the extreme hostility that many nuevo mexicanos evinced toward foreign-born residents during and immediately after the capture of the Santa Fe expedition. The American consul in Santa Fe reported that once definite intelligence of the invading body of Texans had reached the territory, many New Mexicans insulted foreign-born residents on the streets and in public places.[107] Indeed, on the day that regular soldiers and the militia of Santa Fe departed for the frontier to face the Texans, a throng of people and a few soldiers burst into the house of the American consul and wounded

---

[104] Armijo to Ministro de Guerra y Marina, Santa Fe, Jul 12, 1840, MANM 26, 396–8.

[105] See Armijo to Ministro de Guerra y Marina, Santa Fe, Jun 17, 1840, MANM 26, 387–9; Armijo to Colonel Mariano Chávez, Santa Fe, Aug 1, 1841, BHC, 2q175, 339, 40–1; Armijo to Almonte, Santa Fe, Aug 24, 1841, MANM 27, 1135–8; Armijo to Francisco García Conde, Santa Fe, Jun 4, 1841, Herbert E. Bolton Papers, Box 41, no. 688, Bancroft Library.

[106] The wealthy nuevomexicanos included José Chávez, Mariano Chávez, and Antonio Sandoval. Other prominent New Mexicans had their own reasons to join the effort: Diego Archuleta was a protégé of the governor who had received military instruction in Durango, and Captain Pascual Martínez of Taos was a member of the powerful Martínez clan and had long resented the influence of foreigners. Less affluent civil and military officers – such as Juan Lieutenant Colonel Andrés Archuleta, and Captains Antonio Sena, Manuel Doroteo Pino, Teodocio Quintana, Diego Beytia, Miguel Antonio Lovato of Galisteo, and Damacio Salazar of San Miguel del Vado – opted for resistance as well. All of these men (and their followers) had cast their lot with Governor Armijo under the "Liberating Army" to pacify the territory after the violent Chimayo Rebellion. Indian fighters and scouts such as Captains Pedro León Luján and José Francisco Vigil of Abiquiú also joined the anti-Texan coalition. Their fighting experience made them natural candidates to lead the territorial defense. See Armijo to Colonel Mariano Chávez, Santa Fe, Aug 1, 1841, BHC, 2q175, 339, 40–1; and Armijo to Almonte, Santa Fe, Aug 4, 1841, MANM 28, 1443–6.

[107] For an account of the stir that the Texans caused in New Mexico, see Thomas Esteban Chávez, "The Trouble with Texans: Manuel Álvarez and the 1841 'Invasion'," *New Mexico Historical Review* 53:2 (1978), 133–44.

him in the face with a knife.[108] After the Texans surrendered and improvised celebrations broke out, an angry mob cheered as the Texas Constitution was burned in the main plaza of Las Vegas; in Santa Fe, groups of disgruntled nuevomexicanos swept through the streets, insulting foreign-born residents and plundering one of their stores.[109]

The capture of the Texan party gave temporary relief and confidence to a country that had been badly shaken during its short existence as an independent nation. Bustamante, for one, felt confident that such a glorious episode would provide sufficient material to "poets, painters, and speakers who will communicate to future generations a fact worthy of celebration and ennobling of the New Mexican people." He follows up the story of the Texan expeditioners until their final release in Mexico City on President Santa Anna's birthday and ends with a sigh: "God willing these acts of magnanimity on the part of the Mexican government won't be lost and forgotten by these men who are bound to pay us back mounting another charge as soon as they are able!"[110]

The many tales surrounding the Santa Fe expedition show that as late as the 1840s, Anglo Americans, New Mexicans, and Kiowas were immersed in strikingly different literary cultures in spite of their relative geographic proximity to one another. Richard H. Brodhead's contention that writing is inextricably linked to the particularized mechanisms that bring the text to public life is fully validated along the frontier, where independent and highly particular realms for the propagation of texts coexisted, notwithstanding the notable inroads made by print capitalism.[111] Most obviously, texts appeared within specific institutional and cultural settings, where entities like the market and the state shaped these varied literary cultures. The narratives of Anglo-American journalists of the Texan Santa Fe Expedition were filtered through the lens of a fierce journalistic competition that compelled authors to play to the tastes and preconceptions of their readers. In contrast, the Mexican state took the leading role in producing and disseminating texts about the Texan expedition to New Mexico, using all the trappings of governmental power, including public readings of addresses and exhortations, to get its message across. Writing traditions like winter counts and handwritten *bandos* should steer us away from models that univocally and

---

[108] *Memorial* of Manuel Álvarez to Daniel Webster, Washington, Feb 2, 1842, Dispatches from United States consuls in Santa Fe, 1830–46, RG 59, no. 199, NMSRCA.

[109] Diary of Manuel Álvarez, U.S. consul in Santa Fe, Santa Fe, 1840–1, Read Collection, Series II, NMSRCA.

[110] Bustamante, *Cuadro Histórico de la Revolución Mexicana*, 223.

[111] Richard H. Brodhead, *Cultures of Letters: Scenes of Reading and Writing in Nineteenth-Century America* (Chicago, IL: The University of Chicago Press, 1993), 4–10. See also Michael Warner, *The Letters of the Republic: Publication and the Public Sphere in Eighteenth-Century America* (Cambridge, MA: Harvard University Press, 1990).

automatically link the spread of print capitalism and the emergence of national loyalties, as printed material created "an imagined community among a specific assemblage of fellow-readers."[112] As the many narratives of the Santa Fe expedition make clear, printing presses did not generate standard print cultures, but rather became adapted to preexisting and widely diverse literary traditions. And these very diverse cultural milieus both predated the onset of print capitalism and survived long afterward.

[112] Anderson, *Imagined Communities*, 61–5.

8

New Mexico at the Razor's Edge

On August 6, 1846, two thousand men made camp at a plateau near the summit of Raton Pass, over seven thousand feet above sea level. From their tents, they were able to gaze at the enormous expanse of reddish and yellowish prairies below, forbidding but inexpressibly beautiful, eerily biblical.[1] Less than a week later, Colonel Stephen Kearny and his Army of the West marched into Las Vegas, one of New Mexico's first sizeable settlements, boasting some one hundred adobe-built houses. From a rooftop overlooking the plaza, and accompanied by the alcalde and two Mexican militia captains, Colonel Kearny addressed the bewildered people who had not fled to the outlying *ranchos*:

I have come amongst you by the orders of my government, to take possession of your country, and extend over it the laws of the United States. We consider it, and have done so for some time, a part of the territory of the United States. We come amongst you as friends, not as enemies – as protectors, not as conquerors.... I shall not expect you to take up arms and follow me to fight your own people who may oppose me. But I now tell you that those who remain peaceably at home, attending to

[1] My description of New Mexico's military occupation is based primarily on three sources: Lieutenant J. W. Abert. *Report of the Secretary of War, Communicating, in Answer to a Resolution of the Senate, a Report and Map of the Expedition to New Mexico*, Executive Document 23 (Washington, DC: U.S. Senate 1848); "Diary of an Unidentified Officer in the Army of the West," *Saint Louis Republican*, St. Louis, Sep 24, 1846; and W. H. Emory, *Notes of a Military Reconnaissance from Fort Leavenworth in Missouri, to San Diego, California, Including Parts of the Arkansas, Del Norte, and Gila Rivers* (Washington, DC: U.S. House of Representatives, Executive Document No. 41, 1848). In addition, I have used relevant New Mexican sources. Martín González de la Vara and Ángela Moyano Pahissa have gone over much of this ground in González de la Vara, "Los nuevomexicanos ante la invasión norteamericana, 1846–1848," in Laura Herrera Serna, ed., *México en Guerra 1846–1848* (Mexico City: Consejo Nacional para la Cultura y las Artes, 1997), 473–94; Moyano Pahissa, *México y Estados Unidos: orígenes de una relación, 1819–1861* (Mexico City: SEP, 1985), 122–40.

FIGURE 8.1. Town of San Miguel del Vado

their crops and their herds, shall be protected by me in their property, their persons, and their religion. Not a pepper, nor an onion, shall be disturbed or taken by my troops without pay or by the consent of the owner. But listen! He who promises to be quiet and is found in arms against me, I will hang.[2]

Through an interpreter, the American commander turned to the alcalde and two militia captains and asked them, "are you willing to take the oath of allegiance to the United States?" Two of them consented, but one of the militia captains evaded the question. The colonel demanded a categorical answer. The captain said, "sí," but with patently bad grace. Then the three nuevomexicanos made the sign of the cross as the people who kept gathering on the plaza, many on horseback, uncovered their heads. Colonel Kearny administered an oath and then grabbed the alcalde's hand, addressing the people one last time: "I shake hands with you all, through your *alcalde*, and hail you as good citizens of the United States."

As the Army of the West cut a swath through New Mexico in the next few days, variations of this ceremony were enacted in Tecolote and San Miguel del Vado (see Figure 8.1).[3] On the afternoon of August 18, the American troops entered Santa Fe unopposed. After a brief speech, the hoisting of the American flag, and cannon discharges, Colonel Kearny and his top officers disappeared into the inner sanctum of the Palace of the Governors and, together with some nuevomexicanos and foreign-born residents, toasted the

---

[2] Emory, *Notes of a Military Reconnaissance*, 27.

[3] I found the most detailed description of these ceremonies in the diary of an unidentified officer in the Army of the West published in the *St. Louis Republican*, Sep 24, 1846.

night away. The Army of the West had conquered New Mexico "without firing one single shot."

In the early hours of January 19, 1847, a mixed crowd of Pueblo Indians and nuevomexicanos gathered outside the home of Charles Bent, the recently appointed American governor who happened to be visiting Taos, to demand the release of two Pueblo Indians who were being held in the local jail.[4] The people became incensed by Governor Bent's categorical refusal and began making plans at once. One group headed toward the prison building and stormed it, killing Sheriff Stephen L. Lee, Prefect Cornelio Vigil, and Circuit Attorney James W. Leal. The remaining protestors surrounded Governor Bent's house and, after forcing their way in, "filled the body of the fallen man with arrows, three of which he pulled from his head and face as he lay prostrate."[5] The assailants scalped the governor and left him to die. In the next forty-eight hours, similar massacres of Anglo Americans were reported in nearby Arroyo Hondo and across the Sangre de Cristo Mountains in Mora.

The uprising was short-lived, as American troops and volunteers overpowered the ill-organized rebels. In less than a month, scores of Pueblo Indians and nuevomexicanos faced a hastily organized and alien justice system. The Taos District Court worked almost daily through March and April. The proceedings were less than impartial, sometimes outright revengeful, as some of the jurors and the judge were related to the deceased. Lewis H. Garrard, a young English traveler, noted that, "it certainly did appear to be a great assumption on the part of the Americans to conquer a country and then arraign the revolting inhabitants for treason."[6] One of the Taos Indians who killed Governor Bent sat through the trial with lips closed,

---

[4] This was the second rebellious attempt. A month earlier – on the day of the Virgin of Guadalupe on December 12, 1846 – a group of nuevomexicanos had first conspired to drive out the Americans from New Mexico. When everything seemed ready, however, Donaciano Vigil learned of the conspiracy and told Governor Bent, who quickly moved to quell the insurgents. One of the best accounts of this first rebellion is still E. Bennett Burton, "The Taos Rebellion," *Old Santa Fe* 1:2 (1913), 176–92. Accounts of how this first plot was discovered differ. See Myra Ellen Jenkins, "Rebellion Against American Occupation of New Mexico 1846–1847," unpublished paper, University of New Mexico, 1949, 21. See also González de la Vara, "Los nuevomexicanos ante la invasión norteamericana," 482–91; Ángela Moyano Pahissa, *El Comercio de Santa Fe y la Guerra del '47* (Mexico City: SepSetentus, 1976), 143–165; *México y Estados Unidos: orígenes de una relación*, 127–40.

[5] For descriptions of the massacre, see Burton, "The Taos Rebellion," 176–202; Garrard, *Wah-to-yah*, 177. For Lee's death, see David J. Weber, "Stephen Louis Lee," in *Mountain Men*, 3, 181–7.

[6] Garrard, *Wah-to-yah*, 177–8. Opinions differ in this regard. Francis T. Cheetham considered that whereas it took "from two to ten years for the courts to begin to function properly in the other western commonwealths, this court established a record, probably never excelled in the history of the world, for the dispatch and sound discretion exercised in the transaction of the business then before the court." Francis T. Cheetham, "The First Term of the American Court in Taos, New Mexico," *New Mexico Historical Review* 1:1, 23.

"without a show of malice or hatred."[7] An aging and prominent nuevomex-icano, Antonio María Trujillo, could scarcely understand when Judge Joab Houghton began reading the sentence aloud: "... it would appear that old age has not brought wisdom nor purity nor honesty of heart, you have been found seconding the acts of a band of the most traitorous murderers that ever blackened with a recital of their deeds, the annals of history."[8] Trujillo was to be hanged on Friday, April 16, at two o'clock in the afternoon.

Peaceful occupation and fierce resistance are the two polar extremes of a spectrum that consisted of the most varied encounters, as Mexico and the United States went to war and the frontier inhabitants attempted to cope with changing national demarcations. Those who lived through the war wit-nessed myriad episodes ranging from the predictable (Mexican and American soldiers engaged in pitched battles) to the less obvious (American troops fraternizing with Mexicans in long and uneventful occupations that did little more than spawn gambling empires) to the outright unexpected (Irish volun-teers deserting to the Mexican side to defend Catholicism against Protestant aggression, and Mexican politicians urging American diplomats to push for the annexation of all of Mexico).

The Mexican–American War was unquestionably a war of conquest. Af-ter years of ambiguities and delays, the administration of President James K. Polk quite purposefully sought to acquire Texas, New Mexico, and Alta California by military means.[9] Yet, as this book has tried to show, from the perspective of the frontier residents, it was a conquest mediated by Mexico's preexisting core–periphery tensions and a tangle of economic in-terests linking Mexico's Far North with the United States. Conquest thus en-tailed both imposition *and* acquiescence, rivalry *and* complicity. In this light, the Mexican–American War appears less as a one-time event that sealed the fate of this region and more like a catalyst that rekindled longstanding na-tional identity struggles fueled by ongoing and powerful structural transfor-mations. While the war did inject a newfound sense of urgency and drama, these frontier identity struggles continued to revolve around the same mag-netic fields of state power and market persuasion, placing frontier denizens

---

[7] Teresina Bent Scheurich, "Famous New Mexico Trials," unpublished manuscript, Dorothy Woodward Collection, NMSRCA.

[8] *U.S. vs. Antonio María Trujillo*, Taos, Mar 16, 1847, Records of the District Court for New Mexico Territory, First Judicial District, History File No. 166, NMSRCA.

[9] Perhaps the most persuasive document of the deliberateness with which the Polk administra-tion pursued the war to acquire territory is the diary of its president. Luis Cabrera, ed., *Diario del Presidente Polk 1845–1849* 2 vols. (Mexico City: Antigua Librería Robredo, 1948). Both American and Mexican scholars have concluded that it was a war of territorial acquisition. See, among others, González de la Vara, "Los nuevomexicanos ante la invasión norteamer-icana," 491–4; Moyano Pahissa, *México y Estados Unidos*, 122–71; Pletcher, *The Diplomacy of Annexation*; Vázquez, "México y la guerra con Estados Unidos," 17–46.

squarely in the same set of familiar dilemmas of yesteryear. Indeed, the very conquest of New Mexico by the United States reveals the many and subtle ways in which state and market intersected with personal decisions of enormous importance.

NEW MEXICO ON A WAR FOOTING

New Mexicans must have experienced a sense of dejà vu when they found out about the impending American military occupation in the summer of 1846. The preparations that followed – the call to arms, the burst of anti-American and anti-Texan rhetoric, and the military drafts and drills – had been fixtures of life in New Mexico for years. Even without counting the Indian campaigns that periodically disrupted the rhythms of ordinary life, rumors of a foreign invasion of one kind or another had plagued the Department every year going back at least to 1838. It is tempting to assume, given New Mexico's track record of repelling invasions from the outside, that it should have come natural to them to resist the American occupation. Yet a close examination of the strained relationships between national and departmental authorities and the bitter factional disputes unfolding within New Mexico makes clear just how unlikely and heroic any organized resistance would have been.

First, the reactions of New Mexicans to a possible American occupation must be understood against the backdrop of Mexico's national political scene in the 1840s. Mexico's first centralist constitution, known as the *Siete Leyes*, was promulgated at the end of 1836. For the next five years, Mexico lived through a tumultuous period, facing the Texas secessionist movement, a war with France, and continuous federalist uprisings between 1837 and 1841 in peripheral states and territories, including Alta California, New Mexico, Yucatán, and Tamaulipas. By 1840, it was clear that the first centralist experiment had failed.[10] This unsettled situation paved the way for an openly dictatorial regime in 1841–3, headed by Santa Anna and organized under a new constitution known as *Las Bases de Tacubaya*, which, in turn, was replaced by a second centralist regime organized under *Las Bases Orgánicas*, which were promulgated in 1843.[11] The only political actor that truly benefited from this chaotic state of affairs was the military, which was able to extend its access to financial and political resources as it tried to bring stability to the nation. The upshot of all of this was a growing militarization of Mexico's politics and increasing military centralization.

In New Mexico, this process took a tremendous toll as the Department had traditionally enjoyed a measure of autonomy in military matters. Fearful

---

[10] Vázquez, "México y la guerra con Estados Unidos," 31.

[11] For a good examination of the circumstances and political discussions leading up to the promulgation of *Las Bases Orgánicas*, see Cecilia Noriega Elío, *El Constituyente de 1842* (Mexico City: UNAM, 1986).

of increasing Americanization of the Far North, in the early 1840s the national government moved aggressively to consolidate various military organizations of the Far North. In July 1843, President Santa Anna made General Mariano Monterde of Chihuahua commander of all troops in the northern frontier. This supradepartmental military entity was formalized in the spring of 1845 with the creation of Mexico's "Fifth Division" with jurisdiction over the Departments of Durango, Chihuahua, and New Mexico.[12] Regardless of the strategic merits of this reorganization, it severely curtailed the authority of New Mexico's commandant general in matters like appointments and promotions, which now had to go through General Monterde and his successor, General Francisco García Conde. More importantly, this reorganization created a gray area with respect to finances, specifically raising the issue of the military commander's access to New Mexico's tariff resources.

A dramatic showdown in the summer of 1845 between the Chihuahua-based General García Conde and New Mexico's civil administration gives us an inkling of the level of antagonism originated by military centralization. Sounding the alarm of imminent war with the United States, General García Conde went to Santa Fe on an inspection tour and waited until September for the arrival of the caravan from Missouri. His plan from the outset was to channel tariff duties generated by the Santa Fe Trail for military purposes. But he was utterly disappointed when he learned that the resources had already been earmarked to pay for the Department's civil roll, including an outlay of two thousand pesos on behalf of New Mexico's governor. General García Conde became incensed: "... unfortunately, it is well known throughout the country the manner in which public funds have been handled in this department for many years... but I am determined to watch over the interests of the Nation and rescue them from wreckage."[13] The commander of the Fifth Division announced that he would leave for Chihuahua within days, taking with him New Mexico's trade duties. Out of New Mexico's tariff receipts totaling an estimated 62,850 pesos, General García Conde demanded that the treasurer, Ambrosio Armijo, immediately surrender 18,777 pesos. Governor José Chávez y Castillo resolutely refused, instructing the treasurer not to disburse any money. On September 28, General García Conde gave the treasurer until 9:30 P.M. to surrender the funds or he would take them by force. In the end, General García Conde took "a large sum of money to Chihuahua."[14]

[12] Minge, "Frontier Problems," 149.

[13] General García Conde to Treasurer Ambrosio Armijo, reproduced in José Chávez to Departmental Assembly, Santa Fe, Sep 29, 1845, MANM 38, 1045–9.

[14] Controversy in General García Conde to Treasurer Ambrosio Armijo, Santa Fe, Sep 23, 1845, MANM 38, 514; Governor José Chávez y Castillo to Ministro de Relaciones Exteriores y Gobierno, Santa Fe, Oct 1, 1845, MANM 38, 701–5; Governor José Chávez to Departmental Assembly, Sep 29, 1845, MANM 38, 1045–9.

Although no further violence ensued, the underlying problem remained, as military centralization forced New Mexicans to give up resources that would go chiefly to the militaries of Chihuahua and Durango.[15]

The biography of Manuel Armijo, New Mexico's three-time governor during the Mexican era, is very illustrative of the deleterious effects of the national government's centralizing policies on frontier politicians. As recently as 1841–2, Armijo stood at the apex of his political and military career in the wake of his successful capture of the Texan Santa Fe Expedition. By 1842, Armijo's ascendancy over New Mexican affairs was undisputed, as he served as both governor and commandant general of the Department. President Santa Anna even rewarded Armijo and New Mexico for defeating the Texans by ordering a monthly payment of ten thousand pesos on behalf of New Mexico's military.[16] And yet in the course of only a year and a half, his successful career was dramatically cut short by military centralization. The appointment of General Mariano Monterde as commander of all troops in the northern frontier in 1843 delivered a first blow. Although Armijo was formally placed second in command in this new military structure, in reality his military authority both inside and outside New Mexico was fast declining. In October 1843, General Monterde took the additional step of removing Armijo as commandant general of New Mexico, in spite of the latter's distinguished record. Adding insult to injury, General Monterde went on to appoint Colonel Mariano Martínez de Lejanza, a complete outsider who had spent his entire career in Chihuahua, in Armijo's place. New Mexico's military establishment had a long history of clashes with its Chihuahuan counterpart and naturally resented subordination to the latter. Troubled by these developments, Governor Armijo relinquished his civil authority three months later, adducing "unbearable pains making it impossible to continue in charge of the Government in this Department."[17]

Armijo's personal story is deeply entwined with that of New Mexico as a whole in the waning years of Mexican rule. And while his experience can in no way be said to be representative of nuevomexicanos at large, still the

---

[15] See Address of Donaciano Vigil to the Departmental Assembly, Santa Fe, Jun 22, 1846, edited and translated by David J. Weber, in Weber, *Arms, Indians, and the Mismanagement of New Mexico*, 28. General García Conde returned to Chihuahua and left Juan Andrés Archuleta as military commander of New Mexico. Archuleta faced the very same problems. He accused Governor Chávez of putting his private interests ahead of those of the nation and demanded that not half a *real* be spent from the public treasury without his prior approval. Military Commander Juan Andrés Archuleta to Governor José Chávez, Santa Fe, Oct 28, 1845, MANM 38, 521–2.

[16] The treasuries of Chihuahua and Mazatlán would give out the payments that were to commence in 1842. But the funds did not materialize, even after Governor Armijo sent personal representatives to Chihuahua to plead for the money. Minge, "Frontier Problems," 106, 126–7, 135.

[17] Governor Armijo to the Minister of Foreign Affairs, Santa Fe, Jan 15, 1844, quoted in Minge, "Frontier Problems," 159.

predicaments that he faced, specifically with regard to increasing centralization, speak volumes about the contentious relationship between national
and departmental governments. In fact, Armijo's resignation from the governorship merely opened the door for political centralization, as the national
government proceeded to appoint Colonel Mariano Martínez as governor
of New Mexico.[18] New to the ways of New Mexico, he blundered on several occasions, being especially criticized for accidentally provoking a war
with the Utes.[19] The upshot of this military and political consolidation of
power was that by 1845, New Mexico's top military and civil positions
were in the hands of an outsider, a situation that produced unconcealed resentment throughout New Mexico. Addressing the Departmental Assembly
in June 1846, Donaciano Vigil bluntly spoke about the mismanagement of
New Mexico at the hands of outsiders, specifically pointing to the cases of
Governors Albino Pérez and Mariano Martínez and Commander Francisco
García Conde. Representative Vigil insisted that in the future, New Mexico's
top political and military positions should be filled exclusively with native
sons or long-time residents.[20] Thus the rumblings of war a few months later
came at a time when nuevomexicanos were still reeling from Mexico City's
military and political centralizing policies.

Political factionalism was the other main obstacle that kept New
Mexicans from closing ranks in the face of a planned American occupation. In spite of the rapid succession of constitutional changes in 1841 and
1843, a *santanista* government remained in power for the entire period of
1841–4. The political scene at the time consisted of liberals (both radical
and moderate), *santanistas* more or less occupying the center of the political spectrum and always willing to make tactical alliances with the other
groups, and a conservative faction that included a broad range of positions
from moderate to monarchists. On December 6, 1844, the so-called Revolution of the Three Hours resulted in the overthrow of Santa Anna's regime –
and the eventual exile of its leader – and allowed the moderates, led by
General José Joaquín de Herrera, to gain power.

Unfortunately, political infighting only intensified during the new regime,
reaching a climax once the "Texas question" exploded on the political scene.
On March 1, 1845, the United States Congress passed a joint resolution approving the annexation of Texas. President Herrera had spent two months

---

[18] The precise method was somewhat more convoluted. The Departmental Assembly proposed
a list of five candidates from which the president selected a name. In any event, the national
government had the last word.

[19] Governor Martínez received Ute delegates in Santa Fe. The discussion turned heated, and
Governor Martínez, thinking that the Utes were about to take his life, called the guards,
who killed some of the unarmed delegates. This incident ultimately led to an all-out war.
See Donaciano Vigil to the Departmental Assembly, Santa Fe, Jun 22, 1846, in Weber, *Arms,
Indians, and the Mismanagement of New Mexico*, 22–4.

[20] Weber, *Arms, Indians, and the Mismanagement of New Mexico*, 17–28.

making overtures to the American government, seeking a negotiated solution to their mutual disagreements over Texas. But in the wake of the
fateful resolution of the American Congress, President Herrera's administration was assailed from all sides. Indeed, his government barely survived two
overthrow attempts perpetrated in June and September of 1845.[21] General
Mariano Paredes y Arrillaga, generally regarded as one of the more conservative *caudillos*, followed closely these conspiracies from his headquarters
in San Luis Potosí. He was in command of the largest Mexican army in
the country, a force that was intended to be deployed in Texas if necessary.
Shockingly, instead of marching toward the troubled northern frontier, he
directed his men toward central Mexico, entering Mexico City on January 2,
1846. General Paredes then ousted President Herrera, convened new elections, and lashed out against the previous administration for "conspiring
with the enemy to dismember the fatherland." General Paredes made it clear
that after clamping down on internal dissension, he would take appropriate
steps to deal with the external threat.[22]

New Mexicans lived through these events with a great dose of anguish and
uncertainty. Governor and Commandant General Armijo had been a loyal
santanista at least since the early 1840s, but his resignation from the governorship as well as Santa Anna's departure in 1844 introduced considerable instability into the Department. For instance, Governor Martínez, Armijo's successor, received an invitation to join a rebellion launched by General Paredes
early in 1845, leading to great consternation and disagreement within New
Mexico's military establishment and cadre of career politicians.[23] In another
instance, in May the governor of New Mexico informed the ministry of
the interior and exterior of an aborted military mutiny provoked by delays
in the payment of the troops and stoked by opposition forces inside New
Mexico.[24]

Throughout 1845, New Mexico went through a series of short-lived administrations. The paucity of sources and the deliberately ambiguous stance
adopted by many politically active nuevomexicanos prevent us from drawing
a completely satisfactory sketch of the different political factions within the
Department and their connections to other movements in Mexico. Generally,
it seems clear that there was an ill-defined and shifting cadre of liberal politicians that, interestingly, included several of Armijo's close collaborators, such
as Guadalupe Miranda, Donaciano Vigil, the Otero and Pereira families,

---

[21] Pedro Santoni, *Mexicans at Arms: Puro Federalists and the Politics of War, 1845–1848* (Fort Worth, TX: Texas Christian University Press, 1996), 141–50.

[22] Santoni, *Mexicans at Arms*, 191–209. He argues that in spite of General Paredes' bold rhetoric, he still hoped for a negotiated solution.

[23] Minge, "Frontier Problems," 276.

[24] Governor José Chávez to Ministerio de Relaciones Exteriores, Gobernación y Polocía, Santa Fe, May 14, 1845, AGN, Gobernación, caja 304, expediente 9.

and former Governor Francisco Sarracino. This group had established an uneasy alliance (sealed with close business ties, as we shall see) with many politically active, foreign-born residents who also found themselves chafing under New Mexico's conservative regimes. Opposed to them was an even more amorphous conservative faction that clearly included military officers such as Governor Martínez as well as many members of the ecclesiastical hierarchy, beginning with Vicar Felipe Ortiz but most vocally represented by Father Antonio José Martínez of Taos. Because conservatism became so closely identified with the defense of the nation – that is, anti-Americanism – political factionalism in New Mexico cut right through the issue of national identity, rendering politics extremely volatile and making the prospect of an American occupation extremely divisive.

In spite of these obstacles New Mexico began to mobilize in earnest against a possible American occupation early in 1846. At the center of this activity was none other than Manuel Armijo, who had returned to the gubernatorial office on November 16, 1845, for a third and last term. The brand new governor sought to reconstitute New Mexico's ties to the national government and quell internal dissention but did not succeed completely in either endeavor.

Governor Armijo's main priority was to establish a new working relationship with Mexico City and Chihuahua such that he could confidently embark on defense preparations without fear of being suddenly rebuked by his superiors. Armijo knew well that to put New Mexico on a war footing, he needed to take vigorous and controversial actions, including the drafting of men and the allocation of resources, all of which would undoubtedly draw criticism from his local opponents. Strong backing from higher authority was of paramount importance in these circumstances. And yet, barely a few weeks into his term, Governor Armijo learned of General Paredes' military coup in December 1845, rendering the status of the most important political and military authorities of the Department in question. In fact, through his long association with Santa Anna's regime, Armijo was viewed as a *santanista* and therefore unlikely to have a close relationship with General Paredes' regime (among other things Armijo had been among those who had rejected General Paredes' invitation for New Mexico to join his revolution early in 1845[25]). Still, we learn that Governor Armijo pragmatically urged New Mexico's military establishment to pledge allegiance to the new national government, something that took place at the end of February 1846.[26] For the next few months, national and departmental authorities had only sporadic contacts, adding to Governor Armijo's sense of restlessness and lack of support. In June, the embattled governor blamed "envious authorities" of Chihuahua for keeping him in the dark about the impending American invasion and

---

[25] Minge, "Frontier Problems," 276–7.
[26] Plan de adhesión, Santa Fe, Feb 25, 1846, MANM 41, 131–2.

sought reliable information directly from the national government, asserting that New Mexico also belonged "to the great Mexican Family."[27] Thus, to the very end, New Mexico's strained ties to Chihuahua and Mexico City constituted an unwelcome distraction forcing Governor Armijo and his collaborators to wage rear-guard skirmishes with his Mexican administrative superiors.

Governor Armijo's second goal was to try to ease factional disputes within the Department. In at least three speeches, Governor Armijo exhorted New Mexicans to put aside their "petty interests" and "party affiliations." He even invoked divine authority in an address delivered just a few days before the occupation: "...the author and keeper of all societies left in his golden book these peremptory words: 'All kingdoms that are internally divided will be overrun.' Never forget this admonition, nor separate your particular interests from those of the common cause"[28] As had happened before, Catholicism emerged as a crucial unifying theme. Armijo put it tersely in his very first address to New Mexicans in January 1846: "I summon you to rally around our national flag so that all men, children, old people, and even women cooperate with our lives and interests in the defense of our sacrosanct religion that our enemies are trying to destroy."[29] Some evidence suggests that this imagery worked at least in some conservative circles. For instance, Father Antonia José Martínez of Taos, who had been quite critical of Governor Armijo in the previous months, found this rhetoric appealing and began "lauding the Mexican Government and people to the skies in consequence of the proclamation...."[30] In his sermons, Father Martínez had insisted on the same themes and even shared with his parishioners an apocalyptic dream that he had in which the national government "had disposed of New Mexico and heretics on its confines were ready to overrun this unfortunate land."[31] But ultimately, such chiaroscuro distinctions between Catholic and Protestant or between Mexicans and Americans could hardly fit the complex social reality of New Mexico. Protracted political factionalism continued to thrive in the various shades of gray existing in the economic, political, and social life of New Mexico. When the star-spangled banner was raised at the plaza of Santa Fe, the Mexican acting governor, who was soon to give power to Colonel Stephen W. Kearny, somberly pointed out in his speech that internal strife had been the "damned venom" that

[27] Governor Armijo to Secretary of Government, Santa Fe, Jun 30, 1846, Donaciano Vigil Collection, NMSRCA.

[28] Governor Armijo to His Fellow Countrymen, Santa Fe, Aug 8, 1846, MANM 41, 279–82, Benjamin M. Read Papers, NMSRCA.

[29] Manuel Armijo to the people, Santa Fe, Jan 10, 1846, María G. Durán Papers, 10, NMSRCA; Armijo to the people, Santa Fe, Feb 14, 1846, MANM 41, 242–3; Armijo to His Fellow Countrymen, Santa Fe, Aug 8, 1846, Benjamin M. Read Papers, MANM 41, 279–82.

[30] Bent to Álvarez, Taos, Feb 16, 1846, Read Collection, 72, NMSRCA.

[31] Bent to Álvarez, Taos, Feb 26, 1846, Read Collection, 74, NMSRCA.

had brought down one of the greatest nations ever created on the face of the earth.[32]

As the summer approached, news went from bad to worse. The war machines were set in motion. On April 26, 1846, there was a bloody encounter between a Mexican cavalry unit and a squadron of American dragoons along the disputed Texas-Mexico frontier between the Rio Grande and the Nueces. News of this encounter worked its way up to Washington, D.C., in two weeks. On May 11, President Polk read a message in Congress asking for a declaration of war: "Mexico . . . has invaded our territory and shed American blood upon the American soil."[33] By the middle of July, there were no doubts in New Mexico that an expedition was being outfitted in St. Louis, Missouri, to take possession of the Department. In the afternoon of July 17, Governor Armijo held a meeting at the Palace of the Governors, with the most influential men of New Mexico in attendance, to discuss the situation. Governor Armijo broached a delicate subject, openly considering at length the possibility of surrendering the Department to the Americans peacefully. In the end, the group decided to resist and began by issuing orders to enlist all males fifteen years and older, and to make exceptions only for medical reasons.[34]

"TOUCH THEIR MONEY AND YOU REACH THEIR HEARTS"

The Americanization of New Mexico had been long in the making. Since the late 1830s, Governor Armijo's government had been awarding enormous grants of land to mixed groups of Anglo-American and Mexican developers.[35] The size of these grants dwarfed anything that had been seen in New Mexico's entire land history. It is no exaggeration to say that by the mid-1840s, New Mexico's most promising land and settlement ventures had gravitated toward the hands of a small but powerful clique of

---

[32] Juan Bautista Vigil y Alarid, response to Kearny's Proclamation, Santa Fe, Aug 19, 1846, Bloom-McFie Collection, Folder 2, NMSRCA.

[33] Quoted in K. Jack Bauer, *The Mexican War 1846–1848* (Lincoln, NE: University of Nebraska Press, 1974), 66–7.

[34] Secretary of Government to Prefects of the North, Center, and South Districts, Santa Fe, Jul 18, 1846, MANM 41, 232–3; report of the citizens of New Mexico to the President of Mexico, Santa Fe, Sep 26, 1846, translated and edited by Max Moorhead, "Notes and Documents," *New Mexico Historical Review* 26: 1 (Jan 1951), 69–75.

[35] Governor Armijo's relation to Americans was one of love-hate. Contemporary Anglo-American writers such as Josiah Gregg, George Kendall, and W. H. H. Davis portrayed New Mexico's three-time governor decidedly in a bad light, often depicting him as capricious, arbitrary, and ambitious. But this should not obscure the fact that Armijo shared extensive business interests with these men, and conversely, Anglo Americans often relied on Armijo when they were challenged by other nuevomexicanos, such as Father Martínez, who were considerably more hostile to the growing Americanization of the Department. On Armijo and the Americans, see Lecompte, *Rebellion in Río Arriba*, 59–60.

Anglo-American entrepreneurs of Río Arriba together with their Mexican allies (see Chapter 1). These bright prospects briefly hung in the balance in 1844, when Governor Mariano Martínez attempted to backtrack on some of his predecessor's land decisions. But Armijo's return to power in 1845 all but assured the continuation of these land policies.

At the same time, New Mexico became rapidly Americanized because of its continued commercial interaction with the United States. As we saw in Chapter 3, scores of New Mexicans came to depend directly or indirectly on commercial activities with the United States revolving around the Santa Fe Trail. By 1843, the value of the foreign merchandise imported into New Mexico had grown to half a million dollars, by far the largest and most dynamic portion of the Department's economy. And more than a third of this activity was at least nominally in the hands of Spanish-surnamed individuals. In terms of government revenues, New Mexico's dependence on the United States was nothing short of astounding. Revenues from import taxes accounted for more than 70 percent of the state budget. This money went into paying the salaries of the entire New Mexican administration as well as the three militia companies that protected New Mexico from Indian depredations.[36]

In sum, after two and a half decades of vigorous commercial and demographic relations with its northern neighbor, New Mexico was economically far more integrated into the economy of the United States than to that of Mexico. And when the United States government finally decided to occupy New Mexico militarily, it found that it had many nonmilitary levers it could pull to accomplish this end.

On August 12, 1846, Governor Armijo began to have communication with envoys from Colonel Kearny's Army of the West. Santiago (James W.) Magoffin, accompanied by José González Ortega, arrived in Santa Fe at 10:00 P.M. and immediately presented themselves in Armijo's home. Magoffin was a merchant of the Santa Fe–Chihuahua Trail who had lived in Mexico for twenty years. President Polk had commissioned Magoffin to provide supplies to the Army of the West and to use his connections in Mexico's northern provinces to win them over to the American side.[37] The next day, Captain Philip St. George Cooke, with twelve dragoons of the United States Army, reached Santa Fe and went to the governor's house. Magoffin, who was there at the time, came out of the door to receive them and made the introductions between Captain Cooke and Governor Armijo. Then, in full

---

[36] Juan María Alarid, New Mexico's Budget Report for 1832–3, Santa Fe, n.d., MANM 17, 1002–3; Ramón Abréu, New Mexico's Budget Report for 1834–5, Santa Fe, Jun 22, 1835, MANM 21, 420–2; the excellent budget summary from July 1838 through December 1843 in *resúmen estadístico de la tesorería del Departamento del Nuevo México*, n.p., n.d., MANM 34, 1029–31.

[37] Cabrera, ed., *Diario del Presidente Polk*, I: 89–90. See also Magoffin Papers, Twitchell Collection, NMSARC.

sight of all passersby, Cooke reached into his pocket as if to take out some documents; but Armijo stopped him and told him that they would take care of it later.[38]

At night, a group of merchants gathered in the house of José González Ortega. Among those present were Henry Connelly, James Magoffin, Captain Cook, Luciano Frampton, and Manuel Álvarez, the United States consul in Santa Fe. They all spoke English. Late at night, the group visited Governor Armijo. The papers that Captain Cooke had brought with him were letters from Colonel Kearny making Governor Armijo responsible for any bloodshed that would occur as a result of the occupation of Santa Fe. Captain Ignacio Muñoz, who was present in this gathering, stated that the governor spoke to Magoffin and Connelly "in a very reserved manner," and that these proceedings were severely criticized by the Mexican officials who had observed the affair. The witness further stated that the next morning, Magoffin, Connelly, Luciano Frampton, and others attended a picnic in which José Cordero – another Chihuahua merchant and Armijo's main trading partner – made "a very suspicious toast" to New Mexico's happy future.[39]

Cavalry Lieutenant Manuel García de Lara pointed out that although the contents of the talks between Armijo and Magoffin were not known – Magoffin was seen to enter Armijo's home about four or five times – it was easy to surmise the essence. Magoffin himself had told other Mexican officers that they would be happy under the star-spangled banner because their property would be respected, their houses would rise in value, and the political system would change for the better.[40] The consul of the United States confirmed the efforts to persuade Governor Armijo to surrender. Álvarez apparently apprised Armijo of the operations of the Army of the West and attempted to convince him that

... it would be better for himself and the people under his government to capitulate, and far preferable to become an inconsiderable portion of a powerful Republic, than a considerable one of a nation constantly engaged in revolutions, with no stability in the public administration and powerless to defend the citizens of this province from the thousands of hostile Indians who surround them.

Álvarez described Governor Armijo as a man vacillating to the last and passed judgment on him: "... though a great man in small matters, I found him to be a small one in great affairs."[41]

---

[38] See Philip St. George Cooke, *The Conquest of New Mexico and California* (1878; reprint, Albuquerque, NM: Horn & Wallace, [1964]).

[39] Testimony of Captain Ignacio Muñoz, Proceedings Against Armijo, Mexico City, March, 1847, AHSD 2588, copied at Bancroft Library, roll 11.

[40] Testimony of Lieutenant Manuel García de Lara, Proceedings Against Armijo, Mexico City, March, 1847, AHDN 2588, copied at Bancroft Library, roll 11.

[41] Manuel Álvarez to James Buchanan, Santa Fe, Sep 4, 1846, Dispatches from United States Consuls in Santa Fe, 1830–46, RG 59, No. 199.

Even though much of the subsequent historical controversy has revolved around whether Governor Armijo reached a secret agreement with Magoffin and the other American envoys to hand over New Mexico, we should not lose sight of the fact that several members of the nuevomexicano elite, moved by their own pecuniary and political considerations, played a significant role in the decision. Consul Álvarez admitted that in the first interviews with Armijo, he failed to convince him to turn over the Department to the Americans, but reported that he had a lot more success with "other officers" and with the governor's "confidential advisers." In fact, Álvarez stated that they were easily won over because under the new order of things, they could advance in public favor and even occupy higher posts, unlike Armijo, who could never be invested with the same amount of authority that he had enjoyed.[42] Magoffin himself stated that he met many of the "rich" of the Department and the militia officers, with whom he had ample intercourse: "I assured them the only object of our Government was to take possession of New Mexico as being a part of the territory annexed to the U. S. by Texas and to give peace and quietude to the good people of the country *which gave them entire satisfaction.*"[43] His only problem had been to quiet down Colonel Diego Archuleta, second in command, who was bent on fighting the American troops.[44]

In spite of all of this pressure to submit, the governor went through the motions of preparing for the invasion. Among volunteers, draftees, and professional soldiers, Governor Armijo raised a respectable force that has been estimated at more than three thousand and up to four thousand men. It was decided that New Mexico's troops would stop the advance of the enemy at El Cañón, fifteen miles east of Santa Fe. On August 16, 1846, General Armijo left Santa Fe with his dragoons and the civic militia, taking three four-pound pieces of artillery. It was an ambulatory community accompanied by New Mexico's entire government, including the Departmental Assembly. After establishing its camp at El Cañón, Governor Armijo convened the Departmental Assembly and asked whether they should defend the department or treat with the enemy. The Assembly responded that its members were there to serve as soldiers rather than to deliberate and were ready to obey

[42] Ibid.

[43] J. W. Magoffin to Secretary of War W. L. Marcy, Santa Fe, Aug 26, 1846, Magoffin Papers, Twitchell Collection, NMSRCA. My emphasis.

[44] Magoffin's later story is also revealing. After securing the bloodless occupation of New Mexico, he was sent ahead to Chihuahua to do the same for the American forces going there under General John E. Wool. In Chihuahua he was imprisoned, but his sentence was suspended at the request of Governor Armijo. Shortly before the battle of Sacramento, Magoffin was removed to Durango, where the trial continued. He was acquitted of all charges. See Robert B. McAfee to President Polk, Harrodsburgh, Ky, Jun 22, 1847; Proceedings Against Santiago Magoffin, Durango, Apr 30, 1847, quoted in Proceedings Against Manuel Armijo, AHDN. There might be a copy of his sixty-seven-page deposition in Durango. See also Gardner, *Brothers on the Santa and Chihuahua Trails,* 131, 160.

orders. The governor then assembled the militia officers and influential citizens and inquired from them what course of action to take. One of the officers responded that they were there to fight. It appears that Governor Armijo started losing confidence. As he put it, he feared going into battle with people without military discipline.[45] According to a report signed by several eyewitnesses, Governor Armijo suddenly decided to countermarch with the veteran troops, taking the artillery with him. He also ordered the volunteers to go home, so that "even the most unsuspecting knew that Armijo had betrayed them."[46] For his part, the governor claimed that he retreated because, after a thoughtful consultation, all the gathered New Mexicans agreed to withdraw and join the Chihuahua troops that were believed to be marching toward Santa Fe.[47] In a letter sent to Colonel Kearny, Armijo protested, "before God and man," that he did not recognize the Department of New Mexico as part of the United States: "I leave this question to be finally settled by our governments."[48]

Why did Armijo behave in this manner? Did he finally yield to the pressure of the Anglo-American merchants and army officers? Was he protecting his land and trading interests? Was the governor bribed into surrendering, as Donaciano Vigil later claimed?[49] Or did he simply consider any resistance futile? As the tenor of the governor's negotiations with Magoffin and Álvarez reveals, Armijo's considerable pecuniary interests undoubtedly played a part in his decision. But even beyond the governor's personal involvement, many influential nuevomexicanos clearly had similar concerns in mind. Robert B. McAfee, another merchant well acquainted with Magoffin, wrote to President Polk, referring to this phenomenon in a sarcastic manner:

45 Report of the Citizens of New Mexico to the President of Mexico, Santa Fe, Sep 26, 1846, translated and edited by Max Moorhead in "Notes and Documents," *New Mexico Historical Review* 26: 1 (Jan 1951), 69–75.

46 Miguel E. Pino to Facundo Pino, Santa Fe, Nov 14, 1846, in Proceedings Against Armijo, Mexico City, March, 1847, AHDN 2588, copied at Bancroft Library, roll 11; and report of the citizens of New Mexico to the president of Mexico, Santa Fe, Sep 26, 1846, Moorhead, "Notes and Documents," 69–75.

47 Armijo to Ministro de Guerra y Marina, n.p., Sep 8, 1846, in Proceedings Against Armijo, Mexico City, March, 1847, AHDN 2588, copied at Bancroft Library, roll 11. Armijo's claim is supported by Magoffin, who stated that after the military consultation at El Cañón, the officers answered that they were not prepared to defend the territory. Magoffin to W. L. Marcy, Santa Fe, Aug, 26, 1846, Magoffin Papers, Twitchell Collection, NMSRCA.

48 Manuel Armijo to Colonel Kearny, Camp at El Cañón, Aug 15, 1846, Ritch Coll, reel 3, NMSRCA.

49 In his testimony, First Lieutenant Antonio José Apodaca asserted that Donaciano Vigil had claimed publicly to be in possession of documents proving that Armijo had sold the Department. Proceedings Against Armijo, Mexico City, March, 1847, AHDN 2588, copied at Bancroft Library, roll 11. As Martín González de la Vara has observed, various sources have accused Armijo of having been bribed into surrender, but no smoking gun has surfaced in the archival record. González de la Vara, "Los nuevomexicanos ante la invasión norteamericana," 478–9.

"...touch their money and you reach their hearts. Make it their interest to have peace and we will soon have it."[50]

That same day the Army of the West pushed ahead and entered Santa Fe before sunset. At the public square, Colonel Kearny and his staff dismounted and were received by Juan Bautista Vigil, y Alarid who had been left as acting governor. An American flag was hoisted on the staff of the Palace of the Governors, and this was hailed by a salute from the batteries. The next morning, Colonel Kearny gave his well-rehearsed speech and took possession of New Mexico. As before, he reassured New Mexicans of their lives and properties, pledged respect for Catholicism, and proclaimed his intention to establish a civil government "on a republican basis similar to those of our own states."[51] Vigil responded with a brief speech stating the position of at least one faction of his fellow nuevomexicanos to the military occupation. He said that it was not up to them in New Mexico, but up to the governments in Mexico City and Washington, D.C., to determine the boundaries between the two nations. Nevertheless, Vigil warned the military commander not to be surprised by the lack of enthusiasm: "[Mexico] was our mother; and what child will not shed abundant tears at the tomb of his parents?"[52]

SYMBOLIC POWER OF THE STATE, MONTEZUMA, AND THE TAOS REVOLT OF 1847

The American military occupation severed virtually all ties between Mexico and New Mexico. For the duration of the war, a Mexican counterstrike remained a distinct possibility, but it ultimately failed to materialize. Thus the Mexican government henceforth ceased to have any tangible influence on New Mexican affairs in the form of patronage arrangements, political appointments, military activities, exaction of resources, and so on (the one crucial exception occurred in ecclesiastical matters, as New Mexico continued to be a part of the Bishopric of Durango[53]). And yet, notwithstanding this sudden and palpable absence of the Mexican state, by the turn of 1846–7, New Mexico witnessed what we could call a series of "Mexicanist"

---

[50] Robert B. McAfee to President Polk, Harrodsburgh, Ky, Jun 22, 1847, Magoffin Papers, Twitchell Collection, NMSRCA.

[51] Kearny's Proclamation, Santa Fe, Aug 19, 1846, Bloom-McFie Collection, Folder 1, NMSRCA.

[52] Juan Bautista Vigil y Alarid, Response to Colonel Kearny's Proclamation, Santa Fe, Aug 19, 1846, translated and edited by David J. Weber, *Foreigners in Their Native Land: Historical Roots of the Mexican Americans* (Albuquerque, NM: University of New Mexico Press), 127–8.

[53] As late as June 1847, Friar Benigno Cárdenas received instructions from the Bishopric of Durango directing him to conduct rogations asking God for the failure of the "ambitious cabinet of North America," and for aiding the Mexican cause. Fray Benigno Cárdenas to Bishop Zubiría, n.p., Aug 29, 1850, Miscellaneous Records, Church Records, NMSRCA.

insurrections – that is, movements aimed at restoring Mexico's sovereignty over the Department.

The first conspiracy began to take shape on December 12, 1846, on the day of the Virgin of Guadalupe, when various nuevomexicanos from Santa Fe and its vicinity pledged in front of a cross to drive the American intruders out of New Mexico.[54] The rebellion would start on December 19 at midnight, but the plot was exposed and the rebels had to flee.[55] A month later, on January 19, 1847, a second and far more serious rebellion broke out in the northern and western districts of New Mexico. The insurgency directly resulted in the massacre of scores of Anglo Americans and nuevomexicano "collaborationists" in Taos, Arroyo Hondo, and Mora.[56] Although violent outbreaks were restricted only to the northern and western districts, tremors of the movement engulfed all of New Mexico. In Río Abajo, Prefect Francisco Sarracino wrote acting Governor Donaciano Vigil stating that "evil spirits" continually threatened their lives and observing that the pueblos of Cochiti and Santo Domingo were colluded with the rebellious party of Río Arriba.[57] Farther south, Friar Mariano de Jesús López reported that at the pueblo of Isleta there had been some gatherings in support of the Taos movement to expel the Americans and that the pueblos of Acoma, Laguna, and Socorro were likely soon to follow suit.[58] The main protagonists of these movements consisted of a most disparate – almost schizophrenic – social mix: elite nuevomexicanos and Pueblo Indians. In the next few pages, I will try to elucidate the motivations of these two constituencies, a task that requires an appreciation of the many layers of state power (even when the state no longer exists), ranging from straightforward pecuniary calculations to intricate symbolic ties between the Mexican state, organized Catholicism, and Pueblo Indian traditional beliefs.

Members of the nuevomexicano elite clearly understood the Taos Rebellion of 1847 as the latest turn in an ongoing saga of bitter factional disputes that harked back to the Mexican era. In the aftermath of the American takeover, one group of nuevomexicano politicians and prominent families chose to make room for themselves in the emerging political and economic order. Their actions under American rule were hardly unexpected, as for years they had supported or contributed in one way or another in forging

[54] One of the best accounts of this first rebellion is still Burton, "The Taos Rebellion," 176–92.
[55] Accounts of how this first plot was discovered differ. See Myra Ellen Jenkins, "Rebellion Against American Occupation of New Mexico 1846–1847," unpublished paper, University of New Mexico, 1949, 21.
[56] A compilation of accounts is in Michael McNierney, *Taos 1847: The Revolt in Contemporary Accounts* (Boulder, CO: Johnson, 1980). See also James W. Goodrich, "Revolt at Mora, 1847," *New Mexico Historical Review* 47:1, 49–60.
[57] Francisco Sarracino to Donaciano Vigil, Peralta, Jan 26, 1847, Territorial Archives of New Mexico (TANM) 98, 33–4.
[58] Sarracino to Donaciano Vigil, Albuquerque, Feb 12, 1847, TAMN 98, 40–1.

closer economic ties with the United States. They openly talked about "their party" (still clearly reminiscent of their Mexican liberal affiliations), but now further bonded to each other through their open support for of an American regime in New Mexico. Barely a month after his arrival, General Kearny made appointments that confirmed the key roles that these nuevomexicanos were expected to perform. Among others, Donaciano Vigil was named secretary of the newly established American territory of New Mexico, Antonio José Otero was made judge of the Supreme Court of New Mexico, and Francisco Sarracino was named *prefecto*.[59]

This pro-American faction was decidedly opposed by another group of influential politicos who generally kept close ties to the Mexican military and ecclesiastical establishments and whose vague conservative ideals under Mexico now acquired a more precise meaning impelling them to undermine the incipient American regime. The two most visible leaders of this group, Diego Archuleta and Tomás Ortiz, illustrate this phenomenon exceedingly well.

Diego Archuleta was the son of Juan Andrés Archuleta, the aging former military commander of New Mexico whose most famous exploit was the capture of the Texan Santa Fe Expedition in 1841. Diego's military prospects were bright indeed, not only for being the son of the most celebrated warrior of New Mexico, but also for having received formal military training in an academy in Durango, something that few other nuevomexicano officers had. Since the late 1830s, Diego Archuleta rose through the ranks very rapidly. He was promoted even ahead of other officers who had served longer in the army. He did not conceal his resentment of the American military occupation and became a principal leader of the failed conspiracy of December 1846. Should it have succeeded, Diego Archuleta would have become the brand new military commander of New Mexico under a renewed Mexican administration.

For his part, Tomás Ortiz was another member of New Mexico's oligarchy and a successful politician in his own right. He was elected to the Departmental Assembly in 1845. But what set him apart were his close ties to the ecclesiastical hierarchy. He was the brother of the vicar of New Mexico, Juan Felipe Ortiz, and the actions of the two siblings were often interpreted as a good indication of the position of New Mexico's ecclesiastical establishment. During the December conspiracy, Tomás emerged as the main leader of the movement, and in case of success he was slated to become provisional governor.[60]

In short, the involvement of individuals like Diego Archuleta and Tomás Ortiz in anti-American conspiracies has to be placed in the larger context of

[59] These appointments were made on September 22, 1846. See TANM, 98, 4.
[60] Vicar Ortiz was almost certainly aware of the conspiracy, although it is hard to ascertain the extent of his actual participation.

liberal/conservative rivalries and the controversies around the Americaniza-tion of New Mexico.[61] These men articulated a "Mexicanist" political vision aimed at restricting the activities of foreign-born residents and seeking in-stead to strengthen the linkages between Mexico and New Mexico through institutions of national scope such as the military and the Church.

Beyond this handful of New Mexican notables, other sectors of New Mex-ico's society rejected American rule. Anectdotal evidence indicates that a sig-nificant number of non-elite nuevomexicanos remained hostile to the Amer-ican military government. Vicar Juan Felipe Ortiz reported to the Bishop of Durango that no less than one thousand men would be willing to help in the enterprise of reconquering the Department.[62] There were other telltale signs. Animosities ran so high in Santa Fe that Secretary Donaciano Vigil had to take an escort whenever he ventured out into the streets; even then, passersby proffered indignities, and some even cast stones at him and occasionally threatened his life. Smaller towns where the Mexican local administration re-mained intact – especially la Cañada, San Miguel del Vado, and Mora – were rumored to be cold or downright hostile to the American-run territorial gov-ernment and purposefully kept communications to a minimum.[63] But among all of the different groups of New Mexicans that could potentially attempt to restore Mexican rule, the most threatening element by far was paradox-ically the least Mexicanized portion of New Mexico's population: Pueblo Indians.

Any examination of the motives of Pueblo Indians for joining the anti-American conspiracies of 1846–7 leads to the complex economic and sym-bolic nexus between the Mexican state and Pueblo communities and their

---

[61] In his last proclamation, Governor Charles Bent branded the conspirators as "ambitious" and "displaced" men who wished to "keep the people under the yoke of their whims." Charles Bent to the People, Santa Fe, Jan 5, 1847, Ina Sizer Cassidy Collection, NMSRCA.

[62] Vicar Ortiz to Bishop Zubiría, Santa Fe, n.d. (possibly November 1846), Proceedings Against Armijo, Mexico City, March, 1847, AHDN 2588, copied at Bancroft Library, roll 11.

[63] Dámaso Robles to Manuel Álvarez, la Cañada, Sep, 1846, Manuel Álvarez Collection, Folder 17, NMSRCA; Francisco Paula de Robledo to Manuel Álvarez, San Miguel del Vado, Nov 3, 1846, Manuel Álvarez Business Papers, Folder 17, NMSRCA. Indeed, tensions between local and departmental authorities mounted. For instance, the alcalde of Albuquerque, José María Chávez, jailed Ambrosio Armijo – a member of a party that advocated aggregation to the United States – and, with the backing of the local troops, disregarded the authority of Prefect Francisco Sarracino, who had ordered the alcalde to release the prisoner. Sarracino fined Chávez but did not want to press the issue too much, lest the affair end in violence. Francisco Sarracino to Donaciano Vigil, Albuquerque, Oct 15, 1846, Ritch Collection, Reel 3; Francisco Sarracino to Donaciano Vigil, Pajaritos, Nov 16, 1846, Ritch Collection, reel 3, NMSRCA. Both sides distrusted Ambrosio Armijo and his brother Manuel. Ambrosio was taken prisoner by Captain John Burgwin in early December, for he was found carrying out "treasonable correspondence with General Armijo." Incriminating letters found on Ambro-sio and in the rifle barrel of a nuevomexicano soldier informed General Armijo that the province was ripe for revolt. Anonymous letter, Santa Fe, Dec 5, 1846, published in the *St. Louis Republican* and reproduced in the *New York Tribune*, Mar 3, 1847.

transformation under American rule. Like most nuevomexicanos, Pueblo Indians became acquainted with the *americanos del norte* during the Mexican era and for the most part established amicable relations that involved retail trade and occasionally service contracts (see Chapter 3). Yet New Mexico's growing commercialism and closer economic ties to the United States also posed challenges to the Pueblos, especially those in Río Arriba. Commercialism indirectly fueled nomadic raids, as it created a profitable market for plundered objects and increased demand for animals and captives.[64] These raids ultimately strained and complicated the relationships between Pueblo communities and nomadic groups, and prompted New Mexican authorities to retaliate and launch punitive expeditions based largely on Pueblo manpower and resources.

Yet from the standpoint of Pueblo Indians, the most troubling byproduct of economic integration to the United States was land encroachment. The departmental government's drive to encourage settlements and develop lands along the Santa Fe Trail in the 1840s could only impinge on the extensive Pueblo land holdings granted by the Spanish Crown. For instance, the colossal Beaubien-Miranda grant approved by the Armijo administration included an area that the Taos Pueblo Indians had traditionally used for hunting buffalo and was regarded as communal land.[65] Aided by their parish priest, Father Antonio José Martínez, the Taos Pueblo Indians demanded the suspension of the grant, and indeed their efforts met with initial success. Incoming Governor Mariano Chávez suspended the grant on February 22, 1844. Donaciano Vigil, former secretary of government under Armijo, broke the news mockingly to his friend, Guadalupe Miranda: "Father Martínez, the man of letters, the man of learning and sage of the century has managed to dazzle with his knowledge Governor Chávez and has obtained the suspension of Beaubien's possession in the Colorado river...."[66] This suspension, however, lasted less than two months. The Taos Pueblo Indians were back on the defensive. Moreover, the Beaubien-Miranda grant was only the start of a renewed land onslaught as Beaubien and his associates – a group that

[64] Brooks, *Captives and Cousins*, 234–57.

[65] Father Martínez's demand rested on two objections. In addition to encroachment on Pueblo lands, the parish priest objected to the fact that part of the Miranda-Beaubien grant had been sold to Charles Bent, a foreigner, and thus the transaction was illegal because the land was located within the frontier preserve. Data for the Beaubien-Miranda Grant was obtained from the Surveyor General Report, 15, Land Grant Records, reel 14, 141–80, NMSRCA. See also Dunham, "New Mexican Land Grants with Special Reference to the Title Papers of the Maxwell Grant," 1–22; Murphy, "The Beaubien and Miranda Land Grant 1841–1846," 27–47.

[66] Donaciano Vigil to Guadalupe Miranda, Santa Fe, May 31, 1844, Donaciano Vigil Collection, NMSRCA. This is only one example among many. See also the disputes between the Otero family and the Pueblo Indians of San Agustín de la Isleta, in report of the legislative committee to the governor of New Mexico, Santa Fe, Sep 27, 1845, SANM I, 6, 1780–4.

included Charles Bent and other Anglo Americans – unrolled plans to create settlements along the Poñil and Cimarrón rivers, which would only increase demand for land. Two crucial observations stemming from these proceedings are worth emphasizing. First, wealthy foreign-born merchants of Río Arriba, while hardly alone, emerged as principal beneficiaries of the land-developing schemes of the 1840s. Second, Taos Pueblo Indian leaders and the local Catholic Church joined forces *in opposition* to Anglo Americans. This set of alliances proved crucial during the Taos Rebellion of 1847. According to one of Father Martínez's students, after the uprising, a group of Pueblo Indians presented themselves in Father Martínez's house expecting his approval: "Padre, we have killed every one of these heretic Americans, and we command you to write about it in every direction, stating that we performed our duty."[67]

Fear of encroachment was undoubtedly an important consideration that went into shaping the attitudes of Pueblo Indians vis-à-vis the American-run territorial government. But a satisfactory explanation should also strive to examine popular perceptions and rumors, the less tangible but equally crucial symbolic explanations of the American military takeover. The most striking example of this is the so-called legend of Montezuma contained in a mysterious document that appeared in Jemez, San Juan, and probably other pueblos as well. The document was written in the Spanish style current among Pueblo Indians, and it was dated in Mexico City, May 25, 1846. It was the story of Montezuma, "to be told to the Pueblos of the great province of New Mexico, so that they understand that they are and shall be recognized as part of Montezuma's nation to whom they are to render full obedience...."[68] It contained references to a likely war between Mexico and the United States and urged Pueblo Indians to defend their roots. Adolph F. Bandelier, the famous Swiss traveler who "discovered" a written copy of the legend in 1875, considered it a "campaign document" that was widely circulated "in every New Mexican pueblo that could be reached," at a time when war was imminent.[69] The legend is somewhat convoluted, but

---

[67] Biografía del Reverendo Padre Antonio José Martínez, Reel 1, NMSRCA.

[68] Author's translation.

[69] Historia de Montezuma, Mexico City, May 25, 1846, Bandelier Transcripts, Box 2q240, Folder 788, BHC. By the 1870s, several of these 1846 documents were in circulation. William G. Ritch found one copy in Spanish at San Juan Pueblo in 1875 and made a translation of the entire document. In the same year, Samuel Ellison obtained another copy from the Jémez Pueblo. Bandelier made two copies, one in 1886 and another one 1888, from a Spanish document found in Jémez, possibly the same used by Ellison. For a good discussion of the sources, see Charles H. Lange, Carroll L. Riley, and Elizabeth M. Lange, *The Southwestern Journals of Adolph F. Bandelier*, 4 vols (Albuquerque, NM: University of New Mexico Press, 1984) 4: 513–17. See also Twitchell, *The Leading Facts of New Mexican History*, 1: 401–3. The legend of Montezuma is intimately connected to the Pecos pueblo, which was identified as the birthplace of Montezuma. W. H. Emory, J. W. Abert, and the unidentified officer of the Army of the West all took notice of the peculiar ritual performed at that place." "Diary of an

it constitutes a stunning example of the multisecular symbolic ties between the state and Pueblo Indians and how these symbols were deployed to forge national allegiances.

In truth, the allusions to the war constituted merely the last interpretive twist of a multisecular nexus of beliefs that harked back at least to the early-seventeenth century, with some roots extending into the pre-Hispanic period. Pueblo Indians possessed an evolving collective consciousness that incorporated historical events to bolster Pueblo cultural and group affirmation. Indeed, the legend of Montezuma is all the more remarkable because, in the fractious Pueblo world, it transcended deep-running cultural boundaries, as all Pueblos in one linguistic form or another and with only slight variations told the same basic story. In its original Tewa version, the legend concerned itself with the life and tribulations of Pose-yemu (moisture from heaven) or Poseueve (he who walked or came along with the strewing moisture in the morning), a figure who will later become identified with Montezuma.[70] A maiden who became pregnant after eating a *piñón* nut that the Great Spirit had given to her divinely conceived Pose-yemu/Montezuma. But in spite of his heavenly birth, Pose-yemu/Montezuma had a difficult youth, as he was badly treated by his people. One day, the town's old cacique died, and the medicine men gathered to appoint a successor. They could not agree on anyone, so they chose Montezuma on a whim. Pitiful and seemingly powerless, Montezuma was widely mocked and ridiculed. But the Great Spirit came to Montezuma's rescue, giving him a hoof rattle that attracted wild animals and compelled them to surrender. His miraculous hunting abilities and clairvoyance allowed the people of his pueblo to grow rich in corn, turquoises, shells, and other objects. And Pose-yemu/Montezuma himself emerged as a great wizard and was able to exercise power over many pueblos. Here the original Pueblo legend ends.[71]

Unidentified Officer in the Army of the West," *St. Louis Republican*, Sep 24, 1846. Matthew C. Field wrote an article about Pecos and told the tale of how Montezuma had chosen the Pecos as his people and had commanded them to keep a sacred fire burning in a cave until his return. See John L. Kessell, *Cross and Crown: The Pecos Indians and New Mexico, 1540–1840* (Albuquerque, NM: University of New Mexico Press, 1979), 459–61. Montezuma is also tied to the Matachines Dance. See Adrian Treviño and Barbara Gilles, "A History of the Matachines Dance," *New Mexico Historical Review* 66:2 (April 1994), 105–25. For later political usage of the Montezuma legend, see Ramón A. Gutiérrez, "Aztlán, Montezuma, and New Mexico," in Rodolfo A. Anaya and Francisco Lomelí, eds., *Aztlán: Essays on the Chicano Homeland* (Albuquerque, NM: Academia/El Norte, 1989), 172–90.

[70] This version is based chiefly on Twitchell, *Leading Facts of New Mexican History*, 401. See also Elsie Clews Parsons, *Pueblo Indian Religion* (Lincoln, NE: University of Nebraska Press, 1996), 210–13; Alfonso Ortiz, *Tewa World* (Chicago, IL: University of Chicago Press, 1969), 5–7.

[71] Stefanie Beninato has observed that the legend's universal appeal stems partly from the fact that it reinforces deep aspects of Pueblo social structure. For example, Pose-yemu's testing through adversity had been a primary way in which community members had traditionally

In the seventeenth century, Pose-yemu became identified with Montezuma and the mythical tale of the foundation of the Aztec Empire.[72] In this rendition, after establishing himself as a great wizard, Pose-yemu/Montezuma went south to the vicinity of El Paso del Norte in Chihuahua and the nearby indigenous ruins at Casas Grandes and beyond.[73] In time, Montezuma's southern journey acquired paramount historical significance. Post-seventeenth-century versions of the legend explain that God appeared to Montezuma and told him that an eagle would lead him on a long journey. Thus Montezuma and his followers walked for several days following the course of the eagle until they came to a valley where there was a lake with an island in the middle. There the eagle descended onto a prickly pear and devoured a serpent. That was the sign that Montezuma was awaiting, and on that island he founded a great new empire. The legend concludes with Montezuma building a vast kingdom full of gold and silver in central Mexico.[74] We ignore why the legend underwent such transformations, but we know that the figure of Pose-yemu/Montezuma had already emerged as a crucial symbol of Pueblo affirmation in the face of Spanish exploitation. Indeed, Pose-yemu/Montezuma stood at the very epicenter of the Pueblo Revolt of 1680. Various Pueblo Indians confessed to having been led by an Indian who lived in the north, "from which region Montezuma came."[75] The informants also pointed out that Pose-yemu was the leader of the rebellion that ended in the complete expulsion of the Spaniards from New Mexico, but that he acted through Montezuma, who was his *lieutenant*.[76]

gained esteem in Pueblo society, beginning in the pre-Hispanic past. Stefanie Beninato, "Popé, Posé-yemu, and Naranjo: A New Look at Leadership in the Pueblo Revolt of 1680," *New Mexico Historical Review* 65:4, 417–35.

[72] Twitchell, *The Leading Facts of New Mexican History*, I: 401–3. For an excellent discussion of how this association could have occurred, see Richard J. Parmentier, "The Mythological Triangle: Poseyemu, Montezuma, and Jesus in the Pueblos," in *Handbook of North American Indians*, 20 vols. (Washington, DC: Smithsonian Institute, 1979), 9: 609–23.

[73] See Historia de Montezuma, Mexico City, May 25, 1846, Bandelier Transcripts, box 2q240, folder 788, BHC.

[74] Pueblo Indians were hardly alone in establishing a direct link between themselves and the Aztecs. As early as 1610, Spanish chronicler Gaspar de Villagrá wrote: "De la sangre de Christo cuia alteza,/Causa dolor la ignoren tantas almas:/Destas nueuas Regiones es notorio,/Publica voz y fama que decienden,/Aquellos mas antiguos Mexicanos." Gaspar de Villagrá, *Historia de Nuevo México* (1610; reprint, Madrid: Edición de Mercedes Junquera, Historia 16, 1989), 74–5. While Villagrá did not mention Montezuma, in 1664, Pedro de Rivera attributed the foundation of Casas Grandes to Montezuma. Pedro de Rivera, *Diario y derrotero de lo caminado, visto y observado en la visita que hizo a los presidios de la Nueva España septentrional*, edited by Vito Alessio Robles (1664; reprint, Mexico City: Secretaría de la Defensa Nacional, 1946), 45–6.

[75] Charles Wilson Hackett and Charmin Clair Shelby, *Revolt of the Pueblo Indians of New Mexico and Otermín's Attempted Reconquest, 1680–1682*, 2 vols (Albuquerque, NM: University of New Mexico Press, 1942), 1: 15. See also Beninato, "Popé, Posé-yemu, and Naranjo, 417–35.

[76] Parmentier, "The Mythological Triangle," 618.

FIGURE 8.2. Ruins of the Pecos pueblo

In the years leading up to the Mexican–American War, the legend of Montezuma conveyed an unmistakable sense of Pueblo resistance and tenacity in the face of extremely adverse conditions. The legend had somehow become associated with the dwindling pueblo of Pecos (see Figure 8.2). The most common version of the legend stated that Pose-yemu/Montezuma had chosen the Pecos pueblo as his own and had commanded the few remaining families to keep a sacred fire burning in the kiva until his next coming.[77] Various Anglo-American travelers visited the Pecos during the Mexican period. Even the Army of the West, on its way to Santa Fe, took time to visit Montezuma's shrine:

We passed to day the ruins of the ancient town of Pecos. I visited it with some Mexicans and an interpreter, who gave me a full account of it. It was said to have been built long before the conquest – it stands on an eminence. The dwellings were built of small stones and mud; some of the buildings are still so far perfect as to show three full stories. There were four rooms under ground, fifteen feet deep, and twenty-five feet across in a circular form. In one of these rooms burned the "holy fire" which was kindled many centuries before the conquest; and when the Pecos Indians were converted to the Catholic faith, they still continued their own religious rites, and among them the sacred fire which never ceased to burn till seven years since, when the village was broken up.[78]

---

[77] Matthew C. Field wrote an article about Pecos and told the tale of how Montezuma had chosen the Pecos as his people and had commanded them to keep a sacred fire burning in a cave until his return. See Kessell, *Cross and Crown*, 459–61.

[78] Diary of an unidentified officer in the Army of the West, *St. Louis Republican*, Sep 24, 1846.

A Swiss physician was allowed to go inside the kiva and witnessed the travails of the Pecos Indians bent on keeping the fire alive. He went through a square opening in the plaza and descended through the ladder that gave access to a clean and spacious "subterranean apartment." There he saw a raised bank or mound of earth in the middle, and a furnace or brazier with the vestal flame on top of it. Two Pecos Indians, an old man and a boy, who kept guard all the time, tended the kiva. Their task was to prevent the fire from ever becoming extinguished. When the physician asked the old Indian why they maintained the fire, he replied that it was with the hope of seeing the return of Montezuma.[79]

Pecos was completely abandoned in 1840, and the fire finally died out. But the legend lived on and became entangled with the Mexican–American War. The document told the conventional story of Montezuma from his divine conception to the founding of the Aztec Empire, but it bore new and revealing elements. First, the legend itself was briefly introduced with an admonition:

[T]his sketch of the birth of the Great Monarch, Montezuma, was copied in order to lay it before the Pueblos situated in the great province of New Mexico, that they may understand that they are and shall ever be recognized as the nation of that Great Monarch to whom they shall render full obedience.[80]

This supports the idea that Mexican authorities may have deliberately attempted to manipulate Pueblo traditions to enlist their support against American troops.

Other elements also point in this direction. Catholic elements, for instance, loom large in this 1846 version of the legend. Since the colonial period, the story had been progressively Christianized; indeed Montezuma's life in many ways came to resemble that of Jesus Christ – both having been conceived magically by maidens, both being from humble backgrounds, both being destined to rule their peoples, and both departing suddenly and promising to return to usher in a new era.[81] But in the 1846 version, the biblical references became more obvious. For instance, when Montezuma first beheld the island of Tenochtitlán, where he was to establish the seat of his new empire, God opened a path through the water so he could get across with his people. The text also explained that Montezuma's current whereabouts were unknown, "even though some prophecies placed him at the bottom of the Atlantic," but that God would revive him – Lazarus-like – at the appropriate time. Furthermore, interwoven in Montezuma's tale, we find vignettes of the Virgin

---

[79] Enrique Masure, *Santa Fe Republican*, Sep 24, 1847.

[80] The translation is mine.

[81] To explain the fusion of Pose-yemu/Montezuma and Jesus Christ, Parmentier advances the notion that these two figures had some structural and symbolic similarities that became more pronounced over time. Parmentier, "The Mythological Triangle," 622.

of Guadalupe: Juan Diego – the Mexican Indian to whom the Virgin of Guadalupe repeatedly appeared in the sixteenth century – and María de Agreda – a seventeenth-century Spanish mystic who reportedly was able to bilocate or divinely transport herself from Agreda, Spain, to various places in New Spain's Far North, where she ministered to the Indians. Finally, the Catholic imprint is most obvious in the way the 1846 version of the legend ends. Having successfully established his empire in Mexico City, Montezuma one day had a dream in which God appeared and told him that the children of the sun, the Spaniards, would come to conquer his great empire – and so they did. Montezuma received the holy water and learned the teachings of Jesus Christ, and all the Indians under Montezuma did likewise. This is why the Spanish established missions first in central Mexico and then in New Mexico and converted the Pueblos to the Catholic religion that they now profess. Here the legend ends.

The general tenor of the document leaves no doubt that it was intended to cement the ties between Pueblo Indians and Spaniards/Mexicans, possibly to forge a common front against Anglo Americans. Ralph E. Twitchell believed that the document had been circulated for the purpose of justifying the Mexican possession of New Mexico. Adolph Bandelier became enraptured with the legend of Montezuma. He regarded the 1846 rendition squarely as a propaganda document. Lieutenant John G. Bourke, Bandelier's contemporary and fellow ethnologist, concluded that the 1846 Montezuma story had to do mostly with Mexicans and Americans.[82] The 1846 rendition of the legend of Montezuma – with its exuberant Catholic imagery and convoluted ties between New Mexico and Old Mexico – constituted yet one more adaptation of Pueblo identity against the backdrop of rapid Anglo-Americanization. The legend of Montezuma sought to appeal to the Pueblo Indians by casting them not as subjugated peoples but as the divine founders of the Mexican nation. It created an instant bridge between Hispanics and Pueblos and remained a powerful myth long after the Taos Rebellion of 1847. Amado Chávez, writing at the close of the century, left a poetic testimony of this phenomenon:

. . . at dawn numerous Indians climb their *azoteas* and stand there looking towards the east, expecting the Emperor Montezuma to return in a halo of glory to restore them to their old possessions. When he fails to appear they go down to their kitchens and eat their breakfasts and then they go to work in their fields to await another day.[83]

---

[82] Twitchell, *The Leading Facts of New Mexican History*, I: 472.
[83] Amado Chavez, "The Legend of Padre Juan de Padilla," n.d., n.p., Amado Chávez Collection, NMSRCA.

9

Conclusion

Traditional histories of the U.S.–Mexico borderlands have tended to assume that frontier residents had clear national loyalties since inception: Americans were Americans since 1776, and Mexicans were Mexicans since 1821. And the two peoples fought over control of large areas of North America during the first half of the nineteenth century. The scholarship on the Mexican–American War has lent support to such an interpretive shortcut. The war has been portrayed as pitting one fully constituted nation against another, one civilizational project against another, and one people against another (with some indigenous auxiliaries thrown in on each side for good measure). This is hardly surprising. Given that the Mexican–American War became a crucial milepost for both the American and the Mexican national projects, it has been made to conform to clear-cut sides for didactic purposes. In the process, the early histories of places like Texas, New Mexico, Arizona, and California have been reduced to mere antecedents, small skirmishes of the larger national confrontation.

Here I have followed a different tack. Instead of assuming preexisting or fully formed identities, I posit that nations had to be constructed where they hardly existed, and thus I have focused on the contradictory forces swirling around the peoples of the frontier and how they impinged on their loyalties and sense of collective selves. This approach reveals not only an enormously rich, ambiguous, and changing landscape of identities, but it also points to a few specific conclusions that I hope will contribute to move forward the discussion of the history of the U.S.–Mexico borderlands beyond simplistic, billiard-ball-like clashes between nations and ethnicities.

First, the cases of Texas and New Mexico point to the urgent need – borrowing a phrase from Theda Skocpol et al. – to "bring the Mexican State back in[to]" the history of the U.S.–Mexico borderlands. As noted in Chapter 2, the histories of places like Texas and New Mexico – with some exceptions – tend to downplay the Mexican context, giving short shrift to the Mexican institutional arrangement and glossing over the crucial connections between frontier provinces and the rest of Mexico. There are many reasons for this state of affairs. The seductive notion of frontier, a liminal space beyond the pale of governmental control, already implies the absence of such institutional control and has naturally influenced the thinking of frontier scholars. The overwhelmingly Anglo-American sources – used to write the history of the U.S.–Mexican borderlands, especially in the past, are naturally less attuned to the Mexican context. Yet another reason is the enormous influence of the Boltonian school, with its emphasis on Spanish colonial institutions like missions and presidios – institutions that had entered a period of rapid decline even before 1821. All of this has contributed to the impression of institutional decay during the Mexican period.

Yet, a close examination of the political histories of Texas and New Mexico under Mexico shows a completely different reality. Although Mexico lacked a fully formed state at this time, the civil administration, the military, and the Church worked actively to fashion vast and parallel patronage networks all attempting to bind the frontier firmly to the rest of the nation and promote a sense of Mexicanness. In Texas, for example, the mechanism for disposing of vacant lands produced an impressive administrative apparatus linking dispersed frontier communities to the state capital in Saltillo and all the way to Mexico City. Similarly, a priestly network tied various New Mexican communities to the ecclesiastical hierarchy leading to Durango and Mexico City. These enormous chains of command that involved local, regional, and national power holders were able to influence the loyalties of frontier peoples by offering tangible economic or political resources. Public speech, rituals, and symbols also played roles in spreading such influence. Much of the evidence offered in this book points to the conclusion that the Mexican era was a period of fruitful political exploration when colonial institutions were adapted to new circumstances and new administrative networks were created from scratch. This is very much in keeping with recent findings in other regions of early Mexico attesting to the vitality of its institutional development and how it anchored the lives of its early citizens. Similar work carried out on frontier communities is beginning to restore the Mexican institutional context to its proper place, making the tales that we tell about frontier peoples more credible and human.[1]

Second, at the same time that we bring more clearly into focus Mexico's political and cultural institutions, it is important to appreciate the protracted center–periphery tensions that existed even before the arrival of foreign-born indigenous groups and Anglo-American colonists. The most contentious aspect of the Mexican government's attempt to build the nation at the frontier was the relationship between the center and the provinces. Texans and New Mexicans, along with the rest of the country, splintered into several factions

---

[1] For specific citations, refer to the historiographical discussion in the introduction, especially footnotes 7, 12, and 13.

over the issue of the degree to which the national government should be involved in local and state affairs. This tension between municipal and state authorities at one level, and between state and national officials at another, was fought out on several fronts, from elections of officials to the regulation of the economy and the organization of the military.

In its most basic form, the split between centralists and frontier federalists acquired a clear national dimension, as the center worried about territorial disintegration of the country and branded radical federalists operating in peripheral areas as separatists. According to reports filed by Mexican local and regional military authorities, all of Mexico's frontiers were rife with rebellions that merited the label of "secessionist" or "independentist" at this time. A brief rundown of such movements includes the following: in Coahuila and Texas the Fredonia Rebellion of 1826–7, the disturbances of 1830–2, and the Texas Rebellion of 1835–6; in the Texas–Tamaulipas border, the rebellion seeking to establish the Republic of the Rio Grande in 1838–40, and the rebellion supported by New Orleans adventurers seeking to create the Republic of the Sierra Madre in 1848–9; in New Mexico, the Chimayó Rebellion of 1837–8; in Alta California, the separatist movement of 1841–4; in Baja California, the plan to achieve the annexation of that territory to the United States in 1852; in Tabasco, the secessionist movement of 1846; in Yucatán, the de facto separation of 1841, and the petition for annexation to the United States in 1846, and so on.[2]

All of these movements bespeak of bitter and protracted power struggles between a determined center and its wayward peripheries. As we contemplate this rich tableaux of rebellions, we must bear in mind that these movements went far beyond the mere banality or incompetence of Mexico's early political and military leaders (a megalomaniac and histrionic General Santa Anna is a recurrent figure in the borderlands literature). Whatever else

---

[2] A very impressive list of secessionist movements can be compiled from the AHSDN, files 1289, 1351, 1573, 1625, 1654, 1659, 1885, 2273, 2900, 3007, 3142, microfilm edition at the Bancroft Library. These *expedientes* bear titles such as "Documentación relativa al movimiento separatista de la Alta California, encabezado por José Antonio Carrillo, Juan Bandini, William Hinckley, Pio Pico, Santiago Arguello, José María Echandía y José María Padrés," "Expedición organizada en la isla de Gatos, con aventureros contratados en New Orleans, EUA para invadir el puerto de Tampico, Tamaulipas y proclamar la separación de los estados fronterizos," or "Comunicaciones del Ministerio de Relaciones al de Guerra y Marina, dando cuenta del movimiento rebelde en Matamoros, Tamaulipas, y Broconsoilla para formar la República de la Sierra Madre." It goes without saying that the actual scope and aims of each of these movements need to be assessed carefully. For instance, Josefina Z. Vázquez has argued that the Republic of the Río Grande was in fact a creation of the Texas press rather than a real political movement in northeastern Mexico. Vázquez, "La supuesta República del Río Grande," *Historia Mexicana* 36:1 (Jul–Sep 1986), 49–80. In contrast, Leslie A. Jones Wagner more recently has found sufficient evidence to argue for the existence of the Republic of the Río Grande. Wagner, "Disputed Territory: Río Grande/Río Bravo Borderlands, 1838–1840," M.A. thesis, University of Texas at Arlington, 1998, 1. The point to bear in mind is that, given the precedents of Texas and Yucatán, these frontier movements opposing the Federation could conceivably escalate into full-blown secessionism.

these struggles may have been about, they erupted over real issues of spatial distribution of power and longstanding federal–state rivalries. Indeed, as already noted, sectional disputes were not only endemic to Mexico but also to the United States, as both national projects were headed for destruction in this period. Fully acknowledging and exploring the nature and depth of these core–periphery tensions is especially crucial for the story of how Mexico's Far North became the American Southwest, as such tensions constituted the backdrop for such events as the Texas Revolution, the Chimayó Rebellion, and the Mexican–American War. The arrival of foreign-born indigenous groups and Anglo-American colonists to these Mexican provinces exacerbated and changed the dynamics of an *already existing* sectional dispute. The Texas Revolution of 1835–6, for example, would be unthinkable without an understanding of the bitter conflict between the State of Coahuila and Texas and the supreme government that had been brewing at least since 1834. Similar tensions were obvious in New Mexico in the years leading up to the Chimayó Rebellion. Without reference to these protracted core–periphery confrontations, frontier episodes like those described in this book become implausible stories in which a handful of foreign-born individuals were able to wrest entire provinces from Mexico's control, and Mexican and indigenous actors are depicted as mere spectators as their lands are being taken away.

Third, this book seeks to move beyond simplistic notions of American expansionism and Manifest Destiny, and instead tries to examine how specifically American power – with its many facets – affected frontier peoples. As noted in the introduction and elsewhere in the book, vague notions of expansionism and Manifest Destiny are bandied about in much of the frontier literature to describe everything from the psychology of early Americans, to the policies pursued by the United States government, to the relations between different ethnic groups; such notions are even posited to justify territorial acquisitions at the expense of other nations. No one denies that American expansionism existed, but this amorphous American "mood" or "mindset" needs to be dissected if it is to retain some interpretive power.

Here I argue that in the beginning, American expansionism did not materialize at the Mexican frontier as a force of naked conquest. It did not start as a great conspiracy directed from Washington, D.C., and carried out by a succession of scheming presidents, diplomats, and on down to the lowly colonists, all with a clear vision of how things would turn out in the end.[3]

---

[3] Having studied the Texas case in great detail, Andreas V. Reichstein reached the same conclusion:

> ... the idea of Manifest Destiny was only one part of the evolution of Texas; on account of its religious-philosophical content, it was applied like a hastily donned veil that developed into a second skin at an explanation for their deeds (Reichstein, *Rise of the Lone Star*, 202).

For a taste of the grand conspiracy approach, see José Fuentes Mares, *Poinsett, historia de una gran intriga* (Mexico City: Ediciones Océano, 1977).

Instead, expansionism worked in far more interesting, devious, and unexpected ways. Initially, the inhabitants of Mexico's Far North came in contact
with American expansionism in the guise of a powerful economic and cultural phenomenon that proceeded to alter their livelihoods and loyalties.
The economy of Mexico's northern frontier changed dramatically in the aftermath of Mexico's independence from Spain as a result of liberalization
policies pursued by the early Mexican governments. As frontier inhabitants
began participating in a market economy largely dependent on the United
States, they started making personal and collective choices that, while seemingly inconsequential at first, would acquire great significance in the end. In
the course of the Mexican period, this process deepened, as Texas and New
Mexico fell largely within the orbit of the United States economy, and therefore native elites in these provinces saw their fortunes increasingly tied to
the continuation of economic relations with the United States that revolved
around commerce and land. Such economic integration provided the medium
in which crosscultural alliances were forged and loyalties and national attachments were debated. To be sure, the ultimate fate of Mexico's entire
frontier was decided in a war. Direct military intervention sealed the outcome. But the scope of America's territorial acquisition had already been
foreshadowed in previous decades, as the rise of a market economy had
given rise to influential Anglo-American communities across Mexico's Far
North and had realigned the interests of other frontier residents, making
them dependent on the United States.

Finally, beyond addressing aspects of the history of the United States–
Mexico borderlands, this book seeks to contribute to the fast-growing scholarship on borders and identities. This scholarship departs from the notion
that ethnic/national identities do not derive from simple impositions from
the center on peripheral areas and groups, but instead that this process is
better described as two-way exchanges, as frontier peoples appropriate and
bring the nation to the frontier to further their own local interests.[4] Furthermore, this scholarship's literature emphasizes that frontier identities are far
from marginal to the overall emergence of national and nationalist projects
but constitute an integral element of this process.[5]

The existing corpus of frontier/identity studies has already provided a
rough sketch of commonalities as well as variation through space and time.
For a thousand years or so, European Christian society has expanded outward in all directions, venturing beyond its original heartland roughly coinciding with the contours of the Carolingian Empire.[6] This millennium of

---

[4] See Sahlins, *Boundaries*, 267–76.
[5] For recent comparative work on this field, see Thomas M. Wilson and Hastings Donnan,
   eds., *Border Identities: Nation and Sate at International Frontiers* (Cambridge, UK: Cambridge
   University Press, 1998).
[6] Muldoon, *Identity on the Medieval Irish Frontier*, xii, 13–14.

relentless European expansion (with occasional retrenchments, of course) has given rise to numerous frontiers in the most diverse settings and has brought into contact multifarious peoples. Scholars working on European frontiers during the medieval and early-modern period have stressed the centrality of Christianity, a shared religious culture, as an anchor of European identity and as a key determinant in their relations with peoples beyond the Mediterranean/Christian world. For instance, James Muldoon's work on the medieval Irish frontier makes clear that European Christians classified peoples in their immediate surroundings as "degenerates," "half-breeds," and "middle nations," depending on their level of Christianity and acceptance of European standards of civility that included living in settled agricultural communities, possessing a written language, engaging in commercial activities, and having other cultural traits associated with European/Christian culture.[7]

The consolidation of nation-states beginning in the seventeenth century marked a new plateau in the frontier experience. Modern nations emerged only when centralized states were strong enough to launch a process of institutional and cultural integration that resulted in higher levels of effective control of national frontiers than had been previously possible. Peter Sahlins's insightful study of the Spanish–French frontier along the Pyrenees from the seventeenth through the nineteenth centuries describes the frontier experience in the modern era, highlighting that although boundaries may have been arbitrary state impositions at first, frontier peoples in certain instances found it convenient to uphold and maintain such demarcations in order to further their own interests.[8] Regardless of specific frontier circumstances, the activism of nation-states in asserting their territorial claims led to the intensification of frontier clashes and negotiation of identities not only in Europe but in frontiers around the world, as independent nations in Latin America, Asia, and Africa sought to uphold, resist, or change old colonial boundaries.

At the same time that nation-states consolidated their power, the market economy has spread since the eighteenth century. Many frontier studies reveal the paramount importance of economic transactions in shaping borders and identities. Paul Nugent's recent work on the Ghana-Togo frontier, for instance, shows the extent to which the exploitation of cocoa has affected the mental geography of Togolanders and how smuggling – and state efforts to stop this practice – has given meaning and concreteness to the border.[9] Similarly, Kim M. Gruenwald has shown the inextricable linkage between the commercial development of the Ohio valley since the late-eighteenth

---

[7] Ibid., passim.

[8] Sahlins, *Boundaries*, passim.

[9] Nugent, *Smugglers, Secessionists and Loyal Citizens on the Ghana-Togo Frontier*, esp. ch. 2, 3.

century and peoples' understandings of the region and its role in the larger national context.[10]

The U.S.–Mexican borderlands exemplify a particular variation of the frontier experience in the modern era. The consolidation of state power and the intensification of capitalism occurred at different rates in different parts of the world, thus giving rise to encounters in which frontier residents had widely different levels of access to state and market resources. Indeed, some of the most contentious borderlands arise precisely in situations when there are disjunctures between states and markets. In our own hemisphere, the prodigious growth of the economy of the United States in the nineteenth century cast a long shadow over large swaths of the continent precisely at the time of the birth of numerous Latin American nations. Cuba's painful status as a U.S. semiprotectorate because of America's overwhelming economic presence is the best-known example of this phenomenon (at the turn of the century, the New Orleans press openly and unabashedly encouraged planters to invest in Cuba: " . . . little by little the whole island of Cuba is passing into the hands of U.S. citizens, which is the simplest and safest way to obtain annexation to the United States"[11]). The situation was not much different in other Caribbean and Central American nations. In South America, state and market tensions are obvious in places like the Atacama Desert, where Bolivia's claims were thwarted by Chile's expanding nitrate industry. Even in Europe, so neatly parceled out among nations, we can find areas like Alsace-Lorraine formally administered by one nation (France) but economically integrated into another one (Germany). My point is that disjunctures between states and markets – and the type of frontier that this situation generates – are hardly aberrations but all-too-common historical occurrences.

In the case of Mexico and the United States, this disjuncture has an enduring interest, as the economic asymmetry between the two countries has only widened in the intervening two hundred years. There is no question that today's Mexican nation-state is incomparably more successful than its early-nineteenth-century predecessor. The Mexican state is now firmly entrenched, its frontiers are secure, and its political stability is proverbial. Moreover, the true measure of Mexico's success as a nation does not reside in effective exercise of power alone, but on the acceptance of this authority and identity by an overwhelming majority of citizens. One can find innumerable traces of popular nationalism in school textbooks, civic celebrations, football matches, children's bedtime stories, ceramics, and in virtually every other place. By all measures, Mexican identity is profoundly rooted among the many peoples living between the Rio Suchiate in the south and the Rio Grande in the north, and in many communities in the United States. And yet, in spite of the

---

[10] Gruenwald, *River of Enterprise*, passim.

[11] *Louisiana Planter*, cited in Eduardo Galeano, *Open Veins of Latin America* (New York: Monthly Review Press, 1973, 1997), 71.

stunning success of this identity, the pull of the American economy and its impact on immigration patterns, fashions, language, political ideology, and many other realms has never been stronger than today. And this pull affects both the millions of Mexicans who spend part or all of their lives in the United States and those who stay in Mexico. This situation does not necessarily lead to antagonism and open confrontation as in the past. Unlike the early-nineteenth century, when matters of territorial integrity and national survival were at stake, today Mexico's (and the United States') vital national interests appear to be safe, and thus state officials and many citizens – somewhat reminiscent of Japan's Meiji Restoration – can afford to cast themselves as open to the world. I am the first to admit that we humans are capable of living happily with contradictory beliefs, mutually incompatible dreams, and schizophrenic impulses. As Pierre Bordieau has insightfully observed, there's nothing peculiar about flagrant inconsistencies of the mind.[12] American Founding Fathers were known to display an inordinate fondness for British tea sets, Soviet leaders were seduced by tsarist paraphernalia, and patriotic Mexicans have been prone to wearing San Francisco 49ers sweatshirts at Independence Day celebrations. But below the patina of such outward – and often unintended – displays of cosmopolitanism, a certain tug of war persists, and in North America it harks back to the time when Mexicans and Americans first came to terms with one another.

[12] Pierre Bordieau, *Distinction: A Social Critique of the Judgment of Taste* (Cambridge, MA: Harvard University Press, 1987), passim.

Bibliography

Archival Sources

New Mexico

Center for Southwest Research (CSR), University of New Mexico, Albuquerque
Antonio José Martínez Papers
LeBaron Bradford Prince Papers
Miguel Antonio Lovato Papers
New Mexico Imprints Papers
New Mexico Passport Records Papers
Ortiz and Pino Family Papers

New Mexico State Records Center and Archives (NMSRCA), Santa Fe
Benjamin M. Read Collection (series 1 and 2)
Bishop Zubiría's visitation of New Mexico in 1833 (one roll of microfilm)
Bloom-McFie Papers
Delgado Family Papers (Dingee Collection)
Dispatches from United States Consuls in Santa Fe, 1830–46.
Donaciano Vigil Papers
E. Boyd Collection
Francisco Sarracino Family Papers
Getty Family Papers
Historical Society of New Mexico
L. Bradford Prince
Manuel Alvarez Papers
Manuel Armijo Papers (microfilmed)
María G. Durán Collection
Márquez y Melo Papers
Miscellaneous New Mexico Documents
Ritch Papers
Seligman Collection
Sender Collection

Twitchell Collection (series 1 and 2)
United States Archives, RG 59, M199
Valentín Armijo Collection
Woodward Collection

Museum of New Mexico, Santa Fe
Abeyta Manual

New Mexico State University Library, Las Cruces
Archivos Históricos del Arzobispado de Durango (AHAD)

Texas

Bexar County Clerk's Office, San Antonio
Bexar County Probate Records

Daughters of the Republic of Texas Research Library (DRT), San Antonio
Bustillo Family Collection
Casiano-Pérez Family Collection
Garza Family Collection
John W. Smith Collection
Juan N. Seguín Collection
Navarro Family Collection

Eugene C. Barker Texas History Center (BHC), University of Texas at Austin
Archivo General de México
Bandelier Documents
Dimitt Papers (DP)
Documents for the Early History of Coahuila and Texas
Eberstadt Collection
José Antonio de la Garza Papers
José Antonio Menchaca Reminiscences or Memoirs
Maverick Papers
Nacogdoches Archives
San Antonio City Records
Zavala Papers

General Land Office (GLO), Archives and Records Division, Austin
Original Land Grant Collection
Spanish Collection

Nettie Lee Benson Latin American Collection, University of Texas at Austin
Gómez Farías Papers
Hernández y Dávalos Papers

Texas State Library, Archives and Library Divisions, Austin

Comptroller of Public Accounts Collection
Juan N. Seguín Papers
Santa Fe Papers

California

Bancroft Library, University of California at Berkeley

Archivo Histórico de la Defensa Nacional (AHDN) (microfilm edition)
Herbert E. Bolton Papers (BP)
New Mexico Originals

Illinois

Newberry Library, Chicago

Ayer Collection
Graff Collection

Connecticut

Beinecke Rare Book and Manuscript Library, New Haven

Collection of Western Americana

Mexico

Archivo General de la Nación (AGN)

Ramo gobernación
Ramo justicia

Archivo Histórico de la Secretaría de Relaciones Exteriores

Microfilm Collections

Bexar Archives
Mexican Archives of New Mexico (MANM)
Spanish Archives of New Mexico (SANM)
Territorial Archives of New Mexico (TANM)
Thomas W. Streeter Collection

Newspapers

Austin City Gazette
Columbia Patriot
Diario del Gobierno de la República Mexicana
El Látigo de Tejas
El Mercurio de Matamoros
El Mosquito Mexicano
El Payo de Nuevo México

El Telescopio
Gaceta Imperial de México
La Verdad
Natchitoches Courier
New Orleans Daily Picayune
Niles Register
Santa Fe Republican
Siglo XIX
Telegraph and Texas Register
Texas Gazette
Texas Republican

Bibliographical Sources

Abert, J. W. *Report of the Secretary of War, Communicating, in Answer to a Resolution of the Senate, A Report and Map of the Expedition to New Mexico.* Senate Ex. Doc. 23. U.S. Congress: Washington, DC, 1848.

Adelman, Jeremy and Aron, Stephen. "From Borderlands to Borders: Empires, Nation-States, and the Peoples in Between in North American History." *American Historical Review* 104:3 (Jun 1999), 814–41.

Agnew, Jean-Christophe. *Worlds Apart: The Market and the Theater in Anglo-American Thought, 1550–1750.* Cambridge, UK: Cambridge University Press, 1986.

Aguirre Beltrán, Gonzalo, *Regions of Refuge.* Washington, DC: Society for Applied Anthropology, 1979.

Alamán, Lucas. *Historia de México: desde los primeros movimientos que prepararon su independencia en el año de 1808.* 5 vols. Mexico City: Publicaciones Herrerías, n.y.

Alessio Robles, Vito. *Coahuila y Texas desde la consumación de la independencia hasta el Tratado de Paz de Guadalupe Hidalgo.* 2 vols. Mexico City: Porrúa, 1979.

Alonzo, Armando C. *Tejano Legacy: Rancheros and Settlers in South Texas, 1734–1900.* Albuquerque, NM: University of New Mexico Press, 1998.

Anderson, Benedict. *Imagined Communities: Reflections on the Origin and Spread of Nationalism,* 2 ed. London: Verso, 1991.

Andrews, Thomas. "Tata Atanasio Trujillo's Unlikely Tale of Utes, Nuevo Mexicanos, and the Settling of Colorado's San Luis Valley." *New Mexico Historical Review* 75:1 (Jan 2000), 57–72.

Anna, Timothy E. *Spain and the Loss of America.* Lincoln, NE: University of Nebraska Press, 1983.

_____. *The Mexican Empire of Iturbide.* Lincoln, NE: University of Nebraska Press, 1990.

_____. *Forging Mexico 1821–1835.* Lincoln, NE: University of Nebraska Press, 1998.

Annino, Antonio "El pacto y la norma: los orígenas de la legalidad oligárquica en México." *Historias* 5 (Jan–Mar 1984), 3–42.

Archer, Christon. "The Royalist Army in New Spain: Civil–Military Relations, 1810–1821." *Journal of Latin American Studies* 13 (1981), 57–82.

Arrangoiz, Francisco de Paula de. *México desde 1808 hasta 1867.* Mexico City: Editorial Porrúa, 1985.

Baca, Oswald G. "Infectious Diseases and Smallpox Politics in New Mexico's Rio Abajo, 1847–1920." *New Mexico Historical Review* 75:1 (Jan 2000), 107–27.

Bacarisse, Charles A. "The Union of Coahuila and Texas." *Southwestern Historical Quarterly* 61 (Jan 1958), 341–9.

Bancroft, Hubert Howe. *History of Arizona and New Mexico, 1530–1888.* vol. 18. San Francisco, CA: History Company, 1889.

_____. *History of Texas and the North Mexican States.* San Francisco, CA: Bancroft and company, 1890.

Barker, Eugene C., ed. *Austin Papers.* 3 vols. Washington D. C. and Austin: Government Printing Office and University of Texas Press, 1924, 1927, 1928.

_____. *Mexico and Texas, 1821–1836.* Dallas, TX: P. L. Turner, 1928.

_____. *The Life of Stephen F. Austin, Founder of Texas, 1793–1836.* Austin, TX: University of Texas Press. 1969.

Bauer, K. Jack. *The Mexican War 1846–1848.* Lincoln, NE: University of Nebraska Press, 1974.

Baxter, John O. *Las Carneradas: Sheep Trade in New Mexico, 1700–1860.* Albuquerque, NM: University of New Mexico Press, 1987.

Beezley, William H., Martin, Cheryl English, and French, William E., eds. *Rituals of Rule, Rituals of Resistance: Public Celebrations and Popular Culture in Mexico.* Wilmington, DE: Scholarly Resources, 1994.

Beninato, Stefanie. "Popé, Posé-yemu, and Naranjo: A New Look at Leadership in the Pueblo Revolt of 1680." *New Mexico Historical Review* 65:4 (1990), 417–35.

Bennett, Burton E. "The Taos Rebellion." *Old Santa Fe,* vol. 1:2. Santa Fe, NM: Old Santa Fe Press (1913), 176–92.

Benson, Nettie Lee. "Texas as Viewed from Mexico, 1820–1834." *Southwestern Historical Quarterly* 90 (1987), 219–91.

_____. "Territorial Integrity in Mexican Politics, 1821–1833," in Jaime E. Rodriguez O., ed., *The Independence of Mexico and the Creation of the New Nation.* Los Angeles, CA: UCLA Latin American Center, 1989, 275–307.

_____. *La diputación provincial y el federalismo mexicano,* 2d ed. Mexico City: El Colegio de México, 1994.

Berger, Max. "Education in Texas During the Spanish and Mexican Periods." *Southwestern Historical Quarterly* 51 (1947), 41–53.

Berninger, Dieter George. *La inmigración en México, 1821–1857.* Mexico City: SepSetentas, 1974.

Binkley, William C. *The Texas Revolution.* Reprint. Austin, TX: Texas State Historical Association, 1979.

Bloom, John P. "Note on the Population of New Mexico, 1846–1849." *New Mexico Historical Review* 34 (1959), 200–2.

Bloom, Lansig. "New Mexico Under Mexican Administration, 1821–1846." *Old Santa Fe,* vols. 1–3. Santa Fe, NM: Old Santa Fe Press, 1913–15.

Bocanegra, José María. *Memorias para la historia de México independiente, 1822–1846,* 3 vols. Mexico City: ICH-INEHRM-FCE, 1986.

Boyle, Susan Calafate. *Los Capitalistas: Hispano Merchants and the Santa Fe Trade.* Albuquerque, NM: University of New Mexico Press, 1997.

Brack, Gene M. *Mexico Views Manifest Destiny, 1821–1846.* Albuquerque, NM: University of New Mexico Press, 1975.

Brading, David A. *The Origins of Mexican Nationalism.* Cambridge, UK: Centre of Latin American Studies, University of Cambridge, 1985.

_____. *The First America: The Spanish Monarchy, Creole Patriots, and the Liberal State 1492–1867.* New York: Cambridge University Press, 1991.

Brayer, Herbert O. *Pueblo Indian Land Grants of the "Río Abajo," New Mexico.* Albuquerque, NM: University of New Mexico Press, 1939.

Briggs, Charles L. and Van Ness, John R. *Land, Water, and Culture: New Perspectives on Hispanic Land Grants.* Albuquerque, NM: University of New Mexico Press, 1987.

Brooks, James F. *Captives and Cousins: Slavery, Kinship, and Community in the Southwest Borderlands.* Chapel Hill, NC: University of North Carolina Press, 2002.

Broussard, Ray F. *San Antonio During the Texas Republic: A City in Transition.* El Paso, TX: Texas Western Press, 1967.

Burkholder, Mark A. and Johnson, Lyman L. *Colonial Latin America,* 2 ed. Oxford, UK: Oxford University Press, 1994.

Bustamante, Carlos María de. *Cuadro histórico de la revolución mexicana de 1810.* Mexico City: INEHRM, 1985.

Buve, Raymond. "Political Patronage and Politics at the Village Level in Central Mexico: Continuity and Change in Patterns from the Late Colonial Period to the End of the French Intervention (1867)." *Bulletin of Latin American Research* 11 (1992), 1–28.

Cabrera, Luis, ed. *Diario del Presidente Polk, 1845–1849,* 2 vols. Mexico City: Antigua Librería Robredo, 1948.

Campbell, Randolph B. *An Empire for Slavery: The Peculiar Institution in Texas, 1821–1865.* Baton Rouge, LA: Louisiana State University Press, 1989.

Cantrell, Gregg. *Stephen F. Austin: Empresario of Texas.* New Haven, CT: Yale University Press, 1999.

Carroll, H. Bailey and Haggard, Villasana J., eds. *Three New Mexico Chronicles.* Albuquerque, NM: Quivira Society, 1942.

Carter, James David. *Masonry in Texas: Background, History, and Influence to 1846.* Waco, TX: Committee on Masonic Education and Service for the Grand Lodge of Texas, 1955.

Castañeda, Carlos E., ed. *The Mexican Side of the Texas Revolution, 1836, by the Chief Mexican Participants.* Austin, TX: Graphic Ideas, 1970.

_____. ed. *Our Catholic Heritage in Texas, 1519–1936,* 7 vols. Reprint. New York: Arno, 1976.

Castillo Crimm, Ana Caroline. "Success in Adversity: The Mexican Americans of Victoria County." Ph.D. dissertation, University of Texas at Austin, 1994.

_____. *De León, A Tejano Family History.* Austin, TX: University of Texas Press, forthcoming.

Chabot, Frederick C. *With the Makers of San Antonio.* San Antonio, TX, 1937.

Chávez, Angélico. "Doña Tules, Her Fame and Her Funeral." *El Palacio* 58 (1950), 127–41.

_____. "New Names in New Mexico, 1820–1850." *El Palacio* 64:9–12 (1957), 290–380.

_____. "The Penitentes of New Mexico." *New Mexico Historical Review* 29:2 (1954), 97–123.

_____. "José Gonzales, Genízaro Governor." *New Mexico Historical Review* 30:3 (1955), 190–4.

_____. *But Time and Chance: The Story of Padre Martínez of Taos, 1793–1867*. Santa Fe, NM: Sunstone Press, 1981.

_____. "A Nineteenth-Century New Mexico Schism." *New Mexico Historical Review* 58:1 (1983), 35–54.

Chavez, Thomas E. *Manuel Alvarez, 1794–1856: A Southwestern Biography*. Niwot, CO: University Press of Colorado, 1990.

Cheetham, Francis T. "The First Term of the American Court in Taos, New Mexico." *New Mexico Historical Review* 1:1 (1926), 23–41.

Coatsworth, John. "Obstacles to Economic Growth in Nineteenth Century Mexico." *American Historical Review* 83 (1978), 8–100.

_____. "Patterns of Rural Rebellion in Latin America: Mexico in Comparative Perspective," in Friedrich Katz, ed., *Riot, Rebellion and Revolt: Rural Social Conflict in Mexico*, 21–62. Princeton, NJ: Princeton University Press, 1988.

Colley, Linda. *Britons: Forging the Nation 1707–1837*. New Haven, CT: Yale University Press, 1992.

Combs, Franklin. "Narrative of the Santa Fe Expedition in 1841." *New Mexico Historical Review* 5:3 (1930), 305–10.

Connaughton, Brian F. *Dimensiones de la identidad patriótica: religion, política, y regiones en México*. Mexico City: UAM-Miguel Ángel Porrúa, 2001.

_____. *Clerical Ideology in a Revolutionary Age: The Guadalajara Church and the Idea of the Mexican Nation, 1788–1853*. Calgary: University of Calgary Press, 2003.

Cooke, Philip St. George. *The Conquest of New Mexico and California*. 1878; reprint, Albuquerque, NM: Horn & Wallace, 1964.

Copeland, Fayette. *Kendall of the Picayune*. Norman, OK: University of Oklahoma Press, 1997.

Corrigan, Philip and Sayer, Derek. *The Great Arch: English State Formation as Cultural Revolution*. Oxford, UK: Oxford University Press. 1985.

Costeloe, Michael P. *La primera república federal de México (1824–1835)*. Mexico City: Fondo de Cultura Económica, 1975.

_____. *The Central Republic in Mexico, 1835–1846*. Cambridge, UK: Cambridge University Press, 1993.

Craver, Rebecca McDowell. *The Impact of Intimacy: Mexican-Anglo Intermarriage in New Mexico, 1821–1846*. El Paso, TX: Texas Western Press. 1982.

Crisp, James Ernest. "Anglo-Texan Attitudes Toward the Mexican, 1821–1845." Ph.D. dissertation, Yale University, 1976.

Cutter, Charles R. *The Protector de Indios in Colonial New Mexico, 1659–1821*. Albuquerque, NM: University of New Mexico Press, 1986.

Davis, W. W. H. *El Gringo: New Mexico and Her People*. 1857; reprint, Lincoln, NE: University of Nebraska Press, 1982.

De la Teja, Jesús F. "El problema de México con los indocumentados en Texas: el distrito de Atascosito, 1821–1836," in *Memorias del primer encuentro de historiadores fronterizos México-Texas*. Saltillo: Universidad Autóno de Coahuila (UAC) (1990–1), 35–40.

_____. *San Antonio de Béxar: A Community on New Spain's Northern Frontier*. Albuquerque, NM: University of New Mexico Press. 1995.

———. "The Colonization and Independence of Texas: A Tejano Perspective," in Jaime E. Rodríguez O. and Kathryn Vincent, eds., *Myths, Misdeeds, and Misunderstandings: The Roots of Conflict in U.S.–Mexican Relations.* Wilmington, DE: SR Books (1997), 79–95.

———. "St. James at the Fair: Religious Ceremony, Civic Boosterism, and Commercial Development on the Colonial Mexican Frontier." *Americas* 57:3 (2001), 395–416.

———. ed. *A Revolution Remembered: The Memoirs and Selected Correspondence of Juan N. Seguín.* Austin, TX: Texas State Historical Association, 2002.

De la Teja, Jesús F. and Wheat, John. "Béxar: Profile of a Tejano Community, 1820–1832." *Southwestern Historical Quarterly* 89:1 (1985), 7–34.

De León, Arnoldo. *The Tejano Community, 1836–1900.* Albuquerque, NM: University of New Mexico Press, 1982.

———. *They Called Them Greasers: Anglo Attitudes Toward Mexicans in Texas, 1821–1900.* Austin, TX, 1983.

De Palo, William A. Jr. *The Mexican National Army, 1822–1852.* College Station, TX: Texas A & M University Press, 1997.

Deutsch, Sarah. *No Separate Refuge: Culture, Class, and Gender on an Anglo-Hispanic Frontier in the American Southwest, 1880–1940.* Oxford, UK: Oxford University Press, 1987.

Di Tella, Torcuato. *Política nacional y popular en México, 1820–1847.* Mexico City: FCE, 1994.

Downs, Fane. "The History of Mexicans in Texas, 1820–1845." Ph.D. dissertation, Texas Tech University, 1970.

Dublán, Manuel and Lozano, José María. *Legislación mexicana o colección completa de las disposiciones legislativas expedidas desde la independencia de la República.* 34 vols. Mexico City: Imprenta del Comercio, 1876–1904.

Ducey, Michael T. "Village, Nation, and Constitution: Insurgent Politics in Papantla, Veracruz, 1810–1821." *Hispanic American Historical Review* 79:3 (Aug 1999), 463–93.

Dunham, Harold H. *Government Handout: A Study in the Administration of Public Lands.* New York: Edwards Brothers Press, 1941.

———. "New Mexican Land Grants with Special Reference to the Title Papers of the Maxwell Grant." *New Mexico Historical Review* 30:1 (1955), 1–22.

Dysart, Jane. "Mexican Women in San Antonio, 1830–1860: The Assimilation Process." *Western Historical Quarterly* 7:4 (1976), 365–89.

Edward, David B. *The History of Texas or, the Emigrant's, Farmer's, and Politican's Guide to the Character, Climate, Soil and Productions of That Country: Arranged Geographically from Personal Observation and Experience.* c1836; reprint, Austin, TX: Texas State Historical Association, 1990.

Emory, Deborah. "Running the Line: Men, Maps, Science and Art of the United States and Mexico Boundary Survey, 1849–1856." *New Mexico Historical Review* (Apr 2000), 221–65.

Emory, W. H. *Notes of a Military Reconnaissance from Fort Leavenworth in Missouri, to San Diego,* in California, Including Part of the Arkansas, Del Norte, and Gila Rivers. Washington, DC: U.S. House of Representatives, Executive Document No. 41, 1848.

Escalante Gonzalbo, Fernando. *Ciudadanos imaginarios*. Mexico City: El Colegio de México, 1995.

Etulain, Richard W. ed. *New Mexican Lives: Profiles and Historical Stories*. Albuquerque, NM: University of New Mexico Press, 2002.

Everett, Dianna. *The Texas Cherokees: A People Between Two Fires, 1819–1840*. Norman, OK: University of Oklahoma Press, 1990.

Falconer, Thomas. *Expedition to Santa Fe: An Account of Its Journey from Texas Through Mexico with Particulars of Its Capture*. New Orleans, LA: Lumsden, Kendall, 1842.

_____. *Letters and Notes on the Texan Santa Fe Expedition, 1841–1842*. New York: Danber and Pine Bookshops, 1930.

Faulk, Odie B. *The Last Years of Spanish Texas, 1778–1821*. The Hague: Mouton, 1964.

Fehrenbach, T. R. *Lone Star: A History of Texas and Texans*. New York: Wings Books, 1968.

Filísola, Vicente. *Memorias para la historia de la guerra de Tejas*. 2 vols. Mexico City: Editora Nacional, 1968.

Fisher, Lillian Estelle. "Early Masonry in Mexico (1806–1828)." *Southwestern Historical Quarterly* 40:3 (Jan 1939), 198–214.

Frank, Ross H. "Changing Pueblo Indian Pottery Traditions: The Underside of Economic Development in Late Colonial New Mexico, 1750–1820." *Journal of the Southwest* 33:3 (1991), 282–321.

_____. *From Settler to Citizen: New Mexican Economic Development and the Creation of Vecino Society, 1750–1820*. Berkeley, CA: University of California Press, 2000.

_____. "Making New Mexico Santos: Franciscans and Vecino Dominance in Late Colonial New Mexico." *New Mexico Historical Review* 75:3 (Jul 2000), 369–96.

Fritz, Naomi. "José Antonio Navarro." M.A. thesis, St. Mary's University of San Antonio, 1941.

Gammel, Hans Peter Nielson, comp. *The Laws of Texas, 1822–1897*, 10 vols. Austin, TX: Gammel, 1989.

García Canclini, Néstor. *Consumers and Citizens: Globalization and Multicultural Conflicts*. Minneapolis, MN: University of Minnesota Press, 2001.

García Cantú, Gastón. *Las invasiones norteamericanas en México*. Mexico City: Era-SEP, 1986.

Gardner, Mark L. ed. *Brothers on the Santa Fe and Chihuahua Trails: Edward James Glasgow and William Henry Glasgow, 1846–1848*. Niwot, CO: University of Colorado Press, 1993.

Gardner, Mark L. and Simmons, Marc, eds. *The Mexican War Correspondence of Richard Smith Elliott*. Norman, OK: University of Oklahoma Press, 1997.

Garrard, Lewis H. *Wah-to-yah and the Taos Trail*. Norman, OK: University of Oklahoma Press, 1955.

Gellner, Ernest. *Nations and Nationalism*. Ithaca, NY: Cornell University Press, 1983.

Gelo, Daniel J. "'Comanche Country and Ever Has Been': A Native Geography of the 19th Century Comanchería." *Southestern Historical Quarterly* 103:3 (Jan 2000), 273–307.

George, Catherine "The Life of Philip Dimmitt." M.A. thesis, University of Texas, 1937.

Gonzales, Manuel G. *The Hispanic Elite of the Southwest.* Southwestern Studies Series 86. El Paso: Texas Western Press, 1989.

Gonzales-Berry, Erlinda and Maciel, David R. *The Contested Homeland: A Chicano History of New Mexico.* Albuquerque, NM: University of New Mexico Press, 2000.

González, Deena J. *Refusing the Favor: The Spanish-Mexican Women of Santa Fe, 1820–1880.* New York: Oxford University Press, 1999.

González de la Vara, Martín. "La corta mexicanidad de Nuevo México, 1821–1848: un caso de las relaciones entre el gobierno central y la frontera norte." B.A. thesis, Universidad Nacional Autónoma de México (UNAM), 1986.

———. "La política del federalismo en Nuevo México, 1821–1836." *Historia Mexicana* 36:1 (1986), 81–112.

———. "Los nuevomexicanos ante la invasión norteamericana, 1846–1848," in Laura Herrera Serna, ed., *México en Guerra (1846–1848).* Mexico City: CONACULTA (1997), 473–94.

González y González, Luis. "El optimismo inspirador de la independencia," in *Todo es historia.* Mexico City: Cal y Arena (1989), 69–83.

Goodrich, James W. "Revolt at Mora, 1847." *New Mexico Historical Review* 47:1 (1972), 49–60.

Graf, LeRoy P. "The Economic History of the Lower Rio Grande Valley, 1820–1875." Ph.D. dissertation, Harvard University, 1942.

Gregg, Josiah, *The Commerce of the Prairies.* Lincoln, NE: University of Nebraska Press, 1967.

Gruenwald, Kim M. *River of Enterprise: The Commercial Origins of Regional Identity in the Ohio Valley, 1790–1850.* Bloomington, IN: Indiana University Press, 2002.

Guardino, Peter F. "Identity and Nationalism in Mexico: Guerrero, 1740–1840." *Journal of Historical Sociology* 7:3 (1994), 314–42.

———. *Peasants, Politics, and the Formation of Mexico's National State: Guerrero, 1800–1857.* Stanford, CA: Stanford University Press, 1996.

Gutiérrez, David G. "The Third Generation: Reflections on Recent Chicano Historiography." *Mexican Studies/Estudios Mexicanos* 5:2 (1989), 281–96.

———. *Walls and Mirrors: Mexican Americans, Mexican Immigrants, and the Politics of Ethnicity.* Berkeley, CA: University of California Press, 1995.

Gutiérrez, Ramón A. "Aztlán, Montezuma, and New Mexico," in Rodolfo A. Anaya and Francisco Lomelí, eds., *Aztlán: Essays on the Chicano Homeland.* Albuquerque, NM: Academia/El Norte Publications, 1989.

———. *When Jesus Came, the Corn Mothers Went Away: Marriage, Sexuality, and Power in New Mexico, 1500–1846.* Stanford, CA: Stanford University Press, 1991.

Gutiérrez, Ramón A. and Orsi, Richard J., eds. *Contested Eden: California Before the Gold Rush.* Berkeley, CA: University of California Press, 1998.

Gutiérrez Ibarra, Celia, ed. *Cómo México perdió Texas: análisis y transcripción del informe secreto (1834) de Juan Nepomuceno Almonte.* Mexico City: Instituto Nacional de Antropología e Historia, 1987.

Haas, Lisbeth. *Conquests and Historical Identities in California, 1769–1936.* Berkeley, CA: University of California Press, 1995.

Hafen, LeRoy R., ed. *The Mountain Men and the Fur Trade of the Far West.* 10 vols. Glendale, CA: A. H. Clark, 1965–72.

Hale, Charles A. *Mexican Liberalism in the Age of Mora, 1821–1853.* New Haven, CT: Yale University Press, 1968.

Hall, Emlen G. *Four Leagues of Pecos: A Legal History of the Pecos Grant, 1800–1933.* Albuquerque, NM: University of New Mexico. 1984.

Hall, Emlen G. and Weber, David J. "Mexican Liberals and the Pueblo Indians, 1821–1829." *New Mexico Historical Review* 4 (1984), 5–31.

Hall, Thomas D. *Social Change in the Southwest, 1350–1880.* Lawrence, KS: Unversity Press of Kansas, 1989.

Hamnett, Brian R. "Factores regionales en la desintegración del régimen colonial en la Nueva España: el federalismo de 1823–24," in Inge Buisson et al., *Problemas de la formación del Estado y de la nación en Hispanoamérica.* Bonn: Bolhau Verlag (1984), 305–17.

_____. *Roots of Insurgency: Mexican Regions, 1750–1824.* Cambridge, UK: Cambridge University Press, 1986.

_____. "Partidos políticos mexicanos e intervención militar, 1823–1855," in Antonio Annino et al., eds., *America Latina: Dallo Stato Coloniale allo Stato Nazione,* vol. 2, Milan: Franco Angeli (1987), 573–91.

Hardin, Stephen L. *Texian Iliad: A Military History of the Texas Revolution.* Austin, TX: University of Texas Press, 1994.

Hatcher, Mattie Austin. *The Opening of Texas to Foreign Settlement, 1801–1821.* Austin, TX: University of Texas Press, 1927.

Haynes, Sam W. *Soldiers of Misfortune: The Somervell and Mier Expeditions.* Austin, TX: University of Texas Press, 1990.

Henderson, Mary Virginia. "Minor Empresario Contracts for the Colonization of Texas, 1825–1834." *Southwestern Historical Quarterly* 31:4 (1928), 295–309.

Hendricks, Rick, ed. *New Mexico Prenuptial Investigations from the Archivos Históricos del Arzobispado de Durango, 1800–1893.* 2 vols. Las Cruces, NM: Rio Grande Historical Collections, New Mexico State University Library, 2000.

Henson, Margaret Swett. *Juan Davis Bradburn: A Reappraisal of the Mexican Commander of Anáhuac.* College Station, TX: Texas A & M University Press. 1982.

_____. *Lorenzo de Zavala The Pragmatist Idealist.* Forth Worth, TX: Texas Christian University Press, 1996.

_____. "Understanding Lorenzo de Zavala: Signer of the Texas Declaration of Independence." *Southwestern Historical Quarterly* 102:1 (Jul 1998), 1–27.

Himmel, Kelly F. *The Conquest of the Karankawas and the Tonkawas, 1821–1859.* College Station, TX: Texas A & M University Press, 1999.

Hinojosa, Gilberto Miguel. *A Borderlands Town in Transition: Laredo, 1755–1870.* College Station, TX: Texas A & M University Press, 1983.

Hobsbawn, Eric J. *Nations and Nationalism Since 1780: Programme, Myth, Reality.* Cambridge, UK: Cambridge University Press, 1990.

Hogan, William R. *The Texas Republic: A Social and Economic History.* Austin, TX, 1969.

Huson, Hobart. *Captain Phillip Dimmitt's Commandancy of Goliad, October 15, 1835–January 17, 1836.* Austin, TX: Von Boeckmann-Jones, 1974.

Hutchinson, C. Alan. "Mexican Federalists in New Orleans and the Texas Revolution." *Louisiana Historical Quarterly* 39 (1956), 1–47.

_____. "General José Antonio Mexía and His Texas Interests." *Southwestern Historical Quarterly* 86 (Oct 1978), 110–51.

Hyslop, Stephen G. *Bound for Santa Fe: The Road to New Mexico and the American Conquest, 1806–1848*. Norman, OK: University of Oklahoma Press, 2002.

Jackson, Jack, ed., and Wheat, John, trans. *Texas by Terán: The Diary Kept by General Manuel de Mier y Terán on His 1828 Inspection of Texas*. Austin, TX: University of Texas Press, 2000.

Janicek, Ricki S. "The Development of Early Mexican Land Policy: Coahuila and Texas, 1810–1825." Ph.D. dissertation, Tulane University, 1985.

_____. "The Politics of Land: Mexico and Texas, 1823–1836." Paper presented at the Texas State Historical Association meeting, 1986.

Jaramillo, Sandra. "Bound by Family: Women and Cultural Change in Territorial Taos." Unpublished paper, 1994.

Jenkins, Myra Ellen. "Rebellion Against American Occupation of New Mexico 1846–1847." Unpublished paper, University of New Mexico, 1949.

_____. "Taos Pueblo and Its Neighbors, 1540–1847." *New Mexico Historical Review* 41:2 (1966), 85–114.

Jenkins John J., III, ed. *The Papers of the Texas Revolution*, 10 vols. Austin, TX: Jenkins Publishing, 1973.

Johannsen, Robert W., *To the Halls of the Montezumas: The Mexican War in the American Imagination*. New York: Oxford University Press, 1985.

Katz, Friedrich. "Labor Conditions on Haciendas in Porfirian Mexico: Some Trends and Tendencies." *Hispanic American Historical Review* 54:1 (1974), 1–47.

_____. "Rural Rebellions After 1810," in Friedrich Katz, ed., *Riot, Rebellion and Revolt: Rural Social Conflict in Mexico*. Princeton, NJ: Princeton University Press (1988), 521–60.

Kavanagh, Thomas W. *The Comanches: A History 1706–1875*. Lincoln, NE: University of Nebraska Press, 1996.

Kendall, George Wilkins. *Narrative of the Texan Santa Fe Expedition*. 2 vols. New York: Harper and Brothers, 1844.

Kessell, John L. *Kiva, Cross and Crown: The Pecos Indians and New Mexico, 1540–1840*. Washington, DC: National Park Service, 1979.

Knight, Alan. "Peasants into Patriots: Thoughts on the Making of the Mexican Nation." *Mexican Studies/Estudios Mexicanos* 10:1 (Winter 1994), 135–61.

Lack, Paul D. *The Texas Revolutionary Experience: A Political and Social History, 1835–1836*. College Station, TX: Texas A and M University Press, 1992.

Lamar, Howard R. *The Far Southwest, 1846–1912: A Territorial History*. New York: W. W. Norton, 1970.

Lamar, Howard and Thompson, Leonard. *The Frontier in History: North American and Southern Africa Compared*. New Haven, CT. Yale University Press, 1981.

Lange, Charles H. et al., eds. *The Southwestern Journals of Adolph F. Bandelier*. 4 vols. Albuquerque, NM: University of New Mexico Press, 1984.

Lavender, David. *Bent's Fort*. Garden City, NY: Doubleday, 1954.

Lecompte, Janet. "La Tules and the Americans." *Arizona and the West* 20:1 (1978), 215–35.

_____. "Manuel Armijo and the Americans," in *Spanish and Mexican Land Grants in New Mexico and Colorado*. Santa Fe, NM: Center for Land Grant Studies, 1980.

_____. "The Independent Women of Hispanic New Mexico, 1821–1846." *Western Historical Quarterly* 12:3 (1981), 20–37.

_____. *Rebellion in Río Arriba, 1837*. Albuquerque, NM: University of New Mexico Press, 1985.

Limerick, Patricia N. *The Legacy of Conquest: The Unbroken Past of the American West.* New York: W. W. Norton, 1987.

Lomnitz Adler, Claudio. *Exits from the Labyrinth: Culture and Ideology in the Mexican National Space.* Berkeley, CA: University of California Press, 1992.

Loomis, Noel M. *The Texan–Santa Fe Pioneers.* Norman, OK: University of Oklahoma Press, 1958.

Loyola, Mary. "The American Occupation of New Mexico, 1821–1852." *New Mexico Historical Review* 14 (1939), 34–75, 143–99, 230–86.

McClure, Charles R. "The Texan–Santa Fe Expedition of 1841." *New Mexico Historical Review* 48:1 (1985).

McLean, Malcolm D., ed. *Papers Concerning Robertson's Colony in Texas.* 16 vols. Fort Worth and Arlington, TX: University of Texas at Arlington Press, 1974–90.

McNierney, Michael. *Taos 1847: The Revolt in Contemporary Accounts.* Boulder, CO: Johnson Publishing, 1980.

Maciel, David R. *El México olvidado: la historia del Pueblo Chicano.* 2 vols. Ciudad Juárez: Universidad Autónoma de Ciudad Juárez, 1996.

Magoffin, Susan Shelby. *Down the Santa Fe Trail and into Mexico: Diary of Susan Shelby Magoffin, 1846–1847.* Edited by Stella M. Drumm. Lincoln, NE: University of Nebraska Press, 1982.

Mallon, Florencia E. "Peasants and State Formation in Nineteenth-Century Mexico: Morelos, 1848–1858." *Political Power and Social Theory* 7 (1988), 1–54.

_____. *Peasant and Nation: The Making of Postcolonial Mexico and Peru.* Berkeley, CA: University of California Press, 1995.

Martin, Cheryl English. *Governance and Society in Colonial Mexico: Chihuahua in the Eighteenth Century.* Stanford, CA: Stanford University Press, 1996.

Matovina, Timothy M. *The Alamo Remembered: Tejano Accounts and Perspectives.* Austin, TX: University of Texas Press, 1995.

_____. *Tejano Religion and Ethnicity: San Antonio, 1821–1860.* Austin, TX: University of Texas Press, 1995.

Maverick, Mary A. *Memoirs.* Edited by Rena Maverick Green. Lincoln, NE: University of Nebraska Press, 1989.

Meining, D. W. *Imperial Texas: An Interpretive Essay in Cultural Geography.* Austin, TX: University of Texas, 1969.

Menchaca, Antonio. *Memoirs.* San Antonio, TX: Yanaguana Press, 1937.

Merk, Frederick. *Manifest Destiny and Mission in American History: A Reinterpretation.* New York: Alfred A. Knopf, 1963.

Miles, George. "To Hear an Old Voice: Rediscovering Native Americans in American History," in William Cronon, et al., eds., *Under an Open Sky: Rethinking America's Western Past.* New York: W. W. Norton (1992), 52–70.

Miller, Thomas Lloyd. *Bounty and Donation Land Grants of Texas, 1835–1888.* Austin, TX: University of Texas Press, 1967.

Minge, Ward Alan. "Frontier Problems in New Mexico Preceding the Mexican War." Ph.D. dissertation, University of New Mexico, 1965.

Mocho, Jill. *Murder and Justice in Frontier New Mexico, 1821–1846.* Albuquerque, NM: University of New Mexico Press, 1997.

Montejano, David. *Anglos and Mexicans in the Making of Texas, 1836–1986.* Austin, TX: University of Texas Press, 1987.

Montoya, María E. *Translating Property: the Maxwell Land Grant and the Conflict over Land in the American West, 1840–1900.* Berkeley, CA: University of California Press, 2002.

Mooney, James. *Calendar History of the Kiowa Indians.* Washington, DC: Smithsonian Institution Press, 1979.

Moorhead, Max L. *New Mexico's Royal Road: Trade and Travel on the Chihuahua Trail.* Norman, OK: University of Oklahoma Press, 1958.

Morton, Ohland. "Life of General Don Manuel de Mier y Terán as It Affected Texas-Mexican Relations." *Southwestern Historical Quarterly* vol. 46, 22–46, 239–54; vol. 47, 29–47, 120–42, 256–67; vol. 48, 193–218, 499–546 (July 1942–April 1945).

_____. *Terán and Texas: A Chapter in Texas–Mexican Frontier, 1836–1841.* Austin, TX: Texas State Historical Association. 1948.

Moyano Pahissa, Ángela. *El Comercio de Santa Fé y la Guerra del '47.* Mexico City: SepSetentas, 1976.

_____. ed. *México y Estados Unidos: orígenes de una relación 1819–1861.* Mexico City: SEP, 1985.

_____. *La resistencia de las Californias a la invasión norteamericana 1846–1848.* Mexico City: CONACULTA, 1992.

_____. *La pérdida de Tejas.* Mexico City: Planeta, 1999.

Muldoon, James. *Identity on the Medieval Irish Frontier: Degenerate Englishmen, Wild Irishmen, Middle Nations.* Gainesville, FL: University Press of Florida, 2003.

Murphy, Lawrence R. "The Beaubien and Miranda Land Grant 1841–1846." *New Mexico Historical Review* 42: 1, 27–47.

Nance, Joseph M. *After San Jacinto: The Texas–Mexican Frontier, 1836–1986.* Austin, TX: University of Texas Press, 1963.

_____. *Attack and Counter-Attack: The Texas–Mexican Frontier, 1842.* Austin, TX: University of Texas Press, 1964.

Noriega Elío, Cecilia. *El Constituyente de 1842.* Mexico City: UNAM, 1986.

Nostrand, Richard L. *The Hispano Homeland.* Norman, OK: University of Oklahoma Press, 1992.

Nugent, Daniel. "Rural Revolt in Mexico, Mexican Nationalism and the State, and Forms of U.S. Intervention," in Daniel Nugent, ed., *Rural Revolt in Mexico and U.S. Intervention.* San Diego, CA: Center for U.S.–Mexican Studies (1988), 1–2.

Nugent, Paul. *Smugglers, Secessionists and Loyal Citizens on the Ghana–Togo Frontier.* Athens, OH: Ohio University Press, 2002.

Ocampo, Javier. *Las ideas de un día. El pueblo mexicano ante la consumación de su Independencia.* Mexico City: El Colegio de México, 1969.

Olavarría y Ferrari, Enrique *Episodios históricos mexicanos.* 4 vols. Mexico City: ICH-FCE, 1987.

Olmstead, Frederick Law. *A Journey Through Texas: Or, A Saddle-Trip on the South-western Frontier.* Austin, TX: University of Texas Press, 1978.

Olmstead, Virginia Langham, ed. *New Mexico Spanish and Mexican Colonial Censuses, 1790, 1823, 1845.* Albuquerque, NM, 1975.

Ortega y Medina, Juan A. *Zaguán abierto al México Republicano, 1820–1830*. Mexico City: UNAM, 1987.

Ortíz de Ayala, Tadeo. *México considerado como nación independiente y libre: o sea algunas indicaciones sobre los deberes más esenciales de los mexicanos*. Edited by Fernando Escalante Gonzalbo. Mexico City: CONACULTA, 1996.

Pacheco, José Emilio and Reséndez, Andrés. *Crónica del 47*. Mexico City: Editorial Clío, 1997.

Padilla, Genaro, *My History, Not Yours: The Formation of Mexican American Autobiography*. Madison, WI: University of Wisconsin Press, 1993.

Perea, Francisco. "Santa Fe as It Appeared During the Winter of the Years 1837 and 1838." Transcribed by W. H. H. Allison. *Old Santa Fe* 2:2 (1914), 170–83.

_____. "Santa Fe in 1846." Transcribed by W. H. H. Allison. *Old Santa Fe* 2:4 (1915), 392–406.

Pitts, John Bost, III. "Speculation in Headright Land Grants in San Antonio from 1837 to 1842." M.A. thesis, Trinity University, 1966.

Pletcher, David M. *The Diplomacy of Annexation: Texas, Oregon, and the Mexican War*. Columbia, MO: University of Missouri Press, 1973.

Poyo, Gerald E., ed. *Tejano Journey, 1770–1860*. Austin, TX: University of Texas Press, 1996.

Poyo, Gerald E. and Hinojosa, Gilberto M. "Spanish Texas and Borderlands: Historiography in Transition: Implications for United States History." *Journal of American History* 75:2 (Sep 1988), 395–416.

Poyo, Gerald E. and Hinojosa, Gilberto M., eds. *Tejano Origins in Eighteenth-Century San Antonio*. Austin, TX: University of Texas Press, 1991.

Prince, L. Bradford. *A Concise History of New Mexico*. Cedar Rapids, IA: The Torch Press, 1912.

Putnam, Jackson K. "The Turner Thesis and the Westward Movement: A Reappraisal." *Western Historical Quarterly* 7 (1976), 377–404.

Radding, Cynthia. *Wandering Peoples: Colonialsm, Ethnic Spaces, and Ecological Frontiers in Northwestern Mexico, 1700–1850*. Durham, NC: Duke University Press, 1997.

Ramón, Regino F. *Historia general del estado de Coahuila*. 2 vols. c1917; reprint, Saltillo: Universidad Autónoma de Coahuila, 1990.

Ramos, Raúl Alberto. "From Norteño to Tejano: The Roots of Borderlands Ethnicity, Nationalism, and Political Identity in Bexar, 1811–1861." Ph.D. dissertation, Yale University, 1999.

Read, Benjamin M. *Illustrated History of New Mexico*. 2 ed. New York: Arno Press. 1976.

Reichstein, Andreas V. *Rise of the Lone Star: The Making of Texas*. College Station, TX: Texas A & M University Press, 1989.

Reno, Philip. "Rebellion in New Mexico, 1837." *New Mexico Historical Review* 40:3 (1965), 197–213.

Reséndez, Andrés. "Caught Between Profits and Rituals: National Contestation in Texas and New Mexico, 1821–1848." Ph.D. dissertation, University of Chicago, 1997.

_____. "Guerra e identidad nacional." *Historia Mexicana* 47:2 (Oct–Dec 1997), 411–39.

_____. "National Identity and the Shifting U.S.–Mexico Border, 1821–48." *Journal of American History* 86:2 (Sep 1999), 668–88.

_____. "Getting Cured and Getting Drunk: State Versus Market in Texas and New Mexico, 1800–1850." *Journal of the Early Republic* 22:1 (Spring 2002), 77–103.

_____. "An Expedition and Its Many Tales," in Samuel Truett and Elliott Young, eds., *Continental Crossroads: Remapping U.S.–Mexico Borderlands History*. Durham, NC: Duke University Press, forthcoming.

_____. "Masonic Connections, Pecuniary Interests, and Institutional Development Along Mexico's Far North," in Jaime E. Rodriguez O., ed., *La Niña Bonita – The Pretty Girl: Constitutionalism and Liberalism in Nineteenth-Century Mexico*. Wilmington, DE: SR Books, forthcoming.

_____. ed. *A Texas Patriot on Trial in Mexico: José Antonio Navarro and the Texan Santa Fe Expedition*. Fort Worth, TX: De Golyer Library and the William P. Clements Center for Southwest Studies, forthcoming.

Rivera, Pedro de. *Diario y derrotero de lo caminado, visto y observado en la visita que hizo a los presidios de la Nueva España septentrional*. Edited by Vito Alessio Robles. 1664; reprint, Mexico City: Secretaría de la Defensa Nacional, 1946.

Rodríguez, José María, *Rodriguez Memoirs of Early Texas*, 2nd ed. San Antonio: Standard Printing, 1961.

Rodríguez O., Jaime E., ed. *The Independence of Mexico and the Origins of the New Nation*. Los Angeles, CA: UCLA Latin American Center, 1989.

_____. "La Constitución de 1824 y la formación del estado mexicano." *Historia Mexicana* 40 (1991), 507–35.

_____. ed. *Patterns of Contention in Mexican History*. Wilmington, DE: SR Books, 1992.

_____. ed. *The Evolution of the Mexican Political System*. Wilmington: SR Books, 1993.

_____. ed. *Mexico in the Age of Democratic Revolution*. Boulder, CO: Lynne Reinner, 1994.

_____. *The Independence of Spanish America*. Cambridge, UK: Cambridge University Press, 1998.

Rodríguez O., Jaime E. and Vincent, Kathryn, eds. *Myths, Misdeeds, and Misunderstandings: The Roots of Conflict in U.S.–Mexican Relations*. Wilmington, DE: SR Books, 1997.

Rorabaugh, W. J. *The Alcoholic Republic: An American Tradition*. New York: Oxford University Press, 1979.

Rosenbaum, Robert J. *Mexicano Resistance in the Southwest: The Sacred Right of Self Preservation*. Austin, TX: University of Texas Press, 1981.

Ruxton, George Frederick. *Adventures in Mexico and the Rocky Mountains*. Edited by Ross Calvin. New York: Harper, 1848.

Sahlins, Peter. *Boundaries: The Making of France and Spain in the Pyrenees*. Berkeley, CA: University of California Press, 1989.

Sánchez, José María. "A Trip to Texas in 1828." Edited and translated by Carlos E. Castañeda. *Southwestern Historical Quarterly* 29 (1926), 249–88.

Sánchez, Pedro. *Memorias del Padre Antonio José Martínez.* Santa Fe, NM: Companía Impresora del Nuevo Mexicano, 1903.

Sánchez Lamego, Miguel A. *The Second Mexican–Texas War 1841–1843.* Hillsboro, TX: Hill Junior College Press, 1972.

Santoni, Pedro. "A Fear of the People: The Civic Militia of Mexico in 1845." *Hispanic American Historical Review* 68 (1988), 269–88.

_____. *Mexicans at Arms: Puro Federalists and the Politics of War, 1845–1848.* Fort Worth, TX: Texas Christian University Press, 1996.

Santoscoy, María Elena, Villarreal, Arturo Eduardo, and Soto, Miguel, eds. *La independencia y el problema de Texas: dos eventos en Coahuila.* Saltillo: Archivo Municipal de Saltillo-Patronato de Amigos del Patrimonio Histórico de Saltillo, 1997.

Saragoza, Alex M. "Recent Chicano Historiography: An Interpretive Essay." *Aztlán* 18:1 (1990), 1–77.

Sellers, Charles, *The Market Revolution: Jacksonian America, 1815–1846.* New York: Oxford University Press, 1991.

Shearer, Ernest C. "The Carbajal Disturbances." *Southwestern Historical Quarterly* 55:2 (1951), 201–30.

Simmons, Marc. *Spanish Government in New Mexico.* Albuquerque, NM: University of New Mexico Press, 1968.

_____. *The Little Lion of the Southwest: A Life of Manuel Antonio Chaves.* Chicago, IL: Swallow Press, 1973.

_____. *Murder on the Santa Fe Trail: An International Incident, 1843.* El Paso, TX: Texas Western Press, 1987.

Smith, Anthony D. *Theories of Nationalism,* 2 ed. New York: Holmes and Meier, 1983.

_____. *The Ethnic Origins of Nations.* Oxford, UK: Blackwell, 1986.

_____. "State-Making and Nation-Building," in John Hall, ed., *States in History.* London: Basil Blackwell (1986), 228–63.

_____. *National Identity.* Reno, NV: University of Nevada Press, 1991.

Sordo Cedeño, Reynaldo. *El Congreso en la primera república centralista.* Mexico City: El Colegio de México-ITAM, 1993.

_____. "El General Tornel y la Guerra de Texas." *Historia Mexicana* 42:4. (1993), 919–53.

Soto Estrada, Miguel Enrique. *La conspiración monárquica en México, 1845–1846.* Mexico City: EOSA, 1988.

_____. "La disputa entre Monclova y Saltillo y la independencia de Texas," in María Elena Santoscoy, Arturo Villarreal, and Miguel Soto, eds., *La Independencia y el problema de Texas: Dos eventos en Coahuila.* Saltillo: Archivo Municipal de Saltillo (1997), 45–109.

_____. "Tejanos y texanos en la Guerra entre México y Estados Unidos," in Laura Herrera Serna, ed., *México en Guerra (1846–1848).* Mexico City: CONACULTA (1997), 625–34.

Spellman, Paul N. *Forgotten Texas Leader: Hugh McLeod and the Texan Santa Fe Expedition.* College Station, TX: Texas A & M University Press, 1999.

Spicer, Edward H. *Cycles of Conquest: The Impact of Spain, Mexico, and the United States on the Indians of the Southwest, 1533–1960.* Tucson, AZ: University of Arizona Press, 1962.

Staples, Anne. "Clerics as Politicans: Church, State, and Political Power in Independent Mexico," in Jaime E. Rodríguez O., ed., *Mexico in the Age of Democratic Revolutions, 1750–1850*. Boulder, CO: Lynne Reinner Publishers (1994), 223–41.

_____. *La Iglesia en la primera república federal mexicana 1824–1835*. Mexico City: SEP, 1976.

Suárez Argüello, Ana Rosa, Terrazas Basante, Marcela, Soto, Miguel, et al., eds., *Política y negocios: ensayos sobre la relación entre México y los Estados Unidos en el siglo XIX*. Mexico City: UNAM-Instituto José María Luis Mora, 1997.

Swadesh, Frances Leon. *Los Primeros Pobladores: Hispanic-Americans of the Ute Frontier*. Notre Dame, IN: University of Notre Dame Press, 1974.

Taylor, William B. *Magistrates of the Sacred: Priests and Parishioners in Eighteenth-Century Mexico*. Stanford, CA: Stanford University Press, 1996.

Tenenbaum, Barbara. *The Politics of Penury: Debts and Taxes in Mexico, 1821–1856*. Albuquerque, NM: University of New Mexico Press, 1986.

Theisen, Gerald, ed. "Opinions on the Newly Independent Mexican Nation: Documents from the Archives of the Archdiocese of Santa Fe, New Mexico, 1820–43." *Revista de Historia de América* 72 (1975), 27–52.

Thomson, Guy. "Bulwarks of Patriotic Liberalism: The National Guard, Philharmonic Corps and Patriotic Juntas in Mexico, 1847–88." *Journal of Latin American Studies* 22:1 (Feb 1990), 31–68.

Tijerina, Andrés. *Tejanos and Texas Under the Mexican Flag, 1821–1836*. College Station, TX: Texas A & M University Press, 1994.

Tilly, Charles. *Coercion, Capital, and European States, AD 990–1992*. Cambridge, MA: Blackwell, 1992.

Torres Bautista, Mariano E. "De la fiesta monárquica a la fiesta cívica: el tránsito del poder en Puebla, 1821–1822." *Historia Mexicana* 45:2 (1996), 221–39.

Turner, Frederick Jackson. "The Significance of the Frontier in American History," in *Annual Report of the American Historical Association for the Year 1893*. Washington, DC: Government Printing Office (1894), 199–227.

Twitchell, Ralph E. *The Military Occupation of New Mexico, 1846–1851*. Denver, CO: Smith-Brooks, 1909.

_____. *The Leading Facts of New Mexican History*. Cedar Rapids, IA: Torch Press, 1912.

Tyler, Daniel. "New Mexico in the 1820s: The First Administration of Manuel Armijo." Ph.D. dissertation, University of New Mexico, 1970.

_____. "Anglo-American Penetration of the Southwest: The View from New Mexico." *Southwestern Historical Quarterly* 75 (1972), 325–88.

_____. "The Personal Property of Manuel Armijo, 1829." *El Palacio* 80 (1974), 45–58.

_____. *Sources for New Mexican History, 1821–1848*. Santa Fe, NM: Museum of New Mexico Press, 1984.

Valdez, Santiago. *Biografía del Reverendo Padre Antonio José Martínez*. Taos, NM, 1877. Unpublished transcript at New Mexico State Records Center and Archives (NMSRCA).

Van Young, Eric. *The Other Rebellion: Popular Violence, Ideology, and the Mexican Struggle for Independence, 1810–1821*. Stanford, CA: Stanford University Press, 2001.

Vázquez, Josefina Zoraida. *Mexicanos y norteamericanos ante la Guerra del 47.* Mexico City: SEP, 1972.

———. "Una tragedia que reafirmó la identidad: La Guerra del 47 (A Tragedy that reaffirmed our identity: The War of 1847)." Conferencia sustentada el día 14 de octubre de 1981 en el Centro de Estudios de Historia de México (Conference on October 14, 1981, at the Centro de las Relaciones México–Estados Unidos), CONDUMEX. Mexico City: El Centro, 1983.

———. "The Texas Question in Mexican Politics, 1836–1845." *Southwestern Historical Quarterly* 89 (1986), 309–44.

———. "La supuesta República del Río Grande." *Historia Mexicana* 36:1 (Jul–Sep 1986), 49–80.

———. "Santa Anna y el reconocimiento de Texas." *Historia Mexicana* 36:3 (Jan–Mar 1987), 553–62.

———. "Iglesia, Ejército y Centralismo." *Historia Mexicana* 29:1 (1989), 205–34.

———. ed. *Interpretaciones del siglo XVIII mexicano: el impacto de las reformas borbónicas.* Mexico City: Nueva Imágen, 1992.

———. "El federalismo mexicano, 1823–1847," Marcello Carmagnani, ed., *Federalismos latinoamericanos: México/Brasil/Argentina.* Mexico City: FCE-Colmex, 1993, 15–47.

———. "Un viejo tema: El federalismo y centralismo." *Historia Mexicana* 42 (1993), 621–31.

———. "Colonización y pérdida de Texas," in Esther Schumacher, ed., *Hitos en las relaciones México–Estados Unidos.* Mexico City: SRE-FCE, 1994.

———. ed. *De la rebelión de Texas a la Guerra del 47.* Mexico City: Nueva Imágen, 1994.

———. "The Colonization and Loss of Texas: A Mexican Perspective," in Jaime E. Rodríguez O. and Kathryn Vincent, eds., *Myths, Misdeeds, and Misunderstandings: The Roots of Conflict in U.S.–Mexican Relations.* Wilmington, DE: SR Books (1997), 47–77.

———. "México y la Guerra con Estados Unidos," in Josefina Zoraida Vázquez, ed., *México al tiempo de su Guerra con Estados Unidos 1846–1848.* Mexico City: SRE-El Colegio de México-FCE (1997), 17–46.

Vázquez, Josefina Zoraida and Annino, Antonio. *El primer liberalismo mexicano: 1808–1855.* Mexico City: Museo Nacional de Historia-Miguel Ángel Porrúa, 1995.

Vigness, David M. *The Revolutionary Decades, 1810–1836.* Austin, TX: Steck-Vaughn, 1965.

Villagrá, Gaspar de. *Historia de Nuevo México.* 1610; reprint, Madrid: Edición de Mercedes Junquera, 1989.

Villalpando César, José Manuel. *Las balas del invasor: la expansión territorial de los Estados Unidos a costa de México.* Mexico City: Miguel Ángel Porrúa, 1998.

Voss, Stuart F. *On the Periphery of Nineteenth-Century Mexico: Sonora and Sinaloa, 1810–1877.* Tucson, AZ: University of Arizona Press, 1982.

Wagner, Leslie A. Jones. "Disputed Territory: Río Grande/Río Bravo Borderlands, 1838–1840." M.A. thesis, University of Texas at Arlington, 1998.

Walker, Cheryl. *Indian Nation: Native American Literature and Nineteenth-Century Nationalisms.* Durham, NC: Duke University Press, 1997.

Warren, Richard A. "Ashes and Aerostats: Popular Culture Meets Political Culture in Nineteenth Century Mexico." Paper presented at Latin American Studies Association (LASA), Chicago, IL, 1998.

_____. *Vagrants and Citizens: Politics and the Masses in Mexico City from Colony to Republic*. Wilmington, DE: SR Books, 2001.

Webb, James Josiah. *Adventures in the Santa Fe Trade, 1844–1847*. Edited by Ralph P. Bieber. Glendale, CA: Arthur H. Clark, 1931.

Weber, David J. ed. *A Letter From Taos, 1826*. Albuquerque, NM: Historical Society of New Mexico and the University of New Mexico, 1966.

_____. ed. *The Extranjeros: Selected Documents from the Mexican Side of the Santa Fe Trail, 1825–1828*. Santa Fe, NM: Stagecoach Press, 1967.

_____. *The Taos Trappers: The Fur Trade in the Far Southwest, 1540–1846*. Norman, OK: University of Oklahoma Press. 1971.

_____. ed. *Foreigners in their Native Land: Historical Roots of the Mexican Americans*. Albuquerque, NM: University of New Mexico Press, 1973.

_____. ed. "An Unforgettable Day: Facundo Melgares on Independence." *New Mexico Historical Review* 48:1 (1973), 27–44.

_____. ed. *Northern Mexico on the Eve of the United States Invasion: Rare Imprints Concerning California, Arizona, New Mexico, and Texas, 1821–1846*. New York: Arno Press, 1976.

_____. *The Mexican Frontier, 1821–1846: The American Southwest Under Mexico*. Albuquerque, NM: University of New Mexico Press, 1982.

_____. ed. *Arms, Indians, and the Mismanagement of New Mexico: Donaciano Vigil, 1846*. El Paso, TX: Texas Western Press, 1986.

_____. *Myth and the History of the Hispanic Southwest*. Albuquerque, NM: University of New Mexico Press, 1987.

_____. ed. *The Idea of Spanish Borderlands*. New York: Garland, 1991.

_____. *The Spanish Frontier in North America*. New Haven, CT: Yale University Press, 1992.

_____. *On the Edge of Empire: The Taos Hacienda of los Martínez*. Santa Fe, NM: Museum of New Mexico Press, 1996.

_____. "Conflicts and Accommodations: Hispanic and Anglo-American Borders in Historical Perspective, 1670–1853." *Southwestern Historical Quarterly* 39:1 (Spring 1997), 1–34.

Weber, David J. and Winn, Conchita Hassell, eds. *Troubles in Texas, 1832: A Tejano Viewpoint from San Antonio*. Austin, TX: Wind River Press for the Degolyer Library, 1983.

Weber, David J. and Rausch, Jane M., eds. *Where Cultures Meet: Frontiers in Latin American History*. Wilmington, DE: SR Books, 1994.

Weigle, Marta. *Brothers of Light, Brothers of Blood: The Penitentes of the Southwest*. Santa Fe, NM: Ancient City Press, 1976.

White, Gifford, ed. *Census of the Republic of Texas, 1840*. Edited by Gifford White. Austin, TX:, Pemberton Press, 1966.

White, Richard. *'It's Your Misfortune and None of My Own': A New History of the American West*. Norman, OK: University of Oklahoma Press, 1991.

_____. *The Middle Ground: Indians, Empires, and Republics in the Great Lakes Region, 1650–1815*. New York: Cambridge University Press, 1991.

Will, Martina E. "God Gives and God Takes Away: Death and Dying in New Mexico, 1760–1850." Ph.D. dissertation, University of New Mexico, 2000.

Wilson, Thomas M. and Donnan, Hastings, eds. *Border Identities: Nation and State at International Frontiers*. Cambridge, UK: Cambridge University Press, 1998.

Winders, Richard Bruce. *Crisis in the Southwest: The United States, Mexico, and the Struggle over Texas*. Wilmington, DE: SR Books, 2002.

Windham, Margaret L., ed. *New Mexico 1850 Territorial Census*, 2 ed. Albuquerque, NM, 1985.

Zavala, Lorenzo de. *Ensayo crítico de las revoluciones de México desde 1808 hasta 1830*. c1831; reprint, Mexico City: Editorial Porrúa, 1969.

Index